FOURTH EDITION

Strategies for Teachers

Teaching Content and Thinking Skills

Paul D. Eggen
University of North Florida

Donald P. Kauchak
University of Utah

Allyn and Bacon

Boston ■ London ■ Toronto ■ Sydney ■ Tokyo ■ Singapore

Series Editor: *Traci Mueller*
Editorial Assistant: *Bridget Keane*
Marketing Manager: *Brad Parkins*
Editorial–Production Service: *Matrix Productions Inc.*
Composition and Prepress Buyer: *Linda Cox*
Manufacturing Buyer: *Chris Marson*
Cover Administrator: *Jenny Hart*
Electronic Composition: *Cabot Computer Services*

Copyright © 2001, 1996 by Allyn and Bacon
A Pearson Education Company
160 Gould Street
Needham Heights, Massachusetts 02494

Internet: www.abacon.com

Between the time Website information is gathered and then published, it is not unusual for some sites to have closed. Also, the transcription of URLs can result in unintended typographical errors. The publisher would appreciate notification where these occur so that they may be corrected in subsequent editions.

Library of Congress Cataloging-in-Publication Data

Eggen, Paul D.
    Strategies for teachers : teaching content and thinking skills / Paul D. Eggen, Donald P. Kauchak.—4th ed.
        p.   cm.
    Includes bibliographical references and index.
    ISBN 0-205-30808-2
        1. Teaching.   2. Education—Experimental methods.   3. Thought and thinking—Study and teaching.   4. Learning, Psychology of.   I. Kauchak, Donald P.   II. Title.

LB1027.3 .E44 2000
371.102—dc21   00-035591

Printed in the United States of America

10 9 8 7 6 5 4 3 2 1   05 04 03 02 01 00

CONTENTS

PREFACE

Major changes continue to occur in the field of instruction, and we remain immersed in one of most exciting periods in the history of education. Instruction continues to be strongly influenced by cognitive views of learning. This foundation is reflected in greater emphasis on the social nature of learning, the impact of context on comprehension, the need for domain-specific knowledge in higher-order thinking, expert-novice differences in problem solving, and the belief that learners construct their own understanding of the topics they study. Teachers continue to use the effective teaching literature popular in the 1970s and 1980s as a foundation, but they now go beyond it to focus on helping their students acquire a deep understanding of the topics they study while developing critical-thinking abilities. We have attempted to reflect these advances as we revised this text.

Major changes in the fourth edition reflect continued development in both learning and instruction. Two new chapters translate these changes into new instructional models. They are:

- Chapter 3, Social Interaction Models
- Chapter 7, Problem-Based Learning Models

In addition, the fourth edition includes:

- Increased coverage of constructivism as a framework for guiding instruction
- Expanded discussion of Vygotsky's theory of learning
- A section on motivational aspects of each model
- Groupwork strategies
- Developmental considerations in implementing the models
- Discussion strategies
- Technology and problem solving

In writing the fourth edition, we continued to rely on three primary sources. The first is the continuing advance of cognitive psychology that provides a clearer picture of how students learn. This advance has important implications for teachers that are reflected in the models in this text. The second is research on classroom instruction that continues to identify links between teacher actions and student learning. The third source is experience. Since writing the last edition, we continue to spend a great deal of time in classrooms observing teachers, working with students, and studying the complex interactions that take place between them. This experience has helped us understand that while the cognitive revolution is in full swing, teaching continues to be eclectic, reflecting a broad variety of conceptions of effective instruction. This experience is reflected in the scope of the text.

Like the third edition, this book continues to focus on instruction, using a models approach. A models approach links prescriptive teaching strategies to specific content and thinking goals while acknowledging that no approach to instruction replaces the wisdom or professional judgment of an effective teacher. Reflecting research suggesting that coverage of carefully selected content in depth is preferable to broad, superficial coverage, we have consciously decided not to deal with every topic commonly presented in a general methods text. Instead, we present and illustrate specific models in detail — those we feel to be most powerful and useful to classroom teachers — and include suggestions for modifications to make them flexible, allowing teachers to express their own styles and preferences.

The book exists in two main parts. The first two chapters provide a frame of reference by outlining advances in effective teaching and the teaching of thinking. The remaining chapters are devoted to detailed coverage of the individual models, including suggestions for modifications that make them adaptable to a variety of teaching-learning situations.

In making our revision, we have attempted to ground the models in the most recent theory and research, making it a conceptually sound yet highly applicable text. We hope it provides you with opportunities for professional growth.

In preparing this manuscript, we want to thank the people who have supported its development, particularly Virginia Lanigan, our editor for many years, and Merrill Peterson, our production editor. We want especially to thank the many teachers in whose classrooms we've worked and visited, and on whose instruction the case studies in the text were based. This experience has brought to the book an authenticity that would have been otherwise impossible. Last but not least, we want to thank the following reviewers, whose comments and suggestions were of tremendous value to us as we prepared the fourth edition: Dr. Saouma BouJaoude, Syracuse University; Ken Martin, University of Cincinnati; and John R. Zelazak, Central Missouri State University.

P.E.
D.K.

CHAPTER

1

Cognitive Learning and Models of Teaching

This is a book about teaching strategies. As you study the text, you will examine several models, each designed to help students develop a deep understanding of the topics they study and improve their higher-order and critical-thinking abilities. The strategies are all grounded in cognitive learning theory, one aspect of which is the premise that students learn more when they're actively involved in learning activities than they do when they passively listen to teachers. Active involvement results both in deeper understanding of the content and in an improved ability to think.

When you have completed your study of this chapter, you should be able to meet the following objectives:

- Describe differences between behaviorist and cognitive views of learning.
- Identify the important elements of the teacher-effectiveness research.
- Describe differences between a models approach to instruction and other approaches.
- Identify factors influencing the choice of a teaching model.

Learning: A Cognitive Perspective

In the introduction we said that each of the models in this text is grounded in cognitive learning theory. What does this mean? What are the differences between cognitive views of learning and other approaches? We answer these questions in this section.

Psychology attempts to explain how we learn and develop, and understanding learning is obviously critical for teachers. Early views of learning, unfortunately, were not able to explain some important school goals, such as critical thinking and problem solving. This state of affairs is now changing and we have a rapidly expanding body of knowledge that helps guide professional practice. In this section, we examine two views of learning—behaviorism and cognitive theory. Behaviorism helps provide historical context; cognitive theory gives us additional insight into learning and what we as teachers can do to promote it.

Behaviorist Views of Learning

According to behaviorism, **learning** *is a change in observable behavior that occurs as the result of experience*. For behaviorists, learning has occurred, for example, when students consistently give specific, observable, desired responses to questions. The way they learn to give these responses is determined by reinforcement and punishment. (Being reinforced or punished is the *experience* that changes the behavior.) For example, if a teacher asks, "How do you spell *Tennessee*?" and the student responds "T-e-n-n-e-s-s-e-e," the teacher smiles and says, "Right!" Spelling *Tennessee* is specific, the teacher can observe (hear) the correct spelling, and the teacher's smile and comment reinforce the student; the response is strengthened.

However, if the student responds, "T-e-n-e-s-s-e-e," the teacher corrects it by saying, "Not quite," or, "You'd better check your list." Saying, "Not quite," or, "You'd better check your list," is a punisher, since the comments decrease the likelihood that the student will give the same response in the future.

The goal of instruction, according to behaviorism, is to increase the number, or strength, of correct student responses. The amount of learning is measured by observing changes in behavior, such as seeing that students correctly spell twelve of twenty words on a list on Monday but correctly spell sixteen words on Wednesday.

When using behaviorism as a guide for planning and conducting instruction, the teacher designs learning activities that require students to produce specific, observable responses to questions and exercises. Then, during learning activities, the teacher reinforces desired responses, as we saw in the correct spelling of *Tennessee*.

Let's look now at a lesson based on behaviorism.

Kevin Lageman is an eighth-grade English teacher at Ridgeview Middle School, where he teaches five sections of standard English.

We look in on his first period on Monday as he begins a unit on pronoun cases with one of his standard classes.

It's 9:08 and the students are filing into the room. Kevin greets them at the door and hurries them along. "Hurry everyone, 2 minutes until the bell rings. Anyone who's late gets a detention if they're tardy."

Kevin finishes taking roll as the last students slide in their seats, and he hangs the slip outside his door as the bell begins to ring at 9:10.

"All right, listen, everyone," Kevin begins as the bell stops ringing. "Today, we're going to begin a study of pronoun cases. . . . Everybody turn to page 484 in your text."

He waits for a moment as students find the page.

"This is important," he continues, "because we want to be able to use standard English when we write, and this is one of the places where people get mixed up. . . . So when we're finished with our study here, you'll all be able to use pronouns correctly in your writing."

He displays the following rules on the overhead:

Pronouns use the nominative case when they're subjects and predicate nominatives.

Pronouns use the objective case when they're direct objects, indirect objects, or objects of prepositions.

"Let's review briefly," Kevin continues. "Give me a sentence that has both a direct and indirect object in it. . . . Anyone?"

"Mr. Lageman gives too much homework," Leroy offers to the laughter of the class.

Kevin smiles and writes the sentence on the chalkboard, then continues, "Okay, Leroy. Good sentence, even though it's incorrect. I don't give you *enough* work. . . . What's the subject in the sentence?"

Leroy doesn't answer.

"Go ahead, Leroy."

"Ahh . . . er . . . *Mr. Lageman.*"

"Yes, good. *Mr. Lageman* is the subject," Kevin replies as he underlines *Mr. Lageman* in the sentence.

"Now, what's the direct object? . . . Joanne?"

". . . *Homework.*"

"All right, good. And what's the indirect object? . . . Anya?"

". . . *Us.*"

"Excellent, everybody."

Kevin continues by reviewing predicate nominatives and objects of prepositions.

He continues, "Now, let's look at a few more examples up here on the overhead."

He displays ten sentences written on it. The following are the first four.

1. Did you get the card from Kelly and (I, me)?
2. Will Antonio and (she, her) run the concession stand?
3. They treat (whoever, whomever) they hire very well.
4. I looked for someone (who, whom) could give me directions to the theater.

"Okay, look at the first one. Which is correct? . . . Omar?"

". . . *Me.*"

"Good, Omar. How about the second one? . . . Lonnie?"

". . . *Her.*"

"Not quite, Lonnie. This one is a little tricky, but it's the nominative case," Kevin responds.

Then Kevin points up at the overhead and says, "How about the third one. . . . Cheny?"

". . . I don't know. . . . *whomever,* I guess."

"Excellent, Cheny. Indeed, that's correct."

Kevin continues with the rest of the sentences and assigns a page of similar exercises from their books as homework.

On Tuesday, Wednesday, and Thursday, Kevin covers the rules for pronoun-antecedent agreement (pronouns must agree with their antecedents in gender and number) and for using indefinite pronouns as antecedents for personal pronouns—*anybody, either, each, one, someone.* Then he has the students work examples as he had done before.

On Friday Kevin gives a test composed of thirty sentences, ten of which deal with case, ten more with antecedents, and the final ten with indefinite pronouns.

The following are some items from the test:

For each of the items below, mark *A* on your answer sheet if the pronoun case is correct in the sentence and *B* if it is incorrect. If it is incorrect, supply the correct pronoun.

1. Be careful *who* you tell.
2. Will Renee and *I* be in the outfield?
3. My brother and *me* like water skiing.

Let's look at Kevin's lesson now and see how it is based on behaviorism. To elicit observable responses, he displayed exercises, such as:

1. Did you get the card from Kelly and (I, me)? and then he asked, "Okay, look at the first one. Which is correct? . . . Omar?" Omar responded by saying "Me," and Kevin reinforced him by saying, "Good, Omar." Kevin had designed the learning activity so that students could give specific, observable responses, which he could reinforce if they were correct, as he did with Omar.

Learning to provide specific, observable responses is desirable for some forms of fact learning, such as a learner's ability to respond, "54," quickly and effortlessly when asked, "What is 6 times 9?" Knowing multiplication facts, for example, helps with problem solving, and being able to identify words quickly and efficiently helps when students read (Mayer, 1998; Singley & Anderson, 1989).

For many other kinds of learning, however, behaviorism isn't a satisfactory basis for guiding instruction. For instance, being able to write effectively was Kevin's goal for his students, as indicated by his comment, "This [using pronoun cases correctly] is important, because we want to be able to use standard English when we write. . . . So when we're finished with our study here, you'll all be able to use pronouns correctly in your writing." Writing, however, is a complex process, and being able to provide specific, observable responses to exercises involving grammar rules is unlikely to result in significantly improved writing ability (Mayer, 1999; Kellogg, 1994). Students learn to write by practicing strategic planning, translating their plans into drafts, and revising; the more they practice and think about their writing the better their writing becomes (Hayes, 1996).

In math, similarly, because they don't focus on the logic behind problems, students often use superficial and ineffective strategies to solve word problems. Looking for key words that indicate the operation to use is one of these ineffective strategies. For example, when students are faced with the following problem:

LeAnn has 24 jelly beans in a small package. She eats 5 of them and gives 3 to her friend, Andrea. How many jelly beans does LeAnn have altogether?

they commonly conclude the answer is 32, because the word *altogether* usually suggests that the operation is addition.

A problem with behaviorism is that it treats learners as *passive recipients of reinforcers and punishers rather than thinking, strategic learners*. For instance, students who conclude that LeAnn now has thirty-two jelly beans are passively responding to the word *altogether*; they're ignoring the fact that it's impossible to eat some, give some away, and still have more at the end than at the beginning. Learners tend to use these superficial strategies because they're reinforced for using them; they frequently get correct answers. Even though they deliver correct answers, however, students often acquire little understanding of the reasoning or logic behind the problems (Shoenfeld, 1991).

Over time, researchers found the behavioristic perspective to be oversimplified. While reinforcers and punishers do indeed influence behavior, much of learning is the result of students' active attempts to make sense of what they study. In addition, student characteristics such as background knowledge, motivation, and learning strategies all influence how much students learn (Bruning et al., 1999). These findings lead us to cognitive views of learning.

Cognitive Views of Learning

To begin this section, let's look at Suzanne Nelson, another teacher, also working with her students on pronoun cases.

> As with Kevin, Suzanne greets her students pleasantly and says loud enough so Kevin and his students can hear, "Hurry up, everyone. We've got lots of work to do. Let's see if we can beat Mr. Lageman's students to our seats."
>
> "Pretty tricky way to get us in the room, Mrs. Nelson," Leroy smiles as he walks in the classroom.
>
> Other students comment as they come in and are in their seats before the bell rings.
>
> Suzanne finishes taking roll as the bell stops ringing and the students are in their seats. Suzanne steps to the front of the room and says, "We're making progress on the editorial section of the school newspaper we've been working on. I've read the essays you turned in on Friday. Your writing is getting better and better, but we have some things to work on today that will improve it even more. She turns on two overheads, with a paragraph displayed on each. On the left overhead, the first paragraph appears as follows:
>
> > Katrina and Simone were talking. "Did you get the information *from Kelly and me*?" Simone asked.
> >
> > "No, I didn't," Katrina responded. "What was it about?"
> >
> > "Kelly wanted to know if it's okay *that Molly and she* run the concession stand on Friday night at the game."
> >
> > "Sure, that's fine with me," Katrina responded. "The teachers treat *whoever works there* very well, so everything will be fine. By the way, *to whom* do I give the list of people who are working that night?"

On the right overhead, the second paragraph looks like this.

> Katrina and Simone were talking. "Did you get the information *from Kelly and I?*" Simone asked.
>
> "No, I didn't," Katrina responded. "What was it about?"
>
> "Kelly wanted to know if it's okay *that Molly and her* run the concession stand on Friday night at the game."
>
> "Sure, that's fine with me," Katrina responded. "The teachers treat *whomever works there* very well, so everything will be fine. By the way, *to who* do I give the list of people whom are working that night?"

Suzanne gives students a moment to read the paragraphs, then says, "Get together with your partner and see if you can figure out how these passages are similar and different. You've got 2 minutes." After 2 minutes she calls the class back together and continues, "Look at the parts of the paragraphs that are italicized. . . . Let's start with the first one. What do you notice about them? . . . Devon."

After a couple of seconds, Devon offers, "*Me* over there (pointing at the left screen) and *I* over there" (pointing at the right screen).

"Okay," Suzanne nods. "What else? . . . Tonya?"

"Both . . . have *Kelly.*"

"Okay, good. . . . What else? . . . Carlo?"

"*From.*"

"What do you mean, *from*?"

"Both have *from* in the . . . like . . . different kind of letters."

"All right, good observations everyone. . . . Now, . . . look at the one on the left again. What part of speech is the word *from*? . . . Andrew?"

" . . . A . . . preposition, I . . . think."

"Yes, excellent, Andrew. It is a preposition. . . . So let's take a look at this." She takes the paragraph off the right overhead and displays the following:

> Pronouns use the nominative case when they're subjects and predicate nominatives.
>
> Pronouns use the objective case when they're direct objects, indirect objects, or objects of prepositions.

Suzanne gives them a few seconds to read the rules, then continues, "I'd like you to work with your partner again and decide, based on these rules, which of the two versions up here is correct. Again, I'll give you 2 minutes." When the 2 minutes are up, she continues, "So, which do you believe is correct . . . *from Kelly and me* or *from Kelly and I*? . . . Jon?"

"I . . . think it . . . should be *from Kelly and I.*

"And why do you think so."

". . . It . . . sounds better . . . I think."

"Listen to this and tell us which one sounds better. *Kelly and me got some soft drinks,* or *Kelly and I got some soft drinks.*"

"*. . . Kelly and I.*"

"Okay, good. . . . So let's go back to *from Kelly and me* or *from Kelly and I.* What do you think? . . . Katrina?"

". . . Must be . . . *from Kelly and me,*" Katrina says hesitantly.

"Why do you think so?"

"Well, they're . . . not the subject . . . and . . . *I* was used when it was the subject . . . so . . . it must be *me.*"

"Yes . . . makes sense, doesn't it? . . . *Kelly and I* are what part of the sentence?" . . . April?"

". . . The . . . subject."

"Yes, good. Indeed they are. So . . . let's go back to the other example. Which is correct?"

Suzanne continues the discussion until 20 minutes are left in the period. Students then begin revising their paragraphs in light of the information they learned that day and turn them in the next day. On Tuesday and Wednesday, Suzanne continues the discussion with two additional paragraphs; on Thursday, she returns the students' writing assignments and completes the discussion of pronouns, their antecedents, and indefinite pronouns.

On Friday, Suzanne assigns an additional paragraph to be written as a quiz. The students have to embed at least two examples each of pronoun cases, pronouns and antecedents, and indefinite pronouns in the paragraphs. In addition, she has students read each other's essays, checking for the content they've just been studying.

Let's compare Suzanne's lesson to Kevin's. Their goals were the same; they wanted their students to apply the rules for nominative and objective cases correctly in their writing. Their approaches were very different, however. Whereas Kevin focused on isolated items of information, such as the sentence, "Did you get the card from Kelly and (I, me)?" Suzanne made her examples more realistic by embedding them in the context of paragraphs; that is, they were like information we find in books, newspapers, and magazines. Second, instead of reinforcing and punishing specific responses, Suzanne led a discussion of the rules, why they made sense, and how they were used. Her approach emphasized a deep and thorough understanding of the rules. It was more sophisticated and demanding than Kevin's, but it was also likely to result in more student learning. Her instruction was guided by cognitive views of learning; his was based on behaviorism.

Let's look a little further at some of the dialogue in Suzanne's lesson.

SUZANNE: So which do you believe is correct . . . *from Kelly and me* or *from Kelly and I?*" . . . Jon?"

JON: I . . . think it . . . should be *from Kelly and I.*

SUZANNE: And why do you think so?

JON: It . . . sounds better . . . I think.

SUZANNE: Listen to this and tell us which one sounds better. *Kelly and me got some soft drinks,* or *Kelly and I got some soft drinks.*"

JON: *Kelly and I.*

SUZANNE: Okay, good. . . . So let's go back to *from Kelly and me* or *from Kelly and I.* What do you think? . . . Katrina?

KATRINA: (hestitantly) Must be . . . *from Kelly and me.*

SUZANNE: Why do you think so?

KATRINA: Well, they're . . . not the subject . . . and . . . *I* was used when it was the subject . . . so . . . it must be *me*."

KATRINA: Yes . . . makes sense, doesn't it?

We see that Jon initially had a misconception about correct pronoun usage. He hadn't been taught the misconception, and he wasn't reinforced for expressing it. He created, or *constructed,* the idea on his own. As researchers began to systematically examine students' thinking in cases like this one, they arrived at an inescapable conclusion: *Learners don't passively respond to the environment; they actively seek to make sense of it.* Researchers' efforts led to what is called the "cognitive revolution." It began about the middle of the twentieth century and continues to this day.

The cognitive revolution led to a definition of learning that differs from behaviorists' definition. From a cognitive perspective, **learning** *is an active process in which learners attempt to make sense of what they study.* The idea that learners are mentally active lies at the core of cognitive learning theory, and it has important implications for teaching. For example, teachers can clearly explain an idea to students, but students don't mentally "record" the idea as presented (Resnick, 1989). They try to make sense of it and link it to what they already know. Let's see how this works.

A Cognitive Learning Model. Cognitive learning is commonly described using a model similar to the one presented in Figure 1.1 (Eggen & Kauchak, 1999; Mayer, 1998).

From Figure 1.1 we see that stimuli from the environment enter **sensory memory,** *the part of our cognitive system that briefly holds information until we attend to it* (Mayer, 1998). For instance, when we read, we briefly retain the words at the beginning of a sentence in sensory memory until we have read the entire sentence. If this remembering didn't occur, we wouldn't be able to make sense of the sentence, because the words at the beginning would have been lost before we could make sense of it.

We then select some of the information that enters sensory memory by attending to it, perceiving its meaning, and transferring it to working memory. **Working memory** *is the conscious, "thinking" part of our cognitive learning system*, and this is where new information is organized and encoded.

Finally, we retrieve some information from **long-term memory,** *which is our permanent information store,* and we integrate the retrieved information with the information we have in working memory (Mayer, 1998). This process of integrating new and old information is how learning is made meaningful. The term **meaningfulness,** while overused in the educational literature, has a precise definition: *It refers to the number of links or associations between an idea and other ideas.* The more links, the more meaningful the idea.

Let's see how this definition applies to Suzanne's students. They read the passages, which were the stimuli from the environment. She encouraged their attention to important parts by italicizing these words, and to see if they did pay attention, she asked the students

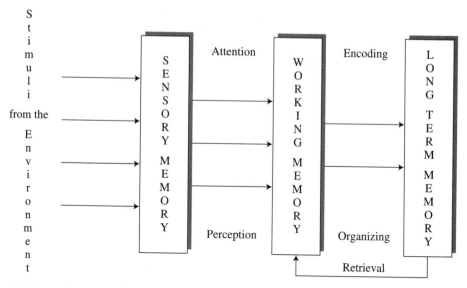

FIGURE 1.1   A Cognitive Model of Learning

to describe their observations of the paragraphs. This information entered their working memories.

As Suzanne led the discussion, the students retrieved information from long-term memory and gradually integrated it with the specific examples. For instance, Katrina said, "Well, they're . . . not the subject . . . and . . . *I* was used when it was the subject, . . . so . . . must be *me.*" To make the information meaningful, she had integrated several items—her understanding of a sentence's subject, the examples, the rules for nominative and objective cases, and the specific information that *from* was a preposition. This process is the essence of cognitive learning.

The cognitive revolution has resulted in a shift in focus away from learners who passively listen to teachers and toward their active involvement in the learning process. As we better understand learning, and as instruction increasingly involves learners, we realize that teaching and learning are very complex and a number of factors come into play. Some of these factors are:

- *Learner background knowledge.* The amount and quality of learning depend on what students already know (Bruning et al., 1999; Mayer, 1999). Effective teachers find out what their students know and continually monitor student learning during the course of the lesson. Suzanne used the essays her students wrote to assess their background knowledge.

- *Realistic learning tasks.* To see connections between the idea they're studying and their lives, students need learning tasks that relate to the real world. If we want students to become better at writing and problem solving, we need to involve them in activities that allow them to practice writing and solving problems.

TABLE 1.1   **Comparison of Behaviorist and Cognitive Views of Learning and Teaching**

	View of Learning	View of Learners	Role of the Teacher
Behaviorism	Increase in number of desirable responses resulting from reinforcement	Passive recipients of stimuli (reinforcers and punishers) from the environment	Present reinforcers to increase desirable behaviors, and punishers to decrease undesirable behaviors
Cognitive	Developing understanding by searching for patterns in what they study	Constructors of knowledge through actively processing information from the environment	Guide learners in their efforts to make sense of the world

■ *Examples and representations*. Since students construct—rather than record—understanding, the experiences they have will determine how valid their understanding becomes (Spiro et al., 1992). Examples and other representations, such as graphs, charts, maps, and case studies, provide those experiences. Again, Suzanne's essays and paragraphs provided these concrete experiences.

■ *Interaction*. Questions and answers and discussions help students understand the topics they study (Lambert & McCombs, 1998). Skillful teacher questioning helps students see connections between the ideas they're studying and helps them see how abstract ideas relate to real-world examples (Brown, 1994; Eggen & Kauchak, 1999). Discussions encourage students to verbalize their own thinking and share it with others.

The shift toward active learners makes teachers' jobs more complex and demanding. Questioning and guiding students is much more difficult than simply lecturing as students passively listen. However, it also results in much more learning. The models in this book are designed to promote active learners and help teachers acquire the abilities to guide this activity.

Table 1.1 summarizes differences between behaviorist and cognitive views of learning.

Research and the Teacher's Role in Learning

We saw in the last section that instruction that promotes active learing is more demanding than instruction that allows students to remain passive. This kind of instruction emphasizes the role of the teacher in promoting learning. In this section, we want to look at the teacher's role more closely.

A large body of research underscores the importance of the teacher in helping students learn (Gage, 1985; Brophy & Good, 1986). Findings from this research consistently indicate that the teacher is the most important factor, outside the home environment, that affects student learning and development. We saw this effect illustrated in the differences between Kevin's and Suzanne's approaches to their topics.

Educators haven't always been optimistic about the ability of research to guide classroom practice. In fact, before the 1970s, both research and teachers themselves were given little credit for contributing to student learning. This pessimism was caused by a number of factors, including faulty research designs and inefficient research procedures (Rosenshine, 1979; Gage and Giaconia, 1981).

One of the oldest traditions in research on teaching focused on teacher characteristics and was based on the implicit assumption that teachers were "born, not made." (This idea is dying but is not completely dead today.) The strategy that followed this assumption looked at teacher characteristics, such as warmth and humor, and investigated whether the presence or absence of these characteristics made any differences in student learning. However, the researchers often failed to determine whether these characteristics, typically measured on paper-and-pencil tests, produced any differences in actual teaching behaviors, let alone differences in student achievement. As we would expect, this approach proved unproductive and was ultimately abandoned.

Another line of research originating in the 1960s and extending into the 1970s focused on the relationship between home- and school-related factors and student learning (Coleman et al., 1966; Jencks et al., 1972). Largely refinements of earlier work, these studies searched for factors that correlated with student achievement. Results suggested that the most important variables impacting school learning were outside the classroom and even the school; they included factors such as parents' income and educational background, which were unalterable and outside education's sphere of influence. Needless to say, both researchers and teachers were discouraged by the results. The data seemed to suggest that the most important variables in learning were beyond educators' control. In addition, these results led to sharply reduced national and state funding for educational research. With reduced economic support, research efforts were made even more difficult.

Teachers Do Make a Difference: The Teacher-Effectiveness Research

However, a new and productive paradigm—one focusing on teacher actions in the classroom—emerged. It resulted from the convergence of two separate lines of research. One was a reanalysis of the data of Coleman and his associates (1966). This reanalysis focused on individual schools and teachers and found that there were large differences in the effectiveness of both; some promoted much more student learning than did others (Brophy and Good, 1986; Good and Brophy, 1986).

The second line of research came when researchers began to compare the teachers whose students learned more than expected for their grade and ability levels with teachers whose students scored as expected or below. The researchers analyzed the teachers' classrooms in both groups to see what differences existed. The results were striking. Investigators found wide variation in the ways the two groups taught, and a *description of these patterns—the patterns of teacher skills and strategies that influence student learning—makes up the body of knowledge that we now call the* **teacher-effectiveness research.** The overriding conclusion from this research is that teachers do indeed make a difference. (We will examine specific teacher-effectiveness behaviors in Chapter 2.)

Beyond Effective Teaching

The literature on effective teaching made an invaluable contribution to education because it both confirmed the critical role teachers play in student learning and provided "education with a knowledge base capable of moving the field beyond testimonials and unsupported claims toward scientific statements based on credible data" (Brophy, 1992, p. 5). It provides, however, only a threshold or a base line above which all teachers should be. Expert teachers go beyond this threshold to construct lessons that help students learn content in a meaningful way. Further, critics have argued that the behaviors specified in the teacher-effectiveness research are too fragmented and simplistic in their orientation, focusing on isolated skills that fail to transfer to new situations. Deep student understanding may or may not result (Marshall, 1992).

Teaching for Understanding

The subtitle of this book, "Teaching for Understanding," may seem ironic; no teacher teaches for lack of understanding. However, when we examine the term *understanding* a little more closely, we see that it is not as simple as it appears on the surface. Perkins and Blythe (1994) describe understanding as "being able to do a variety of thought-demanding things with a topic—like explaining, finding evidence and examples, generalizing, applying, analogizing, and representing the topic in a new way" (pp. 5–6). The teaching models described in this text are designed to help teachers ensure that their students' learning is at the level of understanding instead of mere memorization, which is so prevalent in schools today.

Teacher questioning provides a beginning to this process, with questions such as:

"Why?"

"How do these compare?" ("How are they alike or different?")

"What would happen if . . . ?"

and particularly,

"How do you know?"

These questions can do much to promote student understanding. Surprisingly (and disturbingly), teachers ask questions such as these less than 1 percent of the time (Boyer, 1983).

Teaching for understanding depends both on cognitive views of learning and the teacher skills and strategies identified by the teacher-effectiveness research. Some of the implications of this theory and research include:

- Identifying clear learning goals for students.
- Selecting teaching strategies that will most effectively help students reach the goals.

- Providing examples and representations that help students acquire a deep under-standing of the topics they study.
- Requiring that students are actively involved in the learning process.
- Guiding students as they construct their understanding of the topics being studied.
- Monitoring students for evidence of learning.

While the focus is on learners and learning, these characteristics demonstrate the critical role teachers play in guiding this process.

A repertoire of effective teaching strategies is essential if teachers are going to pro-mote deep understanding. Teachers must be able to select and use strategies that are most effective for different learning goals. We analyze this idea in the next section.

The Need for Instructional Alternatives

Arguments over questions about the best way to teach have absorbed educators' energies since the beginning of formal education. Attempts to answer this question have focused on authoritarian versus democratic techniques (Anderson, 1959), discovery versus expository approaches (Keislar and Shulman, 1966), teacher- versus student-centeredness (Dunkin and Biddle, 1974), and direct versus indirect approaches to teaching (Peterson and Walberg, 1979). Thousands of studies have been conducted in an attempt to answer this question in its various forms. The overriding conclusion from this research is: *There is no single best way to teach.* Some goals are better reached with teacher-centered approaches, for example, whereas learners are better able to reach others with learner-centered approaches.

Bruce Joyce and Marsha Weil first formalized the notion of varying procedures for different teaching situations when their book *Models of Teaching* was published in 1972. At that time, the idea was new and perhaps even controversial. Since then, however, the logic of teachers' use of different instructional strategies to meet different goals has be-come so widely accepted that it is no longer an issue. In fact, the need for teachers to be able to use different strategies is even more important today given the growing diversity of learners in our schools (Villegas, 1991).

While a number of factors influence the choice of strategy, three lie at the core of the decision-making process:

- The teacher
- The students
- The content

Selecting Teaching Strategies: The Role of the Teacher

Teachers may be the most important factor influencing the question of how to teach. Di-recting student learning at any level is a personal enterprise. How we teach depends to a large extent on who we are (Kagan, 1992). The goals we select, the strategies we use to reach the goals, and the way we relate to students all depend on what we bring to the classroom as human beings.

Attempts to identify an ideal teacher type have proved fruitless. Hundreds of research studies investigating different types of teachers have indicated that there is no best personality pattern. Energetic, thoughtful, humorous, serious, traditional, and unorthodox teachers have all proven effective in different situations. Much of teachers' effectiveness lies in understanding their own strengths and preferences and adopting compatible teaching strategies.

Selecting Teaching Strategies: The Impact of Learners

Students are a second factor influencing the choice of a teaching strategy. Individual students respond differently to various instructional strategies (Corno and Snow, 1986). This effect has been called by some researchers an "aptitude-treatment interaction," with aptitude reflecting what students bring to a learning situation and treatment describing our attempts to accommodate these differences (Cronbach and Snow, 1977). In some instances, practices found effective with one type of student are ineffective with others (Brophy & Good, 1986). Researchers have found that what a student brings to the classroom may be as important as any other factor in determining the effectiveness of a method.

Students differ in academic abilities, background experience, and motivation. In addition, a student's culture, including the values, attitudes, and traditions of a particular group, can also have an important influence on learning (Cushner et al., 1992). These individual differences can influence the effectiveness of a particular instructional strategy.

Content and Teaching Strategies

A third factor influencing a teacher's choice of teaching strategy is the content being taught. For example, a social studies teacher may want the class to remember basic facts concerning the American Revolution in one lesson, to understand the assimilation problems encountered by immigrants to a country in another, and to analyze the strengths of a democracy compared to those of a totalitarian society in a third. Though these tasks all involve American history, the goal for each is different. The teacher is trying to teach factual information to one class, have the students understand the process of assimilation in the second, and develop analytical skills in the third. Since the goals are different, the strategies needed to reach the goals are also different; we don't, for example, teach factual information in the same way that we teach analytical skills.

Teachers' goals vary even within a class period. In a single lesson, for example, a literature teacher discussing "The Raven," for example, might want students to remember the poem's author, to relate the poem to the author's life, and to learn the concepts of *meter, rhyme,* and *imagery.* These goals are different, and each requires a different teaching strategy.

Similar situations exist in elementary schools. In teaching reading, for instance, the teacher will want students to be able to pronounce words correctly, identify the major theme of a story, explain cause-and-effect relationships, and predict the consequences of certain events in the story. Again, the teacher's goals are different. Trying to reach all of the goals in the same way is impossible.

The Models Approach to Teaching

Teaching models *are prescriptive teaching strategies designed to accomplish particular instructional goals.* They are prescriptive in that the teacher's responsibilities during the planning, implementing, and assessment stages of instruction are clearly defined. In addition, they can be used as guides for curriculum design or for choosing and constructing instructional materials.

Models differ from general teaching strategies in that models are designed to reach specific goals. The use of models requires an ability to specify precise learner outcomes so that a specific model can be selected to match a particular goal. To better understand this process and how a teaching model relates to it, let us compare the role of a teacher using a model to that of an engineer. In considering a project, an engineer first identifies the type of structure to be built, such as a building, a bridge, or a road. Having done so, the engineer selects an appropriate design or blueprint. The specifications of the blueprint determine the actions the builder takes and the kind of building that will result. Similarly, teachers considering a model first identify what is to be taught and then select a strategy to reach that goal. The model is designed to achieve a specified goal and will determine in large part the actions of the teacher.

A teaching model, then, is a type of blueprint for teaching. Just as a blueprint provides structure and direction for the builder, the model provides structure and direction for the teacher. However, a blueprint does not dictate all of the actions of a builder, and a model cannot dictate all of the actions taken by a teacher. A blueprint is not a substitute for basic engineering skill, and a teaching model is not a substitute for basic teaching skills. A model cannot take the place of qualities good teachers must have, such as an understanding of the subject matter, the ability to ask effective questions, creativity, and sensitivity to people. It is, instead, a tool to help good teachers teach more effectively by making their teaching more systematic and efficient. Models provide enough flexibility to allow teachers to use their own creativity, just as the builder uses creativity in the act of construction. As with a blueprint, a teaching model is a design for teaching within which teachers use all of the skills and insights at their command.

The number of possible teaching goals is so large and diverse that it is impossible to discuss them all in depth in one book. Each of the models discussed in this text is based on cognitive learning theory, and they are designed to reach cognitive goals. Let's look briefly at them.

Cognitive Learning Goals

Educational goals are typically divided into three families or domains: affective, psychomotor, and cognitive. *Emotional and social development goals are in the* **affective domain; psychomotor goals** include *acquisition of manipulative and movement skills. Goals that address the development of the student's intellect and understanding are in the* **cognitive domain.**

Each family is important. The affective domain considers a student's self-concept, personal growth, and emotional development; it deals with students' attitudes and values.

Teachers who work in this area focus on helping students understand who they are and diagnose and find solutions to personal and social problems. Goals such as the "ability to work with peers," "consideration of the elderly," or "willingness to listen to other people's ideas" all fall within this domain.

The psychomotor family is concerned with the development of muscular skill and coordination. This area includes goals such as "learning how to sew a buttonhole," "developing a good tennis serve," or "learning to operate a wood lathe." While intellectual abilities enter into each of the psychomotor tasks, the primary focus is on the development of manipulative skills rather than on the growth of intellectual capability.

Cognitive goals center on the intellectual growth of the individual. They include the acquisition of basic skills such as reading, writing, and mathematics, as well as higher-order goals, such as the ability to solve problems, identify relationships, examine cause and effect, and the other abilities we described as *understanding*. The primary explicit focus of schools is predominantly in this domain.

The three domains are interdependent. For instance, while this book focuses on cognitive goals, we also emphasize the importance of a classroom environment in which students feel safe to conjecture and describe their thinking without fear of embarrassment or criticism. Further, cognitive learning theory stresses the importance of social interaction in learning, and Chapter 3 describes a family of models designed to capitalize on this social interaction while promoting cognitive learning.

Teachers who focus on cognitive learning have two sets of objectives. One is to help students develop a deep understanding of specific topics taught in schools; the other is to help them develop the cognitive skills that will allow them to learn on their own.

Cognitive Skills in the Classroom

Our students' ability to "think" has been and continues to be an ongoing concern (Bransford et al., 1991; Sternberg, 1998). Educators realize that it is no longer sufficient simply to teach students what they should know, but *how* to know as well. Psychology in general, and cognitive learning specifically, provide a framework for addressing the development of students' thinking skills and abilities (Rosenshine and Stevens, 1986; Sternberg, 1998). Students' higher-order and critical thinking abilities develop when they are provided opportunities to practice these skills across the curriculum.

As illustrations of activities that develop students' cognitive skills, consider the following:

■ A teacher wants her class to understand the concept of participatory democracy. She begins the lesson by providing the students with descriptions that range from their student government to the United Nations. She also includes cases of nonparticipatory governments for contrast. Students examine and discuss the similarities in the examples and identify the ways they are different from those that are nonparticipatory. They continue until they can specify the features of participatory democracy that are consistent with the examples.

- A field trip to the zoo is followed by the teacher's request that the class list all of the animals seen. The class groups the members of the list in terms of similarities, and they discuss the basis for the groups.

- A biology teacher wants students to know how the human circulatory system operates. To reinforce the idea, students are asked to form an analogy with the water and sanitary systems of a city. Students make comparisons between analogous parts such as large water mains, pumping stations, and sewage-treatment plants.

- As an introductory activity in the reading of *Silas Marner,* a freshman literature class is given a handout describing two seemingly dissimilar characters. When they are told the descriptions are of the same person, students attempt to explain the disparity. The teacher uses these explanations as a basis for discussing the book.

Let's look now at the similarities in the examples. First, each teacher wanted the students to acquire a deep understanding of a particular topic. The topics ranged from understanding participatory democracy and the circulatory system to identifying the similarities among zoo animals and characters within a novel. Acquiring understanding of important concepts was a central goal in each of the lessons. Development of higher-order and critical thinking was not pursued at the expense of content.

Second, the students were presented with information and were involved in making comparisons, finding patterns, forming and documenting conclusions, and developing generalizations. Instead of being passive listeners, they found their own relationships in the topics they studied with guidance from the teacher.

The most effective way to teach cognitive skills is to provide students with ongoing opportunities to practice these skills in the context of the topics they study (Bransford et al., 1991). Students are given enormous amounts of experience in developing the basic skills of reading, writing, and various components of math. It should be no less the case with cognitive skills and strategies.

The most efficient way to provide this experience is by integrating the skills into the regular curriculum. This approach allows teachers to help students develop cognitive strategies without sacrificing content, and it is the approach taken with the models in this book.

We examine higher-order and critical thinking in more detail in Chapter 2.

Summary

Learning: A Cognitive Perspective

As we better understand learning, we realize that learners are mentally active in their efforts to understand the topics they study. Viewing learners as active is a basic principle of cognitive learning theory, and this theory informs the teaching practices presented in this text. Background knowledge, the use of examples and other representations, realistic learning tasks, and high levels of teacher-student and student-student interaction are all factors that influence the amount students learn.

Research and the Teacher's Role in Learning

Other than the home environment, teachers are the most important influence on student learning. Effective teachers promote learning to a much greater extent than do those who are less effective. The models presented in this text are designed to help teachers improve their effectiveness.

The Need for Instructional Alternatives

Research has consistently demonstrated that there is no one best way to teach. The characteristics of teachers, the type of learners, and the topics being taught all influence the strategy that will be most effective in producing learning in the classroom.

The Models Approach to Teaching

Since learning goals differ, the teaching strategies that we use to reach those goals must also differ. A teaching model is a strategy designed to help students reach specific goals. It prescribes the general actions that will help students learn, but it doesn't dictate a teacher's every move. A model is a general guide for instruction, but it doesn't replace the skill and professional judgment of an expert teacher.

Cognitive Learning Goals

The models presented in this text are designed to help students reach goals in the cognitive domain, the domain that focuses on thinking, problem solving, and intellectual development. Attitudes and values—goals in the affective domain—are important, however, as are those in the psychomotor domain, which deals with physical abilities. The three domains are interdependent, and a focus on the cognitive domain doesn't mean that the others are ignored.

Cognitive Skills in the Classroom

Higher-order and critical thinking involve the ability to use information to find order in the world and solve problems. These goals are an essential part of the modern school curriculum. Cognitive approaches to learning provide an effective means of teaching these cognitive goals without sacrificing content.

The organization of the text is represented in Figure 1.2. We will develop these ideas as the text evolves.

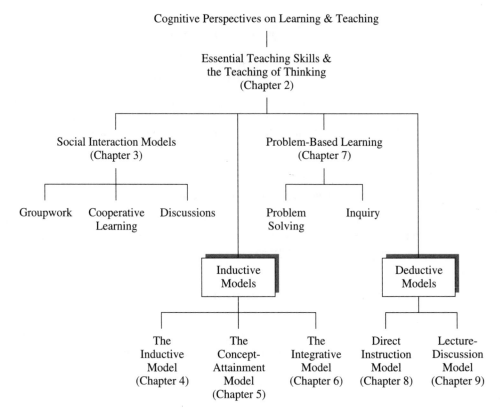

Cognitive Perspectives on Learning & Teaching

Essential Teaching Skills &
the Teaching of Thinking
(Chapter 2)

Social Interaction Models
(Chapter 3)

Problem-Based Learning
(Chapter 7)

Groupwork Cooperative Discussions
Learning

Problem Inquiry
Solving

Inductive
Models

Deductive
Models

The
Inductive
Model
(Chapter 4)

The
Concept-
Attainment
Model
(Chapter 5)

The
Integrative
Model
(Chapter 6)

Direct
Instruction
Model
(Chapter 8)

Lecture-
Discussion
Model
(Chapter 9)

FIGURE 1.2 Organization of the Text

IMPORTANT CONCEPTS

Affective domain (p. 16)
Cognitive domain (p. 16)
Learning (behaviorism) (p. 3)
Learning (cognitive) (p. 2)
Long-term memory (p. 9)
Meaningfulness (p. 9)

Psychomotor domain (p. 16)
Sensory memory (p. 9)
Teacher-effectiveness research (p. 12)
Teaching models (p. 16)
Working memory (p. 9)

DISCUSSION QUESTIONS

1. Describe a class you've been in that used a cognitive approach to learning. In your description, explain how the characteristics of cognitive learning were either present or missing.

2. One criticism made of the effectiveness research is that teaching effectiveness was defined in terms of student performance on standardized achievement tests. What other important school outcomes might be missed or ignored by these tests?

3. Are there some times when a teacher doesn't want to take an active teaching role? If so, when would this be and what would the alternate role be?

4. Choose two content areas of the curriculum (e.g., science versus language arts). Discuss how the content in each area might influence the choice of teaching methods.

5. Briefly describe your own personal goals for teaching and discuss how these might influence your choice of teaching methods.

6. How does the age or ability of a student influence the choice of a teaching strategy? Imagine that you are responsible for teaching the same basic content to three classes, ranging from remedial to accelerated. How would your teaching methods differ? (See Corno and Snow [1986] and Rosenshine and Stevens [1986] for discussions of this problem.)

7. Describe a type of higher-order or critical thinking skill that you believe is important at your level or in your area of the curriculum. How would you teach this type of thinking? How would you measure whether or not students adopted it?

2 Essential Teaching Skills and the Teaching of Thinking

I. Essential Teaching Skills: The Foundation for Teacher Effectiveness
  A. Essential Teaching Skills: What Are They?
  B. Essential Teaching Skills and Classroom Management: Creating Productive Learning Environments
  C. Essential Teaching Skills: A Theoretical Perspective

II. Beyond Effective Teaching: Teaching for Thinking and Understanding
  A. Teaching Thinking: An Enduring Concern

B. Teaching Thinking: Increasing Learner Motivation
  C. A Climate for Thinking

III. Critical Thinking
  A. Critical Thinking: Attitudes and Dispositions
  B. Critical Thinking in Day-to-Day Living

In Chapter 1, you examined the history of the teacher-effectiveness research and its most important finding: that teachers can have a profound influence on student learning. The teacher-effectiveness research describes abilities that all teachers should have and identifies the foundation for teaching expertise. Building on that foundation, we now move beyond effective teaching to examine instruction that results in learners' deep understanding of content and their ability to think critically.

When you've completed your study of this chapter, you should be able to meet the following objectives:

- Identify in case studies examples of teachers displaying essential teaching skills.
- Demonstrate essential teaching skills in your own instruction.
- Describe factors that have contributed to educators' continued interest in teaching thinking.
- Identify characteristics of higher-order and critical thinking.

To begin our discussion of essential teaching skills and higher-order and critical thinking, let's observe an American history class.

Teri Bowden is beginning a unit on the colonization of North America with her American history students. We join her class as she is standing at the door greeting the students at 10:13 A.M. as they file into class for her third period.

"Good morning Suzanne, nice haircut. . . . Hey José, how are you doing today?" she interjects as Suzanne and José walk into the room.

"David, that goes in your locker. . . . Hurry up. You have 2 minutes," she directs as David starts through the door with a basketball in his hand.

"Aw, Mrs. Bowden," he protests, walking away with a little grin on his face.

"Take your seats quickly," Teri reminds them. "You have 5 minutes to answer the questions on the overhead."

The bell stops ringing at 10:16. The students are peering at the overhead and hunching over their desks as Teri takes roll.

At 10:20, Teri asks, "How are you all coming?" Amidst "Fine," "Okay," and "Just about done," Teri says, "Okay, one more minute."

The students finish and pass their papers forward. Teri quickly goes over the exercises and says, "Get these out of your folders as you come in tomorrow morning."

"Now," she announces, turning to the class and shaking her finger for emphasis, "let's shift our thinking a little and begin to focus on the colonial period, which began in the 1600s. This is a very important part of American history, but what's most interesting about all of this is that what we're studying has ramifications for the entire world, even today. Today's topic is one of the most important ideas of the entire colonial period, so let's see what kind of job we can do in figuring it out."

Damon smiles wryly and whispers to Charlene, "Bowden thinks everything is interesting."

Teri continues, "To get us started, I want you to look at the three short passages that I'm going to display on the overhead, and I want you to read them carefully and look for any patterns that might exist in them. So . . . our goal in this lesson is to look for patterns, and then we'll relate these patterns to the events we've been studying in American history."

She displays the following information:

In the mid-1600s, the American colonists were encouraged to grow tobacco, since it wasn't grown in England. The colonists wanted to sell it to France and other countries but were forbidden to do so. In return, the colonists were allowed to import textiles from England but were forbidden from making their own. All of the materials were carried on British ships.

Early French colonists in the New World were avid fur trappers and traders. They got in trouble with the French monarchy, however, when they attempted to make fur garments and sell them to Spain, England, and other countries. They were told that the produced garments would be sent to them from Paris instead. The monarchy also told them that traps and weapons must be made in France and sent to them as well. Jean Forgé complied with the monarchy's wishes but was fined when he hired a Dutch ship to carry some of the furs back to Nice.

India was the "jewel in the crown" of the nineteenth-century British empire, producing large quantities of materials such as raw linens, foodstuffs, and salt. As the Indians became more nationalistic, however trouble began. England wanted to manufacture clothing from the Indian raw materials in the British Isles. When the Indians tried to establish stronger ties with other countries to increase the scope of their trade, their endeavors were quickly squelched by their English rulers, who argued that the British homeland was more than capable of providing for

India's needs and, further, it had a large and efficient fleet. This policy eventually led to Indian protest and ultimately to independence.

"Now, let's take a look," Teri says. "What kinds of reactions do you see up here? . . . Ann?"

Ann begins hesitantly: "Each of the examples deals with some type of colony."

"Good start, Ann," Teri smiles. "And what, specifically, were the colonies? . . . Lenore?"

"The French and British colonies in North America, and the British colony in India."

"Looks like there were some problems," Rasheed volunteers.

"Good observation, Rasheed. What do you mean?"

". . . In each case the colony wanted to do something, but England and France wouldn't let colonists do it."

"Give us some specific examples if you can. . . . Eric?"

"The colonists produced something the parent country wanted, such as tobacco, or furs, or raw linen."

"Very observant, Eric!" Teri enthuses. "Go on, Pam."

". . . They sent the stuff to their parent country," Pam responds after carefully inspecting the information.

"And they couldn't send it anywhere else!" Steve jumps in, adding to the idea.

"That's very good, both of you. Where do you suppose Steve got that idea? Connie?"

". . . It says it right in the first two examples," Connie responds. "And in the third one it says that when India tried to establish stronger ties with other countries to expand the scope of its trade, colonists got in trouble."

"Excellent, everyone! Connie, good use of information to support your ideas. You've all improved a great deal in that regard. Keep going. . . . Mary?" When Mary does not answer, Teri asks: "What did they get in return in each case?"

". . . They got textiles from England . . . and fur garments, traps, and stuff from France . . . and clothing from England," Mary responds, looking from case to case.

"And what did each get from other countries? Liz?"

". . . Nothing."

"They weren't allowed to," Bob adds.

"And what made you say that, Bob?"

"It says in the second example that they were told that their traps and weapons would be sent from France, and in the third example it says that the British argued that the homeland was more than capable of providing for India's needs."

"Does this tell us for certain that they weren't allowed to import goods from other countries?"

". . . Not exactly," Jill adds. "We're sort of assuming it from the information, although it's really implied in the description."

"Very good, Jill. Class, notice that Jill used the word *assume*. Actually she made a conclusion, and the term we use for that kind of conclusion is *infer*. Here the information wasn't directly in the data; she had to go beyond the data to form her conclusion. That's an inference. Nice job," Teri smiles, gesturing positively to the class. "Now let's go a bit farther. What other patterns do you see in the descriptions? Kim?" When Kim does not answer, Teri asks: "How were the goods shipped, Kim?"

"On ships," Kim says, bringing laughter from her classmates.

"Yes, good, Kim!" Teri laughs with them. "What ships, or whose ships?"

". . . In each case it was the ships from the parent country. It says that directly in the first case and in the second one it says that Jean Forgé got into trouble when he hired a Dutch ship to carry some furs back to Nice."

"What evidence is there in the third case? Melinda?"

"They argued that they had a large and efficient fleet," Melinda answers quickly.

"Okay, good, Melinda. Now anything else? . . . What do you think, Cherrie?"

". . . I think that they also couldn't make their own manufactured goods. It says in each case that when the colonists tried to make their own materials from the raw materials they couldn't do it."

"They couldn't make any manufactured goods, not just those from the raw materials they provided," Kathy adds.

"What made you say that?" Teri queries.

"The British colonists grew tobacco, but they weren't allowed to manufacture anything, not just something that you might make out of tobacco," Kathy answers.

"Yes, but you can't make anything out of tobacco," Gregg retorts.

"Oh, yes, you can," Kathy responds. "They could have made cigars and stuff."

"Those are both good points," Teri interjects. "Everyone, remember this." Teri raises her voice. "This is important. Do you see how both Kathy and Gregg used information to support their arguments? Nice job! . . . Do we have any other evidence that supports either Kathy's or Gregg's position, even though they're not really at odds?"

"I think so," Jack volunteers. "In the second case the French colonists were told not to manufacture traps and weapons, and they produced furs, so it wasn't just fur coats that were not allowed."

"That's excellent, everyone! Excellent analysis of the information we have here. Now let's look back and see what we've found."

At this point Teri has the class look back at what they have done, summarizes common characteristics, and then continues: "We've examined the three cases, and now we want to take a broader look at the information in general. Let's begin. We have a situation where . . . ? Toni?"

". . . Colonists related to a country producing only raw materials, no manufactured stuff," Toni begins hesitantly.

"Good," Teri smiles as she writes what Toni said on the board. "Go on."

". . . And they can only be sold to the mother country."

"Who in turn provided the manufacturing and the shipping," Gregg adds.

"Excellent!" Teri praises. "Very clear, succinct description of what we've been discussing. Now we know the features of this policy," she goes on. "Does anyone know what it's called?"

When no one answers, Teri continues. "This is called mercantilism. It was a colonial economic policy designed to make money for the parent country by taking colonial raw materials in exchange for manufactured products." After a brief pause, she asks, "What other countries besides England and France have been guilty of mercantilism?"

The class analyzes additional examples, such as Belgium and the Netherlands, and discusses their mercantile policies.

Teri continues, "Let's look again at the question I asked: 'What other countries have been guilty of mercantilism?' What assumption is being made in that question?"

". . . It looks like you're suggesting that mercantilism is bad," Anthony offers tentatively.

"Good thinking," Teri smiles and gestures for emphasis. "That's exactly what it implies. Now, mercantilism may very well have been bad . . . exploitation of colonialized lands and that kind of thing. However, the question I asked had in it an unstated assumption. Recognizing unstated assumptions is part of the thinking process, and we all need to be on the lookout for that kind of thing. . . . Again, that's good thinking, Anthony."

Teri continues, "Now look at another case and see if it illustrates mercantilism or not. Remember, be ready to explain why or why not when you've made your decision." She displays the following description on the screen:

> Canada is a member of the former British Commonwealth. Canada is a large grain producer and exporter, deriving considerable income from selling grain to Great Britain, France, Russia, and other countries. This trade has also enhanced the shipping business for Greece, Norway, and Liberia, which carry most of the products. Canada, however, doesn't rely on grain alone. It is now a major producer of clothing, high-tech equipment, and heavy-industry equipment.

"What do you think? Is this mercantilism? . . . Someone? Amy, we haven't heard from you," Teri says.

"I would say no," Amy responds after a few seconds of studying the description.

"Okay, now tell us why."

". . . Well, there are several reasons. Canada trades with several countries according to the information, uses a variety of ships to carry the goods, and produces a lot besides raw materials."

"Excellent analysis, Amy," Teri smiles. "Now that we're comfortable with that part, let's go a step farther and examine our thinking in this activity. What are some things you had to do in order to arrive at the conclusion?"

"First we had to observe, so we would eventually recognize the essential characteristics," Amy responds.

"Good beginning! What else? Bob?"

"We hunted for a pattern in the three paragraphs."

"And we had to make comparisons before we could find the patterns," Amy adds.

"Good. All of you! What else? Jack?"

"We had to separate out the relevant from the irrelevant information," Jack answers.

"For example?" Teri probes.

". . . Well, whether it was guns, or traps, or clothing, or whatever, really didn't matter. The important point was that the colonists weren't allowed to manufacture anything."

"Excellent, Jack! Now go on. Patty?"

". . . We didn't see everything in the examples, so we had to infer some of it, and then you asked us for evidence to support our inference."

"Very good, Patty. Can you remember an example of where we did this? . . . Can anyone think of an example of where we made an inference and then had to back it up?"

"I . . . think so," Patty volunteers. "Bob said that he bet that the colonies weren't allowed to get materials from other countries, and then used the example where France said the traps and weapons would be sent from there."

". . . Jill also said that it didn't tell us for sure, but that it was strongly implied and we inferred it from the information that we were given," Becky adds.

"We also generalized when we formed the definition of mercantilism," Lisa Jo says. "We talked about those parts of mercantilism working in all cases, so that's generalizing, isn't it?"

"Yes, it is. Your point is a good one; generalizing is a form of inference. Very well done, Lisa Jo," Teri responds, then continues. "Let's move on. We now want to examine the impact of mercantilism on other events during the colonial period, and we want to think about mercantilism in other parts of the world, such as Africa. . . . So, for tomorrow, I want you to read this article that I copied from one of the news magazines recently. As you read the article, think about how the information in it relates to what we discussed today. Your warm-up activity at the beginning of the class will ask you about some of the information in the article."

Teri sums up: "You did a very nice job today. Your analysis of your own thinking is getting better and better. I'm proud of all of you."

To begin our discussion, let's look back at Teri Bowden's lesson and examine its implications for teaching. Three important features were demonstrated in the lesson:

1. She displayed teaching abilities that all teachers—regardless of content area, grade level, or topic—should be able to demonstrate. We call these abilities *essential teaching skills.*
2. Her goal for developing thinking and her content goal were integrated. Neither was "tacked onto" the other, and her instruction throughout the lesson was directed at both goals simultaneously.
3. Her lesson focused on deep understanding of a particular topic—the role of mercantilism in colonialization.

We examine each of these elements in detail in the following sections of the chapter. We begin with a discussion of essential teaching skills.

Essential Teaching Skills: The Foundation for Teacher Effectiveness

Imagine that you're sitting unnoticed at the back of a classroom. This could be a first-grade class studying basic math facts taught by a veteran teacher; a junior high life science class studying different types of worms taught by someone in her first year; or a high school English class reading and discussing one of Shakespeare's plays taught by a teacher with several years of experience. Regardless of the teacher's personality or background, the grade level of the students, or the topic being studied, some teacher behaviors increase the amount students learn more than others. We call these behaviors essential teaching skills, and they are derived from the teacher-effectiveness research described in Chapter 1. Let's look at them.

Essential Teaching Skills: What Are They?

We're all familiar with the notion of basic skills. These are the essential abilities in reading, writing, and mathematics that all learners must possess to function effectively in the world. Increasing evidence indicates that in order to function in the new millenium, basic skills also include technology and critical thinking (Blanton, Moorman, & Trathen, 1998). We discuss this evidence later in the chapter. **Essential teaching skills** are analogous to basic skills and can be described as *the critical teacher attitudes, skills, and strategies necessary to promote student learning.*

While we discuss these skills separately for the sake of clarity, they are interdependent, and none is as effective alone as it is in combination with the others. The integration and appropriate application of the skills—in the context of particular lessons—are critical.

The essential teaching skills are outlined in Figure 2.1.

Teacher Characteristics.   While teacher characteristics are admittedly not skills, we begin with them to emphasize how important they are to teaching. Teachers set the emotional tone for the classroom, design instruction, implement learning activities, and assess student progress. Their attitudes and orientations toward teaching are critical in this process.

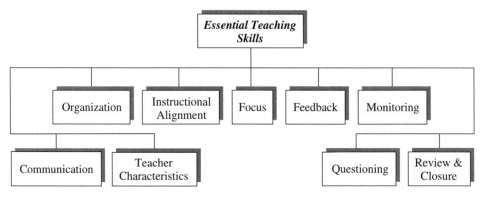

FIGURE 2.1   Essential Teaching Skills

In this section we examine four teacher characteristics:

- Teaching efficacy
- Modeling and enthusiasm
- Caring
- Positive expectations

Teaching Efficacy.   To begin this section, let's turn again to Teri's lesson. She identified clear goals and had an effective strategy to reach the goals, she provided examples to help students acquire a deep understanding of her topic (her cases illustrating mercantilism), and she guided students' active involvement throughout the learning activity. Hers was a positive, proactive orientation, based on the belief that all students can learn and that it's her responsibility to try her hardest to be sure that all reach their maximum potential. Teri was high in **personal teaching efficacy,** *which is the belief that teachers can have an important positive effect on students* (Bruning et al., 1999). Teachers high in personal efficacy increase student achievement by accepting students and their ideas, using praise rather than criticism, persevering with low achievers, and using their time effectively. In contrast, low-efficacy teachers are less student centered, spend less time on learning activities, "give up" on low achievers, and use criticism more than do high-efficacy teachers (Kagan, 1992). High-efficacy teachers also tend to be more flexible, adopting new curriculum materials and changing strategies more readily than low-efficacy teachers (Poole et al., 1989).

Modeling and Enthusiasm.   **Modeling** *occurs when people imitate behaviors they observe in others* (Bandura, 1986), and teachers' attitudes and beliefs about teaching and learning are communicated through their behaviors. Student motivation is virtually impossible if teachers model distaste or lack of interest in the topics they teach, and when motivation decreases, so does learning. Statements such as the following serve no useful purpose and are devastating for motivation:

"I know this stuff is boring, but we have to learn it."

"I know you hate proofs."

"This isn't my favorite topic, either."

In contrast, if teachers display a pattern of statements such as Teri's—"but what's most interesting about all of this is that what we're studying has ramifications for the entire world, even today"—motivation and learning can be increased over time.

Teachers model enthusiasm; they communicate their own interest in the topics they teach through the behaviors they display. Research indicates that teachers who present information enthusiastically increase learners' beliefs in the importance of effort and in their own capabilities, and they increase achievement more than do less enthusiastic teachers (Pintrich & Schunk, 1996).

We see the effect of Teri's enthusiasm in Damon's comment, "Bowden thinks everything is interesting." What did she do to elicit that comment? Most significantly, she demonstrated her own interest in the topic. It didn't include a pep talk or theatrics; rather, it clearly identified the reasons why she found the topic interesting and meaningful. A teacher's goal in projecting enthusiasm is to induce in students the feeling that the information is valuable and worth learning, not to amuse or entertain them (Good & Brophy, 1997).

Teacher Caring.   Let's look again at how Teri began her class period. She made an attempt to greet the students personally as they walked in the door, and even when she told David that he had to take his basketball back to his locker, she did it in a nonpunitive way.

A growing body of research confirms the importance of learners' relationships with their teachers in promoting motivation (Stipek, 1996). "Learners' natural motivation to learn can be elicited in safe, trusting, and supportive environments characterized by . . . quality relationships with caring adults that see their unique potential" (McCombs, 1998, p. 399).

Caring *refers to teachers' abilities to empathize with and invest in the protection and development of young people* (Chaskin & Rauner, 1995). In addition to understanding how students feel, caring teachers are committed to their students' growth and competence. They're attempting to do their very best for the people under their care (Noddings, 1995).

The importance of caring is captured in a fourth grader's comment, "If a teacher doesn't care about you, it affects your mind. You feel like you're a nobody, and it makes you want to drop out of school" (Noblit et al., 1995, p. 683).

How do teachers communicate they care? Although individuals differ, a common thread is *time*. We all have 24 hours a day, and the way we choose to allocate those hours communicates a great deal about our priorities. Willingness to spend time with a student to talk about a personal problem, helping someone with an assignment, or calling parents after hours communicates that the student is important enough to a teacher that she will allocate some of her 24 hours to help that individual. Nothing communicates caring more effectively.

Let's look at a letter a ninth-grade student wrote to her geography teacher to see an example taken from an actual classroom. (The teacher's name has been changed, but the student's note is verbatim.)

Mrs. Hanson,

I want to thank you for everything you have done for me this year. I think that you're the only teacher I've had who believed in me and gave me the confidence I really needed. In a sense, I went to you when I couldn't turn to my own family and I want to thank you for always having time for me and my problems.

I don't want this letter to sound "cheesy" or "sucking up." It's just that I would have never gotten through the year without you and your advice.

You never treated me just as a student, but as a person, unlike most teachers have and that's what makes a great teacher, and Mrs. Hanson you certainly are a great teacher.

Sincerely,

Lisa Zahorchak

Positive Teacher Expectations

Mrs. Cummings watches as her new fifth-grade class files into her room. She notices a girl named Nicole and recalls that she had Nicole's brother Mike two years earlier. Mike was an above-average student with excellent study habits, and a pleasure to work with in class. Their parents were very involved in their children's schoolwork, and the home environment was positive.

Mrs. Cummings doesn't know, however, that Nicole has few of her brother's study habits. She is a happy-go-lucky girl interested in socializing, and she is already developing an interest in boys. Schoolwork is not a high priority for her.

Mrs. Cummings greets Nicole with a big smile, tells her it's nice to have her in class and that she's sure they will have a very good year.

Partway through the grading period, Mrs. Cummings is scoring some math papers and notices that Nicole's is missing. In checking her book, she finds that two other assignments are also missing and that Nicole has been scoring a bit lower on the tests than Mrs. Cummings had anticipated.

The next day she calls Nicole to her desk before class, puts her arm around her, and says, "Nicole, I can't imagine what happened to your homework papers. Please find them and turn them in. If you get them in by tomorrow, you'll get credit."

To be on the safe side, she calls Nicole's parents that evening. They were unaware of the missing homework and comment that Nicole has been rather vague when they ask if she has any homework for the next day.

Nicole's parents take immediate action. They postpone television and telephone conversations until they see that all her homework is finished and correct, and they call Mrs. Cummings, at Mrs. Cummings's request, to check on Nicole's progress. Mrs. Cummings reports that things are much better and that Nicole has improved considerably on the last test (adapted from Kauchak & Eggen, 1993).

Consider Mrs. Cummings's responses to Nicole. Because of her positive experiences with Nicole's brother, she had similar positive expectations for Nicole and her behavior. Because of these expectations, she greeted Nicole warmly, and when Nicole's behavior was less industrious than Mike's had been, she acted immediately. As a result, Nicole's work improved. Mrs. Cummings expected Nicole to learn and behaved in a way that promoted that learning.

Teacher expectations *are inferences that teachers make about the future behavior, academic achievement, or attitudes of their students* (Good & Brophy, 1997). They exert a powerful influence on teachers' behaviors. Believing that students can and will learn (positive teacher expectations) is a key variable that separates teachers who produce high student achievement from those who don't (Good, 1987a, 1987b).

The effects of expectations on the ways teachers treat students can be grouped into four areas: emotional support, teacher effort and demands, questioning, and feedback and evaluation. They are summarized in Table 2.1 (based on reviews by Good, 1987a, 1987b; and Good & Brophy, 1997. Adapted from Eggen & Kauchak, 1999).

We see from Table 2.1 that teachers can be discriminatory, treating students they perceive to be high achievers more favorably than those they perceive to be low achievers. Students are sensitive to this discrimination, and children as young as first grade are aware of differential treatment of high and low achievers (Stipek, 1996). In one study, researchers concluded that "after ten seconds of seeing and/or hearing a teacher, even very young students could detect whether the teacher talked about or to an excellent or a weak student and could determine the extent to which that student was loved by the teacher" (Babad et al., 1991, p. 230).

Unfortunately, expectations tend to be self-fulfilling. "Such low expectations can serve as self-fulfilling prophecies. That is, the expression of low expectations by differential treatment can inadvertently lead children to confirm predictions about their abilities by exerting less effort and ultimately performing more poorly" (Weinstein, 1998, p. 83). Being treated differently affects the way learners feel about themselves. Students "learn" that they have lower ability or are less worthy if they are consistently left out of discussions or

TABLE 2.1   Characteristics of Differential Teacher Expectations

Characteristic	Teacher Behavior Favoring Perceived High Achievers
Emotional support	More interactions; more positive interactions; more eye contact and smiles; stand closer; more direct orientation to student
Teacher effort and demands	Clearer and more thorough explanations; more enthusiastic instruction; require more complete and accurate student answers
Questioning	Call on more often; allow more time to answer; prompt more
Feedback and evaluation	More praise; less criticism; provide more complete and lengthier feedback; more conceptual evaluations

have interactions with teachers that are brief and superficial. Students are acutely aware of differences in treatment, and these differences can have a powerful effect on both motivation and achievement. High expectations communicate that the teacher believes students can learn and cares enough to make the effort to promote that learning. Over time, learning is increased.

Communication.   The importance of teachers' ability to communicate clearly is intuitively sensible, and research documents a strong link between communication and student achievement (Cruickshank, 1985; Snyder et al., 1991), as well as student satisfaction with instruction (Snyder et al., 1991).

Clear communication can be classified into four elements:

- Precise terminology
- Connected discourse
- Transition signals
- Emphasis

Precise Terminology.   If we look again at Teri Bowden's instruction, we see that she described her ideas clearly, and her explanations and answers to questions avoided the use of terms such as *perhaps, maybe, might, and so on, probably,* and *usually.* These vague phrases leave students with a sense of uncertainty, resulting in lowered achievement (Smith & Cotten, 1980).

Precise terminology *means that teachers define ideas clearly and eliminate vague terms from presentations and answers to students' questions.* While it's impossible to eliminate all vague terms from presentations, with effort teachers can make their language much more precise, which in turn contributes to increased achievement by students.

Connected Discourse.   **Connected discourse** *means the teacher's lesson is thematic and leads to a point.* Teri Bowden's lesson is a clear example of connected discourse. The theme of the lesson was the concept *mercantilism,* and the entire lesson was developed around that theme.

In contrast, let's look at another example.

A teacher is beginning a lesson on the Civil War with a group of fifth graders. She tells students that the goals of the lesson are to understand the dynamics of the war, to understand what caused the war and why the North won. Prior to the lesson, she lists several terms on the chalkboard, such as *Appomattox, amendment, free state, Underground Railroad, sectionalism, abolitionists,* and *secede.*

After she states her goal, she begins by explaining the concept of sectionalism and shows the students different sections of the United States on a small map. She continues with a question-and-answer activity in which she asks students how they think it would feel to be a slave, then a brief discussion of Abraham Lincoln, an equally brief discussion of why students think the North won the war, and some information on reconstruction.

Here we see that the teacher discussed sectionalism, what it would feel like to be a slave, Abraham Lincoln, why the North won the war, and reconstruction all in the same lesson. The lesson was not thematic and it didn't lead to a particular point. Her instruction would be described as disconnected or "scrambled" discourse.

There are two major obstacles to the goal of connected lessons: (1) The presentation can be sequenced inappropriately, or (2) information can be added to the discussion without clearly indicating how it relates to the topic. Both problems existed in the lesson on the Civil War, while neither was a problem in Teri Bowden's instruction.

Transition Signals.   Transition signals also contribute to clear communication. A **transition signal** *is a verbal statement that communicates that one idea is ending and another is beginning.* As an illustration, let's look again at Teri Bowden's comment, "Now let's shift our thinking a little and begin to focus on the colonial period, which began in the 1600s." This comment prepared students to move from the warm-up exercises to the lesson for the day.

During any lesson, students are at different places mentally. Transition signals focus students' attention, increasing the likelihood that they will be concentrating on the appropriate topic.

Emphasis.   A fourth aspect of clear classroom communication is emphasis. **Emphasis** *alerts students to important information in a lesson and can occur through vocal and verbal behavior or repetition* (Eggen & Kauchak, 1999). We see from the cognitive learning model in Chapter 1 that learners begin processing information by attending to it, and emphasis promotes this attention. Research confirms the role of emphasis in increasing achievement (Mayer, 1983). When Teri said, "Those are both good points. Everyone, remember this. . . . [raising her voice]. . . This is important. Do you see how both Kathy and Gregg used information to support their arguments? Nice job!" she was emphasizing the fact that providing evidence was important in the lesson. Use of this type of emphasis increases the clarity of communication and helps students follow the theme of the lesson.

Repeating a point also signals that an idea is important. For instance, statements such as, "Remember when Juanita said that amphibians have a three-chambered heart? That tells about their position in the chain of evolution," or, "What did Juanita say about the structure of the heart of amphibians?" are forms of repetition that serve to emphasize important ideas.

Language and Knowledge of Content.   Our discussion of clear language has two important implications for teachers. First, we should try to monitor our own speech to ensure that our presentations are as clear and logical as possible. Videotaping, reviewing, and developing lessons with many questions are simple and effective ways to improve on the clarity of our speech. Second, we must thoroughly understand the content we teach. If the content is unfamiliar, or our own grasp of it is uncertain, we should spend more time studying and preparing. Teachers whose understanding of topics is thorough use clearer language and form better explanations than those whose background is weaker (Carlsen, 1987; Cruickshank, 1985).

Clear understanding is particularly important when using instructional models that emphasize teachers guiding learners rather than lecturing to them. Guiding learning requires that teachers keep their goals constantly in mind, keep students involved, and ask appropriate questions at the right times. These are sophisticated abilities that require a deep and thorough understanding of the topics.

Organization.   Organization is intuitively sensible. We have all complained at one time or another about our lack of organization, and many of us have probably made conscious efforts to improve it. It affects the way we live and also, of course, our teaching. Teachers who are "organized" have students who learn more than their less organized counterparts (Bennett, 1978; Rutter et al., 1979).

Time is a key factor. Effective teachers manage to squeeze more minutes of instruction into the amount of time they have allocated than do less effective teachers.

Important characteristics of effective organization are outlined and illustrated in Table 2.2.

Each of the characteristics in Table 2.2 allows teachers to maximize the time available for instruction. Beginning classes promptly, having materials prepared in advance, using warm-up activities at the beginning of classes, and having students trained to perform routine tasks without being told all help teachers use their time well.

Instructional Alignment.   **Instructional alignment** *refers to the match between objectives and learning activities* (Cohen, 1987). In looking again at Teri Bowden's instruction, we see that her goals were clear and concise: She wanted students to understand the concept of mercantilism and at the same time practice higher-order and critical thinking. Her instruction was pointed directly toward those goals, and her assignment for the next day—to read a news article and relate the information to mercantilism—was also directly related to her goals.

While the notion of instructional alignment seems simple, a surprising number of teachers have goals and learning activities that are not congruent. Even worse, in some cases the instruction doesn't seem to be pointed to any particular goal.

As a contrasting example, let's look again at the teacher in the lesson on the Civil War. We said earlier that she described her goals as understanding the dynamics of the

TABLE 2.2   Characteristics of Effective Organization

Characteristic	Example
Starting on time	Teri's students were at their desks and working on her "warm-up" activity when the bell rang to begin the period.
Materials prepared in advance	Teri's materials were displayed on the overhead as her students walked in the door. The examples for her lesson were at her fingertips.
Established routines	The students knew how to pick up their papers from their folders without being told.

war—to understand what caused the war, and why the North won. We found that she also listed several terms on the chalkboard and then discussed sectionalism, what the students thought it would feel like to be a slave, Abraham Lincoln, why students think the North won the war, and some information on reconstruction. After the discussion, the teacher assigned an in-class essay on the war using the terms she had listed on the chalkboard. Finally, she gave students a homework assignment in which they were supposed to write a paragraph describing what the term *indivisible* meant to them, and the lesson ended.

This is a case of instruction that was almost completely out of alignment. The only part of the learning activity that related to the teacher's goal was the brief discussion of reasons why the North had won the war. At no point in the lesson did she use or refer to any of the terms on the chalkboard, yet her seatwork assignment focused on those terms. Her homework assignment dealt with the concept *indivisible,* to which no part of her instruction referred.

Instructional alignment is more sophisticated and subtle than it appears. For example, on the surface this teacher's instruction looked acceptable, perhaps even good. Her students were orderly and the teacher involved the students in a question-and-answer activity. The lack of alignment wasn't obvious or apparent. In fact, in a research study examining preservice, first-year, and veteran teachers' concepts of effective instruction, most of the preservice and first-year teachers missed the fact that the instruction in this lesson—which was on videotape—was not aligned, while veteran teachers quickly identified the alignment problem (Harris & Eggen, 1993).

Focus.   In reviewing what we've discussed to this point, we see that we have examined teacher attitudes, effective communication, teacher organization, and the need for instruction to be aligned if student achievement is to be as high as possible.

For these elements of instruction to be most effective, students must be engaged or "with us" in the lesson. Lesson focus attracts and holds students' attention throughout the learning activity.

As we saw in our discussion of cognitive learning in Chapter 1, and earlier in our discussion of *emphasis*, learning begins with attention, and attention must be maintained if learning is to continue. **Focus** *is the process teachers use to attract and maintain attention throughout the lesson.* Focus exists in two forms: introductory and sensory. Though the two forms are interrelated, we discuss them separately for the sake of clarity.

Introductory Focus.   To understand introductory focus, let's look again at Teri Bowden's lesson. As soon as students finished their warm-up activity, she said:

> Let's shift our thinking a little and begin to focus on the colonial period, which began in the 1600s. This is a very important part of American history, but what's most interesting about all of this is that what we're studying has ramifications for the entire world, even today. Today's topic is one of the most important ideas of the entire colonial period, so let's see what kind of job we can do in figuring it out.

Teri used this statement as her **introductory focus,** *which is the set of teacher actions designed to attract students' attention and provide an umbrella for the rest of the* *lesson.* While it is similar to an "advance organizer" (Ausubel, 1968; Corkill, 1992), the function of introductory focus is attention getting and motivational, whereas the function of an advance organizer is conceptual. Introductory focus is designed to enhance motivation by arousing curiosity and making lesson content attractive.

Sensory Focus. **Sensory focus** *is the use of stimuli—concrete objects, pictures, models, materials displayed on the overhead, and even information written on the chalkboard—to maintain attention.* The more concrete and attractive the materials, the better they serve as forms of sensory focus. In addition to supplementing her introductory focus, Teri displayed examples on the overhead that helped maintain attention by giving students something to look at and think about.

The simplest form of sensory focus is the chalkboard, but it's often underused, particularly in elementary schools. Teachers commonly deliver their lessons verbally instead of using the board as a supplement; as a result, lessons lose focus and students become inattentive. This is a particular problem for students with special needs or those who have trouble focusing their attention on verbal information.

Feedback. **Feedback** *is information about current behavior that can be used to improve future performance* (Eggen & Kauchak, 1999), and its importance is confirmed by both theory and research. From a theoretical perspective, we know that learners are active in their attempts to construct understanding of the topics they study. They can't be sure, however, that their initial constructions are valid. Feedback gives them information they can use to assess the validity of their understanding.

This theoretical perspective is confirmed by research. Feedback is so important that it is sometimes cited as a learning principle. Regardless of the topic, grade level, or task, learners benefit from feedback about their performance (Good & Brophy, 1997; Rosenshine & Stevens, 1986).

Effective feedback has five characteristics, which are illustrated in Figure 2.2. These characteristics are equally important for both written and verbal feedback.

When teachers provide feedback, it is important to include corrective information. Let's look at an example:

> A teacher is working with students on simplifying arithmetic expressions and displays the following expression on the board:
>
> 4 + 3 (6 − 2) − 5
>
> The teacher asks, "What must we do first to simplify the expression? Leon?"
> "Add the 4 and the 3."
> "Not quite, Leon. Can someone help out?"

Even though the feedback was immediate, it was not specific, and it provided Leon with no additional information. Contrast that response with the following exchange:

> "What is the first step in simplifying the expression? Emilio?"

"Add the 4 and the 3."

"Look again, Emilio. If we first add the 4 and the 3, we would have 7 times the 6 minus 2 in parentheses. What does the expression imply?"

". . . That it's 3 times the numbers in parentheses."

In the second example, the teacher gave a specific response based on Emilio's answer and provided information that helped him answer correctly. Both strategies enhance learning. In contrast to Leon, the feedback both helped Emilio understand why his first answer was incorrect and gave him the opportunity to answer correctly.

In addition to the characteristics we've already described, the emotional tone of feedback is important. To be motivated, students must feel safe. Criticism, sarcasm, or ridicule detracts from this safety, destroys motivation, and decreases learning (Murphy et al., 1986).

Monitoring.   **Monitoring** *is the process of checking students' verbal and nonverbal behavior for evidence of learning progress.* It is important during all learning activities, and particularly during seatwork, when students may be making repeated errors. Monitoring also includes being aware of students' reactions during learning activities. Monitoring, in short, is the ability to be flexible and responsive to students (O'Keefe and Johnston, 1987).

Alert teachers immediately recognize when students become inattentive; they move near these students or call on them to bring them back into lessons. Less alert teachers don't notice the inattention. A sensitive teacher also responds to students' nonverbal behaviors and makes statements (or asks questions) such as, "José, I see your eyes look puzzled. Do you want me to repeat what I just said?" Careful monitoring followed by appropriate responses can strongly contribute to a climate of support while simultaneously demonstrating high expectations both for behavior and learning.

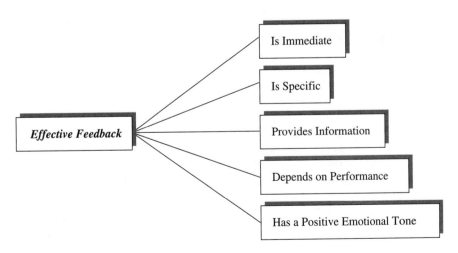

FIGURE 2.2   Characteristics of Effective Feedback

Review and Closure.   **Review** *summarizes previous work and forms a link between what has been learned and what is coming.* **Closure** *is a form of review that occurs at the end of a lesson.* Review emphasizes important points and can occur at any point in a learning activity, although it most commonly occurs at the beginning and end of a lesson.

The value of review is well documented by research (Rosenshine & Stevens, 1986). Dempster (1991) explains its effectiveness in this way: "Reviews may do more than simply increase the amount learned; they may shift the learner's attention away from verbatim details of the material being studied to its deeper conceptual structure" (p. 71). This deeper conceptual structure is especially important when we teach for understanding.

When a topic comes to closure, it is summarized, structured, and completed. The notion of closure is intuitively sensible and it is often used in everyday discussions, such as, "Let's try to get to closure on this." In learning activities, it pulls together the lesson content and signals the end of a lesson.

Teri's closure was thorough and complete. Let's look again at a portion of the dialogue in the lesson.

> **TERI:**   That's excellent everyone! Excellent analysis of the information we have here. Now let's look back and see what we've found. [She goes on] We've examined the three cases, and now we want to take a broader look at the information in general. Let's begin. We have a situation where . . . ? Toni?
>
> **TONI:**   . . . Colonists related to a country produce only raw materials, no manufactured stuff.
>
> **TERI:**   Good. . . .Go on.
>
> **TONI:**   . . . And they can only be sold to the mother country.
>
> **GREGG:**   Who in turn provided the manufacturing and the shipping.
>
> **TERI:**   Excellent! Very clear, succinct description of what we've been discussing. . . . Now we know the features of this policy. Does anyone know what it's called?

At this point, Teri provided the term *mercantilism,* since the students had identified the essential characteristics of the concept.

Coming to closure at the end of a lesson is important. This is the last information that students take away from the class, and if the ideas aren't clear, they may develop misconceptions that can be difficult to eliminate.

Questioning.   In Chapter 1 we saw that cognitive views of learning emphasize interaction, both teacher-student and student-student, to help learners understand the topics they study (Lambert & McCombs, 1998). Questioning is the most important skill teachers have for promoting this interaction (Wang et al., 1993). Skillful teacher questioning helps students see connections between the ideas they're studying and helps them see how abstract ideas relate to real-world examples (Brown, 1994; Eggen & Kauchak, 1999). Questioning also helps students maintain sensory focus, helps emphasize concepts through repetition, and is effective for informally assessing student understanding. In addition, teachers use questioning to ensure success, involve reluctant and inattentive students, and enhance students' self-esteem.

Becoming skilled at questioning is difficult because it involves several things at once (Eggen & Kauchak, 1999):

- Remembering the goals of the lesson
- Monitoring students' verbal and nonverbal behaviors
- Maintaining the flow and development of the lesson
- Preparing the next question

With practice, however, teachers can become skilled at questioning, and this skill is highly developed in expert teachers (Kerman, 1979; Rowe, 1986).

Effective questioning has four characteristics:

- Frequency
- Equitable distribution
- Prompting
- Wait-time

Frequency.   In thinking back to Teri Bowden's lesson, we see that she asked a large number of questions, In fact, she developed much of her lesson with questioning. **Questioning frequency** *refers to the number of questions teachers ask,* and research indicates that effective teachers ask a large number of questions (Morine-Dershimer, 1987). Interactive questions increase student involvement, which increases achievement (Lambert & McCombs, 1998; Eggen & Kauchak, 1999).

Equitable Distribution.   Merely asking a lot of questions isn't enough, however. If the same students are answering all of the questions, others become inattentive, and overall achievement is lowered. Kerman (1979) used the term **equitable distribution** to describe *a questioning pattern in which all students in the class are called on as equally as possible.* We saw earlier in the chapter that teachers sometimes treat students differently based on their expectations. Because teachers expect less from lower than from higher achievers, they call on them less, often unconsciously. Further, most teacher questions are not directed to particular students (McGreal, 1985). This means that a student who wants to volunteer, or even "shout out" an answer is allowed to do so, and those who don't are allowed to remain passive. This practice results in lowered achievement (Brophy & Evertson, 1974). When this occurs, less vocal or aggressive students fall into a pattern of not responding, become inattentive, and achievement decreases.

One solution is to call on all students as equally as possible, and direct questions to students by name. This promotes equitable distribution and prevents a vocal minority from dominating the activity. Equitable distribution communicates to students that the teacher expects them to be involved and able to answer. When this becomes a pattern, both achievement and motivation improve (McDougall & Granby, 1996).

To make the process work, however, the classroom must be managed to prevent student **call-outs,** *which are answers given by students before the students have been recognized by the teacher.* Callouts usually come from the higher-achieving or more aggressive students in the class, and if this becomes a pattern, the less aggressive and lower-achieving students are often left out, equitable distribution is reduced, and general achievement is lowered.

In looking again at Teri's lesson, we see that she was effective in applying this research. She directed her questions to specific students by name, and her instruction never strayed from the goal of her lesson.

Equitable distribution is a simple idea but difficult to put into practice. It requires careful monitoring of students and a great deal of teacher energy. Unfortunately, we don't often see it practiced in classrooms. However, its effects can be very powerful for both learning and motivation, and we strongly encourage you to persevere and pursue it rigorously.

Prompting.   In attempting equitable distribution, an important question arises: What do you do when the student you call on doesn't answer or answers incorrectly? The answer is prompting. A **prompt** *is a teacher question or directive that elicits a student response after the student has failed to answer or has given an incorrect or incomplete answer.* As an illustration, let's look again at some dialogue from Teri's lesson.

> **TERI:** That's very good, both of you. Where do you suppose Steve got that idea [that the colonists couldn't send goods anywhere other than the parent country]? Connie?
>
> **CONNIE:** It says right in the first two examples, and in the third one it says that when India tried to establish stronger ties with other countries to expand the scope of its trade, it got in trouble.
>
> **TERI:** Excellent, everyone! Connie, good use of information to support your ideas. You've all improved a great deal in that regard. Keep going. . . . Mary?
>
> **MARY:** (No response)
>
> **TERI:** What did they get in return in each case?
>
> **MARY:** . . . They got textiles from England . . . and fur garments, traps, and stuff from France . . . and clothing from England.

When Mary was unable to respond, Teri asked another question that helped Mary answer successfully. Let's look at one more example.

> **TERI:** Now let's go a bit farther. What other patterns do you see in the descriptions? Kim?
>
> **KIM:** (No response)
>
> **TERI:** How were the goods shipped, Kim?
>
> **KIM:** On ships.
>
> **TERI:** Yes, good, Kim! What ships, or whose ships?
>
> **KIM:** . . . In each case it was the ships from the parent country.

As with Mary, when Kim didn't respond correctly, Teri asked another question, then asked Kim to expand on her answer with an additional question. This is the essence of prompting.

Prompting and Classroom Climate.   Consider the effects on students if a pattern of prompting is established. It communicates that the teacher expects a successful answer and will provide assistance to ensure success. As a result, on succeeding questions students are likely to increase their effort.

Wait-Time.   Let's look once more at Teri's lesson. While it's hard to see in a written case study, after asking a student a question Teri waited a few seconds for an answer, giving students time to think. *This period of silence, both before and after a student responds,* is called **wait-time,** and research indicates that in most classrooms, it is too short, typically less than 1 second (Rowe, 1986).

A more intuitively sensible label for wait-time might be "think time," because in reality waiting actually gives the student a little time, ideally about 3 to 5 seconds, to think. There are at least three benefits to this practice (Rowe, 1974, 1986):

- Equitable distribution improves and responses from cultural minorities increase as teachers become more responsive to students.
- Students give longer and better responses.
- Voluntary participation increases, and fewer students fail to respond.

Wait-time must be implemented judiciously, however. For example, if students are involved in practice, such as multiplication facts, quick answers are desirable and wait-times should be short (Rosenshine & Stevens, 1986). Also, if a student appears uneasy, we may choose to intervene earlier. On the other hand, students need time to respond to questions asking them to compare, apply, analyze, or evaluate information. In general, increasing wait-time reduces student anxiety rather than increasing it, because a climate of support is established. All students are expected to participate, they're given time to think about their responses, and they know that the teacher will help them if they're unable to answer.

Essential Teaching Skills and Classroom Management: Creating Productive Learning Environments

Teachers and lay people alike believe that **productive learning environments,** *classrooms that are orderly and focus on learning,* are essential. From 1968 until 1986, those surveyed by the Gallup polls identified school discipline as the most important problem teachers face; from 1986 to 1992, it ranked only behind drugs and inadequate funding as the biggest educational problem; and in 1994 and 1995, it returned again to top position (Elam & Rose, 1995). Classroom management is a particularly acute problem for beginning teachers, who often don't feel prepared to deal with these problems (Kher-Durlabhji et al., 1997).

Commonly overlooked in discussions of management and discipline is the role of effective instruction. Research indicates that it is virtually impossible to maintain an orderly classroom in the absence of effective instruction and vice versa. This is where the essential teaching skills are important. Let's look at this relationship in more detail.

Organization and Classroom Order.   A large body of research indicates that teachers' ability to maintain orderly classrooms is one of the most important factors influencing student achievement (Blumenfeld et al., 1987; Evertson, 1987). Good (1979), in a review of this research, observed, "Teachers' managerial abilities have been found to relate positively to achievement in every process-product study conducted to date" (p. 54).

Organization is an important factor in classroom management. As an illustration, let's look again at Teri's class. First, we see that students had a task waiting for them when they walked in the room, which they completed while Teri took roll. This prevents "down time" at the beginning of the period—one of the times that management problems are most likely to occur. Second, she had well-established routines that made the environment predictable for students and allowed her to devote her energy to instruction instead of having to spend it on maintaining order.

Classroom Order and Student Involvement.   It should be emphasized that classroom order doesn't mean teacher lecture and passive students. We saw that Teri's class was very orderly but that a great deal of interaction took place throughout the lesson. Order implies that the students are spending as much of their time focused on learning as possible; it doesn't mean that they sit quietly while a teacher does all the talking.

Involvement, Order, and Student Motivation.   Involvement and order also increase student motivation. Brophy (1987), in describing what he calls "essential preconditions for motivating students," concluded, "Nor is such motivation likely to develop in a chaotic classroom. Thus we assume that . . . the teacher uses classroom organization and management skills that successfully establish the classroom as an effective learning environment" (p. 208). Classroom order and effective teaching are interdependent; it is impossible to be a truly effective teacher without being an effective manager, and it is also impossible to maintain order (without serious coercion) in the absence of effective instruction.

Essential Teaching Skills: A Theoretical Perspective

In the last section we described essential teaching skills as the abilities that every teacher should possess—a foundation on which all other skills are based. This description implies that a first-year teacher should possess these abilities, which is not a simple task.

To understand the challenges that teachers face, we need to look again at the cognitive model we discussed in Chapter 1. There we saw that our processing systems include three memory stores: *sensory memory,* which receives stimuli from the environment; *working memory,* the conscious part of our cognitive system; and *long-term memory,* our permanent memory store (Eggen & Kauchak, 1999; Mayer, 1998).

An important aspect of our processing system is the fact that working memory is limited in capacity (Sweller et al., 1998). This limitation means that we are able to consciously process only a certain amount of information at a time; if we're faced with too much, some will be lost or ignored in an effort to reduce the load. (This is where the term *cognitive overload* originated.)

This problem is common in classrooms with students who haven't mastered basic operations in math or skills in reading, for example. When a student is required to solve a word problem, too much of his or her working memory's limited capacity is required to simply read the problem or perform the basic mathematical operations, leaving an inadequate amount of thinking space to actually find the solution. In reading, similarly, if students use too much working memory space to decode words, they don't have enough left to comprehend what they're reading.

Automaticity: Saving Memory for Decision Making.   The solution to this problem is **automaticity,** *which refers to mental operations that can be performed with little awareness or conscious effort* (Bloom, 1986; Case, 1978). Skills that are automatic take up virtually no working memory space. For example, remember when you learned to drive a car, particularly if it had a stick shift. Initially, the process was quite labored, and a great deal of conscious effort was spent on simply depressing the clutch, shifting, and releasing the clutch without killing the motor. In time, the process became nearly effortless, allowing conversation while smoothly shifting through the gears; the process of driving and shifting became "automatic."

So what does this have to do with essential teaching skills? Teaching is very complex and demanding. In a single learning activity, teachers are expected to maintain order, reengage inattentive students, maintain the pace and flow of the lesson, and help students clarify ideas they don't understand. This is difficult, if not impossible, unless essential teaching skills are virtually automatic. Unless teachers' questioning skills are nearly automatic, for example, the models presented in Chapters 3 through 9 will be very difficult to use. As another example, if teachers are using much of their working memory simply to maintain order in their classrooms, they will also find it difficult to implement these strategies.

Lack of automaticity helps explain why we see so much lecture and seatwork in schools. Lecture is simple; the teacher has to focus only on organizing and delivering content. Since students are passive, management problems are usually minimal. Seatwork is similar. The teacher only needs to monitor students for signs of disruption or confusion; demands on teachers' working memory and energy are low.

In contrast, actively involving students in questioning is much more complex and demanding. Teachers must organize the content, ask the right questions at the appropriate times, and refocus the class when it has drifted away from the original goal. All of this must be done while calling on all students equally, asking the question before identifying the student, watching for signs of confusion, and maintaining classroom order.

The solution is conceptually simple, but demanding in reality. Developing automaticity requires practice. These abilities can be learned if the teacher is willing to make the effort, and the outcomes can be enormously rewarding. Both learning and motivation increase, and the sense of satisfaction that comes with truly guiding student learning can be tremendous.

Beyond Effective Teaching: Teaching for Thinking and Understanding

In Chapter 1, and earlier in this chapter, we said that effective teaching provides only a foundation upon which excellence is built and that expert teachers go beyond this threshold to construct lessons that help students acquire a deep and thorough understanding of the topics they study. Resnick and Klopfer (1989) use the term **generative knowledge,** or *"knowledge that can be used to interpret new situations, to solve problems, to think and reason, and to learn"* (p. 5), to describe this deep understanding.

Generative knowledge involves learning both content and thinking skills. David Perkins (1992) underscores the relationship between thinking and knowledge of content by saying, "Learning is a consequence of thinking. Retention, understanding, and the active use of knowledge can be brought about only by learning experiences in which learners think about and think with what they are learning" (p. 8). The implications for teaching are clear: If deep understanding of content is a goal, emphasis on thinking must also be a goal. The models presented in Chapters 3 through 9 of this text are designed to capitalize on these two interrelated goals.

Teaching Thinking: An Enduring Concern

The crucial need for teaching for thinking and understanding arises from current practice in today's schools. In a comprehensive and widely publicized study of American schools, John Goodlad concluded:

> Only rarely did we find evidence to suggest instruction (in reading and math) likely to go much beyond merely possession of information to a level of understanding its implications and either applying it or exploring its possible applications. Nor did we see activities likely to arouse students' curiosity or to involve them in seeking a solution to some problem not already laid bare by teacher or textbook.
>
> And it appears that this preoccupation with the lower intellectual processes pervades social studies and science as well. An analysis of topics studied and materials used gives not an impression of students studying human adaptations and exploration, but of facts to be learned (Goodlad, 1984, p. 236).

Another study found that

> many students are unable to give evidence of a more than superficial understanding of concepts and relationships that are fundamental to the subjects they have studied, or of an ability to apply the content knowledge they have acquired to real-world problems. The general picture of the thinking ability of U.S. students that is painted by these reports [national assessments of education progress and studies from the National Commission on Excellence in Education] is a disturbing one (Nickerson, 1988, p. 5).

Teaching Thinking: Increasing Learner Motivation

The need for teaching the skill of thinking is well documented. Without an emphasis on thinking, deep understanding of content is virtually impossible. The reverse is also true. In order to think effectively in an area, a person must possess a great deal of generative knowledge about the area (Bransford et al., 1991; Nickerson, 1988; Resnick & Klopfer, 1989).

What receives much less emphasis, however, is the fact that goals that increase critical thinking also lead to increased learner motivation (Brown, 1988; Stipek, 1998).

Teaching for thinking emphasizes learner autonomy and independent inquiry. Because of this emphasis, students' needs for control, competence, and achievement are more likely to be met than they are when passive approaches focusing on teacher lecture and student memorization are used. Autonomy, student self-direction, and self-regulated learning are all factors that increase students' motivation to learn (Bruning et al., 1999; Pintrich & Schunk, 1996).

To see the motivational effects of teaching for thinking, we can look again at Teri Bowden's instruction. The students were in a learning environment where their answers were based on their own thoughts as they interpreted information, not what they thought Teri wanted to hear or what they had memorized. Being allowed the freedom to say what you actually think rather than what you believe someone expects to hear is intellectually liberating. This freedom, combined with learning to defend your position based on evidence, can lead to a personal sense of power and satisfaction. The combination can be intellectually exciting and motivating.

A Climate for Thinking.   As with other aspects of teaching, teaching for thinking requires supporting elements. To illustrate these elements, let's look again at Teri's lesson and the intellectual climate that she established with her students:

- She provided students with information and began the lesson in an open-ended and nonthreatening way.
- She promoted a spirit of cooperation rather than competition and avoided any comparisons of performance among students.
- She focused on improvement rather than displays of ability, as indicated by her comments, "Excellent, everyone! Connie, good use of information to support your ideas. You've all improved a great deal in that regard . . ."
- She emphasized that success was evidenced by improvement and progress rather than high grades and performance compared to others.

Each of these factors created a climate in which the students felt safe and willing to take risks. This type of classroom climate is critical for both thinking and learner motivation (Maehr, 1992).

Critical Thinking

We have discussed the need for teaching thinking and the relationships among teaching for thinking, deep understanding of content, and learner motivation. We now want to look at what critical thinking means. As with other aspects of human cognition, thinking is a complex activity, and we readily acknowledge that what you are about to read may oversimplify the processes. However, we offer this description of thinking as a starting point and foundation for your growth in this area.

In this text we define **critical thinking** *as the ability and disposition to make and assess conclusions based on evidence.* In some cases critical thinking is quite simple. For example, when we shop for a new vehicle, we consider price, economy, reliability, and other factors such as style. If one vehicle is advertised to make 22 miles per gallon whereas another makes only 16, we use that evidence as one factor in making a decision about which is a better buy. This is a form of critical thinking that's common in our shopping habits.

In other instances, critical thinking is more complex and sophisticated and can include such abilities as:

- Confirming conclusions with facts
- Identifying bias, stereotypes, clichés, and propaganda
- Identifying unstated assumptions
- Recognizing overgeneralizations and undergeneralizations
- Identifying relevant and irrelevant information

To illustrate some of these dimensions, let's look again at a portion of the dialogue in Teri's lesson:

STEVE: And they couldn't send it [the raw materials colonies produced] anywhere else!

TERI: . . . Where do you suppose Steve got that idea? . . . Connie?

CONNIE: It says it right in the first two examples. . . . And in the third one it says that when India tried to establish stronger ties with other countries to expand the scope of their trade, they got in trouble.

Steve made a conclusion—colonies couldn't send their raw materials to any country other than their parent country—and Connie provided factual evidence from the examples that supported Steve's conclusion. Teri capitalized on this process at several points in the lesson.

Let's look at another example:

BOB: They weren't allowed to [get finished goods from other countries].

TERI: And what made you say that, Bob?

BOB: It says in the second example that they were told that their traps and weapons would be sent from France, and in the third example it says that the British argued that the homeland was more than capable of providing for India's needs.

Teri's lesson focused on a deep understanding of the concept of *mercantilism* while simultaneously giving students practice in critical thinking—making conclusions based on evidence.

We saw students practicing making and confirming conclusions with evidence in the preceding dialogue. Let's look now at additional dialogue where they demonstrate more sophisticated thinking:

JACK: We had to separate out the relevant from the irrelevant information.

TERI: For example?

JACK: . . . Well, whether it was guns, or traps, or clothing, or whatever, really didn't matter. The important point was that the colonists weren't allowed to manufacture anything.

Jack evidenced critical thinking by identifying some irrelevant information.

Let's look now at how Teri helped her students recognize an unstated assumption in her question about countries being "guilty" of mercantilism:

TERI: Let's look again at the question I asked: "What other countries have been guilty of mercantilism?" What assumption is being made in that question?

ANTHONY: . . . It looks like you're suggesting that mercantilism is bad.

TERI: Good thinking. . . . That's exactly what it implies. Now, mercantilism may very well have been bad . . . exploitation of colonialized lands and that kind of thing. However, the question I asked had in it an unstated assumption. Recognizing unstated assumptions is part of the thinking process, and we all need to be on the lookout for that kind of thing. . . . Again, that's good thinking, Anthony.

Teri's lesson and the dialogue we taken from it represent an ideal. Getting students to think the way hers did won't happen in every classroom, and it may not happen often. However, knowing that it is possible gives us something to strive for, and it's an incentive to raise our expectations for our students. Seeing improvement in our students' thinking indicates progress and is a measure of success. It helps us move beyond the "preoccupation with the lower intellectual processes" Goodlad (1984) found so pervasive in most classrooms.

Critical Thinking: Attitudes and Dispositions

Perhaps most important for critical thinking are the *attitudes, dispositions,* and *inclinations* that we hope to develop in our students. The ability to use evidence, for example, is limited if learners have to be continually reminded that evidence is required. Ultimately, our goals are for students to be "inclined" to use evidence *on their own.* These inclinations develop in time if students are required to practice them.

Critical Thinking in Day-to-Day Living

The following simple example illustrates how such an inclination operates in everyday life.

Terry and Tabatha are walking down the hall when they meet Andrea coming the other way.

"Hi, Andrea," Terry and Tabatha say in unison.

Andrea barely glances at the two girls and keeps walking.

"Is she stuck up or what?" Terry grumbles.

"We don't know that," Tabatha returns. "Maybe she isn't feeling well, or maybe something happened to her this morning."

Tabatha demonstrated the *inclination* to *remain open minded* and *reserve judgment*. Opportunities to promote and encourage these inclinations regularly show up in classrooms, and if teachers are aware of the possibilities, they can capitalize on them when they do occur.

A number of attitudes and inclinations associated with critical thinking have been identified. Some include:

- A desire to be informed and look for evidence
- An attitude of open-mindedness and healthy skepticism
- The tendency to reserve judgment
- Respect for others' opinions
- Tolerance for ambiguity

Students learn these attitudes through teacher modeling and by experiencing them in classroom learning activities.

Summary

Essential Teaching Skills:
The Foundation for Teaching Effectiveness

Teacher effectiveness describes patterns of teacher actions that result in increased student achievement. Essential teaching skills, the abilities that all teachers should have, are based on the teacher-effectiveness research. These skills provide the foundation on which the models in this book are based.

Beyond Effective Teaching:
Teaching for Thinking and Understanding

Expert teachers go beyond essential teaching skills to promote deep understanding of the topics they teach together with thinking. Much instruction in our schools focuses on knowledge and recall, and the ability of our students to think is a matter of ongoing concern. Fortunately, teaching for thinking also increases learner motivation.

Teaching thinking requires a classroom environment where learners feel free to offer their thoughts and ideas without fear of reprisal or embarrassment.

Critical Thinking

Critical thinking is the ability to make and defend conclusions based on evidence. It also includes an attitude of open-mindedness, tolerance for ambiguity, respect for others' opinions, the ability to separate relevant from irrelevant information, and other attitudes and dispositions. Opportunities to practice critical thinking abilities abound, both in classrooms and in everyday living.

IMPORTANT CONCEPTS

Automaticity *(p. 45)*
Call-outs *(p. 41)*
Caring *(p. 31)*
Closure *(p. 40)*
Connected discourse *(p. 34)*
Critical thinking *(p. 47)*
Emphasis *(p. 35)*
Equitable distribution *(p. 41)*
Essential teaching skills *(p. 29)*
Feedback *(p. 38)*
Focus *(p. 37)*
Generative knowledge *(p. 46)*
Instructional alignment *(p. 36)*

Introductory focus *(p. 37)*
Modeling *(p. 30)*
Monitoring *(p. 39)*
Personal teaching efficacy *(p. 30)*
Precise terminology *(p. 34)*
Productive learning environments *(p. 43)*
Prompt *(p. 42)*
Questioning frequency *(p. 41)*
Review *(p. 40)*
Sensory focus *(p. 38)*
Teacher expectations *(p. 33)*
Transition signal *(p. 35)*
Wait-time *(p. 43)*

EXERCISES

Read the following case study illustrating a fourth-grade teacher involved in a math lesson with her students and answer the questions that follow.

1. Entering the kitchen, Jim Barton saw his wife, Shirley, hard at work at the kitchen table. "What are you doing with those cake pans? We've already eaten dinner."

2. "What do you think?" she grinned at him. "Do they look like cake?" she asked holding up cardboard pieces drawn to resemble cake cut into squares in the two pans.

3. "Actually they almost do," he responded, a bit impressed.

4. "My kids didn't score as well as I would have liked on the fractions part of the SAT last year, and I swore that they were going to do better this year."

5. "But you said that the kids aren't as sharp this year."

6. "I don't care. I'm pushing them harder. I think I could have done a better job last year, so I swore I was really going to be ready for them this time."

7. Jim mumbled something about thinking that teachers who have taught for eleven years were supposed to burn out and, smiling slightly, walked back into the living room.

8. The next day, Shirley walked slowly up and down the aisles, at times stopping for a few seconds to comment on a student's work or offer reassurance as students completed their reading seatwork.

9. Glancing at her watch, she saw that it was 9:58, 2 minutes before her normally scheduled math time, and announced hurriedly, "Let me have your reading papers and please get out your math homework. We're running a little late today."

10. The students stopped their writing and passed the papers forward. She collected them from the first person in each row, and as she walked by Shelli on the way to the chalkboard, she paused and asked, "How are you feeling today, Shelli? Is your cold better?"

11. "A lot better," Shelli replied looking up at her. "I've just got some sniffles now."

12. Shirley put the papers in a folder on her desk and stepped to the chalkboard as she watched the students put their reading materials away and pull their math books out of their desks. She wrote the following problems on the board:

$$\frac{3}{8} + \frac{2}{8} \qquad \frac{3}{7} + \frac{4}{7} \qquad \frac{5}{12} + \frac{6}{12}$$

At 10:01 the children had their math books out and were waiting.

13. "Now," she began, "We've been adding fractions, so for a moment let's look again at what we've been doing. What does the eight mean in the first problem? . . . Elmore?" and she walked to the board, tapped it with her chalk, and then pulled out a drawing from behind her desk:

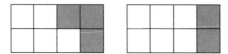

14. "We have eight parts of something altogether."

15. "And what kind of parts? Fernando?"

16. ". . . Equal."

17. "Okay, good.

18. Shirley continued, asking Andrea what the top numbers meant, and went on, "What is the sum in the first problem? Gayle."

19. "Five-eighths."

20. "Good, Gayle. And how did Gayle get that? Tamika?"

21. ". . . She added the top numbers."

22. Shirley continued with the second and third problems on the board and finished by saying, as she tapped her knuckle on the chalkboard, "Now remember, everyone, this is very important. Each of these problems has the same denominator," as she pointed respectively to the 8s, the 7s, and the 12s.

23. "Now," she continued as she strode vigorously across the front of the room, "we're going to shift gears to where we want to add fractions when the denominators are not alike."

24. She then pulled the two cardboard rectangles drawn to resemble the cake that she had made the night before from the shelf, one divided into thirds and the other divided in half.

25. "Now suppose I want to add half of this cake to a third of this one." She pointed to a shaded half and third respectively. "How much cake will I have? How am I going to figure it out?" She paused for a few seconds, then continued, "That's what we're going to begin today."

26. Shirley began by pointing to the shaded third of the cardboard and asking, "How much cake do I have here? Tim?"

27. ". . . A third."

28. "Okay, fine," Shirley smiled. "But now look," and she folded the cardboard in half along the opposite axis. "How many pieces do I have altogether now? Karen?"

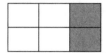

29. ". . . It looks like six," Karen responded uncertainly.

30. "Yes, good, Karen. I saw you actually counting them," Shirley noted and then counted the six squares again herself. "So what portion is now shaded? Michael?"

31. ". . . Two-sixths."

32. "Excellent, Michael!" and she moved to the board and wrote $\frac{1}{3}$ and $\frac{2}{3}$ alongside each other with an equal sign in between.

33. Then Shirley said, "Watch what I do here," and she demonstrated for the students how they could write

$$\frac{(2)\ 1}{(2)\ 4} = \frac{4}{6}$$

and referred again to her cardboard cake as she did it.

34. Then she moved to an example with $\frac{1}{4}$, again folding her cardboard and writing

$$\frac{(3)\ 2}{(3)\ 3} = \frac{3}{12}$$

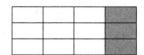

After the two examples, she said, "Now let's stop for a moment. How do we know that the two-thirds and the four-sixths are the same? Ken?"

35. (No response)

36. "How much is shaded here?"

37. (No response)

38. "Look at the cardboard, Andre," Shirley smiled encouragingly. "Tell me what you see here."

39. ". . . Some of the cardboard is a different color."

40. "How much?"

41. ". . . Two-thirds."

42. "And how about this way? Kathy?"

43. ". . . Four-sixths."

44. "So how do they compare? Felix?"

45. "They're the same."

46. "Outstanding!" Shirley smiled and glanced at Ken to see if he appeared to understand.

47. Shirley continued with the process for another 15 minutes, and then said, "Now, everyone, let's look and see what kind of pattern we have in these examples. Give it a try, Ron?"

48. ". . . Well, we're finding fractions that are the same as other fractions."

49. "Explain that a little further, please."

50. ". . . The one-third and the two-sixths were the same, and the one-fourth and the three-twelfths were the same, and the two-thirds and the four-sixths were the same."

51. "Excellent, Ron," Shirley smiled. "And why do we need to do this? Yevgeny?"

52. (No response)

53. "Think about what we did in our last lesson. What were the fractions like there?"

54. ". . . They all had the same denominators," Yevgeny blurted out.

55. "Super, Yevgeny," Shirley responded.

56. She continued, "So what is the purpose in doing what we've done here? Kelly?"

57. "To get fractions with the same denominators so we can add them."

58. "Exactly," Shirley enthused. "Now I'm going to give you the name. They're called *equivalent fractions.*"

59. "Now let's see where we are. What have we been doing here? Toni?"

60. ". . . We're finding equivalent fractions."

61. "Good, Toni, and why do we want to find them? Gary?"

62. ". . . So we can add fractions when the denominators are not the same."

63. Shirley praised Gary and the rest of the students for their good work and gave them a seatwork assignment that involved finding equivalent fractions. "Everyone, do the first one on your sheet."

64. As the students worked the first problem, Shirley walked up and down the rows, checking each student's progress as she went. Periodically, she stopped to point something out to an individual, then moved on.

For each of the following, select the best choice and then *explain why that choice is best.*

1. Of the following, line numbers 2–6 of the case study best illustrate:

   a. effective communication
   b. teacher caring
   c. organization
   d. teaching efficacy

   Explanation:

2. Of the following, line numbers 9 and 10 best illustrate:

   a. organization
   b. communication
   c. academic focus
   d. monitoring

   Explanation:

3. Of the following, line numbers 13–21 best illustrate:

   a. organization
   b. teaching efficacy
   c. modeling
   d. review

   Explanation:

4. Of the following, line number 22 best illustrates:

   a. modeling
   b. organization
   c. communication
   d. closure

   Explanation:

5. Of the following, line number 23 best illustrates:

   a. communication
   b. modeling and enthusiasm
   c. organization
   d. monitoring

   Explanation:

6. Introductory focus is designed to attract students' attention and provide an umbrella for the rest of the lesson. This is best illustrated in Shirley's lesson in line numbers:

   a. 4–6
   b. 12–17
   c. 24–25
   d. 33–34

Explanation:

7. Of the following, line numbers 29–30 best illustrate:

   a. Shirley's effective use of emphasis
   b. Shirley's effective monitoring
   c. Shirley's ineffective feedback
   d. Shirley's use of sensory focus

Explanation:

8. Of the following, line numbers 47–58 best illustrate:

   a. teaching efficacy
   b. emphasis
   c. sensory focus
   d. review and closure

Explanation:

9. Of the following, the question that best promotes critical thinking is in line number:

   a. 34
   b. 38
   c. 44
   d. 53

Explanation:

10. What did Shirley use for sensory focus? How effective was it?

11. Based on the information in the case study, was Shirley's instruction aligned? Explain.

12. Look at line numbers 13, 15, 18, 20, 26, 28, 30, 34, 42, and 47. Which essential teaching skill is best illustrated in these items? Explain.

DISCUSSION QUESTIONS

1. According to Goodlad (1984), teachers tend to conduct most of their instruction at a knowledge/recall level. What explanation would you offer for that tendency?

2. Boyer (1983) found that less than 1 percent of all teacher questions require students to do more than recall memorized information. Why do you suppose this is the case?

3. In the early 1980s and before, the emphasis was on "context-free" thinking skills instruction or, in other words, critical thinking that deemphasized knowledge of specific content.

Why do you suppose there is now a much greater emphasis on thinking combined with deep understanding of content?

4. What implications would an increased emphasis on thinking have for scope and sequence in curriculum design?

5. What implications do the limited capacity of people's working memories and the concept of *automaticity* have for teaching critical thinking?

6. When do you think teachers should begin focusing on critical thinking in students? Should it begin in kindergarten or sometime later? Why?

7. The essential teaching skills were described as a foundation for the learning of other teaching strategies. This implies that first-year teachers should be knowledgeable and proficient in all the essential teaching skills. Is this realistic? Why or why not?

3 Social Interaction Models

Social Interaction Models *are strategies that involve students working collaboratively to reach common goals.* These models have evolved over several years in an effort to increase learner involvement in classroom activities, provide leadership and decision-making experiences, and give students the chance to interact with students from different cultural and socioeconomic backgrounds.

When you've completed your study of the chapter, you should be able to meet the following goals:

- Explain how groupwork can be integrated with other models.
- Identify the characteristics of cooperative learning and how they differ from competitive learning models.
- Plan, implement, and assess learning in lessons using the STAD, Jigsaw II, and Group Investigation Cooperative-Learning Models.
- Describe how the Discussion Model can be used to encourage student learning.

To begin our discussion of Social Interaction Models, let's look at three teachers' experiences.

Isabelle Ortega walks around her fourth-grade classroom as groups of students take turns quizzing each other on the week's spelling words. Isabelle implemented the group work when she noticed that her spelling grades were nearly bimodal; some of her students were doing well, but others are doing very poorly.

As an experiment, she has had the students work in pairs and has arranged the pairs so they are seated together. Before the teams work together, she presents new spelling words in the usual way, describing patterns in their spellings, discussing their origins, and explaining definitions. As students work together, one student asks another to spell a word, their partners write down the word and definition, they discuss it, and then they turn to the next word. They practice for 15 minutes each day, and all students turn in their papers at the end of the practice session. As they work, Isabelle walks among the groups providing brief suggestions and answering questions. At the end of each week she gives the class a quiz on the words and definitions.

Jim Felton grins when he sees the assortment of cereal boxes on the front table in his classroom. He has finally found a topic that interested his middle school students. Jim's health class has been studying nutrition and the class has been discussing breakfasts. Some students claimed that cereal provides a balanced meal; others argued that most were loaded with sugar, salt, and fat. Then the topic of school lunches came up. Some students defended the lunches, but the "brown baggers" claimed the meals were high in calories. Jim decided to do something to capitalize on this interest and energy.

Now he has divided his students into teams, each focusing on a different aspect of nutrition. One group examines cereals, another soft drinks, and a third school lunches. Each group uses cereal boxes, magazine articles, and the school dietitian as sources to gather information about their topic. The groups present their findings, and the class discusses them.

Jesse Kantor watches as her Biology I students silently study the chapter on amphibians. The students each have study guides that help them focus on different aspects of amphibian anatomy. Some study the digestive system, others the circulatory system, and still others the nervous system. The next day, the "experts" on each system get together to pool their knowledge and compare notes. The third day, these "experts" take turns teaching their topics to other members of their group. This session is followed by a quiz that assesses all students' knowledge of all the topics.

How are these teaching episodes similar? How are they different? What characteristics do they share, and how do these characteristics promote learning? What roles do teachers and students play in this process?

In this chapter we present three Social Interaction Models: Groupwork, Cooperative Learning, and Discussion. All are designed to use social interaction as a vehicle to promote learning, but they differ in the goals they are designed to reach and the amount of structure they provide teachers and students. We present these models in this chapter because they are often integrated with the models presented in Chapters 4–9.

We begin with groupwork.

The Groupwork Model

Groupwork *is a strategy that uses students working together to supplement other models.* Groupwork isn't an instructional model per se; rather, it is a strategy designed to increase involvement when another model is used. For example, Isabelle Ortega first used teacher-centered, whole-group instruction to introduce spelling words and then used groupwork as the students practiced. As you study Chapters 4–9 you'll see how some of the teachers use groupwork within the context of the other models.

Groupwork can be used to reach both low- and higher-level goals. Examples of low-level goals include:

- Basic math facts
- Historical names and dates
- Chemical symbols and terms in science
- Punctuation and grammar in language arts

Groupwork can also be used to stimulate students' thinking in the same content areas, such as:

- Improving students' problem-solving skills
- Helping students understand trends and cause-and-effect relationships in social studies
- Teaching students how to design experiments in science
- Providing feedback about written drafts

Planning Groupwork Activities

The goal in using groupwork is to have students work together to think about and discuss lesson content. The quality of the discussion is crucial; research indicates that the way students discuss ideas influences learning (Gillies & Ashman, 1998; King, 1999). Simply put, what students talk about is what they learn. If they talk about a football game, dance, or other social activity, they learn less. Also, if groupwork focuses on getting the right answer at the expense of understanding, learning also suffers.

The focus of groupwork is determined by the tasks and directions teachers give the groups and the training students receive to help them work together effectively.

Helping Students Learn to Learn in Groups.   Though most students like to talk with their peers, working together effectively doesn't automatically happen (Cohen, 1994). Students used to listening quietly to teachers often experience difficulties when they are faced with the freedom of groupwork. They need training and supervision.

The two biggest obstacles to effective groupwork are: (1) off-task behavior, and (2) failure to work together effectively.

Off-Task Behavior.   Some students misinterpret the freedom of groupwork as an opportunity to play and visit with friends. If groups aren't well organized and supervised, a great deal of time can be wasted.

Suggestions for planning and organizing groupwork activities to prevent these problems include the following:

- Introduce your students to groupwork with short, simple tasks.
- Have students practice moving into and out of groups quickly. Group members can be seated together prior to the activity to make the transition from the whole-class activity to groups and back again with little disruption.

- Give students a clear and specific task to accomplish in the groups (Gillies & Ashman, 1998; King, 1999).
- Specify the amount of time students are allowed to accomplish the task (and keep it short).
- Require that students produce a product as a result of the groupwork activity.
- Monitor the groups while they work.

Isabelle implemented each of these suggestions in her work with her fourth graders. She had the pairs sit near each other, the task was very clear, the students wrote the words as they practiced (and turned in their papers), she limited the amount of practice time, and she monitored their work. Each of her actions was designed to keep the students on task.

Working Together Effectively.   The inability of students to work effectively together can also be a problem when groupwork is used. Some simple exercises can help deal with this problem (Slavin, 1995). Some possibilities include:

- *Interviewing.* Rapport among group members can be developed by having them interview each other. They can ask about their favorite foods, TV programs, hobbies, and sports. If you introduce groupwork early in the year, interviewing can also help students learn each other's names.
- *Goal setting.* When you first break students into groups, have them identify the goals of the activity. Ask for feedback after several minutes and have different groups report to the whole group. This strategy focuses each group's efforts and prevents confusion down the line.
- *Quiet voices.* While the noise level in groupwork will be higher than in teacher-centered lessons, excessive noise interferes with learning. Students need to practice using "indoor" and not playground voices. In addition, teachers need a clear signal to capture students' attention when the noise gets too loud or when they want to reassemble the class.

Implementing Groupwork in Your Classroom

Groupwork can exist in different forms depending on the goals of the lesson, the size and composition of the group, and the learning task.

The simplest arrangement consists of learning pairs. When they are seated next to each other, students working in pairs can be easily integrated into existing lessons.

In this section we discuss three options:

- Think-pair-share
- Pairs check
- Combining pairs

Think-Pair-Share.   **Think-pair-share** *is a groupwork strategy that asks individual students in learning pairs to first answer a question and then share it with a partner* (Kagan, 1994). This strategy is most effective when embedded in whole-group, teacher-led instruction. In using this strategy, the teacher asks a question as she normally would but then, instead of calling a particular person, asks all students to think about the answer and discuss it with their partner. After a short period of time, the teacher asks a person in each pair (or several of the pairs) to share his or her thoughts with the whole class.

At least three factors contribute to the effectiveness of this strategy:

- It elicits responses from everyone in the class and promotes active learning.
- Because each member of the pairs is expected to participate, it reduces "free rides," which are sometimes a problem in groupwork.
- It is relatively easy to plan for and implement and can help learners make the transition to more complex groupwork strategies.

Pairs Check. **Pairs check** *is a strategy that involves student pairs in seatwork activities focusing on problems with convergent answers.* The strategy usually follows instruction in which a concept or skill has been taught. It provides students with opportunities to practice on the topic by alternating roles between "solver" and "checker." Pairs are given handouts containing convergent problems or questions (problems or questions with answers that are clearly right or wrong, such as math problems, spelling words, grammar, or punctuation). One member of the pairs works two or three problems, the second member checks the answers, and then the roles are reversed.

As the students work, the teacher monitors the process and encourages the students to discuss, when appropriate, the reasons the answers are correct. If they don't, *pairs check* amounts to little more than individual students checking answers at the back of the book. In addition, time is reserved at the end of the activity to allow whole-class discussion on areas of disagreement or confusion.

Combining Pairs. **Combining pairs** *is a strategy that uses learning pairs as the basic unit of instruction but provides opportunities for the pairs to share their answers with others.* Combining pairs can be used in both interactive teaching and seatwork activities. It has the advantage of encouraging the active participation of pairs while simultaneously helping students develop social skills.

In using the strategy during interactive teaching, the teacher identifies both the learning pairs and the groups of four and has them sit together so instruction can move from small group to whole class efficiently. Each group member is assigned a number from 1 to 4, which will identify students to be called on. The teacher asks the class a question with a convergent answer, such as the solution to a problem. The teacher asks each group to work on the solution and make sure everyone in the group knows the answer. The teacher than asks all the number 1s (or 2s or 3s or 4s) to raise their hand and calls on a student to explain the answer.

Similar arrangements are made with seatwork. Students are seated close to each other to facilitate communication. Students are given convergent problems to complete, and members of the pairs compare their answers. If they agree or can resolve disagreements, they continue. If they can't resolve disagreements, they confer with the other pair in their group. When a dispute arises in the dyads, the pair then compares their answers with the other pair. The teacher intervenes only when disagreements among the four students cannot be resolved.

The Cooperative-Learning Model

Having examined groupwork, we now want to turn to **cooperative learning,** *a group of teaching strategies that provide structured roles for students while emphasizing social interaction.*

Components of Cooperative Learning

Cooperative learning has three essential components:

- Group goals
- Individual accountability
- Equal opportunity for success (Slavin, 1995)

Let's look at them.

Group Goals.   Cooperative learning gets its name from the fact that students are placed in learning situations where they work together to reach common goals.

Classrooms typically operate under one of three goal structures (Slavin, 1995). In *competitive classrooms,* one student's success means another's failure, such as when teachers grade "on the curve," requiring students to compete with each other for grades. In *individualistic classrooms,* each student's efforts have no consequences for others, such as when students work alone. In *cooperative classrooms,* individuals' efforts contribute to others' goal attainment. This last goal structure is similar to the reward that occurs on soccer or basketball teams where individuals of unequal ability work together for team goals. Though individual effort is important, the gauge of this effort is the team's performance. **Group goals** *refer to incentives within cooperative learning that help create a team spirit and encourage students to help each other.*

Contrast this orientation with what often occurs in classrooms:

> The teacher is in front of the class; he or she asks the students questions. Following each question, a number of hands go up. Some students are anxiously stretching their hands in the hopes of being called. Others, of course, do not have their hands up and try not to have their eyes meet those of the teacher in hopes they will not be called on. The teacher calls on Juan. Peter, who sits next to Juan, knows the right answer. As Juan begins to hesitate, Peter becomes glad and stretches his hand higher. Peter knows that if Juan misses, the teacher may call upon him. In fact, the only way in which Peter can obtain a reward in this situation is if Juan fails. It is only natural in this competitive class structure for students to begin to take pleasure in the failure of others. Their own rewards are contingent on the failure of others (S. Kagan, 1986, p. 250).

Cooperative learning tries to avoid these problems by placing students in learning situations where group goals reward cooperation.

Individual Accountability.   Though group goals are emphasized, individual learning is still important in Cooperative-Learning Models. **Individual accountability** *requires that each member of a cooperative learning group demonstrate mastery of the concepts and skills being taught.* The teacher communicates the expectation for individual accountability by emphasizing that all students must understand the content, holding students accountable with quizzes and tests that all students take individually or with individual reports, papers, and projects.

Equal Opportunity for Success.   Group goals build group cohesiveness; individual accountability ensures that each team member learns the content. **Equal opportunity for success** *means that all students, regardless of ability or background, can expect to be recognized for their efforts.* This element is particularly important in heterogeneous classes, where background knowledge and skill levels vary. To promote success, cooperative learning strategies focus on individual effort and improvement. We examine the emphasis on effort and improvement in detail in the next section of the chapter.

Social Structure of Cooperative Learning

Cooperative-Learning Models require different classroom roles for both teachers and students than are found in "traditional" classrooms, where teachers are the center of activity and typically use whole-group instruction to explain content. In these classrooms students are often passive, spending much of their time listening or taking notes. Research indicates that passive students learn less than those who are more active (Eggen & Kauchak, 1999; Wittrock, 1986).

The Teacher's Role.   In cooperative learning activities, teachers often use whole-group instruction to introduce and explain basic concepts and skills, but after this presentation the teacher facilitates group learning. This begins with the organization of groups, continues with building teamwork and cohesion within groups, and includes monitoring the students to ensure that all students are learning.

Students' Roles.   Student roles also change. Cooperative learning requires that students become active and responsible for their own learning. This goal is accomplished by having students act as both teachers and learners. In addition, students also learn to explain, compromise, negotiate, and motivate as they participate as group members. Growth in social interaction skills may be one of the most important outcomes of cooperative learning activities.

Research suggests that cooperative learning can be used to reach a variety of goals ranging from higher achievement, improved motivation, better social skills, and improved relations between students from diverse backgrounds (Emmer & Gerwells, 1998). In addition, it can be used to reach a variety of content goals ranging from automaticity with facts to higher-level goals like problem solving and critical thinking.

Let's look now at *Student Teams Achievement Divisions* (STAD), the first of the models we discuss in this section.

STAD: Student Teams Achievement Divisions

Anya Lozano is beginning a unit on fractions with her fifth graders. She realizes that some of the content is review, so she gives a pretest to help her determine how much her students already know.

As she hands out the pretest, she says, "Class, this week we're starting a new unit in math on fractions and I'm passing out this pretest to help me find out how much you remember from last year." As she walks from aisle to aisle, she hears comments like, "I hate fractions!" and "Not fractions again." Though students often don't care for math, she is surprised at how negative they are. She decides to talk to her friend, co-teacher, and mentor Kay Reilly at lunch.

"What do you do when the kids hate the stuff that you have to teach?" she asks as she rifles through her lunch bag trying to decide where to begin.

"*Hate* is a pretty strong word," Kay grins. "What could prompt those feelings in our fifth graders?"

"Fractions!" Anya responds. "When I gave them a pretest today, I was surprised at the faces and groans I got. Not all of them, granted, but more than usual. . . . I'm not looking forward to this unit."

"Well, be careful about jumping to conclusions, and think for a minute. What are kids usually telling us when they say they hate something?" Kay counters.

". . . Good question," Anya nods after thinking for a few seconds. ". . . Usually it's something like 'I really dislike this stuff and I'm gonna make it miserable for you if you try and teach it to me.'"

"Oh, good, Anya. Very analytical and perceptive," Kay replies drily. "But seriously, usually when they say they hate something it means they don't understand it or they're afraid of it. They may have had a bad experience last year with fractions and are just afraid of having the same thing happen again."

". . . Could be . . . actually, you're probably right," Anya acknowledges. "The ones who were complaining the loudest were the ones who are a little shaky in math anyway. Makes sense . . . but now what? What do I do now? Help help!"

"Well, here's what you might try. I've been doing it for a while now, and it takes some work, but it's starting to pay off. . . . Have you got the pretests graded yet? . . . Good. Let me explain what I'm doing."

The next day Anya begins her math class in the same way she planned to—by passing out squares of paper and having students divide the squares into halves, thirds, and fourths. Using the chalkboard, overhead, and the papers, she guides her students toward a concept of fractions, and the process of adding fractions with like denominators.

When students seem to understood the concept and processes, Anya continues, "You've all been working hard and it looks like you remember a lot about fractions. Now to give you some practice with the ideas we've been discussing, we're going to try something different. Rather than working on our practice sheets alone, like we usually do, we're going to work on them in groups. In a minute I'll tell you how we're going to do this and what group you're in."

She continues, "One of the first things I want you to do when you get in your group is get to know each other and decide on a team name. Your team is important because you will work together for the whole unit. . . . Everyone, look up here for a moment. I'm passing out this worksheet that I want everyone to do. It's important for everyone to do their own work and work hard on the worksheet because I'll be giving you a quiz in a week, and your team's score will depend on how well all the team members do—not just some. Any questions? . . . Hakeem?"

"But how do we know the teams are fair?" Hakeem asks. "Maybe some teams are smarter than others."

"Good question, Hakeem. We'll make sure the teams are fair in two ways. First, everyone took a pretest and I put people on the different teams on the basis of their scores. Second, the teams aren't competing with each other. You can all do well. All teams can win, and no teams have to lose. That's the beauty of what we're going to do."

She goes on, "The way we all win is for team members to improve on their understanding. If we improve, we win, and if we all improve, we all win. I'll explain how this works after the first quiz. For now, let's get into our groups and get started. Listen carefully when I call your name. Team one, over here in this corner. Alysia, Manuel. . . ."

After students move to their groups, Anya spends the next half hour explaining to them how cooperative learning works and modeling for them effective small-group behaviors.

When Kay Reilly first explained cooperative learning to Anya, she stressed the importance of teacher work and attention at this point. "Good cooperative learning groups don't just happen, they need to be developed," Kay stressed. At first Anya was a little skeptical, but she listened anyway and as she listened she became convinced.

As Anya works now with her students in these groups, she is grateful for Kay's advice. Some of the students argue; others have trouble sharing materials. But after some work in these areas, Anya finally has the groups working together.

As students talk in their groups, Anya circulates around the room to be sure all the groups are functioning as smoothly as possible. In some groups, she has to stop some students from dominating the activity; in others, she has to clarify procedures and expectations. Once the groups are working satisfactorily, Anya quietly circulates among them, thinking to herself, "Maybe this will work."

Each math class this week follows a similar format. Anya begins by introducing the concept or skill, then models different computational and problem-solving processes for the students, and finally has students work in their groups to practice. While they work, Anya continues to circulate around the room, monitoring their work and offering suggestions.

The fourth day of groupwork, she interrupts the students to announce: "Class, can I have your attention for a minute? I just wanted to share with you an idea that the Eagle team is trying out. They weren't as confident about the topic today, so they started out by doing the first three problems together. When they thought they all understood what they were doing, they went back to doing them on their own and checking them with each other. This is an idea you might want to try out in your group. However you want to do these is fine with me. The important thing is that everyone should thoroughly understand how to do the problems when you're finished."

Anya checks students' papers each night to monitor her class's learning progress. She is pleasantly surprised by the work students are handing in— especially some of students who were low achievers. After five days of groupwork, Anya decides they are ready for the quiz. She gives the quiz and scores the papers over the weekend. She is pleased and somewhat surprised with the results. The general level of understanding on the quiz is high and, more important, she doesn't have the few scores that are well below those of the rest of the class. Most of her students seem to understand fractions!

Student Teams Achievement Division (STAD) *is a form of cooperative learning that uses multiability teams to teach facts, concepts, and skills.* Developed by Robert Slavin (1995), it is one of the most popular cooperative learning strategies in use in the schools today.

STAD is commonly used with the Direct Instruction Model, which we discuss in Chapter 8. The Direct-Instruction Model follows four steps, *introduction, presentation, guided practice,* and *independent practice.* When STAD is used, the first three steps are identical to those in direct instruction, but independent practice isn't "independent"; rather, it is done in cooperative learning groups. Let's see how this works.

Planning Lessons with STAD.   Planning for the STAD Cooperative-Learning Model is a five-step process that includes the following:

- Planning for instruction
- Organizing groups
- Planning team-building activities
- Planning for team study
- Calculating base scores

Planning for Instruction.   When STAD is used, the teacher plans for presenting the content that students will practice on in groups. This can be accomplished through the Direct-Instruction Model, the Inductive Model, or the Concept-Attainment Model, all of which focus on specific forms of content. As with other models, having clear goals in mind and preparing high quality examples is critical when STAD is used.

Organizing Groups. To effectively implement any kind of cooperative learning, teams must be organized in advance. The goal is to create teams that are mixed by ability, gender, and ethnicity (Slavin, 1995). Slavin suggests that four is an ideal number, but groups of five can also be used effectively. Teachers should form these groups; when they don't, high and low achievers, boys and girls, and minorities and nonminorities tend to be segregated (Webb et al., 1997).

One way to ensure that groups are similar in range of ability is to rank the students, divide them into quartiles, and place one student from each quartile into each group. Students can be ranked according to a pretest, as Anya did, or grades or scores from previous units.

Forming groups based on the rankings is illustrated in Table 3.1 with a sample class of 25 students.

A common way of grouping students is to take the highest achievers from the first two quartiles and pair them with the lowest achievers from the third and fourth quartiles. For example, the first group would then include Natacha, Tolitha, Stephen and Mary, and the second group would include Lucinda, Marvin, Howard, and David. The sixth group, having five members because of the number of people in the class, would then include Juan, Leroy, Gerald, Julia, and Cynthia.

After initially forming the groups, the teacher should check their makeup to see if they're balanced by gender and ethnicity. For example, the first group has three girls and a boy, while the second has three boys and a girl. The teacher might arbitrarily switch two of the students to balance the groups. This is a matter of professional judgment.

Planning Team-Building Activities. Research indicates that merely placing students in groups doesn't ensure trust and cooperation (Emmer & Gerwells, 1998; Scruggs & Richter, 1988). As with groupwork, an important planning task in cooperative learning is to design group building activities that help students learn to accept and trust each other. The purpose of team-building exercises is to help students get acquainted, to develop a team

TABLE 3.1   Grouping Students Based on Rankings

1	Natacha	14	Gerald
2	Lucinda	15	Henrietta
3	Vicki	16	Lawsekia
4	Jerome	17	Tolitha
5	Steve	18	Howard
6	Juan	19	Stephen
7	Tolitha	20	Cynthia
8	Marvin	21	Kevin
9	Enrico	22	Kathe
10	Sara	23	Ron
11	Eugene	24	David
12	Leroy	25	Mary
13	Julia		

identity, and to help students get to know each other as partners and helpmates. Anya began by having each of her teams select a name for their group. Some additional examples of team-building exercises are found in Table 3.2.

A variety of other team-building activities could be used as well. Some teachers identify specific behaviors that they expect from students, such as, "using 'quiet voices,'" "making supporting statements," and "listening while a teammate is talking"; model those behaviors; and then give students experience in practicing these behaviors. Others advocate teaching students how to ask facilitating questions that promote thinking and learning (King, 1999). Examples include:

- Why is _____ important?
- What is _____ an example of?
- How is _____ similar to _____?
- How does _____ relate to _____?

Research indicates that teaching students to ask thought-provoking questions such as these improves the quality of verbal interaction in groups and improves learning (King, 1999).

Planning for Team Study.   The success of STAD learning teams depends on having high-quality materials that guide the interactions within the groups. As teachers plan their lessons, they need to ask themselves, "What specific concepts or skills are students learning, and how can I design materials that will allow them to learn effectively in their groups?" This is where clearly specified objectives are important. They ensure that the group instruction and team study are aligned with the objectives.

A variety of team study materials can be used. In math, as in Anya's case, they might be problems to be solved. In language arts, they could be paragraphs to be punctuated or made grammatically correct. In geography, exercises might require students to identify cities closest to given longitude and latitude coordinates.

The team study materials should require convergent answers—that is, answers that are clearly correct or incorrect, such as the solutions to problems with fractions, or paragraphs that are punctuated properly. If the content doesn't lend itself to convergent answers, STAD isn't the most effective model to be used.

TABLE 3.2   Team-Building Activities

Activity	Description
Favorites	Team members interview each other about their favorites—food, music, hobby, sport, etc.
Biographies	Students interview each other and find out about each others' backgrounds.
Occupations	Students talk about what they might want to be later on in life.
Most interesting topics	Students interview each other about different topics in the class they are interested in.

TABLE 3.3   Calculating Base Scores from Grades

A	90
A–/B+	85
B	80
B–/C+	75
C	70
C–/D+	65
D	60
F	55

Adapted from Kagan, 1992; Slavin, 1995.

Calculating Base Scores.   Earlier we said that *equal opportunity for success* is one of the characteristics of cooperative learning. Equal opportunity for success is accomplished by awarding students *improvement points* if their score on a test or quiz is higher than their *base score*. A base score is the student's average on past tests and quizzes, or a score determined by a previous year's or term's grade. Table 3.3 illustrates a sample calculation of base scores from grades. The teacher determines each student's base score prior to introducing the students to STAD.

Improvement Points.   Improvement points are awarded based on how students perform on a test or quiz compared to their base scores. A sample system for awarding improvement points is illustrated in Table 3.4.

The system shown in Table 3.4 is arbitrary and can be adapted to meet the needs of specific classes. For example, you may choose to award some improvement points for any score that is no more than 5 points below the base score. On the other hand, you may require an improvement of 12, 15, or even more in order to be awarded 30 improvement points. You can also change the system as student motivation and confidence increase. You may want to begin by rewarding virtually any effort—particularly with chronic low achievers—and then raise standards as the students' achievement increases.

Before closing this section, we want to emphasize one point. It is important that students can receive the maximum of 30 points if they get a perfect paper regardless of their base scores. This is important for high-achieving students. For example, if a student has a

TABLE 3.4   Sample System for Awarding Improvement Points

Improvement Points	Score on Test or Quiz
0	Below base score
10	1 to 5 points above base score
20	6 to 10 points above base score
30	More than 10 points above base score, or Perfect paper (regardless of base score)

95 average, it is impossible to improve by more than 5 points, so the student's incentive to improve would be reduced if the perfect-score provision didn't exist.

Implementing Lessons Using the STAD Cooperative Learning Model.   Implementing STAD lessons is much like implementing whole-group instruction that focuses on concepts or skills. The lesson is introduced, the content is explained, and students are involved in guided practice. Then team study takes the place of independent practice. However, STAD differs from the simple Direct-Instruction Model in that some instruction is often required to ensure a smooth transition from whole-group to team study; assessment, improvement points and team recognition are also an integral part of STAD. These phases are outlined in Table 3.5.

Phase 1: Instruction.   When STAD is used, the instruction is identical to typical whole-group instruction focusing on specific concepts or skills. The lesson is introduced by specifying goals; presenting, explaining, and modeling the skills or applications of concepts, principles, generalizations, and rules; and providing for guided practice. Anya's instruction illustrated these steps. She carefully explained and illustrated fractions with her manipulatives and had the students practice under her guidance. When she felt the students had an acceptable grasp of fractions and the procedures for adding them, she moved to team study.

Phase 2: Transition to Teams.   Obstacles to smoothly functioning cooperative lessons are often logistical. Research indicates that whole-group instruction is easier to manage than small-group work for at least two reasons (Good & Brophy, 1997). First, in large-group work the teacher is able to "steer the lesson," speeding up and slowing down based on the students' progress; second, interaction during large-group work allows the teacher to monitor and deal with learning or management problems. When first introducing small-group work, the teacher needs to be carefully organized, anticipating logistical problems in advance.

TABLE 3.5   Phases in Implementing STAD

Phase	Purpose
Instruction	Introduce lesson Explain and model content Provide guided practice
Transition to teams	Move students from whole-group to learning teams
Team study and monitoring	Ensure that groups are functioning effectively
Assessment	Provide feedback about learning Provide basis for awarding improvement points
Recognition of achievement	Increase learner motivation

In first introducing team study, teachers should thoroughly explain how cooperative learning works and the specific procedures to be followed. Let's see how Anya helped her students make the transition to teams:

"Okay, everyone, I think we have a pretty good idea of what fractions mean and how we add them together when the denominators are the same. Now we're ready to practice. The way we're going to do that is by assigning each of you to a team, and each team will practice the new content. Because this is a little new, I'm going to show you how it works before I ask you to do it."

Anya goes on: "In a few minutes I'm going to break you into the groups that you'll be working with for this unit. But before that I want to show you how one group should work. Tanya, Mariko, Willy, can you come up here and sit at these desks? . . . Thanks! Class, this is what your group will look like—it will have four members, and for sake of this illustration, I will be the fourth member. After we break into groups, I'll give each group four worksheets, just like I'm doing here."

Anya then takes a few seconds to give the materials to the group at the front of the room and takes one herself.

She continues, "Now, Tanya and Willy are a pair, and Mariko and I are a pair. Each person does the problem and checks with his or her partner. For example, Tanya does the problem and then checks the answer with Willy, and Mariko and I do the problem and we check with each other. If Tanya and Willy agree on the answer and believe that they both understand it, they move to the next problem. Mariko and I do the same. If Tanya and Willy disagree, they ask Mariko and me, and we do the same with them. We all discuss the problem until we're all sure we understand it. . . . Okay, let's go ahead."

The four of them work the first problem and check with their partners. (Anya intentionally gets a wrong answer for sake of the illustration.)

"I didn't get that," she says loud enough for the class to hear. "Please explain that to me."

Anya discusses ways of providing helpful feedback to each other, and she also models appropriate and inappropriate ways of interacting with partners.

"What happens if we all disagree," Leanne asks after seeing the process modeled.

"Good question, Leanne. If all four of you have thoroughly discussed the problem and cannot come to an understanding, then you can ask me . . . but remember," she emphasizes, "you can only ask me *after* all four of you have carefully discussed the problem."

Anya then assigns the rest of the class to their groups and has them begin.

When introducing students to cooperative learning, the initial directions need to be very detailed and explicit. In Anya's case, we saw that she illustrated and modeled the process with one group before she had all the students begin team study.

Teachers have found it useful to place information, such as the following, on a poster, discuss it with the class, and leave it up for reference:

- Group memberships for different teams
- Location in the room for different teams
- Procedures for obtaining and turning in materials
- Time frames

Spending time on logistics at the beginning of cooperative-learning lessons lays the foundation for smoothly functioning groups later on.

Phase 3: Team Study and Monitoring. As students work in their groups, teachers should monitor their work to ensure they are functioning smoothly but be careful about intervening too soon. One of the goals of cooperative learning is to teach students to work together, and this process isn't always initially smooth. Early intervention may actually be counterproductive, as students often need time and freedom to work through problems. However, if students aren't working together, one is dominating a group or someone isn't participating, intervention is necessary. When to intervene is a matter of professional judgment.

What can be more helpful than individual interventions is calling attention to particularly productive groups. Let's see how Anya did this.

"Class, can I have your attention, please, just for a second. I know you're all working hard but I just wanted to share an idea with you. The Cheetah Team came up with a great idea to work through their problems. They got a box of the blocks, the ones we used earlier, and every time one of the members is having trouble with one of the problems, they use the blocks to explain the answer. I heard one of the group members say, 'Sure you can do this. Just try it again.' That is very helpful and supportive, and that's the way we want to treat our teammates."

Group interventions that focus on positive practice help students understand different roles in the groups and provide models for the other students.

Phase 4: Assessment. Assessment serves at least two functions in the STAD Model. First, it provides both the teacher and students with feedback about learning progress, and second, it can provide incentives for work and effort. The key to the first function is a well-designed instrument that accurately measures understanding of important concepts and skills. Again, clear objectives are critical, because they specify important learning outcomes.

Recognizing Achievement. Assessment results can serve as strong motivators when they are integrated into a scoring system based on improvement points. Improvement scoring systems ensure that individuals compete only against their own past performance and not against each other. When they match past performance, they are given a small number of improvement points; when they exceed it, improvement points increase in proportion.

Team Scoring.   Team scoring is based on the improvement of individual team members. As an example, let's look again at the group composed of Natacha, Tolitha, Stephen, and Mary. Their averages and quiz scores are as follows:

Name	Average	Quiz Score
Natacha	95	96
Tolitha	88	90
Stephen	75	84
Mary	69	80

Based on the system illustrated in the section on planning for improvement points, Natacha would receive 10 improvement points and Tolitha would also get 10 since their scores were in the range of 1 to 5 points higher than their base score (average). In comparison, Stephen would receive 20 improvement points since his quiz score was 9 points above his base score, and Mary would receive 30 points because her score was more than 10 points above her base. Mary, the lowest achiever in the group, actually got the most improvement points. This is how the equal opportunity for success provision is accomplished when STAD is used.

While the use of reinforcers, such as improvement points, is somewhat controversial, research indicates that the system has a positive effect on motivation (Slavin, 1995). The extent to which teachers use the system in their classes is a matter of professional judgment.

Team Awards.   Team scores are determined by averaging the improvement points for the team, and the awards can then be given. The following is one example of a reward system.

Criterion (Average Improvement)	Award
10	Winners
15	Stars
20	All Stars
25	Major Leaguers

Group awards can take a variety of forms; teachers can decide upon the exact form based on what is motivating to students. For example, *Winners* might be asked to stand and be recognized in class, *Stars* could get a certificate of congratulations, *All Stars* a more elaborate certificate, and *Major Leaguers* a group photo on a "hall of fame" section of the bulletin board. Other options could include buttons to wear around school, letters to parents, special privileges, and leadership roles.

Students should be reminded that neither teams nor individuals are competing with each other; individuals only compete with their past performance. If individuals improve, all teams can potentially become *Major Leaguers*. Teams can be changed periodically, such as after four or five weeks, to allow students to work with other classmates and to give students on low-scoring teams a chance for increased success.

Assessing Learning Using STAD.   Assessment of STAD lessons occurs on two levels. The first relates to the content goals of the lesson and is similar to assessing understanding when other content-oriented models are used. As always, assessments should be aligned with objectives, instruction, and team study activities. For example, Anya had as her content objectives:

- Identifying the numerator and denominator in a fraction
- Adding fractions with like denominators

Assessment measures individual students' attainment of these objectives.

Using Improvement Points in Grading.   As with reinforcers, using improvement points in grading is controversial, but teachers often develop grading systems that reflect improvement. For instance, if students average 15 or more improvement points on tests and quizzes, their grade might be raised from a B– to a B, or from a B to a B+. Many teachers feel that seeing improvement reflected in their grades is an added incentive for students; others feel that improvement points unduly penalize top students, who may already be working at the upper limit of the grading system. This decision is a matter of professional judgment.

Assessing Group Work and Cooperation.   At a second, more complex level, assessment of STAD activities attempts to answer questions such as, "Are students getting better at working together and learning to work together as a team?" The best source of information here comes from observing students as they work together in groups. Some questions to ask as you do this include:

- Are all members contributing?
- Are some members dominating?
- Is the group interaction positive and supportive?
- Do boys and girls contribute about equally?
- Are members from different racial and ethnic groups being included?

By attending to these questions, teachers can help individuals and groups learn to cooperate and work together.

As teachers assess cooperation, they can provide feedback to the class, using smoothly functioning groups as models. This may be as simple as noting, "I really like the way this group is taking turns giving feedback," or it may involve role playing, where students publicly work out problems that individual groups are having. The goal is to help students become aware of their interactions in the groups and the effect these interactions are having on their own and others' learning.

This completes our discussion of Student Teams Achievement Divisions. We turn now to a second cooperative learning model, Jigsaw II.

Jigsaw II

Kevin Davis looks out his classroom window on a blustery spring Friday and lets out an audible "Hmmmm." So far the year has gone well for his World

Geography class, but he isn't quite sure where to go from here. The next section of the text is Central America, and Kevin had problems with it last year. Maybe it was the timing—spring fever—and perhaps students were just getting played out with their intellectual journey around the world. Or maybe, he thought, it was the way he taught it last year—minilectures supplemented with small-group discussions. He tried this strategy on Thursday when he presented an overview of the new unit, but the students just didn't seem excited about the content. Kevin knows he has to try something new, if only for his own professional sanity.

He spends part of the weekend going through notes and books from workshops and graduate classes that he has taken. One idea that keeps popping up is student involvement—how to get students actively involved in their own learning? As he thinks about this idea, he keeps flashing on cooperative learning. He has tried learning teams in another class where there were a number of important names and dates that students had to master, but he doesn't feel that would be appropriate here. What he really wants students to know is the "big picture" in terms of the Central American countries, not a lot of facts about each. He decides to try something different.

Monday morning he arrives early, sits down at his computer and prepares several handouts. As he duplicates them, he finalizes plans for introducing the new activity and organizing the groups. He hopes he is ready.

"Class," Kevin begins as the students settle in after the tardy bell, "we're going to try something different for our next unit. I've decided to make each of you the experts on this content and have you teach each other."

He pauses to survey the class to gauge their initial reaction. From their puzzled looks at least they are curious. So far so good.

"To do this," he continues, "I've placed each of you in teams of four. I've tried to divide these teams so that all the teams are about equal. We'll be working in these teams for the next couple of weeks. Your job on these teams is to do two things. First, each of you needs to become an expert on one part of each chapter. Can everyone take out their texts and turn to Chapter 17? That's on page 346. I'll show you what I'm talking about."

He pauses as students turn to the correct page, then goes on, "You'll notice in the introduction to the chapter on Costa Rica that it is divided into four sections—the physical geography of the country, its history, its culture, and its economy. We talked about these on Thursday. I'm going to ask each of you to become an expert in one of these areas and then teach that content to your other group members. To help you become 'experts,' I've got a summary sheet for each of these topics to help you in your note taking. Let's see what one of these looks like."

He walks over to the overhead and displays the transparency shown in Table 3.6 for the class.

"We'll call this our 'expert sheet'; each of you will have one of these when you read the chapter, and it will help you in your note taking. We'll take the rest of today and all of tomorrow to work on this. At the beginning of class

TABLE 3.6   Jigsaw II Expert Sheet

Physical Geography

1. Climate
   a. seasons
   b. temperatures
   c. rainfall
2. Topography
   a. mountains
   b. water
   c. land
      1) soil
   d. prominent features

on Wednesday, the experts on each topic will get together to review their notes and make sure everyone has the essential information. On Thursday the experts in each group will take turns teaching their topics to each other. So, for example, if Miguel has history, he'll teach the other members what he learned about the history of Costa Rica; then, let's say, if Yolanda has culture, she'll learn about history from Miguel and then teach him about the culture of Costa Rica. On Friday we'll take the first part of the class to review and put all this information together, and then we'll take a quiz on this chapter. The quiz will have an even number of questions on each of the topics, so you'll get some questions on the topic that you are an expert on and some on the others. That means you need to learn everything—not just your topic. We'll record team scores and keep a running tally from chapter to chapter. I'll talk more about this later. . . . Any questions? . . . Good.

"Then, let me quickly review our procedures. We'll break into groups in a minute. When you get into your groups, I've got an activity that will help you get to know each other a little better. Then you as a group decide who's going to be the expert in each of the four areas. If you don't get your first pick this time, you will the next. We'll rotate these around. . . .

"All right everyone, look up here for your group assignment. Note that the assignment also tells where in the room your group should meet. Let's go!"

After students quickly move into their groups, Kevin calls for their attention. He has them do a "team-building activity" for 10 minutes. Finally, he announces, "I think you've done a good job with the activity, and we'll do more team building as we continue with the unit. . . . Now, I want the room quiet while each of you reads your section of the chapter and takes notes. We'll finish this on Tuesday and move into our expert groups on Wednesday. I'll be around to help you. Thursday is *expert teach day*. You'll each teach the other members of your group and learn from them about their topic. Make sure you take good notes to study from for the test on Friday. . . . Questions?

... Good. ... Look up at the board. I've written the schedule for the week there as a reminder. ... Okay, let's go!"

Structure of the Jigsaw II Model.   Like other cooperative learning strategies, Jigsaw II derives its effectiveness from the active involvement of students as they work in small groups. **Jigsaw II** *is a form of cooperative learning in which individual students become experts on subsections of a topic and teach that subsection to others.*

Jigsaw II differs from STAD in that it uses a concept called **task specialization,** *which requires that different students assume specialized roles in reaching the goals of a learning activity.* In the case of Jigsaw II, students become experts on a particular portion of a learning task and use their expertise to teach other students. Kevin had his students focus on different aspects of a country's geography as they learned about Central American countries. Then, when they worked as a team, each member contributed a different piece in the knowledge puzzle—thus the name *Jigsaw.* One key to the success of Jigsaw II is the interdependence it fosters in team members; students must depend on each other to learn the content.

Jigsaw II was developed by Robert Slavin (1986) as an adaptation of the original Jigsaw strategy, developed by Aronson and his associates (1978) to encourage interdependence among team members. The original Jigsaw strategy used customized learning materials designed especially for the Jigsaw strategy. These materials were designed so that the expert was the only one who saw the materials for a particular section. Consequently, students *had* to depend on each other to learn the information in each others' sections.

There were two drawbacks to the original Jigsaw that Jigsaw II overcomes. The first was the need for special learning materials that had to be prepared in advance, making the teacher's planning very demanding. The second was the fact that "nonexperts" didn't have access to all the materials. If students didn't learn well from the "expert" presentations, they had nothing to fall back on. Jigsaw II, which uses existing text materials, is designed to eliminate these problems.

Jigsaw II can be used to increase understanding of preexisting written materials such as student textbooks, but it can also be used to supplement other strategies (Kagan, 1992). For example, it could be used to provide background information on controversial issues in social studies, such as a discussion of nuclear energy. Some students might study the history, others the technology, and still others the ecological perspectives. Prior to the discussion, each group could share their expertise on these topics.

As another example, in a unit on poetry, different students might learn about rhyme, meter, symbolism, and authors' lives. Then, in analyses of different poems, each student, or group of students, would contribute their perspective on the work.

Planning for the Jigsaw II Model.   Planning for Jigsaw II lessons is similar to planning for STAD. Objectives and learning materials are specified and prepared, and students need to be assigned to teams. In addition, materials to assess learning progress must also be constructed.

However, because Jigsaw II relies on individual study, planning for whole-group instruction is not required. These steps are summarized in Figure 3.1. In the following sections we'll examine how planning activities are adapted to meet the special goals of Jigsaw II.

1. Specify objectives

2. Design learning materials

3. Form student teams

4. Design evaluation instruments

FIGURE 3.1   Planning for Jigsaw II

Specifying Objectives.   As opposed to STAD, which focuses on learning specific facts, concepts, or skills, Jigsaw II is designed to teach mastery of organized bodies of knowledge. These could be chapters in a text, a story, a biography, or a history of events. The goal for Jigsaw II lessons is to help students understand a topic using available resources.

Designing Learning Materials.   The major tasks during this part of the planning process are the gathering of materials and the construction of expert sheets that guide students' study and teaching efforts. Resource materials can come from a number of sources: present texts, previously used texts, library books, encyclopedias, magazines, and nonprint sources such as videotapes, videodiscs, and the Internet.

In addition to resource materials, teachers also need to design study sheets that help students focus on important information and issues. These can include questions, outlines, matrices, charts, or hierarchies. Kevin used outlines that divided key topics into subcategories. Research indicates that well-organized expert sheets help guide student studying and result in more effective presentations (Eggen & Kauchak, 1999).

Form Student Teams.   In forming student teams, the same considerations that existed for STAD apply here. As with STAD, groups should be balanced in terms of achievement, gender, and cultural background.

Once groups are formed, it is important that members get to know each other and that group identity and cohesion develop. The same strategies described earlier for STAD can also be used here.

Assigning Experts.   An additional factor in forming teams exists with Jigsaw II that didn't exist with STAD. Since each member of a team is required to develop expertise in part of the topic, it is important that the expert teams also be mixed according to achievement. Kevin allowed the students to decide and assured them that if they didn't get their first pick they would get it next time.

Students will be more committed to a topic of their choice than to one that is assigned. On the other hand, if the lowest achievers for each group all happened to be responsible for the cultures of the countries, for example, the quality of learning for that segment of the topic might suffer. In a mixed-ability group, by contrast, since all members of an expert group are responsible for understanding that aspect of the topic, the lower achievers in the group can learn from the higher achievers and then are in a better position to teach the other members of their team.

Topic	Items		
	Knowledge	Comprehension	Application
Physical Geography			
History			
Culture			
Economy			

FIGURE 3.2   Planning for Assessment Matrix

Designing Assessments.   As we've seen, cooperative learning is most effective when all students are held accountable for learning and when hardworking individuals and teams are rewarded for their efforts. Effective assessments can help accomplish both of these goals.

In designing assessments, including a table or planning matrix is helpful to ensure that all topics receive equal weight on the quiz or test and that the items are at an appropriate level of difficulty. A sample for Kevin's class is shown in Figure 3.2.

Implementing Lessons Using Jigsaw II.   Jigsaw II is a five-phase strategy that begins with information gathering, proceeds through a process of disseminating information within groups, and culminates in assessment and recognition (Slavin, 1995). The specific phases in implementing lessons are presented and described in Table 3.7.

Information Gathering.   In the first phase of Jigsaw II, students are assigned to groups and assigned topics in which they are to develop expertise. Since Jigsaw II uses preexisting materials such as chapters from books, the only logistical task is being certain that the learning materials—textbooks, videotapes, and the like—are available for students and that the sheets guiding the experts' study are designed. The first time you use Jigsaw II,

TABLE 3.7   Phases in Implementing Jigsaw II

Phase	Description
Information Gathering	Students are assigned to groups Student experts are assigned topics Experts locate and study essential information
Expert Meetings	Experts meet to compare notes and refine presentations
Team Reports	Experts teach topic to other team members
Evaluation and Recognition	Students take individual quiz on all topics, individual and group performances are recognized

you may have to walk students through one of the expert sheets to help them understand how they can be used to structure and guide their efforts.

The actual study time can be done either in class or as a homework assignment. In first introducing Jigsaw II, it is helpful to do the first few sessions as in-class activities. This strategy provides the teacher with opportunities to monitor the activity and offer suggestions to the groups.

Expert Meetings.   After students have had time to study their individual topics, expert meetings allow experts opportunities to compare notes and clarify areas of misunderstanding. A discussion leader should be assigned to moderate the session and make sure everyone is actively involved. This role can be rotated so that everyone gets an opportunity to lead and participate. The expert sheets passed out earlier help provide structure for this discussion.

Team Report.   During team report meetings, experts return to their groups and take turns teaching the group about their topic. This not only shares the experts' knowledge but also encourages experts to organize and summarize their information. Encouraging and helping experts organize their information and offering suggestions for presentations can increase the learning in these sessions.

Evaluation and Recognition.   The process for evaluating individual student performance and recognizing group achievement can be similar to the process used for STAD. Individual students are held accountable for their understanding of the content, improvement points can be given for continually increasing achievement, and group recognition in the form of certificates, letters to parents, names and pictures on the bulletin board, and privileges can all be used.

Assessing Student Understanding with Jigsaw II.   Assessing student understanding with Jigsaw II lessons occurs on three levels. First, we want to know if groups are functioning smoothly and whether students are growing in their ability to work together. Second, we want to know if students can investigate and organize topics and share this learning with others. Third, we want to know if individual students understand the content. Each of these is discussed in turn.

Assessing Group Processes.   In assessing group processes, we want to know if students are learning to function as productive members of a group. This includes speaking, listening, sharing ideas, and helping the group move in a positive direction. The same kinds of questions asked about STAD lessons apply here:

- Are all members contributing?
- Are some members dominating?
- Is the group interaction positive and supportive?
- Do boys and girls contribute about equally?
- Are members from different racial and ethnic groups being included?

To this list we would add questions about whether experts are explaining content clearly. Again, this skill may need to be taught through modeling and role playing.

Assessing the Development of Expertise.   A second assessment question is whether students are growing as expert presenters and members of each team. Jigsaw II, which involves sophisticated learning skills such as note taking and organization, requires the even more sophisticated ability of teaching content to others. These skills must be taught and monitored. One way to teach the skills is through think-alouds in which the teacher models the skill while talking out loud. As students practice in their groups, teachers should monitor their work and provide feedback.

Assessing Student Understanding of Content.   In terms of content evaluation, the objectives and evaluation matrices (see Figure 3.2) that were used during the planning process help ensure that evaluation instruments are congruent with goals. One of the challenges of assessing Jigsaw II activities is to construct instruments that challenge experts but don't overwhelm nonexperts. A combination of short-answer and essay questions together with actual work samples such as reports about different topics can often be combined into effective assessments.

This concludes our discussion of the Jigsaw II Cooperative-Learning Model. In the next section we describe Group Investigation, a cooperative-learning strategy designed to help students learn to conduct research on specific topics.

Group Investigation

To this point, we have described cooperative learning strategies designed to help students learn facts, concepts, skills, and organized bodies of content. Cooperative learning can also be used to help students learn problem solving and higher-order critical thinking abilities. A cooperative-learning strategy called Group Investigation is designed to reach these goals. Let's see how one teacher implements the strategy in her classroom.

Kim Herron has been teaching junior high science for three years and is generally happy with her teaching. She feels that she gives students a sound foundation for their work in high school and a general understanding of the role of science in their lives. But she isn't quite as happy with her progress in helping students "think." They seem all too happy to memorize the material she gives them rather than thinking on their own. Kim decides that this year will be different.

The school science fair is coming up in two months. She has encouraged her students to participate and most have, but the quality of their projects is uneven. Kim can tell which students received help from parents—which is fine, but what about the rest of the students? She decides to make Fridays in her class group project day, and the focal point for the projects will be the science fair to be held in May.

As she sits down to plan for these Fridays, Kim asks herself, "Where to start? What do they need to get started on their group projects?" After some looking out the window, considerable doodling on her notepad, and occasional thumbing through old science methods texts and teachers' editions, she decides on a two-pronged attack. First, they will need some information about good science projects—what they did, how they were implemented, and how they were reported.

"That shouldn't be too difficult," she thinks. "I've got some winners' projects from the last few years."

Then they will need some background knowledge on the topics they are studying. As she thinks about this, she jots down some possibilities and makes a note to work on them.

The next Friday, she begins her class by saying, "Okay, listen, everybody. . . . We're going to try something different in here today and for the remainder of the Fridays until the science fair, which is May 7. We're going to use Friday's class to work on our science projects, and we're going to do this a little differently than we have in the past. First, I'll give you class time to work on the projects and I'll expect weekly progress reports on how you're doing. Second, I'd like you to do the projects in groups rather than individually. This will result in better-quality work, and I think you'll learn a lot from each other. To divide you into groups, I'm going to ask each of you to write your name and some topics you're interested in studying on a piece of paper. I'll pull this information together and assign you to groups by next Friday. These groups won't be set in stone, but this process will allow us to get started."

The next Friday, she has the different groups listed on the bulletin board by topics and members. Students congregate around the board, buzzing and talking as they enter the room. As Kim observes the excitement, she hopes that the excitement won't interfere with learning.

"Oh, well," she says to herself as the bell rang, "Here goes."

As the class quiets down, Kim walks to the front of the room, pauses briefly, and begins, "You've probably already seen your assignments as you came in the room. If you didn't, you can check up here (gesturing to the bulletin board) when we break into groups. For today, our first job will be to get to know the other members on our teams. To do that, I'd like each person to interview another team member, so when you first get into your groups, select a partner. Then ask your partner why they are interested in that topic and what they know about it. Also, see if you can find any other interesting information about your partner with respect to science. Remember, the interview must focus on your topic and science in general. One person interview the other, then switch. Each person will make a short introduction of that person in your group. Take notes so you can remember all the important points."

Kim pauses, then says, "Before we break into groups, let's quickly review to make sure we know what each person's responsibility will be. What's the first thing you'll do in your groups? Alysha?"

"Find a partner."

"Good, Alysha. Then what? . . . Anyone? . . . Selena?"

"Interview your partner?"

"Fine. And what questions will you ask? . . . Antonia?"

"The ones on the board."

"Good. And what will you do with the interview information? Juan?"

"Report back to the group," Juan replied.

"Excellent, everyone!" Kim exclaims. "Now remember our goal here is to begin to get to know each other so we can work effectively in our teams.

"To avoid congestion, let's have Group 1 over here at the front of the room, Group 2 over here, Group 3 back there, Group 4 over there, Group 5 in the corner, Group 6 over here, and Group 7 up here. If you don't know what group you're in, check up here (pointing to the chart). All set? . . . It's 1:20. I expect you to be done by 1:40. Okay, let's go, move."

Kim watches as students get into their groups. Surprisingly, it goes smoother than she anticipated and the groups quickly settle into the rhythm of interviewing.

A hand goes up. "What do we do if there isn't an even number of students?"

"Good question, Jianna. Class, if there is an odd number in your group due to absence or some other reason, do your interviews in threes."

The class settles again into a low hum as Kim moves around the room. Most of the groups are working well and the others seem to need only a gentle reminder to get back on track.

At 1:30, Kim announces, "Everyone, you should be done with your interviews by now and should be sharing your findings with other members of the group. You've got 5 more minutes and then we'll move on to another activity."

At 1:35, Kim brings the class together again and announces, "Good job, everyone. We're now ready to begin our next task . . . which is to try to understand what a good project looks like. To help us, I've placed several award-winning projects around the room. I'd like the groups to rotate around the room examining each of the projects to try to figure out why they won awards. Take notes and talk about your ideas in your group and then we'll come back together as a class to discuss our findings. Okay, questions? . . . Then let's move."

The class spends the remainder of the period examining the projects and discussing the criteria for good projects.

Near the end of the period, Kim concludes the class by saying, "We've made good progress in trying to understand what a good project looks like. Our job next Friday will be to lay the foundation for one of the components we talked about today—background information. I'd like you all to be thinking about the kind of information you will need to enable you to ask meaningful questions and make interesting hypotheses. I'll try to bring in some reference books for everyone to use, and each of you needs to bring in at least one book on the topic you are studying by Friday. You can get these either at the school library or a public library. Any questions? . . . Okay, then I'll see you on Monday and don't forget your books on Friday."

During the next week, Kim works with the school librarian to build a collection of reference books on the different topics the students are studying. She also raids her own college textbook collection and asks her colleagues to do the same. By Friday, she has over forty books on the different topics that students are investigating.

At the beginning of the period, she calls the class together and explains that their goals for the day are to look at the resources available to the groups and to begin a plan of action for their projects.

As students move into their groups, Kim again circulates around the room, talking to the groups and answering questions. She often sits down with a group and helps them structure the tasks so that members of the group can collaborate and help each other on the different tasks.

During the next few weeks, students work on their projects in their groups. A general topic, like electricity or pollution, serves as the framework for each group while the specific projects direct students' efforts during class. Some of the projects, like the one on electricity, are actually done in school while others, like an investigation of factors affecting plant growth, are done at home.

During the fifth and sixth weeks, students start analyzing their results and writing reports. Kim helps students by again sharing exemplary reports with them and by working with students in their groups. Kim shows them how the computers in the back of the room can be used to describe and display data, and a number of groups use them to write up their projects.

For the next two weeks, students organize poster-board sessions where they present their results to other students. As students circulate from project to project, they evaluate each other's work with a form the class has discussed and prepared. At the end of each session, Kim takes 15 minutes of class time to discuss the different projects, pointing out strengths in each. Using this feedback, students in the groups refine their presentations. The unit culminates in the science fair, where students present their projects to the whole school.

As Kim circulates up and down the aisles of the science fair, she is pleased with the comments she overhears from other people. The projects *are* of higher quality than in any previous year. But more important, Kim feels good about the confidence of the students' presentations. They aren't just going through the motions, they really *do* understand the ideas contained in their projects.

Group Investigation: An Overview. **Group Investigation** *is a cooperative learning strategy that places students in groups to investigate a given topic*. Like other cooperative learning strategies, it uses student interaction as a major learning vehicle. Unlike other strategies, its primary focus is the investigation of a specific subject or topic.

Group Investigation traces its roots to several earlier educational thinkers. John Dewey (1916) viewed the classroom as a microcosm for society. Schools needed to help students learn to work together on meaningful projects so that they could do the same in society. The teacher's role was to help students identify and solve problems that were meaningful to them. Group investigation can help reach this goal.

Herbert Thelen (1960) was another educator who influenced the development of the Group Investigation Model. Thelen stressed the importance of active inquiry in student learning. He felt that learning was most effective when it involved the search for an answer to some question or problem. Like Dewey, Thelen felt that inquiry was most meaningful when pursued in a social context. Group Investigation provides an opportunity for students to pursue meaningful questions in groups of their peers.

More recently, Sharon and Sharon (1988) have used Group Investigation to promote social cohesion between different cultural and ethnic groups. These researchers found that Group Investigation can be effective in helping students from diverse backgrounds learn to work together.

Teachers who use Group Investigation have at least three interrelated goals. First, Group Investigation helps students learn how to investigate topics systematically and analytically; a goal similar to those in Problem-Based Learning Models which we'll discuss in Chapter 7. This results in the development of inquiry and thinking skills, and it helps reach a second goal, which is a deep understanding of content. Third, and perhaps most important, students learn how to work cooperatively toward the solution of a problem. This is a valuable life skill, and unfortunately one that students don't often practice in our schools (Goodlad, 1984). Group Investigation provides teachers with one instructional strategy to reach all three goals—inquiry, content learning, and learning to work cooperatively.

Planning for the Group Investigation Model. Planning for Group Investigation involves five steps, two of which—specifying objectives and designing team-building activities—are similar to planning for the other cooperative learning models. The steps are outlined in Figure 3.3.

Specifying Objectives. As we said earlier, Group Investigation activities are designed to help students meet three interrelated goals—to develop inquiry skills, to develop cooperative learning skills, and to acquire a deep understanding of content. Of the three, the third is least emphasized. If a deep understanding of content is the primary goal, other models

1. Specifying objectives

2. Planning for information gathering

3. Forming student teams

4. Designing team-building activities

5. Planning whole-group activities

FIGURE 3.3   Planning for Group Investigation

are probably more effective. The Group Investigation Model is most effective for helping students develop problem-solving and thinking skills and the ability to work together.

Planning for Information Gathering.   Problem solving and inquiry can't operate effectively in an information vacuum (Bruning et al., 1999). Students need access to information that they can use to guide their inquiry efforts. Kim planned information gathering by collecting used college science texts and working with the school librarian to be sure that school resources were available. Other sources of information include:

- Textbooks from other classes or levels
- Books from the public library
- Encyclopedias and other reference books
- Videotapes, videodiscs, and CD-ROM discs
- The Internet
- Resource people (e.g., doctors, engineers, scientists)

To develop research skills, teachers may want to make this search for information part of the overall investigation—that is, rather than gathering the resources yourself, you may have students do it, so they learn how to access their own information.

Forming Student Teams.   There are at least three factors to consider in forming teams for Group Investigation. Perhaps the most obvious is interest. Kim, for example, formed her teams based on the interest they expressed in different topics. Second, if possible, an equal number of high and low achievers should be on each team, and third, the teams should be balanced in terms of gender and ethnicity. One of the benefits of all cooperative learning strategies is that they help students with varying backgrounds learn to work together. Group Investigation offers unique opportunities for promoting cooperation and teamwork, because it is less structured than other strategies, and consequently it requires higher levels of trust and cooperation. The first step in reaching these goals is forming teams whose members are diverse.

Designing Team-Building Activities.   Group Investigation requires a greater degree of cooperation than does STAD or Jigsaw II; in them, student roles are clearly defined. When Group Investigation is used, students must work together in making decisions about their roles, which will be interdependent. This interdependence makes team-building activities very important.

Team-building activities can take a number of forms. In addition to the general team-building activities described in earlier sections of the chapter, teachers can use the content they're investigating as the focal point for student interviews. For example, Kim had her students interview each other about topics they were interested in and why. This information served as a springboard for their work.

Planning Whole-Group Activities.   The final planning task is to design activities that will introduce the class to the goals for the Group Investigation. This is especially important when it is first used. Because Group Investigations are not highly structured, students must thoroughly understand the process if investigations are to proceed smoothly.

This introduction/orientation is designed to have students understand the goal of the activity and the kinds of products expected. Kim, for example, shared and discussed examples of progress produced in previous years. In a sense, the process is like learning a concept, which is accomplished primarily through the use of examples.

The introduction should also help students understand the procedures they should follow in producing their product. An overview of the process on the first day, together with periodic review and additional reminders, help students gradually become comfortable with the procedures. Also, putting key steps on overheads, charts, or the board can help.

Implementing Group Investigation Activities. As with planning, implementing Group Investigation activities involves five steps or phases. These phases are outlined in Table 3.8 and are discussed in the sections that follow.

Phase 1: Organizing Groups and Identifying Topics. The first phase of Group Investigation lessons involves organizing students into groups and having them identify a topic. The order of these two tasks will vary with the topic and students. In some cases, the teacher may want to select topics first and then form groups based on student interest. This is what Kim did. She first asked students what topic they were interested in studying and formed groups based on these topics. An alternative is to form groups and let the students in each group democratically select the topic. This alternative gives students more experience in negotiating and compromising on the final choice.

Phase Two: Group Planning. During group planning, students determine the scope of their investigation, assess resources, plan a course of action, and assign responsibilities to different members of the group. In some configurations, group planning is easier than in others. If all members of the group are investigating the same topic, the primary task is deciding how to share background information. If pairs or groups of three are investigating subtopics related to the overall project, decisions must be made about coordinating their efforts, such as who will be responsible for background information, gathering data, analyzing the data, combining the different subprojects within the overall project, and writing up the report. Dividing these tasks is not clear cut, and part of the learning process involves making decisions about how they will be handled.

In Kim's class, group planning took several forms. First, groups had to decide on the portion of the overall project that they would be responsible for, how they would pool

TABLE 3.8   Implementing Group Investigation Activities

Phase 1	Organizing groups and identifying topics
Phase 2	Group planning
Phase 3	Implementing investigations
Phase 4	Analyzing results and preparing reports
Phase 5	Presenting reports

their resources, and how to collaborate on gathering data and reporting the results. These deliberations and negotiations are some of the more valuable aspects of learning.

Phase Three: Implementing the Investigation.   Groups are organized, topics for investigation have been identified, and the groups have a plan for accomplishing tasks. The groups are now ready to implement their plans. This is usually the longest phase. Students need time to design data-gathering procedures, gather data, analyze and evaluate data, and reach conclusions.

Keeping all groups working productively during this phase of the activity can be difficult because some projects take longer than others. Progress reports help groups monitor their progress and help the teacher coordinate efforts among the groups.

Phase Four: Analyzing Results and Preparing a Report.   As students gather information, it needs to be analyzed and evaluated. Teachers can help in this process in several ways. One is to continually focus each group's attention on the question or problem they are investigating. In a lengthy investigation, students often lose track of the central focus of their study. A second way to help students analyze results is to encourage them to talk about and share their findings with other group members. A third way is to encourage students to experiment with different ways of displaying data. The construction of charts, diagrams, and tables helps students understand and see relationships in their data. The students in Kim's class used the computer to help them here.

The actual form the report takes is up to the teacher. Options include oral presentations, written reports, poster boards, and demonstrations. If oral presentations are used, they should be supplemented with a written report or some other physical product. The thinking that goes into writing or constructing a report helps students learn to present their findings clearly.

Phase Five: Presenting the Report.   This phase of the project has two goals. The first is to disseminate information; the second is to help students learn to present information in clear and interesting ways. The format for these presentations can vary. Some options include:

- Whole-class presentations
- Presentations to segments of class
- Poster-board presentations
- Demonstrations
- Videotape presentations
- Learning stations or centers

The students' task in this phase of the model is to go beyond the information itself, consider the audience, and create a presentation that is informative and interesting. This is a task that will be useful in later life and one that isn't often encountered in traditional classrooms.

Assessing Group Investigation Activities.   Assessment of a Group Investigation activity should focus on each of the goals that can be met with the model. Let's look at them.

Assessing the Inquiry Process.   One goal of Group Investigation activities is for students to learn about the process of inquiry—its goals, how it proceeds, and its products. Students should be encouraged to reflect on the process and assess their own performance in each of the areas. A rating scale or checklist such as the one found in Figure 3.4 can be a valuable tool to guide self-assessment activities.

A rating scale such as this can help students reflect on the processes they used and learn to be analytical in their thinking. It can also stimulate discussion between group members by providing a concrete frame of reference.

Assessing Groupwork.   A second goal to be assessed in Group Investigations is the efficiency of the group and the extent to which group members effectively work together. The teacher can aid in the process by providing helpful feedback as the investigation progresses. The teacher can also help by discussing the kinds of behaviors that help build effective groups. Rating scales can also help students learning to focus on these critical interaction skills. Figure 3.5 offers a sample.

Rating scales can be used to help students understand how effective groups function, to provide feedback to different groups, or to make decisions about group composition and whether or not to intervene with some groups. They serve as a tangible reminder to both teachers and students that an important goal of Group Investigation is to learn to work together.

Assessing Understanding of Content.   Understanding of content is the third aspect of Group Investigation that needs to be assessed. The teacher wants to know if individual students understand their projects and the conceptual foundation on which they're based.

	Needs Work	Fair	Good	Very Good	Excellent
Clearly stated problem	1	2	3	4	5
Clearly stated hypothesis(es)	1	2	3	4	5
Hypothesis connected to problem	1	2	3	4	5
Variables controlled	1	2	3	4	5
Data gathering appropriate to hypothesis	1	2	3	4	5
Data analyzed clearly	1	2	3	4	5
Conclusions logically connected to hypotheses and data	1	2	3	4	5
Inquiry evaluation instrument	1	2	3	4	5

FIGURE 3.4   Rating Scale for Assessing the Inquiry Process

	Rarely				Always
Group members listened to each other.	1	2	3	4	5
Group members shared information and ideas.	1	2	3	4	5
Group members helped each other clarify ideas.	1	2	3	4	5
Group members asked thought-provoking questions.	1	2	3	4	5
Group members gave each other feedback.	1	2	3	4	5

FIGURE 3.5   Rating Scale for Assessing Group Effectiveness

The report itself, essay questions asking students to explain the project, oral presentations, and interviews can all help the teacher assess this understanding.

Discussions

A **discussion** *is an instructional strategy in which students share ideas with each other and engage in higher level thinking.* It is similar to other Social Interaction Models in that it uses group interaction to promote learning. It is different from other models in its structure and goals. In terms of goals, a discussion is designed to encourage students to think more deeply about a topic while developing their thinking skills. In terms of structure, it provides both teachers and students with more freedom and latitude to pursue ideas and opinions than most other models. Let's see what a discussion looks like in a classroom.

Martha Perez's American government class has been studying the election process at the national, state, and local levels and is preparing for a unit test the next week. Martha wants her class to use the information they have learned to think about some issues that will face them when they become voters. She begins her Thursday's class by saying:

"Class, could I have everyone's attention up here? Thanks. We've been talking about elections and we have some important elections coming up, not only in our city but also in our state next year. An idea that has gathered a lot of attention lately is term limitations. Some people would like congresspeople like senators and representatives to be limited to two terms. The issue I'd like to consider today is [writing the following on the board]:

Should people in Congress be limited to two terms?

To help us think about that question, I'd like us first to explore some of the advantages and disadvantages of this idea."

She now writes "Advantages and Disadvantages" on the board and asks each student to pair up with their partner to brainstorm as many of these as they can. After a few minutes she continues.

"Let's discuss some of these ideas that you've been talking about with your partner. Can we focus on advantages first? What would be an advantage of limiting the terms of people in Congress? Shaylynn?"

"Well, one advantage would be that more people could be in Congress so that we would get different ideas about how our government should be run."

"Okay, who else has an idea?" Martha responds, writing Shaylynn's ideas on the board.

"Kwan?"

"Uh, how about not worrying about reelection all the time. . . ?"

"Say more, Kwan," Martha replied.

"Well, one of the problems we've been reading about is that politicians are always worried about being reelected and have to spend a large part of their time trying to raise money to get reelected. Term limits would reduce this."

"Good, Kwan. Who else has an advantage? Antonio?"

"Umm. How about special interest groups? We read about how special interest groups can influence politics. If politicians weren't worried about special interest groups, then they could do the right thing and not worry about pleasing special interest groups."

The discussion continues with Martha listing additional advantages and disadvantages on the board. After she has a list of each she continues.

"Class, now I'd like us to get into our groups of four and talk about these advantages and disadvantages. What I'd like each of you to do is, first, move your desks so you can talk to each other. Then I'd like each person to examine this list and pick what they think is the most important advantage and disadvantage and think about why. Then I'd like each person to share their most important advantage and disadvantage of term limits with the group. I'll write these steps on the board while you move into groups. Any questions? Miguel?"

"Do you want us to rank all of them or just the top one?"

"Did everyone hear Miguel's question? It was a good one. He asked if you should rank all the advantages and disadvantages."

Martha pauses while she scans the room for students' response.

"No, you only need to identify the most important advantage and disadvantage and share it with your group. Let's do that now."

As students work, Martha circulates among groups, answering questions and listening to the interaction. After 10 minutes, she continues.

"Class, can I have your attention, please? Now I'd like each of you to think about our original question" [pointing to the question on the board]. "Given the advantages and disadvantages that you've been talking about, should the term of people in congress be limited to two terms? Think about that for a moment. Then I want to hear your opinions."

What you've just read is a description of a teacher using the Discussion Model to structure instruction in a social studies classroom. Let's examine the key characteristics of this model.

Overview of the Discussion Model

The Discussion Model involves students in content-oriented interactions as they attempt to resolve some issue or question. The teacher's role in this model, as in other group-inter-action models, is more facilitative than direct. Students learn by using background knowledge gained earlier to discuss thought provoking topics or issues. Let's examine how both teacher and student roles change during discussions.

Social Structure of the Model.   Discussions are most effective when students actively think about and talk about content-oriented topics. Discussions provide opportunities to use ideas they have already learned, integrating them in new and different ways. For this to occur, students need to feel free to explore ideas, share opinions, and exchange views. Teachers facilitate these processes in a number of ways.

Teacher's Role.   Teachers play a central role in successful discussions, but they do this by facilitating student interaction rather than by more direct means. Unlike other strategies where teacher talk predominates, the rule of thumb in discussions in terms of teacher talk is "less is better." The less that teachers talk and still accomplish their objective—which is to have students interact both with content and with each other—the better. Teachers perform several essential roles during discussions:

- Framing the discussion
- Orienting students
- Facilitating student interaction
- Focusing, summarizing, and reviewing

Effective discussions, like all effective lessons, require a focal point—something that attracts and maintains students' thinking. Teachers create a focal point by framing the discussion in such a way that students have something to think about. Martha Perez did this when she posed the question about term limits on the board.

Effective discussions also require that students understand their roles and what they are supposed to do. Too many discussions flounder because students literally don't know what to do. Teachers can prevent this situation through clear directions that orient students to the specific tasks facing them.

Martha did this in several ways. First, she instructed each pair to brainstorm advantages and disadvantages of term limits. Then she asked the members of each group to individually identify the most important advantage and disadvantage and then share it with their group. Finally, she checked to see if there were any questions and used Miguel's question to clarify her instructions. Specific tasks and clear directions effectively focus students' thinking and interactions during discussions.

A third role that teachers perform during discussions is to facilitate interaction. Interaction is essential because it encourages students to:

- Clarify their own thinking.
- Analyze and evaluate their ideas on the basis of others' thoughts.
- Revise their ideas based upon their interaction with others.

Teachers facilitate student interaction in two major ways. First, they encourage student dialogue by the kinds of learning tasks they provide. Martha had her students interact in pairs, then in groups of four, and finally with the whole class.

A second way that teachers facilitate interaction is through the questions they ask. Thought-provoking, open-ended questions that begin with stems like

- Why?
- How?
- Where?
- In what ways?

encourage students to connect ideas and share them with each other.

A final role that teachers perform during discussions is to make sure that discussions stay focused and on track. They do this by asking focusing questions like, "How does that relate to our question?" and by summarizing and reviewing at critical points. In doing these, teachers need to continually guard against dominating the discussion and turning it into a teacher-centered lesson.

Student Roles.   Just as teachers' roles change during discussions, so do students' roles. They become more active than in traditional instruction and also take more responsibility for the direction of the lesson. Discussions work when students are cognitively and emotionally involved in the topics they are talking about. Teachers can encourage their involvement and initiative by creating a classroom environment in which student ideas are accepted and valued.

Goals of Discussions.   Teachers have three interconnected goals when they utilize the Discussion Model in their classroom. They want students to think about content in a deeper, more analytical, and critical manner. They also want to develop students' thinking skills. In addition, they want to help students develop their social interaction skills. Let's examine these different goals.

Content Goals.   Discussions have a definite content focus, and teachers use this strategy to help students develop deeper insights into topics they have been studying. Research suggests that learning increases when students use ideas in meaningful activities (Sternberg, 1998). Discussions provide opportunities for students to connect ideas, take positions, and defend these positions with others.

Thinking Skills.   Students' ability to think increases when thinking skills are embedded in content-rich, meaningful activities (Kuhn, 1999). Discussions provide opportunities for students to:

- Examine and integrate ideas.

- Analyze different perspectives.
- Evaluate alternate solutions.

As students employ these processes on discussion topics, they not only become more knowledgeable but also more competent at playing with ideas, the essence of thinking skills.

Social Interaction.   Discussions also provide opportunities for students to develop their social interaction skills. By participating in discussions, students gain expertise in:

- Expressing ideas and opinions.
- Listening to and reflecting on the ideas of others.
- Respecting differences of opinion.
- Disagreeing with others respectfully.
- Building upon others' ideas.

These are important social interaction skills, and teachers can help students develop them by providing opportunities to practice these during discussions and by providing modeling and feedback.

Planning for Discussions.   Effective discussions don't just happen, they must be planned for carefully. Teachers need to carefully consider their goals when they utilize discussions, ensure that students have sufficient background knowledge to participate successfully in discussions, select appropriate topics, and structure procedures so that student interaction is focused. We discuss these planning tasks in this section.

Goals.   Discussions are designed to accomplish three specific kinds of goals—integration and analysis of ideas, development of student thinking, and social interaction skills. They are not designed to help students initially learn content and are inappropriate for introducing new concepts and skills. In addition, because teachers have less control over the direction of the lesson, this might not be the most time-effective way to integrate large bodies of information. Discussions are optimally useful when teachers want to encourage students to think more deeply about content while learning how to dialogue and exchange ideas with their peers.

Content Background Knowledge.   To discuss a topic, students must know something about the content. Because discussions require student background knowledge, they should either occur at the end of a unit of study or be preceded by specific lessons targeting discussion topics. Martha Perez used her discussion to cap a unit on U.S. politics. Without prior background knowledge about the topic, her students would have been unable to offer insights and take the initiative in integrating and evaluating ideas.

Selecting Topics.   If discussions are to engage students' interest, they must be focused on topics that utilize student background knowledge and require them to engage in issues that are controversial or ego involving. Research shows that discussing controversial issues increases student knowledge about the issues and also encourages deeper under-standing of different sides of the issue (Johnson & Johnson, 1994). Taking a stand on an issue is also motivating because it allows students to become personally involved and cognitively linked to potentially abstract topics. We have observed originally uninterested students become animated and excited when asked to take a personal position on a contro-versial topic. The discussion will often spill over into the hall and even the class the next day. Teachers can capture this motivational enthusiasm by structuring discussions around topics that require students to take a position. Some possible discussion starters in differ-ent content areas are found in Table 3.9.

Structuring Discussions. Teachers have several choices in structuring discussions, and each has advantages and disadvantages. Whole-class discussions allow the teacher to monitor the progress and direction of the discussion but provide fewer opportunities for all students to participate. Small-group discussions provide increased opportunities for all students to participate, but teachers have less control over the tempo and direction of the interaction. Martha Perez combined the best of both options by having students discuss advantages and disadvantages in small groups and then used the products of small-group work to frame large group discussion.

Implementing Discussions

The Discussion Model occurs in three stages. The first stage, Orienting, is designed to introduce the topic, draw students into the discussion, and frame the issues. In the second stage, Exploration, students actively pursue issues surrounding the topic, clarifying their thinking and ultimately taking a position or stand. In the final stage, Closure, the teacher helps students identify major points raised and summarize the progress of the discussion. Let's examine these stages.

Orienting. As with other models, students need to be drawn into discussions and their attention focused on the topic at hand. In addition, student background knowledge needs

TABLE 3.9 Potential Discussion Starters

Content Area	Issue or Question	
Literature:	Shakespeare's *Julius Caesar*	Were Caesar's assassins justified in murdering him?
Science:	Genetics	Should scientists be allowed to use genetic engineering to change plants or animals?
Social Studies:	Political Science	Are gun control laws effective in reducing crime?
Health:	Drugs	Should there be a ban on tobacco products?

to be activated. Teachers do this in several ways. First, a focal question needs to be raised and placed on the board or overhead for students to think about and consider. Martha did this when she wrote, "Should the terms of people in Congress be limited to two terms?" She activated students' background knowledge when she had student dyads brainstorm advantages and disadvantages and share these with the whole class.

Exploration.   During the Exploration phase, students focus their background knowledge on the topic or issue and share their personal perspectives with each other. Whether this occurs in small or large groups, teachers play two essential roles. One is to keep the discussion focused and moving. The other is to facilitate group interaction and help students develop their skills in this area.

Successful lessons have both direction and momentum. Students need to feel that the discussion is heading somewhere and that the class is making progress toward some goal. Because discussions are student centered, the possibility of drift is continually present. Teachers need to carefully monitor discussion progress, refocusing it with questions and making sure that it doesn't become sidetracked into dead ends.

At the same time, teachers need to take advantage of opportunities to help students develop their interaction skills during discussions. Teachers can do this in a number of ways, including comments such as:

> "Class, did you see how Felicia built on Roberta's Point?"
> "So you disagree with Eric's point? You did that clearly. Any other opinions?"

and

> "Good listening, Maria. I think you identified an important difference between those two ideas."

By consciously targeting positive aspects of student interaction skills teachers can help make students aware of their importance in effective discussions.

Obstacles to Effective Discussions.   Research identifies several obstacles to effective discussions (Dillon, 1987). Among these are teacher domination, overparticipation by some, and nonparticipation by others.

Perhaps the biggest obstacle to effective discussions is teachers' inability to allow students to develop ownership for them. Leading discussions in a democratic and noncoercive manner is a difficult task for many teachers, who are used to a more proactive instructional role. If students are to feel ownership of the discussion and learn to effectively participate in them, teachers need to sit back, take a less active role, and let student leadership develop. Some have recommended that teachers stay out of discussions completely, allowing them to develop naturally (Dillon, 1987). While appreciating the intent of their suggestions, we disagree with its practicality. Too many discussions flounder because of lack of direction. We recommend that teachers provide this direction in a sensitive style that still maintains students' central, active role.

Two additional related discussion problems are domination by a few and nonpartici-pation by many. In terms of the former, teachers can help steer the discussion's energy by strategically calling on a wide sample of students with comments like, " Let's hear another point of view from _____ " and, " We haven't heard from _____ yet. What do you think?" A second way to encourage a greater participation by all students is through the use of small-group strategies that not only encourage but require all students to participate.

Closure.   Effective lessons not only need to go somewhere, they also need Closure. Stu-dents need to feel that their efforts have produced something. This is especially true with discussions, where the lesson vector may not be as clear or apparent as it is in more teacher-centered lessons.

Teachers can help students reach Closure in several ways. They can ask for a sum-mary of the major points made. They can also seek consensus on issues through a show of hands. In doing this, teachers must stress that personal opinion and dissent are valued. A simple comment such as, "We found that different people believe different things. That's okay. What is important is that you know what you believe and why," can help students understand that the purpose of discussions is not necessarily conformity or agreement, but the honest exchange of ideas and opinions.

Evaluating Discussions.   Discussions have three goals—the development of interac-tion skills, the development of thinking skills, and the integration and analysis of ideas. We have already discussed evaluating the first two types of skills earlier in the chapter, so we'll focus on the last one in this section.

Measuring Content Outcomes.   We would like our students to leave discussions with two outcomes—a better understanding of the content involved and an increased ability to analyze and evaluate ideas. Short-answer essay items focused on specific outcomes are effective for the first goal, while more traditional essay items are designed to measure the second.

Essay Items.   **Essay items** *require students to make extended written responses to ques-tions or problems.* Essay questions are valuable for two reasons. First, organizing, ex-pressing, and defending ideas require higher-order critical thinking. Second, the essay format is often the only way these goals can be measured (Stiggins, 1997). Also, when students study for an essay exam, they are more likely to organize information in a mean-ingful way (Foos, 1992).

Short-answer essay items target specific content areas and ask students to respond to ideas discussed previously. For example, Martha could assess her students' understanding of the pros and cons of term limitations with the following item:

List and explain three advantages and three disadvantages of term limitations.

An item such as this communicates expectations clearly to students and is relatively simple to score. A drawback to this type of item, however, is that it fails to assess stu-dents' ability to analyze, integrate, and evaluate ideas.

Essay items are ideally suited to these goals. They provide opportunities for students to engage in higher level thinking while focusing on the content of the lesson. For example, Martha might ask her students,

> Would term limits improve the political process in America? In your answer list, analyze, and evaluate the advantages and disadvantages of term limits.

In scoring this item, Martha would construct a scoring rubric that contained essential components (i.e., advantages and disadvantages as well as an evaluation of these) and the point total to be assigned to each. A scoring rubric such as this increases both validity and reliability and can be shared with students to help them become better essay writers.

Increasing Motivation with Social Interaction Models

Anyone who has worked in classrooms and interacted with young children and adolescents soon realizes that students are social beings motivated by the desire to interact with their peers. We consider ways teachers can capitalize on this desire in this section.

Interest in the motivating effects of social interaction goes back to the turn of the twentieth century, when researchers found that the performance of potentially boring tasks could be enhanced by doing them in groups (Pintrich & Schunk, 1996). More recent work in the area has focused on the social nature of learning as well as the role that social groups play in fulfilling basic human needs.

Group processes have also been linked to competence, affiliation and power needs in students (Schmuck & Schmuck, 1997). When they are involved in learning groups, students are concerned about their competence. Each wants to appear knowledgeable, and this is especially important in small groups, which require risk taking and initiative. To accommodate their needs, teachers need to carefully structure group tasks so that all students have opportunities to contribute and succeed (Cohen, 1994).

Groups also satisfy students' needs for affiliation. Participating in groups can be motivating because it fulfills an important students social goal—the need to belong (Maslow, 1968). This need exists at all grade levels but is especially powerful during adolescence. Teachers can capitalize on this affiliation need by making working groups cohesive and supportive. Group-building exercises described earlier can be effective as well as the teacher's emphasis and supportive interaction within groups.

Small groups also help fulfill students' need for power and control (Schmuck & Schmuck, 1997). This need can be negative or positive. For example, it can result in putdowns or other kinds of aggressive behaviors, but it can also promote leadership and individual contributions to the group. Teachers can channel student energies into constructive channels by creating multiple tasks within each group in which all can contribute and succeed (Cohen, 1994). For example, students can take turns being leader, recorder, facilitator, and summarizer. This exchange of roles not only gives students different ways to succeed, but also teaches them different social interaction skills.

Summary

Groupwork Strategies

Groupwork strategies are social interaction models designed to be integrated with other more inclusive, content-oriented models. They divide students into small groups and use these groups to encourage social interaction.

Cooperative Learning

Cooperative learning is an approach to learning that involves students working together to reach a common goal. Several cooperative learning strategies exist, three of which were discussed in this chapter. Each is based on *group goals, individual accountability,* and *equal opportunity for success* as guiding principles. Having students learn to work together effectively is an overriding goal for all cooperative learning strategies.

Student Teams Achievement Divisions (STAD) has teams of four or five work toward understanding of facts, concepts, or skills. Closely related to the Direct Instruction Model, STAD uses team study in place of independent practice. Students compete with their past performance to earn improvement points which contribute to team awards.

Jigsaw II, designed to teach organized bodies of information, develops student experts who in turn teach their teammates. Team members develop deep understanding of content as all team members share their expertise. Improvement points and team awards—as used with STAD—can also be used with Jigsaw II to promote success and provide recognition for team accomplishment.

Group Investigation, the most complex and least structured model of the three, has groups collaborate on inquiry problems. When Group Investigation is used, defining problems, stating hypotheses, gathering data, and assessing hypotheses are similar to processes used with the Problem-Based Learning Models. Group Investigation differs from these in its emphasis on groupwork, collaboration, negotiation, and making written and oral reports that summarize the group's work.

Discussions

Discussion is a social interaction model designed to help students analyze and integrate ideas through interaction with peers. Discussions require sufficient student background knowledge to allow students to discuss ideas freely. In implementing discussions, teachers first need to orient students to the topic, then allow them freedom to explore it, and bring the lesson to closure through summaries and consensus seeking. Teachers evaluate discussions with extended short answer and essay questions.

Increasing Motivation in Social Interaction Models

Social Interaction Models tap into students' need to interact with their peers. As opposed to behaviorist views of learning, social interaction models are more constructivist and cognitively oriented. These models also fulfill students' need for competence, affiliation, and power.

IMPORTANT CONCEPTS

Combining pairs   (p. 63)
Cooperative learning   (p. 64)
Discussion   (p. 92)
Equal opportunity for success   (p. 65)
Essay items   (p. 99)
Group goals   (p. 64)
Group Investigation   (pp. 83, 86)
Groupwork   (p. 60)

Individual accountability   (p. 65)
Pairs check   (p. 63)
Jigsaw II   (pp. 76, 79)
Social Interaction Models   (p. 59)
Student Teams Achievement Divisions
   (STAD)   (p. 68)
Task specialization   (p. 79)
Think-pair-share   (p. 62)

EXERCISES

1. Examine the introductory cases at the beginning of the chapter involving Jim Felton and Jesse Kantor. Which type of model was each using? Defend your answer with specific information from the cases.

2. Analyze the following list of goals and decide whether they are most appropriate for STAD, Jigsaw II, or Group Investigation.

   a. A third-grade teacher wanted his students to know their multiplication facts.

   b. A junior high school social studies teacher wanted to teach his students how to analyze social issues. Since it was an election year, he selected voting and asked each group to design a research project around this topic.

   c. An English teacher was comparing Faulkner, Fitzgerald, and Hemingway and wanted his students to understand similarities and differences between each of the writers.

   d. A junior high science teacher was studying pollution. He assigned students to groups and asked each group to investigate either air, water, or solid waste pollution in their geographic area.

   e. A fourth-grade teacher wanted to develop her students' ability to research a topic. She selected the topic of pets and asked each group to design and implement a project on this subject.

   f. A health teacher wanted his students to know and understand the four major food groups.

   g. A social studies teacher wanted her students to know the names of the states as well as their capitols.

3. Analyze the STAD lesson involving Anya Lozano and identify where each of the following components of cooperative learning were found:

   a. Group goals

   b. Individual accountability

   c. Equal opportunity for success

4. A math teacher is preparing to assign students from her Basic Algebra class into STAD learning groups. Averages of the students' past quiz scores are as follows:

Juan	97	Juanita	81
Bettina	94	Henry	80
Sheri	93	Lisa	79
Akeem	90	Joan	77
Kim	87	Pat	75
Heather	84	Alonza	72
Peter	83	May	70
Marcia	82	Ted	69

   a. She wants to use teams of four. How might the teams be composed?

   b. What factors other than past quiz scores might the teacher consider?

DISCUSSION QUESTIONS

1. What content areas or models are most compatible with integration with groupwork strategies? Least? Why?

2. How are the following essential components of cooperative learning—group goals, individual accountability, and equal opportunity for success—contained in:

   - STAD?
   - Jigsaw II?
   - Group Investigation?

3. Identify at least three similarities among STAD, Jigsaw II, and Group Investigation. Identify at least two ways in which each differs from the other two.

4. Which of the three cooperative learning models presented—STAD, Jigsaw II, or Group Investigation—is easiest to implement? Most difficult? Why? From a student development perspective, what might this suggest about the order in which they're introduced?

5. Researchers have found that cooperative learning is an effective way of breaking down barriers between different ethnic and cultural groups. Which of the following elements is most important for reaching this goal? Explain your answer.

   - Group goals
   - Individual accountability
   - Equal opportunity for success

6. Which of the three cooperative learning models is most widely applicable to different grade levels and across different content areas? Why? Which is least applicable? Explain your answer.

7. How is the form that assessment takes in each of the three cooperative learning models similar? Different? How do these differences correspond to the different goals of each model?

8. In which areas of the curriculum are discussions most valuable? Least? Why?

The Inductive Model

A Constructivist View of Learning

The Inductive Model is a straightforward but powerful strategy designed to help students acquire a deep and thorough understanding of the topics they're studying. Teachers present students with information that illustrates the topics and then guide students as they search for relationships in the information. Grounded in the view that learners construct their own understanding of the world rather than recording it in an already-organized form, the model requires teachers to be skilled in questioning and guiding student thinking. The model is effective for promoting student involvement and motivation within a safe and supportive learning environment.

When you've completed your study of this chapter, you should be able to meet the following objectives:

- Classify topics in the school curriculum as concepts, generalizations, principles, or academic rules.
- Plan and implement lessons using the Inductive Model.
- Adapt the Inductive Model for learners at different ages and with varying backgrounds.
- Assess student understanding of content taught using the Inductive Model.

To begin our discussion, let's look at three teachers, each using the Inductive Model to help students develop a deep understanding of the topic being taught.

Judy Nelson is beginning a study of longitude and latitude in social studies with her fifth graders. Knowing that some of them have limited backgrounds, she plans as if they have virtually no experience with these ideas. In preparation, she buys a beach ball, finds an old tennis ball, and checks her wall maps and globes.

After conducting her beginning-of-class routines, Judy begins the lesson by having students identify where they live on the wall map and then saying, "Now suppose you made some new friends on your summer vacation and you want to describe for them exactly where you live. How might we do that?"

After getting suggestions, she notes that all are good ideas, but none is precise enough to pinpoint the exact location of where they live. Then she says, "Today, we are going to figure out a way to identify where we live precisely. When we're done, we'll be so good at this that we'll be able to pinpoint any city in the world. Keep this in mind as we work today. Okay, ready to go?"

Judy holds up the beach ball and globe and asks her students to compare the two, calling on individual students in each case.

After several comparisons, Judy asks them to identify north, south, east, and west on the beach ball. Then she draws a circle around the center of the ball. "Now what can you tell us about this line? Let's begin. Tara?"

". . . It's . . . a circle."

"Good, Tara," Judy smiles. "What else? Andy?"

"In . . . it's . . . in the middle of the ball."

"Fine, Andy. . . . Now look at the tennis ball. . . . Amy?" she asks holding up the tennis ball, also with a line drawn around its center.

"Also the middle. It's also in the middle . . . of the ball."

Now Judy cuts the ball in half, leading the students to conclude that the center line divides the ball into two hemispheres, as illustrated in Figure 4.1.

Judy identifies the lines as "equators," and continues by drawing other lines on the beach ball, saying, "Now compare the lines to each other. Kathy?"

". . . They're all . . . even."

"Go ahead, Kathy. What do you mean by even?" Judy encourages.

". . . They don't cross each other," Kathy explains, motioning with her hands.

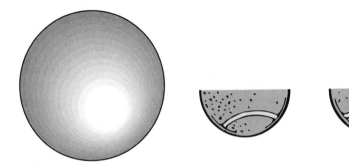

FIGURE 4.1   Beach Ball and Tennis Ball

"Excellent, Kathy," Judy nods, smiling.

She continues with her questioning, guiding students to additional comparisons, such as the fact that the lines all run east and west and get shorter as they move away from the equator, which Judy writes on the chalkboard. When the class is done making comparisons, Judy introduces the term *latitude,* to describe the lines they have been discussing.

Now Judy draws lines of longitude on the beach ball, as shown in Figure 4.2.

She continues by asking, "How do these lines compare to the lines of latitude? Amarilis?"

". . . They go all around the ball."

"Yes, they do," Judy smiles. "What else? Nicola?"

". . . You have the same number of each on the ball."

"Yes, I do," Judy nods, realizing that she has drawn three lines of latitude and three lines of longitude on the ball.

"How do the lengths of the longitude lines compare to the lengths of the latitude lines? Elton?"

It . . . looks . . . sorta like they're the same."

"Same as each other?"

". . . Yes."

"Let's take another look. What do all of the longitude lines do here?" Judy asked pointing the top of the ball toward Elton.

"They all cross there."

"Good," Judy smiles. "So what do we know about the lengths of the longitude lines?"

". . . They're, uh . . . I don't know."

"Okay, wrap this string around the ball," Judy suggests, handing Elton a piece of string that she has on her desk.

Elton measures the circumference of the ball through the poles with the string.

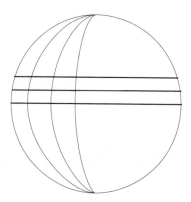

FIGURE 4.2   Beach Ball with Lines of Longitude and Latitude

Judy has Jennifer repeat the process with another piece of string at a different point on the ball but still going through the poles. Then she has Andy and Karen measure the ball, simulating lines of latitude to demonstrate that the latitude lines get shorter near the poles.

"So what do we know about the lengths of the strings? Elton?"

"They're the same," Elton responds, pointing to the longitude strings, "but these got shorter," pointing to the latitude strings.

"And what do these represent?"

"Lines of longitude."

"Excellent! So what do we know about the lines of longitude?"

". . . They're all the same length."

"And how do we know?"

"The strings were all the same length."

"Great! Good thinking," Judy responds enthusiastically.

Finally, Judy reviews by asking students to compare the characteristics of latitude and longitude, and relates both to the globe and her flat-wall maps. Some of their conclusions include:

1. Longitude lines are farthest apart at the equator, while latitude lines are the same distance apart everywhere.
2. Lines of longitude are the same length; latitude lines get shorter north and south of the equator.
3. Lines of longitude intersect each other at the poles, and lines of latitude and longitude intersect each other.
4. Lines of longitude run north and south and measure distance east and west; lines of latitude run east and west and measure distance north and south.

Students then identify the latitude and longitude of different locations on the maps and practice finding the exact location of cities around the world using longitude and latitude.

Sue Grant is beginning a study of Charles's law with her chemistry students. She starts by stating, "We've been studying the kinetic theory of gases, and today we are going to examine another law describing the behavior of gases. This law was originally formed by a Frenchman named Jacques Charles, so the law was named after him. When we're finished today, you'll be able to solve problems using his law."

Sue continues by taking three identical balloons, inflating each with as close to an equal amount of air as possible. She holds them up and asks her students to compare them; the class concludes that they're the same size. As her students watch, she puts the first in a beaker of boiling water, the second in a beaker of water at room temperature, and the third in a beaker of ice, as shown in Figure 4.3.

Now Sue displays three drawings for the students, as shown in Figure 4.4, and a graph, as shown in Figure 4.5.

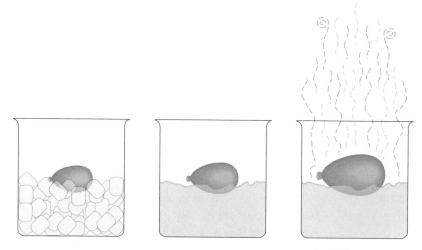

FIGURE 4.3   Beakers with Inflated Balloons

Sue puts the students in pairs and says, "Now work with your partner, and let's carefully observe and compare. Compare the balloons to each other, compare the three drawings to each other and to the balloons, and compare both to the graph. I want you to make as many conclusions as you can, and I want you to be ready to support your conclusions with evidence. I'll give you 5 minutes. Write your conclusions and evidence on your paper."

The classroom gradually becomes a buzz of voices as students study the balloons, drawings, and graph. As they work, Sue walks among them, periodically making a comment or offering a few words of encouragement.

At the end of the 5 minutes, she begins: "Okay, what have we concluded? . . . Steve and Barbara?"

". . . We decided that the masses in each of the balloons were the same."

"Good," Sue nods. "And why did you say that?"

"The number of molecules—dots—in each balloon is the same."

"Excellent. Good thinking, you two."

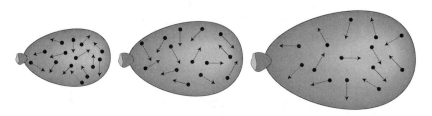

FIGURE 4.4   Models of Balloons at Different Temperatures

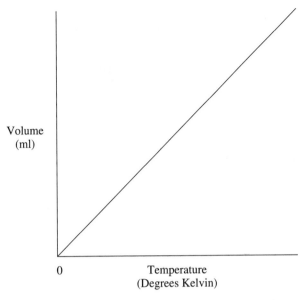

FIGURE 4.5   Graph Relating Temperature and Volume

She continues this process, calling on other pairs. Their conclusions and supporting evidence are summarized in Table 4.1.

Now Sue says, "Look again at the graph. We found that the volume is proportional to the temperature, but what temperature? . . . Greg?"

"I'm not sure what you mean."

"Look at the graph. Is the volume proportional to the Celsius temperature or the absolute temperature?"

"It looks like the absolute temperature."

TABLE 4.1   Conclusions and Supporting Evidence

Conclusions	Supporting Evidence
The masses of air in the balloons are equal.	The number of dots in the three drawings is equal.
The molecular movement increases in the heated balloon.	The arrows in the third balloon are longest.
The volume of the heated balloon increased and the volume of the cooled balloon decreased.	The molecules are closest together in the first drawing and farthest apart in the third drawing.
Temperature and volume appear to be directly proportional.	The graph shows that the volume is proportional to the temperature.

"Yes, it does. That's what we see in the graph. Very good."

Then Sue writes $T_1 \propto V_1$ and $T_2 \propto V_2$ on the chalkboard. "What do the 1s and 2s mean? Debbie?"

"The 1s mean . . . just . . . some . . . temperature and some volume, and the 2s mean some . . . other temperature and another volume."

"Good, so if we know they're proportional, what do we know about their ratios? Mike?"

". . . They're . . . equal."

"Excellent, so how can we write the relationship? Tony?"

". . . It would be $T_1/T_2 = V_1/V_2$."

"Outstanding, everyone. That's Charles's law, and that's what we're after today."

Sue continues, "We see from Charles's law how temperature affects volume. Let's think about how what we just learned relates to what we already know about mass and density. . . . As the temperature increases, what happens to the mass of the gas? Randy?"

". . . Nothing."

"Good. And how do you know?"

". . . The amount didn't change, only the volume."

"Excellent. And how about the density? Jo?"

". . . It . . . it gets . . . less."

"Super. Explain that for us."

". . . The air is expanding, but the mass is the same, so it must be less dense."

"Bravo! Good explanation, Jo."

Sue now gives the students several problems in which temperatures change and they have to determine the change in volume, or a change in volume occurs and they have to determine what temperature caused the change.

Jim Rooney is a teacher in Lakeside Middle School, one of two middle schools in Brooksville, a small town in Florida. Jim is a bit frustrated that his eighth graders seem to be confused and unable to properly punctuate singular and plural possessive nouns in their own writing. He decides he has nothing to lose by trying to help them develop their own understanding of the rules, so he prepares a passage in which the rules are illustrated.

Jim opens the class by saying, "Today, we're going to practice finding patterns. The goal for today's lesson is to identify some patterns in the way words are used in passages. When we're finished, these patterns should help us in our writing. . . . Okay, let's go."

Then he begins his lesson by displaying the following passage.

Jefferson, a rural county in Central Florida, has six **schools**—one high **school,** two middle schools, and three elementary schools. Five of the schools are in Brooksville, the largest **city** in Jefferson **county.** The *city's* schools and the schools in three other **counties** hold an annual scholastic and athletic competition, and students in the *counties'* schools met this year in Brooksville. In all, students from five **cities** were involved, and the *cities'* students did very well.

The two **women** advisors of Brooksville's debate teams were particularly proud, because the *women's* teams won both of their debates. The members of Debate-1 swept the competition. The members of Debate-2 also squeaked out a win, and theirs was perhaps a greater accomplishment, since they haven't competed as long.

Four **girls** and three **boys** won both athletic and scholastic honors. The *girls'* accomplishments were noteworthy in math on the academic side and tennis on the athletic side. The *boys'* achievements were in writing and track. One **boy** set a record in the 100-meter dash; the *boy's* time was a new school record.

Many **children** from the elementary schools participated as well, and the *children's* accomplishments were equally impressive. Several of the children wrote short stories. One **child** wrote a story involving a **woman** and the *woman's* struggle to keep her farm in the face of hardship. The *child's* story and the *story's* plot were very sophisticated. Several *stories'* plots and characters were interesting and well developed. The stories were put in a **display,** and three of the **displays** were photographed for the local newspaper. The *displays'* contents included the stories, as well as some background information on the authors. Lakesha Johnson had her story published in the paper and hers was the first of its type to be presented this way.

Jim asks his students to look at all of the boldfaced terms and see if they have anything in common. The students make a number of observations and in the process recognize that they're all either singular or plural nouns. As part of the process, he leads them to conclude that plural nouns are formed by merely adding an *-s* if the noun ends in a consonant or in *-y* preceded by a vowel, but that the *-y* is removed and *-ies* is added if the noun ending in *-y* is preceded by a consonant. They also see that some nouns, such as *woman* and *child,* become plural by changing the form of the word.

Jim continues the lesson by turning to the italicized words in the passage, following a procedure similar to the one he used with the boldfaced terms. He asks the students what the italicized terms have in common and leads the students to the rules for forming singular and plural possessive nouns based on their observations of the information in the passage.

The Inductive Model: An Overview

Let's begin our study of the Inductive Model by looking back at the episodes we've just read and seeing what they have in common. This will give us a concrete reference point from which to develop our discussion.

- First, the topics the teachers focused on were specific and well defined—longitude and latitude in Judy Nelson's lesson, the relationship between temperature and volume in Sue Grant's, and the rules for forming singular and plural possessives in Jim Rooney's.
- Second, each teacher started with an example or set of examples—Judy's beach ball, tennis ball, and maps; Sue's demonstration and drawings; and Jim's passage.
- Third, the teachers guided the students from the examples to the conclusions in each case.
- Fourth, under the teachers' guidance, the students used basic cognitive skills, such as observing, comparing and contrasting, and finding relationships to reach the teachers' goals.

The examples and conclusions are summarized in Table 4.2.

Social Structure of the Model

Social structure *refers to the characteristics of the classroom environment necessary for learning to take place and the roles of the teacher and students in the environment.* The Inductive Model requires a classroom environment in which students feel free to take risks and offer their thoughts and ideas without fear of criticism or embarrassment. We will discuss specific ways of promoting a safe and supportive climate in the section "Implementing Lessons using the Inductive Model."

The Teacher's Role.   As we saw in our introductory examples, teachers using the Inductive Model establish positive expectations (Good & Brophy, 1997), keep students on task (Emmer et al., 1997; Evertson et al., 1997), and actively guide the learning activity (Good, 1983), all of which increase student achievement.

TABLE 4.2   Examples Leading to General Conclusions

Specific Examples	General Conclusions
Drawings of latitude and longitude on the beachball, and lines on maps.	Latitude lines are parallel, run east-west, measure distance north and south of the equator. Longitude lines intersect at the poles, run north-south, and measure distance east and west of the prime meridian.
Demonstration with balloons and drawings of containers and molecules.	When pressure is constant, volume is directly proportional to absolute temperature. $$\frac{T_1}{V_1} = \frac{T_2}{V_2}$$
Passage containing illustrations of singular and plural possessive nouns.	To make singular nouns possessive we add apostrophe *s*, and to make plural nouns possessive we add an apostrophe (if the plural ends in *s*).

When the Inductive Model is used, the teacher does not display or demonstrate information for students and then explain it, as would be typical in a lecture or demonstration. Rather, the teacher presents carefully chosen examples and guides students as they form their own understanding of the topic. This doesn't imply in any way that the teacher is intentionally vague or withholds information from the students. Clear goals are as critical with the Inductive Model as they are with a lecture or any other format. The difference is that instead of merely *telling* students, the teacher *guides* them.

The essence of the Inductive Model, from the teacher's perspective, is the process of presenting learners with examples that clearly illustrate the topic you want them to understand, and then guiding their thinking until the objective is reached. To use the Inductive Model effectively, teachers must be experts in questioning.

From the learner's perspective, the essence of the learning activity is the process of analyzing the examples to find their essential common elements, ultimately creating meaning from them. Let's look now at the learner's role in a bit more detail.

The Inductive Model: Theoretical Perspectives

The Inductive Model is grounded in the principles of cognitive learning theory, and particularly **constructivism,** *a view of learning suggesting that learners develop their own understanding of the topics they study instead of having it delivered to them by others* (most commonly teachers) in an already organized form (Eggen & Kauchak, 1999). As we saw in Chapter 1, the evidence that learners *do* construct rather than record understanding is overwhelming.

Constructivism places the learner in the center of the learning process. "Current research [on learning] . . . focuses on the role of the student. It recognizes that students do not merely passively receive or copy input from teachers, but instead actively mediate it by trying to make sense of it and to relate it to what they already know (or think they know) about the topic. Thus, students develop new knowledge through a process of active construction" (Brophy, 1992, p. 5).

Real learning "is not simply the parroting back of information. Real learning involves personal invention or construction, and the teacher's role in this process is a difficult one. On the one hand, the teacher must honor students' "inventions," or they will not share them. On the other hand, the teacher needs to guide students toward a more mature understanding" (Prawat, 1992, p. ii).

In contrast, in instruction not informed by constructivist thought, "the teacher lectures and the students listen. Children assume the role of passive, rather than active, participants. It is as if the knowledge the teacher has can be transmitted directly to the students: the metaphor is that of pouring information from one container (the teacher's head) to another (the student's head)" (Brown & Campione, 1990, p. 112). The Inductive Model is designed to prevent this type of passive learning.

The influence of constructivism in teaching and learning has increased over the last several years. The shift toward literature-based approaches to reading, for example, and process approaches to writing are both grounded in constructivism (McCarthy, 1994). The *National Science Education Standards* (National Research Council, 1996) and the *Curriculum and Evaluation Standards for School Mathematics* (National Council of Teachers of Mathematics, 1989) both have a constructivist foundation, and modern school textbooks are also being influenced by constructivist views of learning (e.g., Thompson et al., 1995). The increasing influence of constructivism can be seen across the school curriculum.

Goals for the Inductive Model

The Inductive Model is designed to accomplish two primary goals. The first is to help students acquire a deep and thorough understanding of specific topics, such as longitude and latitude, Charles's law, or the rules for forming possessives, as we saw in the three lessons that introduced the chapter.

Second, it's designed to put students in an active role in the process of constructing their understanding. Each of the teachers provided students with data in the form of examples—the balls with drawings on them in Judy's case; the demonstration, models, and graphs in Sue's; and the passage in Jim's. As students try to make sense of this information—with the guidance of the teacher—they both construct a thorough understanding of the topics and gain skill and confidence in their thinking abilities.

The procedures Judy, Sue, and Jim used were similar, but the specific content they taught was different. We examine this content in the next section, beginning with concepts.

Concepts: Categories with Common Characteristics

Concepts *are categories, sets, or classes with common characteristics.* For example, whenever Judy's students encounter parallel, imaginary lines on a map that run east-west but measure distance north-south, they know they are dealing with latitude. *Latitude* is a concept.

As another example, suppose children see the following blocks:

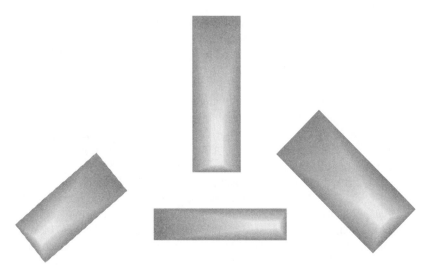

Even though they vary in size, relative dimension, and orientation, the blocks would be classified as rectangles because they all have opposite sides equal and parallel, with interior angles of 90°. *Rectangle* is also a concept.

The number of concepts taught in the school curriculum is nearly endless. Some are listed in Table 4.3.

Similar lists could be generated for other areas, such as *major scale* and *tempo* in music, *perspective* and *balance* in art, or *aerobic exercise* and *isotonic exercise* in physical education.

In addition, many other concepts exist that don't neatly fit into a particular content area, such as *honesty, bias, love,* and *internal conflict.*

Characteristics. A concept's **characteristics** *are its defining features,* and concept learning depends on students' abilities to identify the essential characteristics in the teacher's examples. For instance, Judy helped her students identify the following characteristics of *latitude:*

- Parallel lines
- Lines run east and west
- Lines measure distance north and south of the equator

The students then generalized to conclude that latitude always has those characteristics.

Similarly, the concept *rectangle* has the characteristics:

- Opposite sides equal in length
- Opposite sides parallel
- All interior angles 90°

Other characteristics, such as the size, color, or orientation, aren't essential, and an important part of concept learning is the ability to discriminate between the essential and nonessential characteristics.

Learners "construct" a concept through the process of generalizing. For instance, in the example of the concept *rectangle,* we saw four examples, each with 90° angles and opposite sides equal and parallel. Students then generalize to conclude that all rectangles have these characteristics.

TABLE 4.3   Concepts in Different Content Areas

Language Arts	Social Studies	Science	Math
Infinitive	Culture	Monocot	Quadratic
Pronoun	Republican	Conifer	Pyramid
Plot	Liberal	Arthropod	Triangle
Hyperbole	Pork Barrel	Work	Division
Indirect object	Community helper	Digestion	Equivalent fraction

Many concepts, such as *latitude, longitude,* and *rectangle,* have well-defined characteristics. Others, such as *democracy* or *liberal,* are less precise. For instance, some democracies are more "democratic" or more "like a democracy" than others.

For concepts such as these, the characteristics are much harder to specify. Some researchers believe they are better represented with a prototype, a case that is a good illustration of the concept rather than trying to specify characteristics (Schwarz & Reisberg, 1991). In this case, learners generalize from the prototype in "constructing" the concept.

Concepts: Ease of Learning. The ease of learning a concept depends on the number of characteristics it has and to what degree they are concrete or tangible (Tennyson & Cocciarella, 1986). The concept *rectangle* is easy to learn, because it has only three essential characteristics, all of which are concrete and observable. *Democracy,* in contrast, is much more difficult because of its abstractness and complexity.

These differences are reflected in the school curriculum. Shapes, such as *rectangle,* are taught at the kindergarten level or before, while *democracy* rarely appears until the middle school years or beyond. Further, if you asked people on the street to give you a precise description of *democracy,* few would be able to, which demonstrates how difficult some concepts such as *democracy* are to learn.

Concept Analysis: Clarifying Meaning. Learners shouldn't learn concepts in isolation; rather, their understanding should connect the concept to related concepts. Concept analysis is a useful tool in helping develop these connections. **Concept analysis** *is the process of describing a concept using its characteristics, related concepts, examples, and definition.* A concept analysis for the concept *adverb* is illustrated in Table 4.4.

From Table 4.4 we see that the concept analysis includes a **definition**—*a statement including a* **superordinate concept,** *which is a larger category into which the concept fits and its characteristics.*

A concept analysis also includes **subordinate concepts,** *which are subsets or examples of the concept,* and **coordinate concepts,** *which are also members of the*

TABLE 4.4   Concept Analysis of *Adverb*

Definition	A part of speech that modifies verbs
Characteristics	Modifies verbs Modifies adverbs Modifies adjectives
Examples	Susan <u>quickly</u> jumped to her feet. Kelly revealed her feelings <u>very openly</u>. David, a weightlifter, is <u>incredibly</u> strong.
Superordinate concept	Part of speech, modifier
Subordinate concept	Adverb that modifies another adverb
Coordinate concept	Adjective

superordinate concept. The role of the subordinate and coordinate concepts are outlined in the next section.

Examples: The Key to Concept Learning.   Whether concepts are specified by their characteristics or by prototypes, the key to concept learning is a carefully selected set of **examples,** *which are cases that illustrate the concept,* together with a definition (Tennyson & Cocciarella, 1986). In cases where the concept may be confused with a closely related concept, both positive and negative examples are necessary. For instance, when they are learning the concept *insect,* students should also be shown spiders—which are arachnids—so they won't conclude that spiders are insects. By pointing out differences between the two, such as eight legs for spiders instead of the six found in insects, learners are less likely to confuse the two.

Using concept analysis as a tool for thinking about examples, we see that subordinate concepts provide the positive examples and coordinate concepts supply the negative examples. In the case of *insects,* positive examples—subordinate concepts—would include beetles, butterflies, ants, and others, while the negative examples—coordinate concepts—would include arachnids, such as spiders. *Arthropods* are superordinate to both, since insects and spiders are both arthropods.

Judy Nelson used positive and negative examples in her lesson on longitude and latitude; her examples of longitude served as negative examples for latitude and vice versa.

Quality of Examples.   In order to make learning most effective, teachers want to use the best examples possible. What makes an example a good one? In the case of concept learning, the best examples are those in which *the characteristics of the concept are observable in the examples* (Eggen & Kauchak, 1999). For example, in teaching the concept *mammal,* we would want to use examples that help students learn that mammals have fur, are warm blooded, and give live birth to their young. In the real world teachers will have to compromise in many cases, but this criterion is the ideal for which we always strive. This is why Judy Nelson began her lesson with the beach ball. Drawing lines on it allowed her to illustrate the characteristics of longitude and latitude more clearly than would have been possible with a flat wall map or even the globe. Judy then used the globe and flat maps to help students elaborate on their understanding.

Relationships among Concepts: Principles, Generalizations, and Academic Rules

By extending specific instances to broad categories, such as generalizing from the four examples on page 116 to *rectangle,* concepts help us simplify our world; we remember the categories instead of each individual instance. Imagine how bewildering the world would be, for example, if we had to remember each individual insect among the billions that exist rather than understanding the broad classes. Some practical aspects of our lives, such as pest control, would be literally impossible.

Generalizing can also be used to link individual concepts to each other to form broader patterns than the concepts themselves. These patterns exist as principles, generalizations, and academic rules. Each is a relationship between two or more concepts. Some concepts and the relationships among them are outlined in Figure 4.6.

Let's look at them in more detail.

Principles: Relationships Accepted as True.   **Principles** *are relationships among concepts accepted as true or valid for all known cases.* The terms *principles* and *laws* are commonly used interchangeably, and we saw that *law* was used in Sue Grant's lesson topic. The statement, "When pressure is constant, an increase in temperature results in an increase in volume," is a principle. It describes a relationship between the concept *temperature* and the concept *volume,* and it occurs so consistently that we accept it as true.

Some other examples of principles include:

- The greater the unbalanced force on an object, the greater its acceleration.
- Like magnetic poles repel and unlike poles attract.
- Change is inevitable.

Principles are an important part of the school curriculum, particularly in the sciences. Much of the content in chemistry and physics, for example, is an examination of principles and their applications.

Generalizations: Relationships with Exceptions.   Many of the patterns we observe in the world are generally accurate but have obvious exceptions. These patterns are called **generalizations,** which are *relationships between concepts that describe patterns with exceptions.* For example, look at the following statements.

- People immigrate for economic reasons.
- A diet high in saturated fat raises a person's cholesterol level.
- Teachers increase achievement by calling on all students equally.

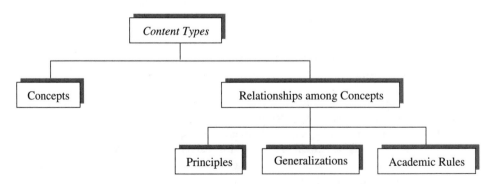

FIGURE 4.6   Types of Content Taught with the Inductive Model

Like principles, each statement describes a relationship between two concepts, but they have obvious exceptions. For example, people also immigrate for religious or political reasons; for some fortunate people a high saturated-fat diet has little impact on their cholesterol; and highly motivated students achieve whether they're called on or not.

Much of what we know about human behavior in general, and teaching and learning in particular, exists in the form of generalizations, as is most of the health-related information that we acquire from the media. For instance, the famous study suggesting that "an aspirin every other day helps reduce the danger of heart attack" is a rough generalization at best, and "taking vitamin C reduces the likelihood of colds" is an even more problematic generalization.

Understanding the difference between principles and generalizations helps students think about the validity of different assertions. The validity of the conclusions that are based on generalizations depends on the validity of the generalizations themselves. The abilities to make and assess these conclusions are basic critical-thinking skills.

Academic Rules: Relationships Arbitrarily Derived by People.   Consider the following statements:

- A pronoun must agree with its antecedent in number and gender.
- In rounding off a number, you round up if the last digit is 5 or more, and round down if it is 4 or less.
- In English, an adjective precedes the noun it modifies.

Each of the statements is an **academic rule,** *which is a relationship between concepts arbitrarily derived by people.* For instance, in both Spanish and French, adjectives follow the nouns they modify, which demonstrates the arbitrary nature of the rule. In the case of rounding, it would be equally valid to round up if the last digit were 6 or more, but it has been arbitrarily set at 5.

While arbitrary, rules are important for consistency, particularly in communication. For example, if we didn't have a rule to consistently communicate both singular and plural possessives—the goal in Jim Rooney's lesson—our writing would be confusing and communication would suffer.

Examples and Applications.   As with concepts, learners "construct" their understanding of principles, generalizations, and academic rules by working with examples. The teacher's role is to provide the best examples possible and to guide students as they attempt to construct meaning from the examples. In the case of principles, generalizations, and rules, a good example is one in which the relationship between the concepts is observable. For instance, Sue Grant was careful to illustrate the relationship between temperature and volume both with her demonstration and with her model. She didn't illustrate differences in temperature or differences in volume alone; she illustrated the relationship between the two. Jim illustrated forming possessives for singular and plural nouns, linking them to the use of apostrophes. In both cases, the teachers did an excellent job of illustrating the relationship they wanted their students to understand.

Planning Lessons with the Inductive Model

The planning process for using the Inductive Model involves three essential steps, which are illustrated in Figure 4.7.

Identifying Topics

Imagine that you're planning a lesson or unit. Where do you start? If you're typical, it's with a topic, and this is where most teachers begin (Peterson, Marx, & Clark, 1978). For example, the teachers in our opening episodes focused on *longitude* and *latitude, Charles's law,* and the *rule for forming singular and plural possessives.* Each topic served as the beginning point for the teacher's planning. Topics may come from textbooks, curriculum guides, or other sources, including teachers themselves. When the topics are concepts, principles, generalizations, or academic rules, the Inductive Model can be used effectively.

Specifying Goals

Having identified the topic, we must then decide what we want students to know about it. Effective teachers have very clear goals in mind and teach directly toward them (Berliner, 1985). For example, Judy Nelson wanted her students to be able to do the following:

- State the characteristics of longitude and latitude.
- Identify the longitude and latitude of cities and other specified locations on a map.
- Identify a city or landmark nearest a given longitude and latitude.

Judy's goals were clear, as were Sue's and Jim's, and this conceptual clarity provides focus during the lesson. Beginning teachers often specify their goals and objectives in writing, and while veterans tend to not write them down, they are no less clear about what they want their students to understand or be able to do (Clark & Peterson, 1986).

Clear goals—whether or not they're stated in writing—are critical because they provide a framework for teachers' thinking as they guide their students' "constructions" of the topics they're teaching. If teachers' goals aren't clear, they won't know what questions to ask, their responses to students' questions will be vague, and they will be less able to offer suggestions to students working collaboratively. Also, clear goals guide teachers as they select examples. If goals aren't clear, teachers don't know what they're trying to illustrate, and the likelihood of selecting the best possible examples is reduced.

Developing Critical Thinking.   The second part of specifying goals in this model focuses on developing students' thinking. While content goals focus on topical outcomes,

FIGURE 4.7   Planning with the Inductive Model

such as identifying the relationships between an animal's characteristics and its habitat, or immigration and economics, critical thinking focuses on making and evaluating conclusions based on evidence. Planning for thinking means that teachers consciously intend to have students practice making conclusions and providing evidence to support their conclusions. Teaching for thinking doesn't change the content objective; rather, it changes the way the teacher and students operate as they move toward it.

We saw in Chapter 2 that "learning is a consequence of thinking" (Perkins, 1992, p. 8), which suggests that content goals and goals for thinking are interdependent. Learners automatically practice making and defending conclusions while they're involved in constructing deep understandings of the topics they are studying. The teacher helps make this process conscious and systematic.

Selecting Examples

Selecting examples is the third step in the process. Once teachers know exactly what they want students to be able to say or do, they must identify examples that illustrate those characteristics. We know that, ideally, examples include observable characteristics if a concept is being taught, or an observable relationship in the case of a principle, generalization, or rule. Selecting examples can be as simple as drawing on a beach ball as Judy Nelson did, or as demanding as creating a simulation and role play to illustrate a concept such as *discrimination* or *relative deprivation*. The importance of good examples is impossible to overstate. Let's examine some different types of examples.

Concrete Materials. Concrete materials are the "real thing." They are the best type of example and should be used wherever possible. For instance, an ideal example of the concept *arthropod* would be a live lobster purchased from a fish store. The children could see and touch the animal, feel its hard, cold shell, and notice its jointed legs and three body parts. The essential characteristics of the concept would be illustrated in this example.

Demonstrations and hands-on activities are another form of concrete examples. Sue Grant's balloons in three different conditions allowed her students to observe the relationship between temperature and volume. When students connect two wires to a battery and make a bulb light up, they are seeing a *real* complete circuit, not a simulation, model, role play, or other indirect method of illustrating the concept.

Pictures. When concrete materials are impossible, pictures can be an acceptable compromise. Since we can't bring young and mature mountains into the classroom, and it is often difficult to go to where we can observe them directly, pictures of the Rocky Mountains and Appalachian Mountains would be an appropriate way of illustrating these concepts. The key is to come as close as possible to reality. Detailed colored slides or photographs are better than black-and-white pictures, which in turn are better than outline drawings.

Models. Some content, particularly in science, is impossible to observe directly. In these cases, **models,** *which allow us to visualize what we can't observe directly,* are effective. Sue Grant's drawings were a type of model because they allowed her students to

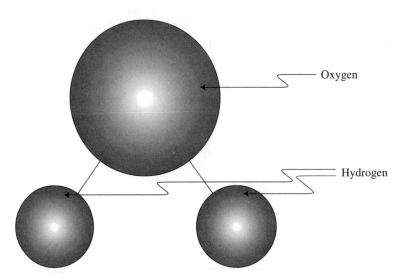

FIGURE 4.8   Model of a Water Molecule

visualize the spacing and motion of the molecules under three different temperature conditions. The molecular motion was impossible to illustrate in any other way. As another example, look at the model of a water molecule shown in Figure 4.8. While the model is obviously not reality, it illustrates accepted characteristics of the water molecule. One atom (the oxygen) is larger than the other two (the hydrogens), which are both equidistant from the oxygen, and the shape is accurate. From this example we can see that while models do not actually illustrate reality, they can help us identify essential characteristics of reality.

Case Studies.   Case studies, particularly minicase studies, can be powerful tools in illustrating topics difficult to illustrate in other ways. For example, consider the following illustration.

> Mary's dream had come true. John, a boy she had wanted to date for some time, had asked her to go to the movies. However, as she thought about her homework assignments for that night, she remembered the term paper that was due on Friday. She had been putting off work on the paper until the last moment, and now she didn't know what to do.
>
> Johnny knew if he cheated off Bill's paper, he'd pass the test, but he also knew if he got caught cheating, he'd be suspended.
>
> Although Mary hated to leave her hometown friends and family, and even her room, which she had lived in since a child, she wanted to go to college in Boston, 500 miles away.

Notice that in each of the three anecdotes, the character is faced with two alternatives that are antagonistic to each other. These brief case studies illustrate the concept *internal conflict*. We can see how hard the concept would be to describe, and an abstract definition such as "to come into collision, clash, or be at variance within oneself," would also do little to clarify the concept for school-age learners. The brief scenarios, however, provide a clear picture of the concept's characteristics. Skill in developing case studies can help teachers communicate many difficult concepts to their learners. Case studies are powerful teaching aids in areas such as social studies or literature, where concrete materials, pictures, and models are often inappropriate.

Simulation and Role Play. *Simulation* and *role play* are forms of examples used when concepts are hard to illustrate in any other way. Because they are often found together, we discuss them at the same time. For instance, consider a concept such as *discrimination*. While students hear a great deal about it, many have little firsthand experience. A simulation where some members of the class are discriminated against because of eye or hair color, height, or some other arbitrary characteristic provides powerful illustrations of an important concept.

Social studies teachers have also used simulations to illustrate our court system, the ways bills become laws, and the drudgery of assembly-line jobs.

We have devoted this space to a discussion of the various forms of examples because they are critical in learning concepts, principles, and generalizations. Without examples, learning is often reduced to mere memorization (Tennyson & Cocchiarella, 1986).

Quality of Examples: Teaching Learners with Diverse Backgrounds. Our learners are becoming more diverse. For example, cultural minorities now range from 70 percent to 96 percent in the nation's fifteen largest school systems, and they bring widely varying background experiences and needs with them to our schools. In addition, one-fourth of U.S. children currently live below the poverty level, and between a fourth and a third of today's children have no adult at home when they return from school (U.S. Bureau of the Census, 1994). As a result, more **at-risk students,** *students in danger of failing to complete their education with the skills necessary to survive in modern society*, attend school than have done so in the past (Slavin et al., 1989). At-risk students are characterized by high dropout rates, low achievement, and low self-esteem (Vito & Connell, 1988), and may lack the school-related experiences that other students often enjoy. For example, we referred to the concepts *young* and *mature mountains* in the last section. Some students may have traveled through the Rockies, Appalachians, or both, so verbally describing the mountains would be meaningful to them. For students without these experiences, however, a verbal description would be meaningless.

The best way teachers have of accommodating students with widely varying experiences is to provide the experiences for them; this is why the quality of examples is so important. Ideally, *all of the information that the student needs to understand the topic is contained in the example*. In essence, the example *becomes* the experience. Realistically, high-quality examples won't eliminate all of the school-related background differences among students, but using these examples is an important first step. Excellent examples make understanding richer and more meaningful for all students.

Quality of Examples: Utilizing Technology.   Some of the topics we teach are difficult to represent, and this difficulty is what makes them hard to learn. It is for these topics that technology can be effectively used (Alessi & Trollip, 1991). We might simply drop heavy and light objects, for example, to demonstrate that all objects fall at the same rate, regardless of weight, but it's virtually impossible to visually illustrate the actual acceleration of a falling object. Here, technology can be a powerful tool. For example, Figure 4.9 illustrates the position of a falling ball at uniform time intervals. We see that the distance between the images is greater and greater, indicating that the ball is falling faster and faster. This presents an excellent example of acceleration, which is virtually impossible to represent in any other way.

Learners can also use computer software to capitalize on the power of simulations. For instance, students might use software to simulate a frog dissection rather than cutting up an actual frog. While the simulation doesn't allow students the hands-on experience of working with a real frog, it is less expensive, since it can be used over and over; it is more flexible, because the frog can be "reassembled"; and it avoids sacrificing a frog for science (Roblyer et al., 1997). As the quality of software improves, representations will become more sophisticated and the simulations will be more interactive, further increasing learner motivation and understanding.

Implementing Lessons Using the Inductive Model

You have identified your topic, carefully specified your goals, and selected or created your examples. You're now ready to begin the lesson. Implementing a lesson using the Inductive Model combines five interrelated phases, illustrated in Figure 4.10.

Phase 1: Lesson Introduction

Teachers *introduce* the lesson by telling students that they are going to look at some examples, and their task is to look for patterns and differences in them. The teacher can do this in a variety of ways. A simple statement such as, "Today, I'm going to show you some examples. I want you to be very good observers and try to see what kind of pattern exists in them." Or the lesson can begin as Judy Nelson did when she posed the problem of specifying for a new friend exactly where the students lived. Sue Grant identified Charles's law by name, linked it to kinetic theory, and told the students that they would be able to solve problems with it when they finished the lesson. Jim Rooney began his lesson by simply elaborating on a review of the previous day's work. Each of these introductions provides a conceptual framework for the lesson.

Phase 2: The Open-Ended Phase

During the *open-ended phase,* students actually begin the process of constructing meaning from the examples. Teachers can start this phase in several ways:

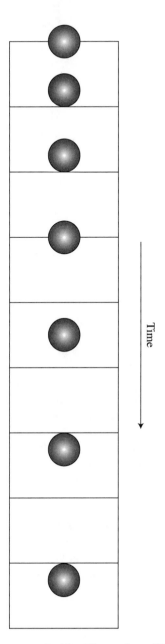

FIGURE 4.9 Illustration of Falling Object

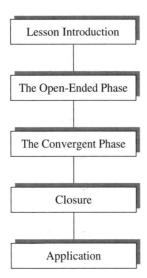

FIGURE 4.10   Steps in Implementing the Inductive Model

- They can present an example and ask students to observe and describe it. This is what Judy Nelson did with her beach ball, and what Sue Grant did with her demonstration.
- They can present two or more examples and ask students what they have in common (search for patterns). This was Jim Rooney's choice in his activity.
- They can present an example and a nonexample and ask the students to contrast the two.
- They can even begin with a negative example and have the students describe it. A teacher wanting the students to understand *exoskeletons,* for example, might begin by having students touch and squeeze themselves to demonstrate that their skeleton is internal.

Whichever option the teacher chooses, the lesson continues by having students respond to **open-ended questions,** *questions (or directives) that ask them to simply describe or compare (and contrast),* so a variety of acceptable answers are possible. For example, the following are some of the questions Judy Nelson asked during this phase:

"Now what can you tell us about this line? Let's begin. Tara?"

and later she said,

"Now compare the lines to each other. Kathy?"

Open-ended questions have several advantages compared to typical questions that require a single, convergent, correct answer:

- They are easy to think up and ask. Teachers can ask students to describe or compare and then use students' responses as the basis for further questions. As a result, questioning is less labor intensive for teachers.

- Because a variety of responses are acceptable, the questions are safe, meaning shy or reluctant learners are virtually assured of success in answering them.

- Since the questions can be asked and answered quickly, it is easy for teachers to call on several different students in a short time period. Research indicates that larger numbers of classroom questions promote students involvement and are related to increased achievement (Pratton & Hales, 1986).

- The questions allow for brisk lesson pacing, which results in greater student attention than slower-paced lessons.

- Open-ended questions have been found effective with cultural minorities and students with limited English language proficiency, encouraging them to participate in lessons (Langer et al., 1990).

- Open-ended questions allow teachers to diagnose students' background knowledge. What the students "observe" in the examples reflects their backgrounds and perceptions of the examples.

The last point is particularly important. As we said earlier in the chapter, students "construct" new understanding based on their background, so diagnosing their existing understanding is important. Asking open-ended questions is a simple, efficient way of obtaining this information.

Learning to keep questions open ended requires some adjustment at first. Because teachers are concerned with time and lesson momentum, they tend to be directive and want to "hone in" on the idea they're after almost immediately. To increase student participation and give students time to think, we're encouraging you to loosen up a little and remain open ended a little longer.

For instance, suppose you are teaching the concept of *direct object* and you have illustrated the concept with the following sentences:

Kelly threw the ball to Jamey.
Jim dumped the cans in the recycle bin.

Teachers, knowing that their objective is for students to understand direct objects, tend to want to ask questions such as, "What did Kelly throw?" or "What did the people do in each sentence?" While these questions are not wrong, they narrow the opportunity for students to respond, and many of the advantages of open-ended questions are lost. A better beginning question in the open-ended phase would be, "What do you notice about the sentences?" or "What are some things that the sentences have in common?" These questions give students a chance to think about the sentences, verbally describe their thoughts, and, perhaps most important, answer without fear of being wrong.

As another example, consider a teacher who wants students to understand the rule, "Nonessential clauses in a sentence are set off by commas." The following sentence might be displayed on the board or overhead:

The boys in this class, who are among the most hard working in the school, did very well on the last test.

The teacher could then continue by saying, "What do you notice about the sentence?" "Tell us something about the sentence," "Describe this sentence for us," or some similar directive. At this point in the lesson, these questions are better than, "What is the subject of the sentence?" or other questions that have a right or wrong answer.

There is no rule that tells you how many open-ended questions to ask. With practice, teachers become comfortable with the process and use their judgment about when to move on. Monitoring students' behavior is important here. If they appear eager to continue describing or comparing the examples, you may continue a bit longer; if they appear antsy or eager to get on with it, you might move on more quickly. This is when Phase 3 begins.

Phase 3: The Convergent Phase

The open-ended phase is designed to increase student involvement, motivation, and ensure success. However, you have a specific content goal, and you must help students reach the goal. To do so, you narrow the range of student responses and assist them in identifying the relationship, if you're teaching a generalization, principle, academic rule; or you assist them in identifying characteristics, if you're teaching a concept. Because the students' responses converge on a specific answer, this is called the *convergent phase*. Because the open-ended phase flows naturally into the convergent phase, the line between the two is often blurred.

Let's return to Judy Nelson's lesson to see how she made the transition from the open-ended to the convergent phase.

> **JUDY:** How do these lines compare to the lines of latitude? Amarilis?
>
> **AMARILIS:** . . . They go all around the ball.
>
> **JUDY:** Yes, they do. . . . What else? Nicola?
>
> **NICOLA:** . . . You have the same number of each on the ball.
>
> **JUDY:** Yes, I did [realizing that she had drawn three lines of latitude and three lines of longitude on the ball].
>
> **JUDY:** How do the lengths of the longitude lines compare to the lengths of the latitude lines? . . . Elton?

Judy began the convergent phase with the question, "How do these lines compare to the lines of latitude?" When Amarilis and Nicola didn't compare the lengths of the lines, Judy asked, "How do the lengths of the longitude lines compare to the lengths of the latitude lines?" While she was still calling for a comparison, it was narrower and required a more specific answer. This narrowing of possible responses occurs during the convergent phase.

Moving toward the goal doesn't always go as planned, however. When Judy asked Elton to compare the lengths of the longitude and latitude lines, she wanted him to say that the longitude lines were all the same length, but he didn't. Let's look again at how she handled it.

JUDY: How do the lengths of the longitude lines compare to the lengths of the latitude lines? Elton?

ELTON: . . . It looks like they're the same.

JUDY: Same as each other?

ELTON: Yes.

JUDY: Let's take another look. What do all of the longitude lines do here [pointing the top of the ball toward Elton]?

ELTON: They all cross there.

JUDY: Good. So what do we know about the lengths of the longitude lines?

ELTON: They're . . . I don't know.

JUDY: Okay, wrap this string around the ball (handing Elton a piece of string).

JUDY: So what do we know about the lengths of the strings [after Elton and Jennifer measure the circumference of the ball through the poles at two different points and Andy and Karen measure the ball simulating lines of latitude]?

ELTON: They're the same [pointing to the longitude strings], but these got shorter [pointing to the latitude strings].

JUDY: And what do these represent?

ELTON: Lines of longitude.

JUDY: Excellent! So, what do we know about the lines of longitude?

ELTON: . . . They're all the same length.

JUDY: Great! Good thinking.

When Elton was unable to provide the correct answer, Judy might simply have told him that the lines were the same length and moved on. This is seemingly more efficient than the process Judy went through. However, Elton's conception of lines of longitude and latitude was that they were all the same length, and it is unlikely that merely telling him otherwise would be convincing. Instead, Judy confronted his misconception directly and convincingly demonstrated the characteristics of both longitude and latitude. This tactic, together with her prompting questions, led him to an understanding of longitude and latitude that was more meaningful than merely telling him about the concept would have been.

Interaction and the guidance of the teacher are critical in confronting student misconception. For example, in spite of an eight-week unit on the topic of photosynthesis, over 90 percent of fifth graders retained the original belief that instead of making their own food, plants get their food from the outside, just as people do (Roth & Anderson, 1991). In another study with eighth graders who had completed a course in physical science, over 75 percent of the students retained the belief that larger objects (objects with greater volume) have more mass and are more dense than smaller objects, in spite of considerable experience in solving problems with the formula *density = mass/volume* (Eggen & McDonald, 1987). While these two studies were both done with science content, we see from Judy Nelson's lesson that misconceptions can exist in all content areas.

As we said earlier in the chapter, all students bring a considerable amount of background knowledge with them to the learning situation, and this knowledge influences their learning. Merely "telling" students typically has little influence in changing previous conceptions. They must have clear examples combined with teacher-student and student-student interaction to help them "reconstruct" misconceptions and accurately construct new conceptions. This is what Judy Nelson did in her work with her class in general, and Elton in particular.

Phase 4: Closure

Closure is the point at which students identify the characteristics of the concept or can state the principle, generalization, or rule. Judy's closure occurred when her students were able to summarize the characteristics of longitude and latitude. Sue Grant reached closure when students were able to state Charles's law and relate it to the balloons, and Jim Rooney did the same when his students could state the rule for punctuating singular and plural possessive nouns.

While a formal statement of closure is generally important (Brophy & Good, 1986), certain exceptions exist. For example, suppose the concept *above* is being taught to a group of young children. It could be defined as "a position in space where one object is at a higher altitude than another." Obviously, young students would be unlikely to generate such a statement even with considerable prompting. In this case, the teacher would move directly to the application phase in lieu of a formal statement of closure.

Phase 4 also provides opportunities to help students develop thinking skills related to recognizing irrelevant information. For instance, in Jim Rooney's case the content of the sentences in each case is irrelevant to the rule. With any topic, it is quite easy to assess the examples for nonessential information, which in turn sensitizes students to this important thinking skill.

Phase 5: The Application Phase

While being able to state a definition of a concept or describe a principle, generalization, or rule reflects understanding at one level, to make the topic meaningful students must be able to apply it outside the classroom. Judy Nelson's students, for example, were asked to find the longitude and latitude of different locations around the world, Sue Grant had her students solve problems with Charles's law, and Jim Rooney asked his to correctly punctuate singular and plural possessive nouns in their writing. Developing these abilities occurs in the *application phase.*

The application phase typically includes a seatwork or homework assignment. However, in spite of careful development of the concept, principle, generalization, or rule, application is a transition that often requires additional help from the teacher. Let's see how Judy handled this part of the learning activity.

> JUDY: Okay, everyone. Suppose now that you were trying to tell someone exactly how to locate Denver, Colorado. How would we do that? Connie?
>
> CONNIE: . . . We would find . . . the longitude and latitude.

JUDY: Good, Connie. Everyone, do that with your maps. [All the students have maps in front of them.]

     Judy walks among the students watching them work. After about a minute she begins again.

JUDY: All right. What did you find? Kim?

KIM: . . . Its about 40°.

JUDY: North or south?

KIM: . . . North.

JUDY: How do you know?

KIM: . . . Because it's north of the equator.

JUDY: Yes. Excellent, Kim. [Judy then continues by discussing Denver's longitude.]

Carefully monitoring and discussing students' initial efforts at application helps solidify ideas in students' minds, makes the topic more meaningful for them, and helps bridge the gap between the teacher-led learning activity and independent practice.

    When you're satisfied that most students can comfortably apply the information on their own, you can give an assignment that requires further application. While most of the students work independently, you can help those who haven't fully grasped the idea or who aren't yet ready for application on their own.

Application: The Role of Context.   The application phase is most effective when students are required to apply their understanding in a realistic context. Judy capitalized on the role of context with her initial problem of trying to specify exactly where the students lived. Jim used paragraphs that related to the students' experiences as the context for applying his rule. This strategy is much more effective than having the students apply the rule to isolated sentences.

    As another example, Sue Grant gave her students the following problem.

    You have a balloon filled with 1000 ml (the same volume as a liter bottle that commonly is filled with water) of air at room temperature, 72° F. Suppose that you put it in the freezer, which is 10° F. What will its volume be? What assumptions are we making when we solve this problem?

Here Sue provided a common household context for her problem, measuring whether or not the students realized that they had to first convert to Celsius and then to absolute temperature. Her problem was easy to write but powerful in its ability to make Charles's law meaningful to students.

Application: Linking New and Old Learning.   The application phase also includes helping learners link new learning with prior understanding. For example, Sue's students connected Charles's law to their earlier understanding of mass, volume, and density; Jim's students linked possessives to earlier understanding of singular and plural nouns; and

Judy's students linked their understanding of latitude and longitude to earlier knowledge about the earth.

If these links don't spontaneously develop during the lesson, the teacher should formally link the information with a review. For example, Sue Grant said,

> "We see from Charles's Law how temperature affects volume. Let's think about how what we just learned relates to what we already know about mass and density."

In this way, she helped link their understanding of Charles's law to their earlier understanding of mass and density.

The Inductive Model:
Emphasis on Thinking and Understanding

As we've studied each of the phases to this point, the explicit focus has been on content objectives. The planning started with content topics, specific content objects were identified, examples that illustrated the topics were created, and teachers guided lessons toward a content goal.

As we saw in our discussion of planning for using the Inductive Model, critical thinking objectives are not an outcome in the same sense as are the content objectives; rather, they're processes the students are involved in as they move to the content objective. For example, in each of our episodes we saw teachers promote thinking in their students in the following ways:

- Each teacher emphasized comparing (and contrasting). This is one of the most important and fundamental thinking skills.
- In each case, students were required to find patterns and generalize—by identifying the characteristics of longitude and latitude (Judy), verbally formulating Charles's Law (Sue Grant), and verbally stating the rule for punctuating possessives (Jim).
- In each case students were required to apply the information they learned in a realistic context.

These are all important thinking skills, the development of which is inherent in the structure of the Inductive Model.

In addition, the teachers capitalized on other opportunities to involve their students in thinking processes. For instance, Judy asked the following questions during her activity:

> "Go ahead, Kathy. What do you mean by even?"
> "Excellent! So what do we know about the lines of longitude?"
> ". . . They're all the same length."
> "And how do we know?

Sue's students worked in pairs; she required them to write their conclusions (inferences) in one column and their supporting observations in another. The following are some of her examples:

Inference	*Observation*
The masses of air in the balloons are equal.	The number of "dots" in the three drawings is equal.
The volume of the heated balloon increased and the volume of the cooled balloon decreased.	The molecules are farthest apart in the first drawing and closest together in the third drawing.

Learning to recognize opportunities to ask questions such as, "How do you know?" "Why?" and "What would happen if—?" requires practice. With effort, teachers develop the inclination to ask these questions, and recognizing and capitalizing on these opportunities gets easier and easier. The payoff is a much higher level of student thinking with little extra class time.

Using the Inductive Model to Increase Learner Motivation

We've just seen how the Inductive Model can be used to promote deep understanding and critical thinking. In addition, however, it can also be an effective strategy for increasing learner motivation, first by developing student *interest,* and second, by increasing *self-efficacy*. Let's consider these motivational mechanisms.

Developing Student Interest

Teachers often think about motivation in terms of the concept of *interest* (Zahorik, 1996), and a body of research examining interest is beginning to emerge (Alexander & Murphy, 1998), researchers having linked it to learner attention, comprehension, elaboration, and the seeking of additional information (Krapp et al., 1992).

Certain topics seem to be universally interesting to students—death, danger, chaos, power, money, sex, and romance (Wade, 1992). Unfortunately, little of the school curriculum focuses on these topics, leaving teachers with the question, "What can I do to increase learner interest?"

The most consistently effective way of promoting interest is by increasing student involvement. Students given a chance to participate also experience a sense of autonomy (Deci & Ryan, 1987), control, and self-determination, all of which are linked to intrinsic motivation (Lepper & Hodell, 1989).

The open-ended phase of the Inductive Model, with its emphasis on open-ended questions, makes this phase uniquely applicable to promoting high levels of involvement. Think again about the characteristics of open-ended questions. Earlier in the chapter we saw that they are easy for teachers to "think up" and ask, reducing the amount of effort required to use questioning as a tool for involving students, and making it easy for teachers to call on several different students in a short time period. The questions also allow brisk lesson pacing, which further increases involvement.

We also saw that open-ended questions virtually ensure success, which increases students' inclination to be involved. Their ability to be successful leads to a second important factor in motivation-self-efficacy.

Increasing Self-Efficacy

Expectancy-value theories of motivation (Feather, 1982) *suggest that learners are motivated to work on a task to the extent that they (a) expect to succeed on the task, and (b) value the task.* If both are present, learners may develop a sense of **self-efficacy,** *which is learners' beliefs about their capability of succeeding in specific activities* (Schunk, 1994).

As with promoting involvement, the open-ended phase of the Inductive Model, with its emphasis on open-ended questioning, also promotes motivation by increasing learners' expectations for success.

Success alone doesn't increase self-efficacy, however. If learners are successful on trivial or meaningless tasks, self-efficacy doesn't increase (Clifford, 1990). Learners readily recognize the difference between learning that emphasizes thinking compared to a focus on facts and memorization, and we saw in the previous section that the Inductive Model emphasizes thinking and deep understanding of the topics being studied. Combining high expectations for success with emphasis on thinking and understanding can be very effective for increasing learner motivation.

Flexibility in the Inductive Model

To this point we have illustrated and discussed the planning and implementation of Inductive Model lessons. Applying the model in different content areas and with students of different ages, however, requires flexibility. We examine the flexibility of the model in this section.

Examples

We have emphasized the role of examples as Inductive Model lessons are planned and implemented. Again, the importance of high-quality examples cannot be overstated. Several considerations in the creation or selection of examples exist, however.

Number of Examples.   How many examples are necessary? The answer is: as many as you need to illustrate the scope of the topic. For instance, if you were teaching the concept of *adverb,* a minimum number would be at least one example each of an adverb modifying a verb, an adjective, and another adverb, plus one or two adjectives as nonexamples.

As another case, if you were teaching the concept *reptile,* you would need at least one example each of an alligator (or crocodile), snake, lizard, and turtle, and a sea turtle (so the students don't conclude that sea turtles are some kind of fish because they live in the water), together with a frog (which is an amphibian) as a nonexample.

Accommodating Individual Differences

Adapting the Inductive Model for use with students at different levels of development and experience depends on two factors—the background of the students and the examples that you choose. For example, Sue Grant's students had experience with concepts such as *mass, volume, temperature,* and *pressure,* indicated by their ability to incorporate these concepts into their conclusions and supporting observations. Had they lacked those concepts, Sue would have had to back up and begin by developing them. (Because the Inductive Model begins open endedly, informal diagnosis of the students' background is built into the process.) Also, the students were able to deal with the abstraction involved in Sue's models of molecular motion and the information in the graph she presented. The illustrations that she used were more abstract than those that would be effective with younger students. In comparison, Judy Nelson used a very concrete beginning, the beach ball with the lines on it, because she knew that several of her students had little experience in this area.

The decisions that teachers make about the kind of examples to use depends upon students' backgrounds. In Judy's case, abstract illustrations would have been less effective because of the students' developmental level and lack of background knowledge. In general, the younger the students or the less experience they have had with the topic, the greater the need for concrete, high-quality examples. High-quality examples are the ideal for everyone; with young children and learners lacking experience, they are essential.

Creativity in Teaching

We have all heard about creative teachers and the need for teachers to be creative. Creativity in teaching often boils down to teachers' ability to motivate students. In terms of the Inductive Model creativity is often how eye catching, attractive, and clever we are in preparing our examples. Children's programs, such as *Sesame Street* and *Barney,* are very effective in this process. For instance, a muppet who runs off into the distance and announces, "Now I'm far," then comes closer and says, "Now I'm near," is doing nothing more than illustrating the concepts *far* and *near.* However, the illustrations are attractive, eye catching, and clever. They are creative.

Judy Nelson was creative in using the beach ball for her illustration of longitude and latitude. It was reasonably eye catching and very clear. Sue Grant's balloons attracted students' attention and posed a problem to solve. This is the essence of creativity.

Teaching "Off the Top of Your Head"

Teaching "off the top of your head" means generating examples on the spot and guiding your students toward an idea that appears spontaneously during the course of a lesson. As your expertise with the model develops, your ability to guide your students will require less conscious effort on your part, and you will be able to recognize opportunities to use mini-inductive lessons in the context of larger topics. Let's look at some examples of this idea.

In the middle of a class discussion, one of Sandy Clark's students raises her hand and says, "I don't get this 'division by zero is undefined.' I just don't understand what they mean by 'undefined.'"

Sandy pauses, thinks a moment, and says, "Okay, look," and she writes the number 12 on the chalkboard.

"Now I'm going to give you each a number to divide into 12, and when I call your name, you give me the answer. Roy, divide by 2; Eddie, 0.03; Karen, 0.01; Jeff, 0.002; Judy, 0.0004; Kelly, 0.000006; John, 0.000000002; Donna, 0.0000000000003."

"We'll go ahead and make a table," and she then writes the following on the board as the students give their answers.

Divided by	Answer
2.0	6
0.03	400
0.01	1,200
0.002	6,000
0.0004	30,000
0.000006	2,000,000
0.000000002	6,000,000,000
0.0000000000003	40,000,000,000,000

"So let's look at the patterns we have here," Sandy directs. "What do you notice about the left column? Terry?"

"The numbers are getting smaller and smaller."

"Good. So imagine now that we kept going with those numbers. Eventually we would be approaching what? Leah?"

"... I'm not following you."

"Imagine that we have many more numbers in the left column," Sandy continues, "and they continued to get smaller and smaller. Eventually, they would be nearly what?"

"... Zero."

"Yes, exactly, good," she smiles at Terry.

"Now look at the right column. What pattern do you see there? Rene?"

"They're getting bigger and bigger."

"Now imagine that the numbers in the left column got incredibly small, so small that we can hardly imagine. What would happen to the numbers on the right?"

"They would be huge," Brent volunteers.

"And ultimately if we actually got to zero, what would happen to those on the right? ... They would sort of what?" Sandy gestured openly as if illustrating an explosion with her arms.

"... They would sort of explode?" Dennis responds uncertainly, reacting to both the pattern and Sandy's gestures.

"Yes, exactly," Sandy nods. "That's what we mean by 'undefined.'"

At least three points should be made about this example. First, Sandy had the insight to be able to generate her examples on the spot. This required clear understanding of her subject matter and what it would take to effectively illustrate this topic for her students. *The ability to represent topics in ways that are meaningful to learners, plus an understanding of what makes topics difficult or easy to learn is called* **pedagogical content knowledge** (Shulman, 1986).

Second, helping students understand that "division by zero is undefined" took less than 10 minutes. This is what we mean by mini-inductive lessons in the context of larger discussions.

Third, and perhaps most important, Sandy could have simply tried to verbally explain division by zero and it would have taken less time. However, the likelihood of an explanation's being meaningful to students is much less than Sandy's illustration was.

An important trend suggested by the research on teaching is that in-depth study of fewer topics is preferable to superficial coverage of many and that students need time and opportunities to think about the topics they're learning. Brophy describes this movement in this way:

> Embedded in this approach to teaching is the notion of "complete" lessons carried through to include higher-order applications of content. The breadth of content addressed, thus, is limited to allow for more in-depth teaching of the content. Unfortunately, typical state and district curriculum guidelines feature long lists of items and subskills to be "covered," and typical curriculum packages supplied by publishers respond to these guidelines by emphasizing breadth over depth of coverage (1992, p. 6).

Inductive lessons that provide opportunities for students to analyze examples and apply new content in realistic settings are one solution to this problem.

Length of Lessons

In working with teachers, we're often asked, "How long should the lesson be?" The answer is the same for all lessons—as long as it takes students to reach the goal. In some cases, it may be rather long; for example, it took Judy Nelson's students about 30 minutes to develop valid characteristics of latitude and longitude, and they spent the rest of the class period practicing identifying the longitude and latitude of various locations around the world. In comparison, Sandy Clark's "spontaneous" lesson also took less than 10 minutes.

Fostering Cooperation

Lessons taught with the Inductive Model provide excellent opportunities for promoting cooperation among students. For example, in the open-ended phase of the activity, Sue Grant had her students work in pairs as they made comparisons of the balloons, her models, and the graph. Jim Rooney had individual students write comparisons on a piece of paper, but he could have as easily had students work in pairs as well.

Using the open-ended phase of the Inductive Model is a good way to introduce students to working together. Since they are only required to make observations and comparisons in most cases, the cognitive task isn't so demanding that the process is frustrating for them. With some practice, students can then be introduced to more demanding tasks, such as making and defending conclusions, as Sue Grant's students did.

Assessing Student Learning

The content outcomes of a lesson using the Inductive Model can be measured in a variety of ways, ranging from standard paper-and-pencil tests to performance measures and portfolios.

Regardless of the type of assessment measure, teachers must be very clear in their thinking to be sure that their goals, learning activities, and assessments are consistent with each other. Each of the teachers in the examples we presented in the chapter had learning activities that were consistent with their goals.

Maintaining this consistency through the assessment phase of teaching can be challenging. It's easy to fall into the trap of thinking you're measuring one level of understanding when in reality you're measuring another. For example, consider the following test item designed to measure students' understanding of the concept *arthropod.*

Circle all of the following that are arthropods.

   a. alligator
   b. shrimp
   c. oyster
   d. dragonfly

In order to respond correctly to the item, students must know characteristics of each of the animals or how each appears. If not, they could understand the concept and still respond incorrectly. This invalidates the item. While it's intended to measure students' understanding of the concept, it more nearly measures students' knowledge of each of the individual animals.

Pictures would be a much better medium than words. If pictures are used (assuming the characteristics are displayed in detail), students could respond to the item without knowing the names of the animals, and those with less experience are not disadvantaged compared to the rest of the class.

Better yet, although admittedly more demanding, would be for the teacher to display two examples, such as a grasshopper and a clam, and have the students explain in writing why the grasshopper is an arthropod and the clam is not. This provides students with an opportunity to apply the knowledge they have acquired, and it also gives the teacher insight into students' thinking.

As another example, suppose that Sue Grant wanted to measure her students' understanding of Charles's law and she presented the following problem.

$T_1 = 50°\text{C}, T_2 = 40°\text{C}, V_1 = 100 \text{ ml. Find } V_2.$

The problem presented in this way measures little more than recall of the procedure. In situations such as this, students commonly memorize formulas, plug in numbers without understanding, and find answers that often have no meaning for them. Regardless of the way a lesson is taught, if the measurement is essentially knowledge and recall, students will study more in response to the way they're tested than to the way they're taught (Crooks, 1988).

A much better alternative would be the following:

It's July 15, and extremely hot outside. You have three closed containers, each filled with 250 ml of air in your kitchen, which is 23°C. (Imagine that the containers are made of an elastic that can expand and contract without changing the pressure.) You put container A in the freezing compartment of your refrigerator, B in the other part of the refrigerator, and C outside your house.

1. Which of the following best describes the volume of each container after they have been in these conditions for an hour?

   a. Since the mass of air for each doesn't change, each container will have 250 ml of air in it.
   b. All three containers will have more than 250 ml of air in them.
   c. A will have less than 250 ml of air, the volume of B will not change, and C will have more than 250 ml of air.
   d. A and B will have less than 250 ml of air, and C will have more than 250 ml of air.
   e. We don't have enough information to make conclusions about the volume of the air in each case.

2. If the freezing compartment of your refrigerator is –6°C, what will be the volume of air in the container placed there?

Notice that the first example is qualitative. This measures a different kind of understanding than does the quantitative problem. Both measurements are necessary. Students often learn to put numbers in formulas and get answers with little actual understanding of the concepts and principles involved. Qualitative measurements help ensure that this doesn't happen.

In both Judy Nelson's and Jim Rooney's cases, simple performance measures would be the most effective form of assessment. For instance, Jim could have his students write paragraphs—just as he did in the application phase of the lesson—to determine the extent to which his students could correctly punctuate singular and plural possessive nouns in the context of one or more paragraphs. Judy could simply have the students find the longitude and latitude of several locations, and also find cities and landmarks when given the coordinates. She could personalize the process by having the students find the longitude and latitude of the city they came from if they lived somewhere else, the city their grandparents live in, or a city they visited.

Judy might also extend the thinking of her students with an item such as the following:

> Look at the map displayed on the overhead and find Chicago. Which of the following is the best predictor of Chicago's longitude and latitude?
>
> **a.** 40° N. latitude, 90° E. longitude
> **b.** 40° S. latitude, 90° W. longitude
> **c.** 40° N. longitude, 60° E. latitude
> **d.** 40° S. longitude, 60° W. latitude
> **e.** 40° N. latitude, 90° W. longitude
>
> Explain the reasons for your choice.

An item such as the preceding one assumes that the latitude and longitude of Chicago have never been discussed in class. The item would require that students:

- Know that latitude measures distance north and south of the equator.
- Know that longitude measures distance east and west of the prime meridian.
- Recognize that Chicago is north of the equator.
- Recognize that Chicago is west of the prime meridian.

As another example, consider the following item (again based on an unmarked map).

> Look at Lisbon, Portugal on the map. Its latitude is approximately 10^0 W. Now look at Madrid, Spain. Based on our understanding of latitude and the location of Lisbon, which of the following is the best predictor of Madrid's latitude?
>
> **a.** 4° W
> **b.** 4° E
> **c.** 14° W
> **d.** 6° E

This item would require that students recognize that Madrid is east of Lisbon but still west of the prime meridian. It is easy to write but requires that students both apply previous understanding to a new problem and predict an outcome. Items such as these measure both deep understanding of the content and students' abilities to think critically.

Summary

The Inductive Model: An Overview

The Inductive Model is a powerful strategy that uses examples to teach well-defined content. Under the teacher's guidance, students find relationships in the examples that lead to general conclusions and applications.

Based on constructivist views of learning, the Inductive Model emphasizes learners' active involvement and the construction of their own understanding of specific topics.

Goals for the Inductive Model

The Inductive Model is used to teach *concepts,* categories with common characteristics; *principles,* relationships between concepts accepted as true; *generalizations,* relationships between concepts that have exceptions; and *academic rules,* relationships between concepts arbitrarily derived by people. At the same time, the model is designed to help students develop their critical thinking abilities.

Planning Lessons with the Inductive Model

Planning lessons with the Inductive Model includes identifying topics and precise goals together with preparing high-quality examples. Examples can include concrete materials, pictures, models, case studies, and simulations and role plays. High-quality examples include all the information students need to understand the topic, and they are the most effective tool teachers have for accommodating background differences among students.

Implementing Lessons Using the Inductive Model

Lessons using the Inductive Model begin with a short introduction followed by an open-ended phase in which students are encouraged to make observations and comparisons among examples. The open-ended phase is followed by students' gradual convergence toward the goal under the guidance of the teacher. Lessons are completed when the students are able to define a concept or state a relationship in a principle, generalization, or academic rule, and apply the topic to a new, and ideally real-world, situation.

The Inductive Model:
Emphasis on Thinking and Understanding

Promoting deep understanding of topics and developing critical thinking abilities is accomplished primarily with teacher questioning. Questions such as, "Why?" "How do we know?" and "What would happen if?" promote both thinking and understanding. Although teachers typically ask few of these questions, with effort and practice using them can become virtually automatic.

Flexibility in the Inductive Model

The Inductive Model easily accommodates different numbers of examples, different lengths of lessons, and background differences in students. Teachers can be creative in the way they use examples, and as their expertise increases they can learn to use the model spontaneously.

Assessing Student Learning

Effective assessments are consistent with teachers' goals. Both traditional and alternative assessments in the form of performance assessments can be used to measure student understanding.

IMPORTANT CONCEPTS

Academic rule   (p. 121)
At-risk students   (p. 125)
Characteristics   (p. 117)
Concept analysis   (p. 118)
Concepts   (p. 116)
Constructivism   (p. 115)
Coordinate concept   (p. 118)
Definition   (p. 118)
Examples   (p. 119)
Expectancy-value theories   (p. 136)

Generalizations   (p. 120)
Models   (p. 123)
Open-ended questions   (p. 128)
Pedagogical content knowledge   (p. 139)
Principles   (p. 120)
Self-efficacy   (p. 136)
Social structure   (p. 114)
Subordinate concept   (p. 118)
Superordinate concept   (p. 118)

EXERCISES

1. Think back to your study of cognitive learning in Chapter 1. Explain how each of the lessons at the beginning of the chapter was based on cognitive views of learning.

2. Identify an instance in her lesson where Judy Nelson was attempting to establish positive expectations for her class.

3. Examine each of the following statements and classify each as a generalization, principle, or academic rule.

   a. People immigrate for economic reasons.

   b. Subjects and verbs in sentences agree with each other in number.

   c. A diet high in saturated fat raises a person's cholesterol level.

   d. Like magnetic poles repel and unlike poles attract.

4. Identify the concepts being related in each of the statements in item 3.

5. For each of the statements in item 3, describe one or more examples that could be used to effectively illustrate the concept or the principle, generalization, or academic rule.

6. Do a concept analysis of the concept *rectangle*.

7. Classify each of the following according to type of example: concrete materials, pictures, models, case studies, or simulation and role play.

    a. Jim Rooney's passage.

    b. Judy Nelson's beach ball with lines drawn on it.

    c. Judy Nelson's maps.

    d. Sue Grant's balloons.

    e. Sue Grant's drawings of the balloons and molecules.

8. Think back to Shirley Barton's lesson on equivalent fractions at the end of Chapter 2. Suppose Shirley has shown the students the following drawings:

Now suppose Shirley has the students shade in one of the three portions on the first paper and one of the four portions on the second. She has the choice of beginning the activity by asking:

    "What do you notice about the two pieces of paper?" or "How many parts are shaded in each paper?"

    a. Which of the two questions is more desirable for beginning a lesson with the Inductive Model? Why?

    Suppose Shirley has the students fold the first paper into fourths and the second one into thirds so they appear as follows:

    She again has the choice of at least two different questions, such as:

    "How do the two papers compare now?"

    "Now how many parts of each paper are shaded?"

    b. Which of the two questions is more desirable when using the Inductive Model? Why?

9. Consider a teacher wanting to teach the principle: "Less dense materials float on more dense materials if they don't mix." The lesson is introduced by displaying two vials of the same volume, one containing water and the other containing cooking oil, and placing them on a balance. The mass of the water is measurably greater than that of the cooking oil. The water and oil are then poured together into a third vial and the oil floats. Answer the following questions based on the information.

    a. How many examples did the teacher use?

  b. What kind of examples were they? (concrete materials, pictures, etc.)

  c. What specific information would the teacher have to prompt the students to identify?

  d. What might the teacher do in Phase 5 of this lesson for application of the principle?

D I S C U S S I O N   Q U E S T I O N S

1. Consider the motivational features of Judy Nelson's, Sue Grant's, and Jim Rooney's lessons. What motivational advantages did each have? How could the student motivation be increased in each case?

2. Teachers obviously do not have time to develop an inductive lesson for every concept, principle, generalization, or academic rule existing in curriculum materials. How do they decide what concepts and relationships to select?

3. Are some concepts and relationships among them more conducive than others to being taught using the Inductive Model? If so, what characteristics do they have in common?

4. Are there instances when verbal examples would be sufficient for teaching a concept, generalization, principle, or rule? If so, what would these instances be?

5. What are the major advantages of inductive teaching? The major disadvantages?

6. We have briefly discussed options for using the Inductive Model with different age groups. What other factors would have to be considered in using the model with younger students? With advanced high school students?

7. An Inductive Model lesson can begin with little or no introduction to the content being taught. What are the advantages and disadvantages of beginning in this way?

5 The Concept-Attainment Model

The Concept-Attainment Model is an inductive teaching strategy designed to help students of all ages reinforce their understanding of concepts and practice hypothesis testing. Developed from concept-learning research (Klausmeier, 1992; Tennyson & Cocchiarella, 1986), the model uses positive and negative examples to illustrate concepts as simple as *square* and *dog* or as sophisticated as *oxymoron* and *socialism*.

The Concept-Attainment Model is also useful for giving students experience with the scientific method and particularly with hypothesis testing, experiences that are often hard to provide in content areas other than science.

When you've completed your study of this chapter, you should be able to meet the following objectives:

- Identify topics most appropriately taught with the Concept-Attainment Model.
- Prepare a list of examples that effectively illustrate a concept and promote hypothesis testing.
- Implement lessons using the Concept-Attainment Model.
- Adapt the Concept-Attainment Model for learners of different developmental levels.
- Assess student understanding of content objectives taught with the Concept-Attainment Model.

To begin our discussion, let's look at a teacher using the Concept-Attainment Model to help students reinforce their understanding of a concept and develop their analytical thinking.

Karl Haynes, a fifth-grade teacher, begins a science lesson by calling students' attention to a bag he holds in his hand.

Karl says, "Today we're going to do something a little different than what we've been doing. I have an idea in mind, and you are going to figure out what it is. To help you figure it out, I'm going to show you some things that *are* examples of the idea, and I'm also going to show you some things that *are not* examples of the idea. Then, based on the things that are examples and the others that are not, you will figure out what the idea is. This is sort of a game and it will give us all some practice in being good thinkers. If you're not quite sure of what we're doing, you will catch on once we get started. Okay, ready? . . . Here we go."

Now Karl reaches into the bag, pulls out an apple that has been cut in half and puts it on the table in front of a cardboard sign that says, "Examples." He also takes a rock out of the bag and places it in front of a sign that says, "Nonexamples."

"Now," he continues, "the apple *is* an example of the idea I have in mind, and the rock *is not* an example of the idea. . . . What do you think the idea might be?"

"We eat apples," Rufus volunteers.

"Good," Karl smiles, "so the idea might be . . . ?"

Rufus does not respond.

". . . Things . . . we . . .?" Karl prompts.

". . . Eat?" Rufus continues hesitantly.

With that, Karl writes the word *Hypotheses* on the board, underlines it, and asks, "What do we mean by the term hypotheses? . . . Anyone?"

". . . It's, like . . . kind of a guess," Mike volunteers after a few seconds.

"Yes," Karl nods to Mike. "For our purposes, that's a good definition. Our *hypotheses* will be our educated guesses about what the idea might be." Then he writes, *things we eat* under the word *Hypotheses.*

"What else might be a possibility?" Karl goes on. . . . "Sharonda?"

"It could also be things that are alive, or . . . were."

"Fine," Karl replies, writing the words *living things* on the board under the list of hypotheses. "Any others? . . . Tenille?"

"Well, this is . . . sort of like Sharonda's . . . but it's a little different. How . . . about 'things that grow on plants'"?

"Okay. . . . Does everyone see how living things and things that grow on plants are different? . . . No? Karen, can you explain that to the class?"

". . . Like . . . well, there are some living things that don't grow on plants. . . . Like animals."

"Excellent thinking, Karen. Do we have any other ideas?"

After pausing for a few seconds, Karl continues, "Well then, let's look at a few more examples." He takes out a sliced tomato and puts it under the Examples sign and places a carrot that has been sliced in half under the Nonexamples sign.

He continues, "What does this new information tell us? Let's first look at the hypotheses we have. Are they still all acceptable? . . . Serena?"

". . . It can't be *things to eat,*" Serena responded.

"Explain why, Serena," Karl encourages.

"...Well ... we eat carrots ... and carrot is not an example."

"Good, Serena," Karl smiled. "Very good, clear explanation. The added information we have requires that we eliminate that hypothesis."

"Now, let's look at the rest of the hypotheses. ... How about *things that grow on plants?* ... Sherry?"

"... Things that grow on plants is out."

"Why? ... Explain," Karl smiles.

"... A carrot grows from a plant."

"And?" Karl probes.

"And ... it's not an example," Sherry adds quickly after Karl's prompt.

"Excellent, Sherry. Good thinking and good explanation."

He turns to the class. "Now, how about *living things?*"

"Also out," Jaime volunteered.

"Go on."

"... Carrot is living and it's not an example," Jaime explains, beginning to see how the process is intended to work.

"Yes! That's fine," Karl waves enthusiastically. "You are really catching on to this."

"How about things that we eat that grow above the ground?" Renita offered.

"Are you suggesting another hypothesis?" Karl asked.

"... I ... think so."

"Very good. Perhaps I should have pointed that out in the beginning. We can always add hypotheses as long as the data support them. ... Now how will we know if the data do indeed support them? ... Anyone?"

No one responds.

"This is a little tough to describe, so I'll try to help you. A hypothesis is supported if *all* the examples fit the hypothesis, *and* if *none* of the non-examples fit the hypothesis."

"For example," he goes on, "do both an apple and a tomato grow above the ground?"

"Yes," the class says in unison.

"Do either a rock or a carrot grow above the ground?"

"Part of the carrot does," Heidi notes.

"Good thinking," Karl nods. "What is your reaction to Heidi's point, Renita?"

"I meant the part that we eat."

"Okay, is that all right with you, Heidi?"

Heidi shakes her head.". . . I think we should say, 'plant parts we eat that are above ground.'"

"Excellent, Heidi. We can also modify hypotheses so that they better fit our data. This is the kind of thinking that we're after. Very well done!"

"Now ... is the hypothesis, *plant parts we eat that are above ground*, acceptable? ... Remember, all the examples *must* fit the hypothesis, and none of the nonexamples *can* fit the hypothesis."

Among a chorus of nods, "Yeses," and "Okays," Karl continues with the process. Shawn offers the hypothesis *things we eat with seeds in them,* and Marsha offers *red foods,* to the giggles of the class.

Karl then asks in a form of admonishment, "Are apples and tomatoes both red, and are either the rock or the carrot red?"

"No," the students respond.

"Good. . . . Now, I want us to have fun with this, of course, but remember that the only thing that determines whether or not a hypothesis is acceptable is whether or not the data support it. . . . And do the data support *red foods?*"

The students nod, a bit sheepishly.

"Good. Now, I know you didn't mean any harm, but keep that in mind."

Karl then adds an avocado to the Examples list, a piece of celery to the Nonexamples list, and again they analyze the hypotheses as they did before.

Karl continues by adding and analyzing hypotheses with a peach, a squash, and an orange as positive examples and a head of lettuce, artichoke, and potato as negative examples.

The students continue the process with Karl's guidance, narrowing their hypotheses to *things with seeds in them* and finally modifying the hypothesis to *seeds in the edible part of the plant.*

Now Karl asks, "Does anyone know what we call foods that have seeds in the edible part of the plant, like the ones we have here?"

After hesitating a few seconds and hearing no response, he says, "We call these foods *fruits,*" and he writes the word *fruit* on the board.

Karl continues, "Excellent, everyone. Now, we need a good clear definition of *fruit.* Someone give it a try. . . . Go ahead, Goeff."

"Okay, . . . Fruits are . . . things we eat . . . that have seeds in them."

"Seeds in what part?"

". . . In the part we eat."

"Very good, Goeff. I'll revise this a tiny bit to smooth it out a little, but we essentially have it."

Karl writes on the board, "Fruits are foods we eat with seeds in the edible part."

Now Karl has the class take out a piece of paper and categorize additional examples as either positive or negative examples of the concept *fruit.*

Let us look now at how another teacher uses the Concept-Attainment Model to help high school students reinforce their understanding of the concept *metaphor.*

Tanya Adin, a ninth-grade English teacher, begins her sixth period class on Friday by saying, "I know that you're all anxious to start the weekend, so to break the routine we're going to do something a little different today. It will both help us review some of the ideas we have briefly dealt with in the past, and it will give us some practice in being good critical thinkers."

"Now, this is what we're going to do. . . . I have a list of sentences on this overhead," she continues, motioning with the overhead in her hand. "Some of the sentences illustrate a concept I have in mind, and others *do not* illustrate the concept. The ones that do I've marked with a *Y,* which stands for *yes,* meaning they *do* illustrate the concept, and the others are marked with an *N,* meaning *no,* they *do not* illustrate the concept. Then you need to figure out what the concept is based on the yeses—the examples—and the noes—the sentences that are not examples.

"Let's try it," she continued. "I'll show you an example and a non-example to start with. Remember, the examples—yeses—illustrate the concept, and the nonexamples—noes—do not illustrate the concept."

Tanya puts the transparency on the overhead and uncovers the first two sentences, which appear as follows:

1. John's Camaro is a lemon. (Y)
2. Hurricane Andrew did a great deal of damage in Florida. (N)

The students look at the examples for a few seconds, and Dean says, "Cars."

"Okay, good," Tanya nods. "The example is about cars and the non-example has nothing in it about cars, so *cars* could be the concept. . . . Any other possibilities?"

". . . I think *linking verbs,*" Antonio adds.

"You mean you think *linking verbs* is the concept?" Tanya asks.

"Yeah, there's a linking verb in the first sentence, but there isn't one in the second one."

"Very good, Antonio. Good thinking. . . . Now this is the kind of thing we're trying to do. We see both a description of a car and a linking verb in the *yes* example, but we don't see either of them in the *no* example, so *cars* and *linking verbs* are both possibilities for the concept.

". . . Now let's go on. Are there any other possibilities?"

"How about *present tense?*" Nancy wonders.

"Good thinking, Nancy. Is present tense acceptable?"

No one responds.

Seeing the uncertainty on the students' faces, Tanya continues, "Does the *yes* example illustrate present tense?"

The students nod that it does, and Tanya goes on, "Is there anything about present tense in the *no* example?"

"No," Bruce says quickly, beginning to see how the process works.

"Very good," Tanya waves briskly. "You see how we do this? . . . Good. Now let's go on."

Tanya then briefly explains that they are *hypothesizing* the possibilities that they have listed, so each is a *hypothesis.* She notes that she will refer to the items on the list as hypotheses from this point on.

Next, Tanya uncovers two more sentences on the overhead, so her list now appears as follows:

1. John's Camaro is a lemon. (Y)
2. Hurricane Andrew did a great deal of damage in Florida. (N)
3. Mrs. Augilar's Lexus is a pearl. (Y)
4. My grandmother's hat is a garden of daisies. (Y)

"I know," Adam said eagerly after looking at the list for a few seconds. "It's *possessives*. Each of the yeses has a possessive in it."

"What does everyone else think?" Tanya queries. "Can we accept Adam's hypothesis?" she wonders out loud, emphasizing the word *hypothesis* as she asks the question.

"How about number 2?" Rachael wonders.

". . . It's a *no*," Karla points out.

". . . Oh, yes," Rachael nods, recognizing Karla's point.

"Good . . . any others?" Tanya continues. "Okay, let's look at our hypotheses so far. . . . How about *cars?* Is it still okay? . . . Heidi?"

". . . I . . . don't think so."

"Explain why for everyone."

". . . Well . . . number 4 has nothing about a car in it."

"And . . ."

". . . It's a *yes* example," Heidi says after realizing what Tanya is after.

"Very good, Heidi," Tanya nods, and she continues, "How about *present tense?* Is it still acceptable? . . . Lisa?"

". . . I . . . think so."

"Please explain," Tanya encourages.

". . . All of the *yes* examples are in the present tense."

"And?" Tanya probes.

". . . The *no* is in the past tense."

"Very good," Tanya nods and smiles.

"Now," she goes on, "Is there anything else we can add?"

". . . How about *metaphors?*" Ramona offers.

"Okay. . . . Is metaphor an acceptable hypothesis?" Tanya asks over her shoulder as she adds *metaphor* to the list she is writing on the board.

The students look at the examples uncertainly, and in response Tanya continues, "Is each of the positive examples a metaphor?"

She smiles as some of the students nod that they are, and she goes on, "Any other hypotheses?"

". . . How about *figures of speech?*" Frank suggests.

"Good! . . . *Figures of speech* okay?"

". . . Yes," several students say simultaneously beginning to get comfortable with the process.

"Any others?"

After waiting a few seconds, Tanya then says, "Okay, let's look at another example."

She uncovers another example, so her list now appears as follows:

1. John's Camaro is a lemon. (Y)
2. Hurricane Andrew did a great deal of damage in Florida. (N)
3. Mrs. Augilar's Lexus is a pearl. (Y)
4. My grandmother's hat is a garden of daisies. (Y)
5. My bedroom is green. (N)

Tanya says, "Now, anything else we can add to our list of hypotheses?" The list appears as follows:

linking verbs

present tense

possessives

metaphor

figures of speech

Hearing nothing, she continues, "Okay, let's look at them. How about *linking verbs?* Is it still okay? . . . Amanda?"

". . . No."

"Why not?"

". . . There's a linking verb in the last one . . . and it's a *no.*"

"Very good analysis, and a good complete explanation," Tanya responds, gesturing at the board. "So how about *present tense?*"

"Also out," Shannon volunteers quickly. ". . . The nonexample is in the present tense," she adds, responding as Tanya gestures for her to continue.

"Excellent. . . . How about *possessives?*"

"Out," Donalee offers.

"Explain why."

"There's no possessive in the last sentence."

"Wait. It's a *no,*" David interjects.

"Go on, David," Tanya nods.

". . . It's a nonexample . . . and it doesn't have a possessive in it . . . so *possessive* is still okay," David says slowly as he is describing his thoughts.

"Do you agree with that, Donalee?"

". . . I guess . . . I see now," she responds after looking at the examples again.

"Excellent. . . . Now how about *metaphor?*"

The students conclude that *metaphor* is still acceptable, since number 5 is *not* a metaphor and it is also *not* an example, and they go through similar reasoning with *figures of speech.*

Tanya then adds the following example to her list.

6. Autumn leaves are the skin of trees, wrinkled with age. (Y)

The students decide that *possessives* must be rejected since the sentence does not illustrate possessives and it is a positive example, and they further conclude that *metaphor* and *figures of speech* are still acceptable.

Tanya then adds a seventh example.

7. I had a million pages of homework last night. (N)

After some discussion the students conclude that *metaphor* is acceptable, but that *figures of speech* is unacceptable, since number 7 is a figure of speech—a hyperbole—and it is a nonexample.

"Now," Tanya interjects, "let's stop for a moment and take a look at what we've been doing. Let's look back at the process that we've been in so far. Let's try and describe it. . . . Go ahead, someone."

". . . Well, we've been trying to guess what the concept is that you have in mind," Alandrea volunteers after several seconds.

"Actually, you haven't been guessing, and I want to emphasize that," Tanya responds, gesturing to the board. "You have made your decisions based on information. In this case the information is in the form of the examples I've given you, but it can apply to nearly everything you do. For example, why did you decide that *figures of speech* wasn't an acceptable hypothesis?"

". . . That sentence—*I had a million pages of homework last night*—is a figure of speech, and you told us it was a nonexample," Sydney suggests.

"Exactly. You made the decision to reject *figures of speech* based on the data, not on a whim. The same thing applies in life in general," Tanya goes on. "Now this may seem like a silly example, but it applies. Your dad decides to fix you cooked oatmeal for breakfast rather than Cream of Wheat. It says on the box that oatmeal has virtually no fat and no sodium, while Cream of Wheat has some of each plus preservatives. Just as you used information in this exercise to direct your thinking, your dad used information about the fat and sodium content of the cereals to reject Cream of Wheat on that basis.

"So we're learning a very fundamental process here that helps us learn to live better as a result of thinking more clearly. Keep the oatmeal and Cream of Wheat example in mind, and we'll remind ourselves of it and others as we do lessons like these."

Tanya then goes back to the theme of the lesson, displaying the following examples one at a time, and asking the students to consider whether or not *metaphor* is still an acceptable hypothesis after each one.

8. At night you are the moonlight floating through my window, lifting the curtains. (Y)

9. So far my life has been like an unmarked chalkboard. (N)

10. He touched her cheek as the sun touches a rose. (N)

11. The blank sheet of paper reclined on my desk and stared at me with its blank eyes, waiting for me to tease it with my pencil. (N)

12. The guns cracked and the bullets squealed as the battle raged for hours. (N)

After displaying and analyzing the last example, Tanya asks, "Now what do you think? Did we prove that the concept is *metaphor?*"

"Yes," several students say simultaneously, and others nod in agreement.

"It looks promising, doesn't it?" Tanya smiles. "But suppose, for instance, that sometime later we found a sentence that we were told was an example, but it wasn't a metaphor. Then what?"

". . . I guess we'd have to cross off *metaphor,*" Wendy offers uncertainly.

"Yes, that's exactly right," Tanya went on. "A hypothesis is acceptable as long as *all* the data—examples of the concept in our case—support it, but we have to reject a hypothesis if *only one* item of data does not support it. . . . So technically you never actually prove a hypothesis. You can only gather more and more data that support it.

"You'll understand the process of analyzing hypotheses better and better as we do more of these," Tanya assures the students, seeing uncertain looks on some of their faces.

Tanya then asks individual students to give additional examples of metaphors to reinforce the concept, discussing each as they are offered. After several examples, she closes the lesson.

The Concept-Attainment Model: An Overview

Let's begin our study of the Concept-Attainment Model by looking back at Karl Haynes's and Tanya Adin's lessons and identifying their key elements. Let's look at their common features:

- First, both lessons focused on a concept—*fruits* in Karl's case and *metaphors* in Tanya's—rather than a principle, generalization, academic rule, or other form of content.
- Second, the teachers began by explaining the procedure that would be followed in the activity.
- Third, they began with an example and a nonexample of the concept—an apple and a rock for Karl and the first two sentences for Tanya.
- Fourth, the activity centered on the process of making and analyzing hypotheses, which resulted in the elimination of some, modification of others, and finally the isolation of a single hypothesis.

Social Structure of the Model

In Chapter 4 we described **social structure** *as the characteristics of the classroom environment necessary for learning to take place and the roles of the teacher and the students in that environment.* Like the Inductive Model, the Concept-Attainment Model requires a classroom environment in which students feel free to think and test their ideas. When Karl admonished the students for laughing at Marsha's offer of *red foods,* he was attempting to maintain that environment. If it is supported by the existing data, no hypothesis is silly or trivial, and Karl communicated this spirit with his comments. He also noted that he knew the students meant no harm, and that he wanted them to enjoy the activity. These elements of respect for each other's ideas are important in capturing the spirit of the process.

This social support was further illustrated in the exchange between Donalee and David in Tanya's lesson. Donalee suggested that *possessives* had to be rejected, and David offered a valid counterargument. Aware of the need for students to feel safe, Tanya returned to Donalee and asked her to respond to David's reasoning rather then merely accepting it and continuing. This sensitivity on the part of the teacher is crucial in using either the Inductive or the Concept-Attainment Model.

The Teacher's Role. As we have already said, one of the teacher's roles is to help create an environment in which students feel free to think and conjecture without fear of criticism or ridicule, and both teachers performed this role very well.

A second role is to explain and illustrate how the model works and to guide the process and help students state and analyze hypotheses and articulate their thinking. Both teachers first carefully introduced the activity—Karl explaining that he had an idea that the students were to figure out based on the examples and nonexamples, and Tanya announcing first that she had a list of sentences, some of which illustrated a concept and others of which did not.

The teachers then guided the activity in three important ways:

- First, they encouraged students to state their thinking as hypotheses rather than observations. In Karl's lesson, for example, Rufus offered an observation when he said, "We eat apples." Instead of recording Rufus's statement, Karl helped him reword it into the hypothesis *things we eat.*
- Second, Karl and Tanya helped guide the students' thinking as they determined whether or not a hypothesis was acceptable.
- Third, they asked the students to explain *why* they accepted or rejected hypotheses—for example, Tanya asking Amanda why *linking verbs* was unacceptable after Tanya displayed the fifth sentence in her lesson.

We need to note a final aspect of the process. Students will sometimes disagree about whether or not a hypothesis is acceptable, or if a new hypothesis can be added. The teacher must maintain the spirit of accepting and rejecting hypotheses based on data while keeping the flow of the activity from bogging down. We saw an example of this in Karl's lesson when Heidi disagreed with Renita's hypothesis, which resulted in its modification. When a disagreement can't be immediately resolved, the teacher can encourage students to leave a hypothesis on the list and allow additional data to resolve the problem.

The essence of the process for students is to suggest hypotheses; accept, modify, or reject them; and ultimately isolate a single hypothesis that best accounts for the data. We saw this sequence illustrated in both lessons.

The Concept-Attainment Model: Theoretical Perspectives

Like the Inductive Model, the Concept-Attainment Model is grounded in cognitive learning theory. The model places the students in *active roles* and emphasizes *interaction* between the teacher and students and among the students themselves. The teacher guides the learning activity instead of merely explaining the concepts to the students.

We also saw that the students in both lessons offered hypotheses based on what they already knew. Cognitive learning theory recognizes that new learning is connected to students' *background knowledge*.

Finally, the learning activity is developed around examples and nonexamples. As we saw in Chapter 1, learners construct understanding based on the examples and representations of the topics they're studying.

The Concept-Attainment Model has an additional feature that isn't explicit in the other models. It provides students with experience in the epistemology of science. **Epistemology** *is the branch of philosophy that examines how we know what we know*, and the scientific method is an important epistemology in our culture. The **scientific method** *emphasizes forming conclusions based on observation, developing hypotheses, and testing them with facts*. Critical thinking and the scientific method fit hand in glove.

Students involved in Concept-Attainment activities are provided with similar experiences at a classroom level. Many school textbooks describe the scientific method, but few provide students with any genuine experiences with it. The Concept-Attainment Model can provide those experiences.

Goals for the Concept-Attainment Model

Content Goals

Content goals for a Concept-Attainment and an Inductive Model lesson are related but not identical. They show two important differences.

- First, while the Inductive Model is designed to teach concepts, principles, generalizations, or academic rules, the Concept-Attainment Model—as the name implies—focuses on concepts.
- Second, while the Inductive Model can be used to teach a topic essentially from "scratch," the Concept-Attainment Model requires that the students have more background knowledge.

For example, Tanya's students had some experience with both metaphors and other figures of speech or they wouldn't have been able to suggest either as hypotheses. For this reason, the Concept Attainment Model can be effective for review or enriching a concept by helping students see relationships between it and closely related concepts. We saw this in Tanya's lesson, where her students examined differences among the concepts *metaphor, simile, personification,* and *hyperbole*.

However, as we saw in Karl's lesson, students don't necessarily have to know the *label* for the concept. His students identified the essential characteristic of the concept *fruit,* and he then supplied the label.

Developing Critical Thinking

The Inductive Model and Concept-Attainment Models also differ in emphasis. The Inductive Model emphasizes students' deep understanding of specific topics, whereas the Concept-Attainment Model focuses more strongly on the development of critical thinking in the form of hypothesis testing, as we saw in the last section. As we saw in both lessons, much of the emphasis was on the students' analysis of the hypotheses and why they were accepted, modified, or rejected. The kinds of conclusions students practice making, such as, "The nonexample is in the present tense," as an explanation for why the hypothesis *present tense* had to be rejected, are as important as understanding the concepts themselves. While Tanya's lesson focused on *metaphors* and other figures of speech, her goal to develop students' critical thinking was equally important. If her primary goal had focused on the concept *metaphor* as a topic, she probably would have chosen a different model.

Planning Lessons with the Concept-Attainment Model

Identifying Topics

Research indicates that teachers usually begin the planning process by identifying a topic (Morine-Dershimer & Vallance, 1976; Peterson et al., 1978). This was an appropriate beginning point with the Inductive Model, it's also appropriate for the Concept-Attainment Model.

Specifying Goals

As we saw in the last section, goals for the Concept-Attainment Model include helping students develop concepts and the relationships among them and giving them practice with forming and testing hypotheses. We also saw that the development of critical thinking strategies can be the dominant goal.

In Chapter 4 we emphasized that the teacher must know exactly what she is trying to accomplish by using the Inductive Model. Being clear about goals is no less important when using the Concept-Attainment Model. Because Karl was teaching a group of elementary students, he had identified *seed contained in the edible part of the plant* as the essential characteristic of the concept *fruit.* A biology teacher would attach a more sophisticated set of characteristics to the concept, such as the fruit being an enlarged and ripened ovary, but Karl was teaching a valid concept for fifth graders. He knew exactly what he wanted from his students.

The same was true in Tanya's case. In her planning she had clearly specified "a nonliteral comparison that avoids the words *like* and *as*" as the characteristics of the concept *metaphor,* and she had these characteristics clearly in mind as she conducted her lesson.

Both teachers were also clear in their intent to provide students with practice in hypothesis testing. Had this not been an important goal for them, they would probably have chosen a different model.

Having a precise content goal in mind and knowing that emphasis will be placed on hypothesis testing and critical thinking, we are now ready to prepare and sequence examples.

Selecting Examples

The principles involved in selecting examples to teach a concept are the same regardless of the model being used. As we saw with the Inductive Model, selecting examples that best illustrate the characteristics of the concept is most important. Karl chose good examples when he used the apple, tomato, squash, peach, and orange. In each case the students could see the essential characteristic—the seeds in the edible part of the plant—in the examples. The same was true in Tanya's case. The students could see a nonliteral comparison in each of the positive examples.

The teachers were also clever in their choices of examples. Karl, for example, used a tomato and squash as examples—fruits commonly thought of as vegetables. Using them as examples helped the students to broaden their understanding of the concept *fruit.*

Examples are selected so that *each* contains the combination of essential characteristics and *none* of the nonexamples contain the same combination. To further illustrate this process, consider the characteristics of the concept *proper noun* and then analyze the following examples based on those characteristics:

1. Mary
2. New York
3. John
4. Chicago
5. United States
6. George Washington

Two aspects of this list are problematic. First, the examples should have included the idea that a proper noun names a specific person, place, or *thing*. There are no specific *things* in the list. To ensure that the concept is complete, we would need to add positive examples such as *German Shepherd, Honda,* and *Old Testament.*

Second, the examples are not presented in context. In Chapter 4 we found that examples in context promote more meaningful learning than examples that are isolated and abstract. Putting the proper nouns in the context of sentences would be easy to do. For instance, the examples could be presented as follows:

1. Mary is one of the most common names that girls are given, and John is one of the most common for boys.

2. New York is the largest city in the United States, and Chicago is the second largest.
3. George Washington is often called the father of our country.
4. The German Shepherd is one of the smartest working dogs that exist.
5. One of the first Japanese cars to be sold in this country was the Honda.
6. The Old Testament is strongly related to the Koran in many ways.

While presenting the examples in the context of a paragraph would be even better, the sentences are more effective than the words in isolation.

Preparing Nonexamples. In selecting nonexamples, an attempt should be made to vary the nonessential characteristics and to represent all the things that the concept is not. For instance, Tanya used the following sentences (in addition to the simple statements, "Hurricane Andrew did a great deal of damage in Florida," and "My bedroom is green.") as nonexamples in her lesson on metaphors.

- I had a million pages of homework last night. (hyperbole)
- So far, I think my life has been like an unmarked chalkboard. (a simile using the word *like*)
- He touched her cheek as the sun touches a rose. (a simile using the word *as*)
- The blank sheet of paper reclined on my desk and stared at me with its blank eyes, waiting for me to tease it with my pencil. (personification)
- The guns cracked and the bullets squealed as the battle raged for hours. (onomatopoeia)

From the list we see that the negative examples served to differentiate *metaphor* from other figures of speech. When both the positive and negative examples are used, the learner can construct a valid concept that is not confused with closely related concepts.

As we see, each of the nonexamples—examples of *hyperbole, simile, personification,* and *onomatopoeia*—illustrated a concept coordinate to the concept *metaphor.* Thinking of concepts that are coordinate to the concept being taught is helpful as the list of examples and nonexamples is being prepared.

Sequencing Examples and Nonexamples

Having selected the examples and nonexamples, the final planning task is to put them in sequence. Since practicing hypothesis testing is an important goal when the Concept-Attainment Model is used, the examples should be arranged so the students are given the most practice with analyzing hypotheses. The shortest route to a concept may not give students this opportunity, and it may not result in the deepest student understanding. Tanya, for example, purposely sequenced her examples so the students could initially offer *cars, possessives, present tense,* and *linking verbs* as valid hypotheses—all of which ultimately had to be rejected—which gave the students considerable practice in analyzing hypotheses.

Notice that the teachers don't necessarily have to alternate examples and nonexamples in their sequences. They may choose to present two or even three positive examples in a row, which might be followed by two or more nonexamples. This is a matter

Karl's Sequence	Tanya's Sequence
1. Apple (Y)	1. John's Camaro is a lemon. (Y)
2. Rock (N)	2. Hurricane Andrew did a great deal of damage in Florida. (N)
3. Tomato (Y)	3. Mrs. Augilar's Lexus is a pearl. (Y)
4. Carrot (N)	4. My grandmother's hat is a garden of daisies. (Y)
5. Avocado (Y)	5. My bedroom is green. (N)
6. Celery (N)	6. Autumn leaves are the skin of trees, wrinkled with age. (Y)
7. Peach (Y)	7. I had a million pages of homework last night. (N)
8. Squash (Y)	8. At night you are the moonlight floating through my window, lifting the curtain. (Y)
9. Orange (Y)	9. So far my life has been like an unmarked chalkboard. (N)
10. Lettuce (N)	10. He touched her cheek as the sun touches a rose. (N)
11. Artichoke (N)	11. The blank sheet of paper reclined on my desk and stared at me with its blank eyes, waiting for me to tease it with my pencil. (N)
12. Potato (N)	12. The guns cracked and the bullets squealed as the battle raged for hours. (N)

FIGURE 5.1   Karl's and Tanya's Sequences of Examples

of teacher judgment. Karl's and Tanya's sequences, for instance, appear as shown in Figure 5.1.

To further illustrate this point, let's look at a simpler example. Suppose the concept is *numbers with perfect square roots*. Consider the sequences illustrated in Figure 5.2. In sequence A, the pattern is quickly and clearly established. Many students would probably hypothesize the concept after two positive examples. On the other hand, the concept is less obvious in sequence B, providing the students with a greater opportunity to practice hypothesis testing. In preparing sequence B, the teacher was not trying to hide information from the students or trick them. Instead, she wanted to maximize the students' opportunity to practice hypothesis testing.

For any set of examples a number of sequences could be designed. The organization depends on the judgment of the teacher and depends on the goals of the lesson and the backgrounds of the students.

Implementing Lessons Using the Concept-Attainment Model

Introducing Students to the Concept-Attainment Model

Since Concept-Attainment lessons are quite different from traditional teaching, the procedure may initially be confusing. Both Karl and Tanya addressed this problem by providing specific directions for the activity and by initially prompting students to form hypotheses based on the examples. (For instance, we saw that Karl nearly put the words in Rufus's mouth as Rufus stated the first hypothesis of the activity.)

Sequence A		Sequence B	
4	Yes	1	Yes
5	No	1/2	No
9	Yes	81	Yes
15	No	7	No
16	Yes	64	Yes
2	No	12	No
25	Yes	9	Yes

**FIGURE 5.2   Two Sequences of Examples
for Numbers with Perfect Square Roots**

To avoid overloading learners' working memories by requiring that they simultaneously learn the procedure and cope with a demanding topic, teachers can help them get
used to "playing the game" by using a familiar topic the first time or two the model is
used. Topics such as *living things, mammals, wooden objects, prime numbers,* or even *students with red hair* are all simple, concrete topics that would help students get used to the
procedure.

Using a simple topic also gives them some initial practice with hypothesis testing.
As we saw in Karl's and Tanya's lessons, the students are required to do some reversals in
their thinking. For example, after Tanya had presented her fifth sentence, the students had
to reason as follows:

The fifth sentence does *not* illustrate a possessive, and it is *not* an example, so
therefore *possessives* is still an acceptable hypothesis.

This kind of reasoning is developed through practice, and students won't initially be good
at it. This is the reason having the students articulate their thinking is so important, and
why using familiar topics to introduce them to the model can be helpful.

We also saw in both lessons that the teachers initially had to prompt students to fully
explain why they accepted or rejected hypotheses. In practice, teachers may have to do
even more prompting than was illustrated in the episodes. We intentionally abbreviated
them because of length.

We turn now to the specific phases of the Concept-Attainment Model.

Phases in the Concept-Attainment Model

The Concept-Attainment Model occurs in four phases. The activity begins when the
teacher presents examples and continues until the students have isolated a single hypothesis. The phases are outlined in Table 5.1 and described in the sections that follow.

Phase 1: Presenting Examples.   After the activity has been introduced or explained,
the lesson begins when the teacher *presents* the students with examples. Typically, it will
be an example and a nonexample, as Karl and Tanya used in their lessons. However, there

TABLE 5.1   Phases in the Concept-Attainment Model

Phase	Description
Presenting examples	Students are presented with positive and negative examples; they generate hypotheses.
Analyzing hypotheses	Students analyze hypotheses based on additional examples.
Closure	Students isolate a hypothesis and form a definition.
Application	Students analyze additional examples based on the definition.

is nothing inherently wrong with only presenting a positive example; not including a nonexample merely results in more initial hypotheses.

Karl began his lesson by presenting an apple as an example and a rock as a nonexample. Using a nonexample that was so distant from the example was designed to keep the possibilities for hypothesizing open. A teacher could as appropriately have chosen something more closely related to the concept, such as *milk,* or another food. This choice would have narrowed the possibilities for initial hypothesizing and would have reduced the emphasis on hypothesis testing.

Phase 2: Analyzing Hypotheses.   After presenting the first example or examples, the teacher asks the students to hypothesize possible concept names. In Karl's lesson, for example, the students initially hypothesized *things we eat, living things,* and *things that grow on plants,* while Tanya's students initially hypothesized *cars, linking verbs,* and *present tense,* then added *metaphors* and *figures of speech* after she presented her third and fourth sentences. These hypotheses are then the focal points for the analysis.

As another case, consider possible hypotheses for the following examples.

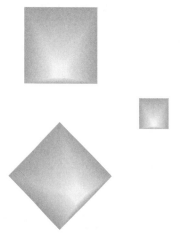

Among others, some hypotheses might include:

> closed figures
> four-sided figures
> squares
> figures with equal sides and equal angles
> figures with straight lines

From the list we see that the hypotheses vary in specificity; *square,* for example, is a more specific hypothesis than is *four-sided figure.* This isn't a problem, because they will be eliminated or modified as new examples are presented and the hypotheses are analyzed.

The Cyclical Process. Having presented the students with the initial examples and solicited the first set of hypotheses, the teacher then *cycles* through Phases 1 and 2 by alternately presenting examples and analyzing the hypotheses. This is what Karl and Tanya did in their lessons. For instance, after presenting her first example and nonexample and calling for students' initial hypotheses, Tanya then added two more examples and asked them to assess the acceptability of each of the hypotheses, in the process asking the students to explain *why* they accepted or rejected the hypothesis.

There are two reasons for asking students to explain why they accept or reject a hypothesis. First, articulating their reasoning helps them develop their thinking. Second, other students benefit from hearing their reasoning described in words. If one student decides that a hypothesis must be rejected, for instance, others may not understand why, or may disagree. Explaining helps keep understanding among the students as uniform as possible (Beyer, 1983, 1984).

Notice also that hypotheses can be revised instead of being totally rejected. For instance, in Karl's lesson Heidi wasn't satisfied with the hypothesis *things we eat that grow above the ground,* based on the argument that part of a carrot grows above the ground and *carrot* had been given as a nonexample. So the hypothesis was revised to *plant parts we eat that are above ground.* In this instance, the students had a concrete experience that was consistent with the philosophy of hypothesis testing.

It is important during the analysis of hypotheses that the teacher refrain from passing judgment. It would be inappropriate at this point to say, "You've got it!" or "That's it!" if a student should hypothesize the name the teacher has in mind. For example, in Tanya's lesson, Ramona offered *metaphor* as a hypothesis after Tanya had displayed two examples and two nonexamples. Tanya then added *metaphor* to the list with no more or less reaction than she gave to other hypotheses. If Tanya had acknowledged that *metaphor* was the concept she had in mind, the lesson would have been a simple guessing game rather than a process where the students learn to make conclusions based on data. Reacting as Tanya did in response to Ramona's hypothesis puts the responsibility for identifying and verifying the concept on students. This is consistent with emphasis on learner-centered learning activities (Lambert & McCombs, 1998).

The cyclical process in Phases 1 and 2 can be summarized in a series of steps:

- The teacher presents positive and negative examples.
- Students generate hypotheses.
- The teacher presents additional positive and/or negative example(s).

- Students analyze hypotheses and eliminate those not supported by the data (examples).
- Students offer additional hypotheses if the data support them.
- Analyzing hypotheses, eliminating those invalidated by new examples, and offering additional hypotheses continues until one hypothesis is isolated.

At this point you might wonder, "What do I do if I get to the end of my list of examples and students haven't isolated one specific hypothesis?" If your set of examples and nonexamples is complete, this possibility will only occur when one hypothesis is a synonym for another. In that case, you can retain both and, when all the others have been eliminated, note that the two are synonymous.

The second is, "What do I do if the students eliminate all the hypotheses but one before all the examples are used?" Here the answer is simple. Simply allow the lesson to come to closure, and use the remainder of the examples as part of the application phase.

Phase 3: Closure.   Once students have isolated a hypothesis, the lesson is ready for *closure*. At that point, the teacher asks the students to identify the critical characteristics of the concept and state a definition. As we saw in Chapter 4, the definition reinforces the students' understanding by including a superordinate concept and the concept's characteristics. Karl, for example, helped his students form the definition, "Fruits are *foods we eat* (superordinate concept) with seeds in the edible part. (*Seeds in the edible part* is the essential characteristic of the concept.)

For the concept *regular polygon* the definition might be as follows:

A *regular polygon* is a *plane figure* (superordinate concept) with all sides and angles equal (characteristics).

Having stated the definition, the students are prepared for the application phase of the model.

Phase 4: Application.   The application phase of the Concept-Attainment Model is designed to increase students' understanding of the concept and help them generalize to new examples. In this phase, students classify additional examples as positive or negative and/or they generate additional examples of their own. In Karl's lesson, the students identified the fruits from additional examples of foods; Tanya asked her students to supply additional examples of metaphors.

This phase of the model is important for both students and the teacher. It provides students with opportunities to test their understanding with additional examples, and it gives the teacher feedback about that understanding.

Using the Concept-Attainment Model to Increase Motivation and Self-Regulation

As learner-centered instruction becomes more prominent, intrinsic motivation and learner self-regulation are more strongly emphasized (Lambert & McCombs, 1998). Let's examine them.

Increasing Learner Motivation. As we said in Chapter 4, learner motivation is at the heart of school success, and anything teachers can do to promote it is positive. Concept-Attainment lessons can be helpful in developing motivation because implementing lessons with the model is flexible and can be fun for both the teacher and the students. The process can be presented as a type of game in which the students try to identify the idea (concept) the teacher has in mind. This can increase learners' **intrinsic motivation,** which is *motivation to engage in an activity for its own sake* (Pintrich & Schunk, 1996). The gamelike features of the Concept-Attainment Model can induce curiosity, one of the characteristics of intrinsically motivating ideas identified by researchers (Lepper & Hodell, 1989). Further, the model can be used to add variety to classroom activities, which also increases student motivation (Stipek, 1998).

Increasing Motivation with Student Groupwork. The Concept-Attainment Model can also be used effectively when students work in pairs or small groups. For example, consider Tanya's lesson again, which was conducted in a whole-class setting. Instead, after presenting her first two examples, she could have had students work in pairs, or groups of three, to brainstorm and write a list of all possible hypotheses. Allowing students to work in groups increases student involvement, which can increase motivation (Blumenfeld, 1992; Eggen & Kauchak, 1999).

The process would be easy to organize; groups could be seated together, and each group could be encouraged to analyze examples and share their thinking. The groups could then report their hypotheses to the whole class, which could be compiled into an overall list. Then, after Tanya presented her second pair of examples, the groups could be asked to decide which hypotheses were acceptable and which ones had to be rejected. To increase accountability and on-task behavior, they could also be directed to *write* the reason they accepted or rejected the hypothesis in each case. This would capitalize on critical thinking, give students practice in working together, and require little extra effort from the teacher.

Developing Self-Regulation. Suppose that you are about to go to a class or a meeting and you say to yourself, "I'm really dragging. I'd better have a cup of coffee before I go in there so I can stay awake." Being aware of your attention and doing something to control it is called *meta-attention.* Meta-attention is one type of **metacognition,** which is *awareness of and control over our mental processes,* attention being one of those processes.

Developing metacognitive abilities in students is a valuable educational goal, because it can help them to become self-regulated learners. **Self-regulation** *is an individual's conscious use of mental strategies for the purpose of improving thinking and learning.* Self-regulated learners take responsibility for their own learning progress and adapt their learning strategies to meet task demands (Bruning et al., 1999). One possible outcome from Concept-Attainment learning activities is the development of student self-regulation.

Tanya attempted to help her students develop their metacognitive abilities when she compared the process of hypothesis testing in her lesson to the simple decision-making process involved in selecting oatmeal instead of Cream of Wheat. This simple example was a first step in helping students become aware of making conclusions and decisions based on information instead of whim, emotion, or something worse, such as stereotyping. In addition, encouraging students to think about their own thinking helped them recognize that the processes they were involved in had utility beyond the classroom. Developing metacognitive abilities and self-regulation would take much more than the one example we saw in Tanya's lesson, of course, but if provided with continued experiences, these abilities would gradually develop. The same applies to the construction of all forms of knowledge and skill.

Implementing Concept-Attainment Activities: Modifications

While Concept-Attainment learning activities exist in four interrelated phases, the procedure need not be rigid and inflexible. It can, in fact, be adapted to a variety of goals and learning situations. In this section we describe some of the modifications that can be used to make the model more adaptable to your own teaching situation.

Developmental Considerations

To implement Concept-Attainment activities most effectively, we must consider the developmental level of the students. In general, the younger the students, the more concrete the examples need to be (Eggen & Kauchak, 1999). Karl's lesson, for example, would be more appropriate for young children than Tanya's, because *nonliteral comparison,* a characteristic of the concept *metaphor,* is much more abstract than *seeds in the edible part of the plant,* the key characteristic of the concept *fruit.*

Increasing the emphasis on the positive examples and using fewer nonexamples is a second adaptation that makes the model more effective with young children; they have difficulty dealing with the notion that something *is not* an example (Berk, 1997). The practice of inferring categories and doing rudimentary analysis of hypotheses is excellent for young children, however, and with modification they can become skilled with the strategy.

As students' facility with the model develops, they usually like it and often ask if they can "play the game." Teachers of young children have found the model effective as a form of review and to add variety to classroom activities. Also, experienced learners become adept at generating their own sequences of examples and "playing the game" with each other.

Concept Attainment II and Concept Attainment III

To this point, we have discussed basic procedures in implementing Concept-Attainment lessons and modifications that can be made for young children. The procedure can be further modified, however, to increase the emphasis on thinking. Let's look at these modifications.

Concept Attainment II.   Concept Attainment II is a modification in the basic procedure designed to increase the emphasis on hypothesis testing and critical thinking. It begins in the same way as the basic procedure (which we'll call CA I for reference); the students are presented with a positive and a negative example, and they hypothesize concept names, which are listed on the board, overhead, or chart paper. Then, instead of presenting subsequent examples one at a time, as with CA I, the teacher displays all the examples. The students are encouraged to scan the list for examples that might substantiate or refute the hypotheses on the list. They choose an example and indicate whether they think it is positive or negative. They also state which hypotheses would have to be rejected if their classification is correct. The teacher verifies the classification. If the classification is correct, the appropriate changes are made in the list of hypotheses; if incorrect, the hypotheses are reanalyzed in light of the new information. The students then select additional examples and continue the process until one hypothesis is isolated.

For example, a Concept-Attainment II lesson might begin like this: The teacher, wanting to teach the concept *carnivores,* might provide pictures of the following animals.

Examples

dog—yes	chair	hamster
car—no	cat	mouse
tree	beaver	
cow	tiger	

Students might respond to this information with the following hypotheses which would be listed.

Examples		*Hypotheses*
dog—yes	cat	living things
car—no	beaver	animals
tree	tiger	domestic animals
cow	hamster	mammals
chair	mouse	carnivores

A goal in using Concept Attainment II is for students to develop efficiency in their hypothesis testing. Efficiency is achieved if an example can be used to test all or several of the hypotheses. For example, one way to test all of these hypotheses is with *cat.* If *cat* is a nonexample, all the hypotheses would be rejected. However, in the case of *carnivore,* cat is a positive example, so none of the hypotheses can be rejected. Even though this example didn't result in the elimination of hypotheses, it provided excellent practice with the process.

The students might then decide to choose *beaver* as the next example. If beaver is an example, all the hypotheses except *carnivores* and *domestic animals* are acceptable, but if beaver is a nonexample, *carnivore* and *domestic animals* would be the only acceptable hypotheses. The teacher would verify beaver as a nonexample, because beaver is not a *carnivore.* Therefore, *living things, animals,* and *mammals* would have to be rejected.

Domestic animals and *carnivores* would be retained as viable hypotheses because *beaver* was a nonexample and *dog* and *cat* have been classified as positive examples. Now look at the list and see if you can determine a way in which students could investigate the hypothesis *domestic animal*.

Examples		**Hypotheses**
dog—yes	cat—yes	domestic animals
car—no	beaver—no	carnivores
tree	tiger	
cow	hamster	
chair	mouse	

Consider the choices *cow* and *tiger*. The two choices provide slightly different information, and the difference is enough to make one a more efficient choice. First, if *tiger* is a *yes, domestic animal* must be rejected because a tiger is not a domestic animal. If *tiger* is a *no,* it merely says that the category cannot be rejected, but it actually isn't supported, either. The data are neutral with respect to the hypothesis, because *tiger* may be a *no* for reasons other than the fact that it is not a domestic animal. Remember that when students select examples and examine hypotheses, they do not know what the concept is; they must infer it from the information provided.

Now consider *cow* as a test of the hypothesis *domestic animal*. If cow is a *no, domestic animal* is rejected, because a cow is a domestic animal, and succinct information about the inference is obtained. However, if *cow* is *yes,* not only is the category not rejected, but it is directly supported (again because a cow is a domestic animal). The choice of *cow* provides more information about the hypothesis than does the choice of *tiger,* so *cow* is the more efficient choice. The reverse would be true if we had wanted to test the hypothesis *carnivore.* In that case, *tiger* would be a more efficient choice.

With practice, students become efficient at gathering data, obtaining maximum information with each example. The primary goal in this case is acquiring experience with the epistemology of science. In a sense, students are designing their own investigation or experiment.

Concept Attainment III. A second modification is designed to extend the process of hypothesis testing even further. The basic strategy and thinking processes are essentially the same for CA II and CA III, but the procedure is slightly different. With CA II, after seeing the first two examples, the students hypothesize concept names, and the remaining examples are displayed. With CA III, after seeing the first two examples identified and labeled, students hypothesize concept names (as with CA II), but then they must supply their own examples to test the hypotheses.

For example, consider the following activity designed to teach the concept *vegetables with edible roots.* The teacher begins by showing the class:

carrot	yes
corn	no

Some possible hypotheses might be:

orange-colored vegetables
vegetables with edible roots
vegetables rich in vitamin A
vegetables that are eaten raw

The responsibility of providing examples to test these hypotheses now rests with the students. The students could test the hypotheses by selecting additional examples of vegetables. An efficient choice might be *radish*. If *radish* is a *yes, orange-colored vegetables* and *vegetables rich in vitamin A* are eliminated, but if *radish* is a *no, vegetables with edible roots* and *vegetables that are eaten raw* are eliminated. For this lesson, *radish* is a *yes,* which leaves *vegetables with edible roots* and *vegetables that are eaten raw* as possible concepts. The students' task would now be to examine these remaining hypotheses further. A choice now might be *potato*. Potato as a *yes* would further support *vegetables with edible roots* but would force rejection of *vegetables that are eaten raw*. Because of the concept being taught, *potato* would be a *yes,* causing the latter hypothesis to be rejected and lending further support to the hypothesis *vegetables with edible roots*. Students would continue to test the hypothesis and, in so doing, would be both reinforcing and enlarging their notion of the concept.

In planning for a CA III activity, the teacher should have additional examples available for use if the students' examples do not provide a complete picture of the concept. If their use is not necessary during the lesson, they could be used to assess the students' understanding.

One additional advantage of CA III is the opportunity it affords learners to gather data. CA III is more authentic or realistic than the other two Concept-Attainment formats because students more actively investigate a concept they don't fully understand. Because students are not limited to the examples the teacher provides, they can use more of their own background knowledge and initiative in investigating hypotheses. This increases their control of the learning activity, which has been identified by researchers as a factor increasing learners' intrinsic motivation (Lepper & Hodell, 1989). In addition, critical thinking is best developed with practice in which students share and explain the thinking processes they use in arriving at their answers.

Assessing Student Outcomes of Concept-Attainment Activities

Two kinds of outcomes result from Concept-Attainment activities. One is a deeper understanding of concepts—often those with which students have had some experience—and the other is increased critical thinking abilities. In this section we address the assessment of both.

Assessing Understanding of Concepts

Students' attainment of a concept can be measured in one or more of four primary ways:

1. They identify or supply examples of the concept not previously encountered.
2. They identify the concept's characteristics.
3. They relate the concept to other concepts.
4. They define the concept.

A simple and effective way of measuring concept attainment is by asking students to identify or provide additional examples of the concept. This type of measurement item is relatively easy to prepare, and—unlike stating a definition or characteristics—if the teacher uses unique examples, it is a valid way of determining whether or not students have constructed a valid understanding of the concept. For instance, consider the following item designed to measure the concept *direct object*.

Read the following passage and underline all the direct objects in it.

> Damon and Kerri were out riding. As they rode, Kerri spotted a funny-looking animal in the bushes.
>
> "Let's catch it," she suggested.
>
> "No way," Damon responded. "I'm not chasing any strange animal. It might bite me."
>
> "C'mon, chicken," she retorted. "I'll bet it's harmless."
>
> "Oh, all right. But, if it jumps you, I'm out of here."
>
> The kids chased the animal. Unfortunately for Kerri, but fortunately for Damon, they had no luck in catching it.

The effectiveness of this item is increased by the fact that the examples of direct objects were presented in the context of a paragraph; presenting examples this way increases the likelihood that students will be able to transfer the information to new settings.

A variation of this format is to ask students to provide examples of the concept rather than identify examples from the list. In that case, the students would be asked to write their own passage containing a specified number of examples.

A second form of measurement is to ask students to identify characteristics of the concept. An illustration could be the following:

Circle all the following which are characteristic of mammals:

a. Naked skin
b. Lays eggs
c. Four-chambered heart
d. Scaly skin
e. Regulated body temperature
f. Nurses young

The disadvantage of this type of measurement is that the item generally measures little more than knowledge, since the characteristics will have already been identified during the activity.

Students' understanding of concepts can also be measured by having students relate them to other concepts. Here the teacher asks the students to identify coordinate, superordinate or subordinate concepts, or a combination of them. The following is an example.

If *figure of speech* is superordinate to the concept *metaphor*, which of the following are coordinate to the concept *metaphor*?

    a. Simile
    b. Personification
    c. Alliteration
    d. Trope
    e. Meter
    f. Iambic pentameter

This item tests students' understanding of the relationship between *metaphor* and other concepts that are also figures of speech. Similar items can be designed to measure superordinate and subordinate relationships. Use of items such as these assumes that the teacher has discussed these relationships in class.

A fourth alternative for measuring for concept learning is to ask students to provide a definition of the concept or to identify the correct definition from a list of alternatives. The disadvantage of this type of measurement item is that it is most like items used to measure students' knowledge of characteristics because it typically involves recall of information.

As this discussion suggests, there is no one best way to measure students' understanding of concepts. Each tells the teacher something different about students' understanding, and the best strategy is to use a combination of them.

Assessing Students' Critical Thinking Abilities

When using the Concept-Attainment Model, assessing learners' critical thinking abilities is perhaps more important than assessing their understanding of the concept itself. This type of assessment is difficult using a paper-and-pencil format, but it can be done. For example, consider the following item:

You have been given the following examples:

Yes	*No*
36	5
81	111

The following hypotheses have been listed:

Two-digit numbers
Composite (not prime) numbers
Perfect squares
Multiples of 3

    1. Are all the hypotheses acceptable?   Yes   No   (Circle one) Explain.

    _____

    _____

    _____

    2. You are given two more examples, so your list now appears as follows:

Yes	*No*
36	5
81	111
49	45

    Which hypotheses are now acceptable, and which must be rejected? Explain why in each case.

    _____

    _____

    _____

    _____

    _____

    As we see from these items, the ability to assess hypotheses requires that students understand the concepts *two-digit numbers, composite numbers, perfect squares,* and *multiples of 3*. Thinking critically does not exist in the absence of knowledge, and assessing critical thinking cannot be done without simultaneously assessing learners' understanding of content. The assessment of critical thinking is a matter of emphasis.

Summary

The Concept-Attainment Model: An Overview

The Concept-Attainment Model is a strategy designed to teach concepts and promote critical thinking. Like the Inductive Model, it requires a classroom environment in which learners feel free to share their thinking without fear of embarrassment.

The Concept-Attainment Model is also based on cognitive views of learning. It emphasizes learners in active roles, depends on their background knowledge, and uses examples to develop understanding. In addition, it provides learners with experience in the epistemology of science.

Goals for the Concept-Attainment Model

While the Inductive Model is designed to teach concepts, principles, generalizations, and academic rules, the Concept-Attainment Model focuses exclusively on concepts. In addition, it is designed to provide learners with extensive experience in the processes of generating and testing hypotheses, and it emphasizes the scientific method, which can be used in all content areas.

Planning Lessons with the Concept-Attainment Model

As with the Inductive Model, teachers plan for Concept-Attainment activities by identifying clear goals and creating or finding positive and negative examples. In addition, teachers carefully sequence the examples to maximize the amount of practice learners get with hypothesis testing.

Implementing Lessons with the Concept-Attainment Model

Because learners are likely to be unfamiliar with the Concept-Attainment procedure, using a familiar topic to introduce the strategy is often effective. When the model is used, lessons begin with the teacher's presentation of a positive and negative example. Students then generate hypotheses, which is followed by more examples, analysis of hypotheses using the additional examples, and continued hypothesis testing until a single hypothesis has been isolated. The lesson comes to closure when the concept is defined and additional examples are examined.

Implementing Concept-Attainment Activities: Modifications

Concept-Attainment activities can be used with young children by making the topics and examples more concrete and decreasing the emphasis on nonexamples.

Concept Attainment II is a modification in the procedure in which learners select examples to test hypotheses. Concept Attainment III is a further modification in which learners generate their own examples to test the hypotheses.

Assessing Student Outcomes of Concept-Attainment Activities

In using the Concept-Attainment Model, teachers assess learners' understanding of concepts as well as their abilities to think critically. Teachers can assess concept understanding by having students classify or produce examples, identify characteristics, or relate the concept to superordinate, coordinate, or subordinate concepts.

Teachers can assess critical thinking by having learners analyze hypotheses in light of additional concepts. Assessing thinking always involves simultaneous assessment of content understanding.

IMPORTANT CONCEPTS

Epistemology (p. 158)
Intrinsic motivation (p. 167)
Metacognition (p. 167)

Scientific method (p. 158)
Self-regulation (p. 167)
Social structure (p. 156)

EXERCISES

1. Look at the content goals listed here. Identify which are appropriately taught with the Concept-Attainment Model. For those that are inappropriate, explain why.

   Goals

   a. An English teacher wants her students to understand *gerund*.

   b. An elementary teacher wants his students to understand *soft*.

   c. A science teacher wants her students to know why two coffee cans released at the top of an inclined plane roll down the plane at different speeds.

   d. A science teacher wants his students to understand *miscible fluids* (fluids that are capable of being mixed).

   e. A literature teacher wants her students to know the time period in which Poe did his writing.

2. For each of the content goals identified in Item 1 as appropriate for Concept Attainment, prepare and sequence a list of examples that would help the students attain the concept.

3. Select a topic of your choice and design a sequence of examples that will maximize the students' practice with thinking skills.

4. Read the following case study illustrating a Concept Attainment activity and answer the questions using information from the scenario.

Michele Scarritt wants her students to practice their abilities to test hypotheses. In order to provide practice with the process, she focuses on the concept *canine*. She has done a number of Concept-Attainment activities with her students, so they are familiar and comfortable with the process, viewing it as a "thinking game."

She cuts pictures of various animals and plants from magazines and pastes them on poster paper.

"Today we are going to do another Concept-Attainment activity, and I've thought up a really good one for you," she says in her introduction to the class. "You're going to have to really think about this one, so I'm curious to see how you'll do."

"You can't stump us, Mrs. Scarritt," the students retort. "We get 'em all."

"We'll see," Michele continues, smiling. "Here we go. . . ." She shows a picture of a German Shepherd as a *yes* example and an oak tree as a *no* example.

1. "I know what you're thinking of, "Mary volunteers. "It's an animal."

2. "It could be *pet*," Tabatha added.

3. "I think it's *mammal*," Phyllis puts in.

4. "Let's take a quick look at those hypotheses to be sure we're all in the same place. Phyllis, where did you get mammal?"

5. ". . . A German Shepherd's a dog, and dogs are mammals."

6. "Okay," Michele nods, "and I think we can all see where Mary and John got pet and animal. Let's go on and look at some more data." She shows a collie *(yes)* and a magnolia tree *(no)*.

7. "I think it's dogs," Judy adds.

8. "Okay, let's put that on the board. Now let's go a bit further," Michele says. She shows a beagle *(yes)* and a Siamese cat *(no)*.

9. "It can't be pet," Kathy quickly says, "because Siamese cat is a *no* and it's a pet."

10. "It can't be animal or mammal either," Mike notes, "because a cat is both an animal and a mammal."

11. "Let's continue," Michele requests. She then shows a fox *(yes)* and a leopard *(no)*.

12. "It can't be just dog," Don asserts. "Maybe it's *dog family*."

13. "I'll show you another picture," Michele says. Then she shows a picture of a wolf *(yes)*.

14. "It must be *dog family*," Denny stated. "All the yeses support the idea of dog family."

15. Michele adds, "What do we call *dog family*?" After hearing no response, she says, "Animals in the dog family are called 'canines.'"

16. Then Michele suggests, "Let's look at these pictures again (the yeses) and see what they have in common."

17. "They all have four legs," Sharon notes.

18. "They bark," Ann adds.

19. "They have sharp, prominent teeth," Jimmy says.

20. "They all have hair," Jane suggests.

The lesson continues as Michele helps the class form a definition for *canine*. Then she shows them some additional pictures and asks the students to classify them as *canine* or not.

Using information from the anecdote, respond to the following questions.

   a. Identify all the positive examples of the concept.

   b. Identify all the characteristics of the concept that were presented in the anecdote.

   c. Identify all the statements in the anecdote that were statements of hypothesizing.

   d. Explain how Michele's sequence of examples promoted the development of students' thinking abilities in the activity.

   e. What could Michele have done to further enrich the concept the children attained?

   f. What did Michele do that did not quite follow the Concept-Attainment procedure?

   g. Where in the anecdote did Michele make students' thinking processes explicit?

DISCUSSION QUESTIONS

1. When Concept-Attainment activities are implemented in classrooms with diverse learners, students who do not typically participate sometimes become quite involved. What might be a reason for this?

2. What would a Concept-Attainment activity be like if only positive examples were used? Only negative? What is the optimal mix of positive and negative examples?

3. What are the advantages of using coordinate concepts as negative examples in Concept-Attainment activities? Disadvantages? What can be done to minimize these disadvantages?

4. The amount of time that a teacher waits after asking a question has been found to be an important determinant influencing the quality of student answers (Rowe, 1974). How important is wait-time in a Concept-Attainment activity? When should it occur?

5. In what areas of the curriculum is it hardest to provide adequate examples for Concept-Attainment activities? Easiest? Why do you think so?

6. In what order should CA I, CA II, and CA III activities be introduced to students? What can be done to help students understand similarities and differences among the different strategies?

7. In comparing CA I, CA II, and CA III, which is easiest to implement in the classroom? Hardest? Which requires the most planning?

8. How could the critical thinking developed in CA II and CA III be assessed?

6

The Integrative Model

Teaching Organized
Bodies of Knowledge

The Integrative Model is an inductive strategy designed to help students develop a deep understanding of organized bodies of knowledge while developing critical thinking skills at the same time. As with the other models in this text, the Integrative Model is grounded in cognitive learning theory.

The Integrative Model is closely related to the Inductive Model. The primary differences relate to the topics taught with each. While the Inductive Model is designed to teach specific concepts, generalizations, principles, and academic rules, the Integrative Model is designed to teach combinations of those forms of content in organized bodies of knowledge.

The historical foundations of the Integrative Model are based on the work of Hilda Taba (1965, 1966, 1967), and we gratefully acknowledge her contributions to our work.

When you've completed your study of this chapter, you should be able to meet the following goals:

- Describe the characteristics of organized bodies of knowledge.
- Identify topics that are organized bodies of knowledge.
- Plan and implement lessons using the Integrative Model.
- Adapt the Integrative Model for learners at different ages and with varying backgrounds.
- Assess learner understanding of topics taught with the Integrative Model.

To begin our discussion, let's look at two teachers, each using the Integrative Model to help students understand organized bodies of information while simultaneously practicing higher level critical thinking.

Kim Soo is involved in a science unit on amphibians with her fourth graders. To this point, the class has read about amphibians and Kim has used a CD-ROM to show a variety of amphibians. As a class project, groups of students found pictures of different frogs and toads and the foods they eat. They brought the pictures to class, and with Kim's help organized them in a matrix. Kim supplied some additional information for the matrix and the result is shown in Figure 6.1.

Kim laminated the matrix so she could use it again later and prepared to guide students' analysis of the information in it.

After directing the class to study the chart for a moment, she begins the activity by saying, "First, let's look at the words at the top of the chart," and

Toads	Characteristics	Food	Habitat
Broad flat back Clumsy No tail	Eggs Tadpoles Dark Colors Shorter back legs Rough warty skin Poison on skin	Earthworms Insects Spiders	Water Land
Frogs	Characteristics	Food	Habitat
Narrow back Moves fast No tail	Eggs Tadpoles Different Colors Long back legs Smooth skin Poison under skin	Insects Spiders Earthworms	Water Land Trees

FIGURE 6.1   Matrix Comparing Frogs and Toads

pointing to *characteristics* continues, "This is kind of a big one. What do you think it means?"

". . . It's . . .kind of . . . the way they look," Andrea responds uncertainly.

"Sure," Kim nods. "It's a way of describing them. The way they look, their color, the way they're built."

Kim also has students describe what *habitat* means to them and she goes on, "Let's start with *food* since we're all familiar with food. Look carefully at the part that tells what toads eat. What do you notice here? . . . Serena?"

"They . . . eat earthworms," Serena responds.

"And what else? . . . Dominique?"

"Spiders," Dominique answers.

"Also grasshoppers," David volunteers.

"Yes, very good, everyone," Kim smiles. "Now look at the frogs. Let's do the same with them. What can you tell me about what they eat? Judy?"

". . . They eat insects," Judy replies.

"Also earthworms," Bill adds.

"Now let's go a bit farther," Kim encourages. "Look at both the frogs and the toads. How would you compare what they eat? Is there any kind of pattern there?"

"They both eat insects," Tim notices.

"Leroy?"

"They both eat earthworms too," Leroy offers.

". . . The food is . . . almost the same," Kristy adds tentatively.

"Why do you suppose that the food seems to be the same? . . . Fernando?" Kim continues, smiling, as she acknowledges Kristy's answer.

". . . The frog and toad live in about the same places," Fernando responds after several seconds of studying the chart.

"How did you decide that?" Kim probes.

" . . . It says on the chart that frogs live on land, in the water and in trees, and it says for toads that they live on land and in the water," Fernando responds, pointing to the chart.

"Yes, excellent, Fernando," Kim nods. "Remember how we have talked about justifying our thinking in some of our work in math. This is exactly the same thing. Fernando provided evidence for his conclusion that their environments are about the same by pointing out where they live on the chart. This is the kind of thinking we're after."

"Also, the frog and toad are a lot alike," Sonya adds, turning back to the chart.

"What do you see that tells you that, Sonya?"

"They look . . . about the same," Sonya replies.

"Also, both start from eggs and then get to be tadpoles. See where there are eggs and tadpoles on the chart," Lakesha adds.

"Very good, everyone!" Kim exclaims. "That is particularly good, Lakesha. You provided evidence for your comment without being asked for it. You're all thinking very well."

"Now here's a tough one," Kim continues. Suppose that frogs and toads were quite different rather than being very similar. What kinds of conclusions might we make about them then? . . . Donna?"

". . . Maybe the food that they would eat would be different," Donna shrugs.

"Can you give us an example of where that would be the case, Donna?" Kim queries.

Donna does not answer.

"Think about some animals that we know about. What do they eat?"

". . . Dogs eat dog food and stuff."

"Sure. There's an example," Kim smiles. "Dogs are different from frogs and toads, and we see that they eat different kinds of foods."

"Wait," Emmitt waves. "Dogs and cats are different, but they eat the same kinds of foods."

"Excellent thought, Emmitt," Kim nods. ". . . Now think about Emmitt's point, everyone. Do you have some other thoughts?"

". . . Dogs and cats *are* different, but a cat is more like a dog than a toad," Tabatha adds to the laughter of some of the other students.

"Some of you are laughing," Kim smiles, "but consider what Tabatha said. What do you think?"

". . . I think she's right," Sylvia adds. "Cows and horses are different, but they eat the same food."

"Okay," Kim waves. "I think you've all come up with some good thoughts. . . . Now let's think some more about all this. Look again at the toad and frog in the first column of the chart. In what ways are they different? . . . Fred?"

". . . It says the toad is clumsy, but it doesn't say anything about the frog."

". . . Suppose the toad wasn't clumsy," Kim continues nodding in acknowledgment of Fred's answer. "How might that affect the food toads eat or where they live? . . . Anyone?"

No one answers.

"Look over at the *food* column and the *habitat* column."

". . . Maybe toads could live in trees if they weren't clumsy," Marcy suggests.

"That's an interesting thought," Kim nods. "Why do you think so?"

". . . They couldn't be clumsy and get up there. . . . If they were clumsy, they might fall out," Andre suggests after studying the chart for several seconds.

"Sounds sensible. What does anyone else think?"

The rest of the class nods and murmurs, and Kim goes on, "How about food?"

"That would be different too," Kathy says quickly.

"Why do you think so, Kathy?" Kim probes.

". . . Well, . . . Well, maybe not?"

"Why not?"

"The frog and toad eat the same food."

"What does that have to do with it?"

". . . If the frog isn't clumsy, and the toad is . . . and they eat the same food . . . it doesn't matter."

"What doesn't matter?"

". . . Whether the toad is clumsy or not?"

"What do you think of Kathy's suggestions, anyone?"

The class discusses Kathy's ideas for a few more minutes and finally conclude that what she says made sense.

Kim then continues, "Now let's summarize what we've found here, and let's think about animals in general. . . . I want you to try and extend beyond the toad and frog, and I'll help you if you need it.

"For instance," she goes on, "what can we say about the characteristics of animals that look a lot alike?"

". . . They're, like . . . mostly the same."

"So how should we write that? Help me out," Kim urges as she moved up to the board.

No one responds.

"I'll get us started." She writes, "Animals that look alike . . ." on the chalkboard.

". . . Will have the same characteristics," Ladonna offers.

"Okay," Kim replies, and she then writes, "Animals that look alike have similar characteristics," on the chalkboard.

"What else?" she urges.

"The also eat the same kind of food," Tonya offers.

"Good. So . . . tell me what to write."

"Animals that look alike . . . "

"And have the same characteristics," Nancy interjects.

"And have the same characteristics," Tonya repeats, "eat the same kind of food."

Kim then writes the statement on the board, then asks the students for any additional summarizing statements.

Finally, they have a list of statements that appears as follows:

- Animals that look alike have similar characteristics.
- Animals that look alike and have similar characteristics eat the same kind of food.
- Animals that are similar live in similar habitats.

Finally, Kim asks the students if they can think of some examples that fit their statements, and they discuss animals such as deer and elk, different kinds of birds, and predators such as lions and leopards. They also discuss exceptions, such as the fact that deer and elk both live in the mountains, but some deer live on the plains as well, until Kim closes the lesson.

Let's look now at another teacher, Tony Horton, using the Integrative Model in his eighth-grade history class. As you read through the second lesson, compare what Tony is doing with what Kim did in her lesson.

Tony Horton is beginning a unit on immigration with his American history students. He asks the students what *immigrant* means and then asks them to suggest some representative immigrant groups from the late nineteenth century until the middle of the twentieth century, saying that they would look at immigration from the middle of the twentieth century to the present later in the unit. Students suggest that they study a group from Europe and another from the Far East. Tony also encourages them to consider one or more groups closer to the United States as well, and at his suggestion they settle on Puerto Rico.

Just as he begins again, Juan interjects, "What about Cuba? I have some relatives in Florida who came from Cuba."

"Sounds good to me," Tony nods. "What do the rest of you think?"

The class agrees that it is a good idea, and Tony comments, "This will extend our study a bit past the middle of the century, but I really like your idea, Juan. Also, everyone, we will extend what we're doing to consider Hispanic Americans in the Southwest, and many other immigrant groups, particularly in California."

Tony draws a matrix on the board that appears as shown in Figure 6.2.

Tony organizes the class into pairs. Each pair is assigned to gather information about different aspects of the four immigrant groups, such as their reasons for coming, characteristics, and assimilation. The pairs work for three days on gathering the information, turn in the notes they made, and Tony compiles the information together with some of his own into the matrix that appears in Figure 6.3.

The next day Tony begins by saying, "All right, everyone, slide your desk next to your partner and we're going to analyze the information that we've put together in our chart," as he passes out a copy to each of the pairs.

	Reasons for Coming	Characteristics	Assimilation
I T			
C H			
P R			
C			

FIGURE 6.2   Matrix Organized for Data Gathering

	Reasons for Coming	Characteristics	Assimilation
I T A L I A N S	Small farms couldn't support families Large estates controlled land Population increases Poor land, little irrigation, wooden plows Few factories, little industry Heavy taxes Stories of wealth in America	Many from low-income backgrounds Religious; Catholic Large families Tight family structure Many from farm occupations Most could not read or write English English language learned quickly by second generation	First generation did not mix Church schools Second generation moved away from home "Little Italy" in New York City Second generation "Americanized"
C H I N E S E	Large population Land controlled by warlords High taxes Crop failures Famine Promise of high wages in America	Many brought to U.S. initially as laborers Religious; Confucianism Most could not read or write English Retained many former customs Tight family structure	Men as job hunters initially lived together "China Towns" established in major cities Major influx from 1868-1890 Little social association with others Large population in western U.S. Eager to preserve customs
P U E R T O R I C A N S	Large population increases Few factories Little land Close to the United States Descriptions of "good life" in America	Many had low-income backgrounds Religious; Catholic Large families Most could not read or write English English language learned quickly by second generation Tight family structure	Major influx in 1940s and 1950s "Spanish Harlem" in New York Many stayed in northeastern U.S. Initially church, then public schools Second generation "Americanized"
C U B A N S	Batista overthrown Castro into power Promises of opportunity to return to Cuba	Many had upper-income backgrounds Religious; Catholic Tight family structure Many could not read or write English Politically powerful in South Florida Economically powerful in South Florida	Major influx in 1960s Large population in south Florida Adapted quickly to American politics Adapted quickly to American business practices

FIGURE 6.3   Matrix Containing Gathered Information

After each pair has received a copy, he continues, "Now here's your assignment. I want you to look in each column of the chart and look for patterns. For instance, when you look at the immigrants' reasons for coming, compare the groups to see what they have in common. Then describe the similarities in writing.

"Let's look at a sample. Everyone take a look at the first column for a minute and see if you find some things that the four groups have in common, or something that two or three of the groups have in common."

After about half a minute, Aurelia volunteers hesitantly, "It looks like the Italians, Chinese, and Puerto Ricans all had population problems, but that didn't seem to be the case for the Cubans."

"Excellent, Aurelia. That's exactly what we're trying to do," Tony praises, and he writes "Population problems for the Italians, Chinese, and Puerto Ricans; not for the Cubans," on the board.

He continues, "Now I want you to work with your partner and find as many patterns as you have evidence for in each of the columns. I want you to work as follows. . . . First you write your own response . . . find your own patterns and write them down. . . . Then share them with your partner. . . . Discuss them with each other and be ready to share them with the class. You have 10 minutes."

"Do we turn these in, Mr. Horton?" James asks.

"Absolutely," Tony nods. "Now get to work quickly and quietly."

The room soon becomes a buzz of voices as the students begin studying the chart and writing information on their papers. At the end of the 10 minutes, Tony says, "Okay, let's take a look. What do you have there?"

"Wait, we're not done," several protests.

"All right, 5 more minutes."

At the end of the 5 minutes Tony says, "Now here we go. What are some of the comparisons you made?"

Each of the pairs reports some of the comparisons that they have found, and Tony records them on the board. When they are finished, they have the following lists:

Reasons for Coming	*Characteristics*	*Assimilation*
Poor agriculture except for Cubans	Tended to come from lower classes except for Cubans	First generation stayed to themselves
Large populations except for Cubans	Most didn't speak English	Chinese assimilated less rapidly than the others did
Promises of a better life in America	All were religious	At least initially, stayed where they first landed
Political problems in Cuba	All except Chinese learned English quickly	

"That's well done," Tony nods, pointing to the lists. "Good work. . . . Now let's look a little more closely at the information. Why do you suppose that the Italians, Chinese, and Puerto Ricans tended to come from the lower socioeconomic classes, while the Cubans did not? . . . Anyone?"

". . . I think . . . it's because of why they came," Antonio offers. "The Italians, Chinese, and Puerto Ricans came so they could have a better life, but the Cubans were escaping from Castro."

"They wanted a better life, too," Kevin interjects.

"Well, that's true, but the reasons were different. The others wanted to make a better living, and in Cuba it was politics mostly."

"Good thoughts, everyone," Tony goes on. "Is there anything that we can say in general about the reasons immigrants move from one country to another?"

". . . I think they think that they will have a better life in the new country," LaQuana puts in. "It might be to make more money, or it might be for political reasons, but they all think they'll be better off in the new country than they are in the old one."

"Does everyone agree with that?" Tony asks, turning to the rest of the class.

Seeing several nods, Tony writes on the board, "Immigrants immigrate in search of a better life."

He continues, "Let's look again at some of the comparisons we've made. We wrote that the Chinese assimilated less rapidly than did the other groups. Why do you suppose that was the case?"

". . . Their culture was . . . like . . . more different than the others," Christine volunteers finally.

"What evidence do we have on our chart that tells us they were more different culturally?"

". . . Their religion, for one thing. The Italians, Puerto Ricans, and Cubans were mostly Catholic, which a lot of people in the United States are, but the Chinese were Confus . . . Confushist . . . whatever that religion is," Christine continues.

"Also, it says in the chart that the Chinese learned English slower than the others," Estella adds.

"And why might that have been?"

"Their language is different. There are letters for each of the languages in the chart, and the Italians, Puerto Ricans, and Cubans use the same letters as English, but the Chinese letters are really different."

"Suppose they weren't different, meaning they used the same letters as we do. How do you suppose that would have affected how fast they assimilated?"

". . . It would have speeded it up," Dean offers.

"What do you think, Gayle? You've been sort of quiet," Tony encourages.

"... It might have speeded it up, but it still would have been slower than for the others."

"Why do you think so?"

"Well, the religion, for one thing."

"And they kept their customs," Shelli adds.

Tony continues with the process of having students explain their comparisons and hypothesize outcomes until the information in the chart has been covered.

Now he says, "Now let's try and make some summary generalizations about the information we have here, and then we'll see if we think it applies to immigrant groups today."

With Tony's guidance, the students offer some generalizations, which he writes on the board. The list appears as follows:

- Immigrants immigrate in search of a better life.
- Immigrants usually immigrate to make a better living. (Tony added, "Usually for economic reasons.")
- Some immigrants immigrate for political reasons.
- Immigrants usually hear stories of how good it will be in the new country.
- If immigrants immigrate for economic reasons, they're usually in the lower economic classes in their native country.
- Immigrants assimilate more easily if their language and customs are similar to the language and customs of the new country.
- Immigrants tend to first settle where they first land in the new country.

"Now let's take a look at our list as see if we think everything we've said is valid. How do they all look?"

"... I don't think that 'economic reasons' is right," Troy says after several seconds.

"Go on, Troy. Why don't you think so?"

"... It looks to me like both the Italians and Chinese also had political problems, sort of like the Cubans. The Puerto Ricans are the only ones that didn't have political problems."

"What evidence do you have for that?"

Troy points to information on the chart, such as "heavy taxes from government," for the Italians and "war lords" and "heavy taxes" for the Chinese.

Tony acknowledges his point, asks the rest of the class if they think the generalization should be revised, does so in response to their comments, and then analyzes each of the other generalizations in the same way.

Finally he says, "Now we're going to keep this list on the board." Tony continues, "And when we study immigrants further, we'll see if our generalizations are still valid. We'll ask ourselves, did we overgeneralize, or maybe even undergeneralize? Did we stereotype any immigrant groups? Then we'll look back at some of the early colonialization, such as the Jamestown and Plymouth Colonies. Can the people that came then even be legitimately called immigrants? We'll start there tomorrow."

The Integrative Model: An Overview

As with the other models, we begin our discussion of the Integrative Model by looking again at the teaching episodes and identifying their similarities and differences.

The lessons were similar in the following ways:

- The topics the teachers taught were **organized bodies of knowledge,** *topics that combine facts, concepts, generalizations, and the relationships among them* (Eggen & Kauchak, 1999).
- The teachers began their lessons by displaying information that the students and teacher had gathered and compiled in a matrix.
- The students, under the guidance of the teachers, analyzed the information in the matrix; they increased their understanding of the topic and practiced critical thinking simultaneously.

Because of the topics, ages of the students, and the teachers' goals, the lessons had some minor differences:

- Kim began the lesson by having students first describe the information in a specific cell of the matrix, while Tony had students make comparisons as the first part of the activity.
- Kim did her lesson as a large-group activity, whereas Tony had the students initially work in pairs, report their findings, and then analyze the findings in a whole group.
- Kim had the students first make observations, which were followed—essentially in order—by making comparisons, forming explanations, hypothesizing, and generalizing. Tony had his students practice the same processes, but they didn't follow a sequence in the same way Kim's did.

The similarities and differences are summarized in Table 6.1.

Social Structure of the Model

As with the Inductive and Concept-Attainment models, the Integrative Model requires a classroom environment in which students feel free to take risks and offer their conclusions, conjectures, and evidence without fear of criticism or embarrassment. Achieving a climate of support in using the Integrative Model is accomplished in much the same way as it is with the Inductive Model. Some examples include:

- Providing virtually all the information students needed to reach the lesson's content goals. Kim and Tony used the information in their matrixes for this purpose.

TABLE 6.1   Comparison of the Two Lessons

Similarities	Differences
Both teachers taught an organized body of information.	Kim's students began by describing information in a single cell. Tony's students began by making comparisons and looking for patterns.
The teachers displayed information in a matrix for the students.	
In both classes, the students' analysis was based on the information in the matrix rather than on information they recalled from reading or lecture.	Kim conducted her lesson as a whole-group activity. Tony's students began working in pairs followed by a whole-group discussion.
The teachers guided the students' analyses with directed questions.	Kim guided her students through the model's phases in order. Tony did not follow a specific sequence.
Both lessons focused simultaneously on deep understanding of content and higher-order and critical thinking.	
Both lessons included all phases of the model.	

- Beginning the lesson open-endedly. Both teachers had the students respond to open-ended questions—the initial observations in Kim's lesson, and the comparisons the students recorded in Tony's.
- Guiding students as they did their analysis. In each case, the teachers prompted when necessary and helped keep the lesson directed toward the goal.

Providing as much information as possible—ideally all the information the students need to reach the content goal—ensures success because students can make their conclusions based on what they see rather than information that they may or may not bring with them to the classroom. This is especially important in working with diverse learners. Since a variety of answers are acceptable, open-ended questions also ensure success, and they allow students to respond based on their own experience and background knowledge. Open-ended questions are especially effective for increasing the participation of cultural minorities and nonnative English speakers (Langer et al., 1990).

The Teacher's Role

As with the Inductive Model, the teacher guides students' analysis of the information displayed for them by starting open-endedly and continuing through a process of explaining, hypothesizing, and generalizing. The biggest task for the teacher is keeping the lesson's goal in mind while maintaining the flow of the discussion.

As with the Inductive Model, the success of a lesson depends on the quality of the data or examples—the matrices in Kim's and Tony's lessons—the teachers use and their ability to guide the students' analysis of the information. As with both the Inductive Model and the Concept-Attainment Models, using the Integrative Model effectively requires teachers who are skilled in questioning and can think on their feet.

The Integrative Model: Theoretical Perspectives.   As with the models we have already discussed, the Integrative Model is grounded in cognitive views of learning. It assumes learners are *active* and *construct* rather than *record* their understanding of the topics they study. Consistent with cognitive learning theory, learners must be presented with effective representations of the topics they're studying, and interaction between the teacher and students and students with each other is critical. Let's look at some dialogue that illustrates this interaction:

> **KIM:**   Why do you suppose that the food seems to be the same?
>
> **FERNANDO:**   . . . The frog and toad live in about the same places.
>
> **KIM:**   How did you decide that?
>
> **FERNANDO:**   . . . It says on the chart that the frog lives on land, in the water, and in trees, and it says for the toad that he lives on land and in the water.
>
> **SONYA:**   Also, the frog and toad are very much alike.
>
> **KIM:**   What do you see that tells you that?
>
> **SONYA:**   From the pictures we see that they look about the same.
>
> **LAKESHA:**   Also, they both start from eggs and then become tadpoles. See where there are eggs and tadpoles on the chart.

In Tony's lesson we also saw instances of the teacher's assisting students in the process of constructing understanding. For example:

> **TONY:**   Why do you suppose that the Italians, Chinese, and Puerto Ricans tended to come from the lower socioeconomic classes, while the Cubans did not?
>
> **ANTONIO:**   . . . I think it's because of why they came. . . . The Italians, Chinese, and Puerto Ricans came so they could have a better life, but the Cubans were escaping from Cuba.
>
> **KEVIN:**   They wanted a better life, too.
>
> **ANTONIO:**   Well, that's true, but the reasons were different. The others wanted to make a better living, and in Cuba it was politics mostly.

Both lessons were developed around students' evolving understanding of the topic, and at least a portion of the discussion broke away from the typical questioning pattern of teacher-student-teacher-student and toward a pattern where students were responding to each other rather than answering direct questions from the teacher. Both Kim and Tony capitalized on the social aspects of learning and the fact that understanding is constructed by learners. This strategy captures critical elements of instruction based on cognitive views of learning in general and constructivism in particular (Brooks & Brooks, 1993; Clements & Battista, 1990).

Goals for the Integrative Model

The Integrative Model is designed to accomplish two interrelated goals. The first is to help students construct a deep and thorough understanding of *organized bodies of knowledge,* and the second is to practice critical thinking. Let's examine these.

Organized Bodies of Knowledge:
Relationships among Facts, Concepts, and Generalizations

In our overview of the Integrative Model we said that Kim and Tony taught **organized bodies of knowledge,** *topics that combine facts, concepts, generalizations, and the relationships among them* (Eggen & Kauchak, 1999). To put *organized bodies of knowledge* into context, let's look back at the lessons we discussed in Chapters 4 and 5. In Chapter 4, for example, Judy Nelson taught *longitude* and *latitude* (concepts), *Charles's law* was Sue Grant's topic, and Jim Rooney wanted his students to understand the *rules for forming singular and plural possessive nouns.* In Chapter 5 topics were the concepts *fruit* and *metaphor.*

Each topic was specific and well defined. Each had precisely described characteristics—parallel imaginary lines that measure distances north and south of the equator for the concept *latitude,* for example, or a specific relationship, such as *as temperature increases, volume increases when pressure is constant* in the case of Charles's law.

By comparison, the topics that Kim and Tony taught were not discrete topics and they didn't have specific characteristics, relationships, or boundaries. For instance, Kim's lesson included several facts—the kinds of foods frogs and toads eat, for example, concepts (such as *habitat*), and generalizations (*animals with similar characteristics tend to each the same kinds of foods,* and *animals with similar characteristics tend to live in similar habitats*).

Tony's lesson was similar. The content contained facts, such as the major influx of Cubans occurring in the 1960s, and there is a place in New York called "Little Italy," among several others; concepts (*socioeconomic status, assimilation,* and *Confucianism*); and generalizations (such as *the Chinese were eager to preserve their customs* and *second-generation Italians quickly learned English*).

The goal in each of these lessons was not to teach these specific facts, concepts, or generalization themselves; rather, it was for students to find and understand relationships among them, form explanations for those relationships, and consider additional possibilities (hypotheses).

Much of the content we teach in schools exists in the form of organized bodies of knowledge. For example, geography teachers compare different cultural regions, such as the climates, cultures, and economies of Brazil, Argentina, and Venezuela. English teachers compare the works of Faulkner, Fitzgerald, and Hemingway. Life science teachers compare different body systems and their functions. Teachers of young children compare food, clothing, and recreation for different seasons of the year. Each of these topics combines facts, concepts, and generalizations into organized bodies of knowledge just as Kim's and Tony's lessons did.

Additional examples of topics that are organized bodies of knowledge include:

- Life science—a comparison of different animal phyla and the characteristics of each.
- Health—a comparison of well-balanced and poorly balanced meals.
- Art—a comparison of art forms in different historical periods.
- Music—a comparison of baroque, Romantic and classical music.
- Early elementary—a comparison of different community helpers.
- History—a comparison of settlements in the northern and southern Colonies.

All of these topics combine facts, concepts, and generalizations, and the teacher would want students to identify and understand relationships among them.

Developing Critical Thinking

A second goal for the model is to develop students' critical thinking. Developing critical thinking requires practice in finding patterns, forming explanations, hypothesizing, generalizing, and documenting them with evidence. We saw in Chapter 2 that, "Learning is a consequence of thinking" (Perkins, 1992, p. 8), which suggests that content goals and goals for thinking are interdependent. Learners automatically use the critical-thinking processes as they are involved in constructing deep understandings of the topics they are studying. The teacher helps make this practice conscious and systematic.

How important is this goal? John Goodlad (1984), in his well-known work *A Place Called School,* reported that, on average, only about 5 percent of class time was spent in thoughtful discussion. He also reported:

> Only rarely did we find evidence to suggest instruction (in reading and math) likely to go much beyond merely possession of information to a level of understanding its implications and either applying it or exploring its possible applications. Nor did we see activities likely to arouse students' curiosity or to involve them in seeking a solution to some problem not already laid bare by teacher or textbook.
>
> And it appears that this preoccupation with the lower intellectual processes pervades social studies and science as well. An analysis of topics studied and materials used gives not an impression of students studying human adaptations and exploration, but of facts to be learned (p. 236).

Further, Boyer (1983) found that fewer than 1 percent of all teacher questions invite students to respond in a way that goes beyond factual information or demonstrating a routine procedure. From the case studies we see that Kim's and Tony's teaching behaviors were in direct contrast with the patterns identified by these studies.

While different from the prevailing patterns in schools, the questioning and guidance Kim and Tony provided are not difficult to accomplish. It takes a little adjustment in thinking—away from teaching as *telling* and toward teaching as *guiding*—and it also requires that students be provided with information to think with, such as Kim's and Tony's matrices.

Let us look now at how we can plan to make this happen.

Planning Lessons with the Integrative Model

The planning process for using the Integrative Model is similar to that for using either the Inductive Model or the Concept-Attainment Model, and the steps are outlined in Figure 6.4.

Identifying Topics

Research indicates that teacher planning most commonly begins with a topic (Morine-Dershimer & Vallance, 1976; Peterson, Marx, & Clark, 1978). This is a practical and intuitively sensible beginning point. The topics in the two lessons at the beginning of the chapter were *frogs and toads* and *immigrants*. Topics may come from textbooks, curriculum guides, and other sources, including the interests of students or teachers themselves. When topics are organized bodies of knowledge, the Integrative Model can be effectively used.

Specifying Goals

The fact that planning typically begins with a topic does not imply that goals are not important. In fact, effective teachers have very clear goals in mind and teach purposefully to them (Berliner, 1985). This is true regardless of the topic being taught.

Content Goals. Having identified the topic, we must then decide what we want students to know about it—the learner outcomes. Specifying student outcomes requires a bit more thought when the topics are organized bodies of knowledge because they are less precisely defined than specific facts, concepts, or generalizations. For example, merely knowing that he wanted his students to understand relationships among the "Reasons for Coming," "Characteristics," and "Assimilation" of the four immigrant groups wouldn't have been precise enough to help Tony guide his students' analysis. He needed to anticipate some of the generalizations that were summarized in his lesson, such as the relationships between *immigration* and *economics, characteristics of immigrants* and *their reasons for coming,* and *characteristics of immigrants* and *their rates of assimilation.* Other generalizations

FIGURE 6.4 Planning with the Integrative Model

may arise as incidental outcomes, which is very desirable, but having specific outcomes in mind is critical to the flow and goals of the lesson.

Planning for Critical Thinking.   Planning for critical thinking is more a matter of awareness than it is actually planning. The instructional steps contained in the Integrative Model involve students in finding patterns, forming explanations, and hypothesizing, all on the basis of evidence. As students use these processes, they practice critical thinking.

Preparing Data Representations

Having identified the topic and goals, we are prepared to move to the third step, capturing information in a way that allows students to process it. As we saw in Kim's and Tony's lessons, the data are often organized in the form of a matrix. We will first examine matrices, and later in the chapter we will discuss how alternate forms of information displays can be effectively used with the Integrative Model.

In each of the examples we have discussed, the topic involved a comparison—toads and frogs in Kim's lesson, and the four immigrant groups in Tony's. We also see that two ideas were compared in Kim's lesson, while four were compared in Tony's. The number depends on the developmental level of the students and the teacher's goal.

Each of the other topics that we illustrated in the last section involved a comparison as well. However, the comparisons don't have to involve closely related concepts, such as *toads* and *frogs,* or different immigrant groups. For example, a teacher might want to compare arthropods to mammals to demonstrate—among other things—that animals with external skeletons are much smaller than animals with internal skeletons.

Student ideas and interests should be used as well in the planning process. In Tony's lesson we saw that he and the students collaborated on the choice of immigrant groups, whereas Kim alone made the decision to study toads and frogs. It also appears that Tony made the decision to include "Reasons for Coming," "Characteristics," and "Assimilation" as the dimensions on which the immigrant groups would be compared, and Kim made the decision to include their appearance, "Food," "Characteristics," and "Habitat," as the dimensions to be examined. Though Tony and Kim made these decisions, they could have solicited student input, helping students see the logic behind the investigation.

Gathering Data.   Once the dimensions for the matrix have been identified, the next step is to gather the data that students will analyze. Here the teacher has at least three options.

- Assign individuals or teams of students to gather the data that will appear in each of the cells of the matrix. A teacher would choose this option if learning to do research on the Internet or library and/or organizing information was part of the goal.
- Have students gather some of the data, and add some additional data yourself. This is the option Kim and Tony chose.
- Prepare the entire matrix yourself. This approach saves classroom time and ensures that the content in the matrix leads to important content goals. The disadvantage is that students aren't as involved in the data and, as a result, their knowledge of and interest in analyzing the data may be reduced.

The process of gathering and organizing data may appear time consuming, and initially it can be, if you do all the preparation yourself. However, if students help gather the initial information, your preparation time is reduced and, once it is gathered, you can store the information in your computer and quickly modify it the next time you teach the topic. So while initial preparation is demanding, once the matrix is prepared additional preparation is minimal.

Let us now look at effective ways of displaying the data.

Effective Data Displays.   While data can be displayed in different ways, some are more effective than others. Two guidelines are important. First, *display the information in as factual a form as possible*. This provides students with increased opportunities to analyze information and practice critical thinking. If this is impossible, next best is a series of relatively narrow generalizations or a mixture of narrow generalizations and facts. Least desirable is a series of broad generalizations. For example, let us consider Tony's lesson again, and compare the matrix he used to the one displayed in Table 6.2.

Because the information in Table 6.2 is already in the form of broad generalizations, the opportunity for students to analyze data and form generalizations themselves is reduced. To be consistent with the principle, "Learning is a consequence of thinking," students must have the opportunity to think about the topics they're studying. Reducing this opportunity decreases the likelihood that they will develop the deep understanding that is so important to learning.

A second guideline is to *provide sufficient information so that students can use data from one part of the matrix as evidence for a conclusion about another part*. For example, Kim asked the students to *explain* why the frog and the toad would eat the same food, and she called on Fernando. He responded by saying that the animals live in essentially the same places. When asked to provide evidence for his response, he was able to point to the

TABLE 6.2   Matrix Containing Broad Generalizations

Reasons for Coming	Characteristics	Assimilation
Italians Economic problems Political problems Overpopulation	Lower socioeconomic class Religious	Relatively rapid assimilation
Chinese Overpopulation Economic opportunity Political problems	Religious Lower socioeconomic class	Relatively slow assimilation
Puerto Ricans Overpopulation Economic opportunity	Religious Lower socioeconomic class	Relatively rapid assimilation
Cubans Political problems	Higher socioeconomic class	Relatively rapid assimilation

section of the chart that showed the habitat for each. If that section hadn't existed, Fernando wouldn't have been able to use the matrix to provide the evidence for his conclusion.

We saw the same kind of processing in Tony's lesson. For instance, we saw the following dialogue in his lesson.

> **TONY:** Let's look again at some of the comparisons we've made. We wrote that the Chinese assimilated less rapidly than did the other groups. Why do you suppose that was the case?
>
> **CHRISTINE:** They were more different than the others were.
>
> **TONY:** What information do we have on our chart that tells us that they were more different?
>
> **CHRISTINE:** Their religion for one thing. The Italians, Puerto Ricans, and Cubans were mostly Catholic, which a lot of people in the United States are, but the Chinese were Confus . . . Confushist . . . whatever that religion is.
>
> **ESTELLA:** Also, it says in the chart that the Chinese learned English slower than the others.

If the information about the immigrant groups' religions or the rate at which they learned English had not been included in the matrix, the students would not have been able to provide evidence based on data they could observe.

Including enough information in the chart so students are able to make links and verify their responses through observation is very important. We illustrate this process in greater detail as we discuss implementing Integrative Model lessons.

As an additional example, let's look at the matrix in Table 6.3 (pp. 200–201). As part of a unit on the solar system, the teacher assigned teams of students to gather the information which appears in the matrix. So while gathering and organizing the data required guidance from the teacher, she did not have to spend her planning time in actually gathering the information.

We see that the information in the matrix is factual. Information in this form gives students opportunities to practice analyzing information, which leads to deep understanding of the content and improved critical thinking. (You will be asked to examine the information in this matrix again when you complete the exercises at the end of the chapter.)

Implementing Lessons Using the Integrative Model

The Integrative Model is implemented in four closely related phases:

- Phase 1: Describe, compare, and search for patterns
- Phase 2: Explain similarities and differences
- Phase 3: Hypothesize outcomes for different conditions
- Phase 4: Generalize to form broad relationships

Though they are listed in order, and teachers will normally start with Phase 1, *the phases are not hierarchical and they do not imply a rigid sequence.* A teacher, for example, may move directly from a comparison in Phase 1 to a hypothesis in Phase 3, and then return to another comparison. Students' abilities to hypothesize in Phase 3 do not require that they have first formed explanations in Phase 2. The order a teacher uses should depend upon content goals, and student interests and responses. This flexibility was illustrated in Kim's and Tony's lessons. Kim conducted her lesson so that the students went through the phases pretty much in order, whereas Tony varied the sequence.

Phase 1: Describe, Compare, and Search for Patterns

Phase 1 is the beginning point for students' analysis. Looking again at Kim's and Tony's lessons, we see that Phase 1 can begin in one of two ways:

- The teacher simply directs students' attention to a cell in the matrix and asks them to observe and describe the information. This is what Kim did.
- The teacher asks students to look for similarities and differences in two or more of the cells. This was Tony's approach.

Kim's students were younger than Tony's, and focusing on a single cell better matched their developmental level.

Both types of beginnings are open ended and capitalize on the advantages that also exist in the beginning of a lesson using the Inductive Model. Because Phase 1 is open ended, it breaks the ice for the students, assures success, promotes involvement, and allows the teacher to quickly and easily involve a number of students by asking a large number of questions, a factor positively correlated with student achievement (Eggen & Kauchak, 1999; Lambert & McCombs, 1998).

The point on the matrix where students begin the analysis is a matter of teacher judgment. Most commonly, it begins with the top left cell, probably because we're in the habit of reading beginning with the upper left. You don't have to begin there, however; any point could be productive.

The time you spend on a single cell (or column) is also a matter of judgment. You most likely wouldn't ask for a single observation or comparison and move on, but you don't want to overdwell on a single portion of the chart to the point of reducing the momentum of the lesson.

After describing information in the first cell or making comparisons in the first column, the teacher moves on to a second, a third, and so on until all the information in the matrix has been examined.

In looking again at Kim's and Tony's lessons, we see a smooth process that promoted high levels of success and interaction. They first asked the students to make observations (in Kim's case) or comparisons (in Tony's). Teachers sometimes feel that they should have to work harder at the initial question, but this isn't the case. Simple, straightforward questions that actively involve students are very effective. To illustrate, let's look again at some of the dialogue from Kim's lesson.

TABLE 6.3   Matrix with Information about the Solar System*

Name	Origin of Name	Diameter in miles	Distance from Sun in miles	Length of Year (orbit)	Length of Day (rotation)	Gravity Compared w/Earth's
Sun	Sol, Roman god of the Sun	865,000				
Mercury	Mercury, messenger of the Roman gods	3,030	35,900,000	88 Earth days	59 Earth days counterclockwise	0.38
Venus	Venus, Roman goddess of love and beauty	7,500	67,200,000	225 Earth days	243 Earth days counterclockwise	0.88
Earth	Terra Mater, Roman earth mother	7.900	98,000,000	365 1/4 days	24 hours counterclockwise	1
Mars	Mars, Roman god of war	4,200	141,500,000	687 Earth days	24 1/2 hours counterclockwise	0.38
Jupiter	Jupiter, Roman king of all gods	88,700	483,400,000	12 Earth years	10 hours counterclockwise	2.34
Saturn	Saturn, Roman god of agriculture	75,000	914,000,000	30 Earth years	11 hours counterclockwise	0.92
Uranus	Uranus, Roman god, father of Saturn grandfather of Jupiter	31,566	1,782,400,000	84 Earth years	24 hours counterclockwise	0.79
Neptune	Neptune, Roman god of the sea	30,200	2,792,900,000	165 Earth years	17 hours counterclockwise	1.12
Pluto	Pluto, Greek god of the lower world	1,423	3,665,000,000	248 Earth years	6 1/2 days counterclockwise	0.43

Continued

TABLE 6.3 *Continued*

Name	Moons	Average Surface Temperature (F)	Other Interesting Characteristics
Sun	0	10,000°	The sun is a star, Earth's star; a gigantic ball of glowing gases; more than 1 million Earths could fit inside the sun; sun's gravity keeps the 9 planets in orbit; sun gives planets light and heat.
Mercury	0	300° below zero to 800° above zero	No atmosphere; no water; many craters.
Venus	0	900° average	Atmosphere mostly carbon dioxide and poisonous sulfuric acid; no water; brightest planet; hottest planet; desert; huge lightning flashes; thick cloud cover; enormous winds.
Earth	1	57° average	Atmosphere contains about 78% nitrogen, 21% oxygen, 1% other gases; water covers about 70% of surface; has plant life, animal life, and people.
Mars	2	67° below zero average	Atmosphere—thin carbon dioxide; no water; white ice caps at poles; salmon sky; frequent dust storms; red, rocky surface (the Red Planet); appears to have no life; home of Earthlings' first space colony(?).
Jupiter	16 or more	162° below zero average	Atmosphere has hydrogen, helium, ammonia; no water; bands of color; Great Red Spot (hurricanes); faint horizontal ring; huge lightning bolts.
Saturn	21 or more	208° below zero average	Atmosphere has hydrogen and helium; no water; has at least four rings tilted from horizontal position; mostly big ball of gas; clouds; some bands of color in shades of yellow. Mostly gas. Small solid core.
Uranus	15 or more	355° below zero average	Atmosphere of hydrogen and helium; no water; greenish color; has at least nine vertical rings. Would float on water.
Neptune	2 or more	266° below zero average	Atmosphere of hydrogen and helium; no water; bands of color in shades of blue.
Pluto	1	460° below zero average	No oxygen; no water; extremely cold and dark; orbiting closer to the sun than Neptune from 1979—1999.

*Matrix adapted by permission of Dr. June Main.

> **KIM:** Let's start with *food* since we're all familiar with food. Look carefully at the part that tells what toads eat. What do you notice here? . . . Serena?
>
> **SERENA:** Well, they eat earthworms.
>
> **KIM:** And what else? . . . Dominique?
>
> **DOMINIQUE:** Spiders.
>
> **DAVID:** Also grasshoppers.
>
> **KIM:** Yes, very good, everyone. . . . Now look at the frogs. Let's do the same with them. What can you tell us about what they eat? . . . Judy?
>
> **JUDY:** They eat insects.
>
> **BILL:** Also earthworms.

Kim began the lesson in a comfortable, open-ended way with the students, which ensured success and built lesson momentum.

In comparison, Tony started his lesson by having the students work in groups, beginning by saying, "Now here's your assignment. I want you to look in each column of the chart and look for patterns." Then he got them started with an example when he said, "Let's look at a sample. Everyone take a look at the first column for a minute and see if you find some things that the four groups have in common, or something that two or three of the groups have in common." Though Kim asked for descriptions and Tony called for comparisons, both lessons started out in an open-ended way by involving students.

Becoming more open ended requires some adjustment for many teachers, because it isn't a natural inclination and few have been taught that way. However, once the adjustment has been made, teachers find it a desirable alternative to the traditional one-question, specific-answer dialogue that is typical of most classrooms.

Recording Information. As students conduct their analysis, the teacher typically writes information on the board, overhead, or chart paper. This provides a public record of the process and reference points for students. Tony recorded both the comparisons the students made in groups and the summarizing generalizations, while Kim recorded only the summary statements. Both teachers made a record of the information, however. Without a public record, students will lose some of the most important points in the analysis, and the understanding that results will be less thorough. The process of recording information typically continues in Phases 2, 3, and 4.

Phase 2: Explain Similarities and Differences

During Phase 2, students are asked to compare and contrast and explain similarities and differences. This is the point where the students are immersed in critical thinking, and once they warm to the task, their analyses can become quite sophisticated. While the questioning in Phase 2 is more demanding than it was in the first phase, with practice teachers can become skilled to the point where their questioning is almost automatic.

In Phase 1 of Kim's lesson, we saw that making comparisons was a natural outgrowth of observing and describing. Moving from comparing to explaining has a similar relationship. To illustrate this process, let's look again at some dialogue from Kim's lesson.

> **KIM:** Look at both the frog and the toad. How would you compare what they eat? Is there any kind of pattern there?
>
> **TIM:** They both eat insects.
>
> **LEROY:** They both eat earthworms, too.
>
> **KRISTY:** . . . The food for each seems to be almost the same.
>
> **KIM:** Why do you suppose that the food seems to be the same?

Asking students to explain why a certain similarity (or difference) exists marks the shift from Phase 1 to Phase 2. The shift is virtually automatic, and the questioning sequence remains smooth. However, the thinking on the part of the students is significantly advanced. In Phase 1, students are merely asked to make an observation or identify a similarity or difference, whereas in Phase 2 they are asked to explain why it exists—a higher level of reasoning.

The transition to Phase 2 in Tony's lesson was a bit more formal, primarily because he had his students work in pairs during Phase 1. Let's look again at some of the dialogue:

> **TONY:** Good work. . . . Now let's look a little more closely at the information. Why do you suppose that the Italians, Chinese, and Puerto Ricans tended to come from the lower socioeconomic classes, while the Cubans did not? . . . Anyone?
>
> **ANTONIO:** . . . I think it's because of why they came. . . . The Italians, Chinese, and Puerto Ricans came so they could have a better life, but the Cubans were escaping from Fidel Castro's revolution.
>
> **KEVIN:** They wanted a better life, too.
>
> **ANTONIO:** Well, that's true, but the reasons were different. The others wanted to make a better living, and in Cuba it was politics mostly.

This type of analysis is what we're looking for in students. They had identified a difference between the Cubans and the other three immigrant groups, and Tony capitalized on this observation by asking them to explain that difference. Antonio offered an explanation, which resulted in additional student-student interaction. This process of developing understanding is consistent with constructivist descriptions of learning. Like Phase 1, the process continues until the opportunities for forming explanations have been exhausted.

Not every comparison is automatically "explainable," however. Let's examine this issue.

Explainable Comparisons. While Phases 1 and 2 are closely related and the move from one to the other should be smooth and comfortable, teacher judgment is required to manage the transition effectively. For example, consider again the topic dealing with frogs and toads. Suppose the teacher asks a question in Phase 1, "Look at the frog and toad in the left column. How would you compare them?"

A student might then respond, "The toad has rough skin with bumps on it while the frog's skin is smooth." This type of comparison is essentially "unexplainable." The difference is characteristic of their physiology, and no data exist on the chart, nor in all probability in students' background knowledge, that could be used to help form the explanation. Asking students to explain "why" the toad's skin is bumpy and the frog's skin smooth is like asking, "Why does gravity make objects fall to the earth?" It is one of the characteristics of gravity that we merely describe; it doesn't have a readily available explanation.

As a contrasting example, Tony's students noted in their comparisons that the Chinese seemed to assimilate less rapidly that did the other immigrant groups. This is an eminently "explainable" comparison. The students explained the slower assimilation for the Chinese by suggesting that differences in culture was a cause, and they could find information in the matrix to support the explanation.

The teacher's task in guiding students' analysis is to recognize comparisons that can be appropriately explained and ask students to provide the explanation, while at the same time leaving "unexplainable" ones as simple comparisons.

Like other aspects of the Integrative Model, recognizing explainable comparisons is not difficult and only requires a little getting used to. The exercises at the end of the chapter offer some practice with this process.

Promoting Critical Thinking: Documenting Assertions. In Chapter 2, we said that critical thinking involves making and assessing conclusions *based on evidence*. Phase 2 of the Integrative Model provides an excellent opportunity for students to practice this ability. To illustrate, let's look again at some dialogue from Kim's lesson.

> **KIM:** Why do you suppose that the food seems to be the same? . . . Fernando? [a question in phase 2]
>
> **FERNANDO:** . . . The frog and toad live in about the same places.
>
> **KIM:** How did you decide that?
>
> **FERNANDO:** . . . It says on the chart that frogs live on land, in the water, and in trees, and it says for toad that they live on land and in the water.
>
> **KIM:** Yes, excellent, Fernando. . . . Remember how we have talked about justifying our thinking in some of our work in math. This is exactly the same thing. Fernando provided evidence for his conclusion that their environments are about the same by pointing out where they live on the chart. This is the kind of thinking we're after.

Kim's question, "How did you decide that?" asked Fernando for evidence when he concluded that the animals' environments were about the same. Teachers can ask students for evidence when they ask questions such as:

"How do you know?"
"Why do you say that?"
"What evidence do we have for that conclusion?"

The exact wording of the question isn't important as long as it asks students to provide evidence for their conclusions.

While asking students for evidence is rare in classrooms (Boyer, 1983), it is not difficult once teachers get used to it. Students quickly warm to the task and begin to provide evidence without being prompted by their teachers. To illustrate, let us look again at Tony's lesson.

> TONY: Let's look again at some of the comparisons we've made. We wrote that the Chinese assimilated less rapidly than did the other groups. Why do you suppose that was the case?
>
> CHRISTINE: They were more different culturally than the others were.
>
> TONY: What information do we have on our chart that tells us they were more different culturally?
>
> CHRISTINE: . . . Their religion, for one thing. The Italians, Puerto Ricans, and Cubans were mostly Catholic, which a lot of people in the United States are, but the Chinese were Confus . . . Confushist . . . whatever that religion is.
>
> ESTELLA: Also, it says in the chart that the Chinese learned English slower than the others.

Here we see that Estella, without prompting from Tony, referred to the matrix for additional information offered as evidence in support of the cultural-differences contention.

Once students get used to providing evidence, teachers can capitalize on these opportunities to promote sophisticated critical-thinking discussions, such as examining the quality of evidence. For instance, Tony could ask the class to examine Estella's comment with questions such as:

- Is learning English less quickly really evidence for cultural differences?
- Why is it, or why is it not, "good" evidence?
- What would be better evidence of cultural differences?

When questions such as these are discussed and analyzed, students obtain valuable critical thinking experience.

Phase 3: Hypothesize Outcomes for Different Conditions

Phase 3 marks another advance in students' abilities to analyze information, and it evolves directly from Phase 2. Let us look again at Tony's lesson.

> ESTELLA: . . . it says in the chart that the Chinese learned English slower than the others. [evidence for a response in Phase 1]
>
> TONY: And why might that have been? [a question marking the transition to Phase 2]
>
> ESTELLA: Their language is different. There are letters for each of the languages in the chart, and the Italians, Puerto Ricans, and Cubans use the same letters as

English, but the Chinese letters are really different. [an explanation—a response in phase 2]

TONY: Suppose they weren't different, meaning they used the same letters as we do. How do you suppose that would have affected how fast they assimilated?

Tony's last question called for a hypothesis on the part of the students. His question asked students to consider the outcome if conditions were changed—a hypothetical situation in which Chinese used the same letters as do the Italians, Puerto Ricans, and Cubans.

Though the dialogue we just read illustrates how Phase 3 can naturally evolve from Phase 2, this isn't a requirement. To illustrate, let's look again at Kim's lesson.

KIM: Look again at the toad and frog in the first column of the chart. In what ways are they different? [a question in phase 1]

FRED: It says the toad is clumsy, but it doesn't say anything about the frog. [a response in phase 1]

KIM: Suppose the toad wasn't clumsy. . . . How might that affect the food toads eat or where they live? . . . Anyone?"

Here Kim asked a question calling for a hypothesis (Phase 3) that followed directly from a comparison (Phase 1). The fact that Kim didn't ask the students to explain "why" the toad is clumsy, which would have been a question in Phase 2, is a matter of teacher judgment. It is part of the decision-making process that makes teaching an art. She might have felt that the toad's clumsiness was an "unexplainable" comparison, or she might have had another reason for choosing not to ask for an explanation.

As with Phases 1 and 2, the process of hypothesizing continues until opportunities for analysis have been exhausted.

Phase 4: Generalize to Form Broad Relationships

The lesson is summarized and comes to closure when students derive one or more generalizations that summarize the content. To illustrate this process, let us look again at Kim's lesson.

KIM: Now let's summarize what we've found here, and let's think about animals in general. . . . I want you to try and extend beyond the toad and frog, and I'll help you if you need it. . . . For instance, what can we say about the characteristics of animals that look a lot alike?

ADELLA: . . . They have mostly the same characteristics.

KIM: So how should we write that? Help me out. . . . I'll get us started. [She writes, "Animals that look alike . . ." on the chalkboard.]

LADONNA: . . . Will have similar characteristics.

KIM: Okay. . . . What else? [after writing, "Animals that look alike have similar characteristics," on the chalkboard]

> TONY: They also eat the same kind of food.
>
> KIM: Good. So . . . tell me what to write. . . . Animals that look alike . . .
>
> NANCY: And have the same characteristics.
>
> TONYA: And have the same characteristics eat the same kind of food.

Kim wrote the statement on the board, asked the students for additional summarizing statements, which resulted in the following list:

- Animals that look alike have similar characteristics.
- Animals that look alike and have similar characteristics eat the same kind of food.
- Animals that are similar live in similar habitats.

Then Kim asked students for some additional examples such as deer and elk, different birds, and predators, such as lions and leopards, plus some exceptions to the patterns, and then she closed the lesson.

We can see from this dialogue that students are not automatically good at making summarizing statements, and the teacher may initially have to do a considerable amount of prompting, as Kim did in her lesson. With practice, however, students' ability to summarize quickly develops.

In comparison, Tony's students were older than Kim's and they had more experience with summarizing information, so Tony didn't have to prompt and guide his students as much as Kim did in summarizing the lesson.

Increasing Learner Motivation with the Integrative Model

In Chapters 3 and 4, we described how the Social Interaction Models and the Inductive Model can be used to increase learner motivation. In Chapter 3 we saw how the Social Interaction Models utilize the motivational benefits of students working together, because "students are social beings motivated by the desire to interact with their peers." This was documented with research which found that tasks, even boring ones, are more motivating when they're done in groups (Pintrich & Schunk, 1996).

The Inductive Model, as a tool for increasing learner motivation, profits from the effects of involvement in increasing student interest, and the emphasis the Inductive Model places on thinking and deep understanding of content can increase learner self-efficacy.

Since the Integrative Model is very similar to the Inductive Model—the primary difference being the content it is designed to teach—it can be used to capitalize on each of these benefits.

First, as we saw in Tony's lesson, the Integrative Model is very compatible with the Social Interaction Models. For instance, Tony had students work in pairs to gather the information that was put in the matrix. Then he said to the students, "Now I want you to work with your partner and find as many patterns as you have evidence for in each of the columns. I want you to work as follows. . . . First you write your own response . . . find your own patterns and write them down. . . . Then share them with your partner. . . . Discuss them with each other and be ready to share them with the class. You have 10 minutes." This was an application of "think-pair-share."

Second, like the Inductive Model, the Integrative Model begins in an open-ended way, which helps promote high levels of involvement, and third, the emphasis on thinking and understanding that exists with the Integrative model makes it effective for increasing learner self-efficacy. The model's flexibility in promoting involvement, both with open-endedness and its compatibility with the social interaction models, together with its potential for increasing self-efficacy makes it a powerful tool for promoting learner motivation.

Modifications of the Integrative Model

Using the Integrative Model with Young Children

Modifying the Integrative Model for use with young children primarily relates to the way information is presented. Tony's matrix—in a lesson designed for eighth graders—had the information presented in words. Kim used both words and pictures in her lesson with fourth graders. A primary teacher, or a teacher whose students lack language skills might choose to present the information exclusively in pictures. As an example, consider the information in Figure 6.5 (pp. 210–211).

Let us examine some dialogue based on analysis of the information in the matrix.

T: How are the foods we eat in the summer different from the foods we eat in the winter? [Phase 1]

S: Foods with ice in summer.

S: Hot drinks in winter.

T: Why do you think we have hot drinks in the winter? [Phase 2]

S: It's cold outside.

T: How do we know it's cold outside?

S: [No response]

T: Do you see anything on the chart that tells us that its cold outside in the winter?

S: They're wearing coats. [pointing to the chart]

T: What else?

S: No leaves on the trees.

T: Suppose we lived in the south, where it's warm all year around. How might the foods we eat in winter be different from what we see on the chart? [a question in Phase 3]

S: Our drinks might not be as hot.

T: What have we learned here about our foods? [a question asking for a summary]

S: We eat different foods.

T: How are they different?

S: We eat warm foods when it's cold outside.

T: And why do we do that?

S: Hot foods help keep us warm.

Special things to do and clothing are analyzed and summarized in the same way. As students develop their skills with the process, the teacher is able to move away from traditional teacher-student-teacher-student interaction and toward a more teacher-student-student-student discussion, which we illustrated at different points in Kim's and Tony's lessons.

In some cases, teachers may choose to develop a matrix together with actual objects or people. For example, a teacher wanting to develop a lesson on community helpers could ask an actual fire fighter and a member of the police to come into the class as guests. After these guests visit the classroom, the teacher and students could list information they had learned, which could be used as the basis for the analysis.

Children's Language Abilities.   A developmental second factor relates to students' ability to analyze information and articulate their conclusions (Kuhn, 1999). With young children, Phase 1 may initially be emphasized more strongly than the other phases, since it focuses on observation and comparison. However, as they acquire experience, even young children learn to form explanations and respond to hypothetical questions. Much of the value in using the model is the opportunity it provides for children to practice their developing language and thinking abilities.

Increasing Efficiency: Reducing Preparation Time

Anyone familiar with classrooms knows that teaching is enormously complex and demanding. Teachers spend a great deal of afterschool time correcting papers, planning, and talking to parents. Anything that can be done to help them reduce the time they spend planning new lessons—and still meet their goals—is beneficial. Let us look at some modifications that can reduce planning time, yet still help students acquire deep understanding of content and develop critical thinking abilities.

Using Existing Materials.   To this point in our discussion, we have focused on data displayed in matrixes. The planning process can be simplified further by using tables, charts, graphs, and maps in textbooks and other already-existing sources of information that provide opportunities for analysis. All you have to do is capitalize on these representations and use them to simultaneously promote thinking and understanding.

To do so, you must be able to recognize existing materials that can be used to help you reach your goals. Virtually any chart, graph, or map that contains raw data can be used for analysis with the Integrative Model. Let us look at some examples.

Table 6.4 contains information in a chart taken from a typical chemistry book. A chart such as this is found in the text, and the teacher would need do nothing more than

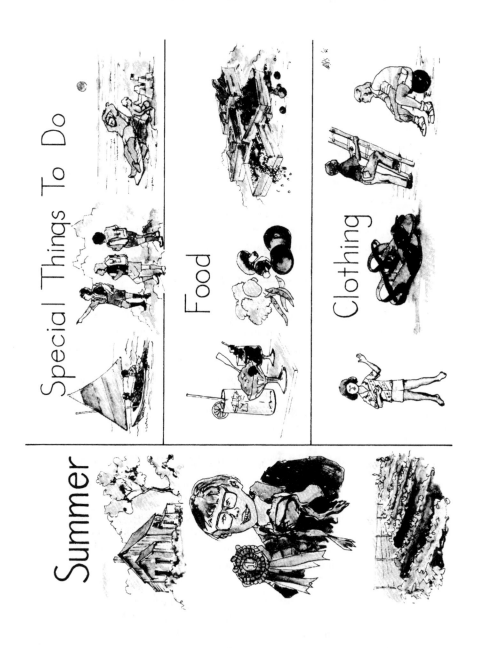

Summer

Special Things To Do

Food

Clothing

FIGURE 6.5 Matrix Containing Information about Winter and Summer

TABLE 6.4   Table of Ionic Radii Taken from a Chemistry Book

Ionic Radii*

IA	IIA	IIIA	VIA	VIIA
Li+	Be^{2}+		O^{2}–	F–
0.60	0.31		1.40	1.36
NA+	Mg^{2}+	Al^{3}+	S^{2}–	Cl–
0.95	0.65	0.50	1.84	1.81
K+	Ca^{2}+	Ga^{3}+	Se^{2}–	Br–
1.33	0.99	0.62	1.98	1.95
Rb+	Sr^{2}+	In^{3}+	Te^{2}–	I–
1.48	1.13	0.81	2.21	2.16
Cs+	Ba^{2}+	Tl^{3}+		
1.69	1.35	0.95		

*Radii given in angstrom units.

direct students to the page on which it occurs, or scan the chart into a computer file, make an overhead, and display it.

Then the teacher could guide the students' analysis based on the chart. For example:

Phase 1

T: What kind of pattern do you see in the Group IA ions?

S: They get bigger as we move down the column.

A: They all have a valence of plus 1.

T: How about the other groups?

S: They all get bigger as they move down the columns.

T: How would you compare the radii in each column to each other?

S: They get smaller for the positive ions and then get bigger for the negative ions.

T: What do you mean?

S: Magnesium (Mg) is smaller than sodium (Na), and aluminum is smaller yet, but sulfur and chlorine are bigger.

Phase 2

T: Why do you suppose magnesium is smaller than sodium?

S: Magnesium loses two electrons, so its ionic radius will decrease more than sodium's, which loses only one electron.

T: Then why isn't the ionic radius for chlorine bigger than the radius for sulfur?

S: Chlorine only adds one electron, so its ionic radius won't increase as much as sulfur's will.

Phase 3

T: Suppose somehow that sulfur was involved in a reaction in which it actually lost electrons rather than gained them. How would its ionic radius be affected?

S: Its ionic radius would maybe be smaller than aluminum's rather than larger.

T: Can we be sure?

S: No; it may not follow that pattern. We would need more information to be sure.

Phase 4

T: What kinds of generalizations can we make about ionic radii?

S: As elements lose electrons, their ionic radii get smaller and the more electrons they lose, the smaller they get.

S: Ionic radii with positive charges tend to be smaller than those with negative charges in comparable rows.

We have abbreviated the interaction for the sake of clarity; it wouldn't go as smoothly as it appears in the illustration, and teachers would probably have to prompt students to recognize some of the patterns. However, since most of the information needed to make the conclusions is available in the chart, students only need some guidance to get them started.

We also see from the dialogue that the chart—which already exists in the text—can be used for a great deal of critical thinking. In fact, a number of patterns, explanations, hypotheses, and generalizations could be added to those in the illustration. In this case, using the Integrative Model requires *no additional preparation*. The teacher only needs to recognize opportunities to capitalize on already existing data.

As another example, consider the maps in Figures 6.6a and 6.6b.

Again, let's look at some sample interaction based on the maps.

Phase 1:

T: Look at the northern parts of the two maps. How do they compare?

S: The northern part of the first one is mostly desert.

T: And the second one?

S: Very little rain, 2 inches a year.

T: How about other parts of the map?

S: There is tropical rainforest around the area near the equator, and there is a lot of rain in that area.

Phase 2:

T: Why is much of the northern part of the continent desert?

S: It gets very little rain.

T: Why do you think the rainfall is so sparse?

S: Maybe it has to do with the direction of the wind. The prevailing winds come from huge land areas, so they don't have much rain in them.

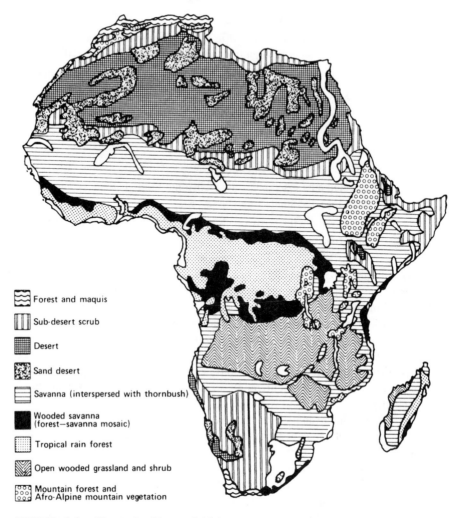

Forest and maquis

Sub-desert scrub

Desert

Sand desert

Savanna (interspersed with thornbush)

Wooded savanna
(forest—savanna mosaic)

Tropical rain forest

Open wooded grassland and shrub

Mountain forest and
Afro-Alpine mountain vegetation

FIGURE 6.6a   Vegetation Zones of Africa

T: What else might impact the amount of rain a region gets? What do you see on
the map?

S: Maybe the direction of the ocean currents has something to do with it.

Phase 3:

T: Suppose the winds over northern Africa came primarily from the west. How
would the climate of that part of the continent be affected?

S: Maybe it wouldn't be a desert.

T: Can you look at any part of the map for some evidence that supports that idea?

S: We see that the winds are from the west over the central portion of the continent.

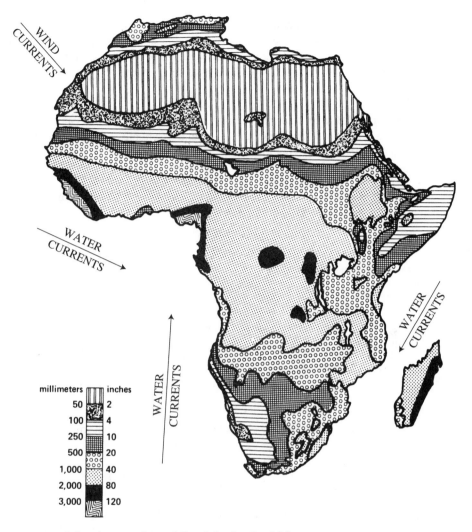

FIGURE 6.6b   Average Annual Precipitation for Africa

Phase 4:

T: What kinds of summary statements can we make based on the map?

S: The ocean currents and wind direction have an important impact on the amount of rain a region gets.

This dialogue only gives us a sample of the possibilities. Much more analysis of the maps could have occurred and the process could have been significantly expanded by adding a map showing physiographic regions on the continent. The students could then consider altitude, latitude, wind direction, and ocean currents as factors impacting climate.

This could all be done with little teacher preparation; teachers need only to be clear about their goals and seize on opportunities like these. As they get used to the process, they will recognize more and more opportunities for using the charts, maps, and other instructional aids in their textbooks as a basis for promoting a great deal of analysis by the students.

Developing Matrices During Class Discussions.   Teachers can also use information gathered in class discussions to capture data essentially on the spot, which can then be used to further analyze the topic being studied. Let us look at an English class that is discussing *Romeo and Juliet*.

> T: Let's think about some of the things we've found from the play. Let's just list anything you can think of based on your reading.
>
> S: The Montagues and Capulets were feuding.
>
> S: Escalus, the Prince, threatened the Montagues and Capulets with death if they didn't stop feuding.
>
> S: Some of the people seemed to be sort of hung up on sex.
>
> T: Why do you say that? Can you give us an example?
>
> S: Sampson and Gregory were always fantasizing about women.
>
> S: And the nurse and Mercutio seemed to be focused on sex.
>
> T: Okay, what else?
>
> S: Tybalt killed Mercutio, and then Romeo killed Tybalt.
>
> S: Romeo and Juliet killed themselves.
>
> T: Let's focus on the characters a little more. What kind of a young man was Romeo?
>
> S: Well, he was actually a kid.
>
> S: He was sort of innocent and naive.

As students made their comments, the teacher listed them on pieces of chart paper, which she rolled up and stored after the discussion. She also prompted them for additional information, such as the question, "What kind of a young man was Romeo?" and she added some information of her own about the themes of the play. She then stored the chart paper, telling the students that they would return to the information after they had read some additional plays. She then repeated the process with *Hamlet* and *Julius Caesar*.

After the students had read and reported on all three plays, the teacher displayed all the information and began a more extensive analysis of the plays by comparing them to each other. The information appears in Table 6.5.

In this case, the teacher used the information students gathered from their reading as the matrix, making her preparation time minimal.

This type of analysis does not have to be the focus of an entire lesson. For example, the illustration with the chemistry chart could be embedded within an overall topic of atomic structure, and the entire sequence may take only a few minutes. The same could be the case with maps.

TABLE 6.5   Matrix Comparing Shakespearean Tragedies

Plot	Key Characters	Themes
ROMEO & JULIET		
Montagues and Capulets feud	Romeo:	Symbolism of "star-crossed lovers"
Escalus, the Prince, threatens	romantic	Love amidst hate
Montagues and Capulets with death	love struck	Innocence amid mature bawdry
Sampson and Gregory fantasize	guileless	Conflicted loyalty to self and family
about women	young	
The nurse and Mercutio	unthinking	
focus on sex	innocent	
Romeo and Juliet fall in love	Juliet:	
Tybalt kills Mercutio	romantic	
Romeo kills Tybalt	love struck	
Juliet takes a potion	guileless	
Romeo kills himself	young	
Juliet kills herself	innocent	
Montagues and Capulets end feud		
HAMLET		
King Hamlet dies	Hamlet:	Ingenuousness and deceit
Claudius marries Gertrude	sentimental dreamer	Moral ambiguity
Hamlet regrets and resents Claudius's	witty	The search for natural justice
and Gertrude's marriage	sensitive	Loyalty and revenge
Hamlet seeks revenge on Claudius	loyal	Private and public conflict
Hamlet mistreats Ophelia	weak	Internal conflict
Laertes wounds Hamlet in a duel	intelligent	Courage and cowardliness
Hamlet wounds Laertes in a duel	romantic	Purging of evil
Hamlet kills Claudius	indecisive	Restoration of morality
Gertrude dies of poison meant	ambitious	
for Hamlet	Claudius:	
Laertes dies	strong	
Hamlet dies	hypocritical	
	skillfully political	
	deceitful	
	adroit	
JULIUS CAESAR		
Caesar defeats Pompey	Caesar:	Power
Caesar becomes a dictator	great soldier	Ambition
Caesar pardons Brutus	great politician	Jealousy
Caesar pardons Cassius	brilliant scholar	Revenge
Romans fear Caesar's growing	arrogant	Idealism
power and ambition	ambitious	
Conspiracy against Caesar develops	Brutus:	
Cassius influences Brutus	quiet	
Brutus feels he must stop Caesar	idealistic	
Brutus kills Caesar	Caesar's friend	
Antony incites citizens	feared Caesar's ambition	
Rome is in chaos	Cassius:	
The armies of Brutus and Cassius engage	thin	
and armies of Antony and Octavius	quick-tempered	
Cassius is stabbed by his servant and dies	practical	
Brutus falls on sword and dies	grudge against Caesar	

As we can see, charts, maps, and even graphs can be very effectively used as the basis for lessons using the Integrative Model, and the Integrative Model is applicable in many grade levels and content areas. We hope this discussion has increased your awareness of the possibilities.

Making the Integrative Model More Learner Centered

To this point, the descriptions of the Integrative Model have focused on teacher-led activities. The teacher has directed the discussions, and the processing has been teacher directed.

As students gain experience, however, teachers can make the lesson more student centered. For instance, instead of first asking students to look for patterns in the information (Phase 1) followed by questions that call for explanations (Phase 2), the teacher could begin the process by having students work in teams and ask each team to generate a series of questions they would like answered based on the information in the chart. Through this process, students are learning to ask their own questions about the data rather than have the teacher ask them.

As students learn to ask questions, they get valuable practice in the process of inquiry. One of the weaknesses in activities that are teacher directed is that students don't learn to generate their own questions.

With respect to development, this is quite advanced; initially students won't know what to look for or what questions to ask. However, as they acquire experience—seeing the teacher model questions in Phase 2—and as they practice, they will learn to look for differences in parts of the matrix, chart, map, or graph and ask why those differences exist. This marks a leap forward in students' thinking abilities and self-directed learning abilities.

Assessing Integrative Model Activities

Of the models discussed so far, the content and thinking outcomes for the Integrative Model are the most complex. As a result, a variety of options exists in preparing items to measure student growth. Keep in mind as you read this section that the information is intended to be illustrative rather than exhaustive. Our goal in presenting these examples is to stimulate your own thinking about assessment.

Measuring Content Outcomes

Earlier in the chapter we saw that the Integrative Model, rather than teaching a single concept or generalization, is designed to teach organized bodies of knowledge, which focuses on relationships among facts, concepts, and generalizations. In the assessment phase, teachers attempt to measure students' understanding of those relationships.

To illustrate this process let's look at some sample paper-and-pencil items. For example, consider how Kim Soo might measure her students' understanding of the generalizations they derived in her lesson. Look at the following item.

Think about the conclusion made about the frog and the toad and their habits. Based on that conclusion, which of the following pairs of animals would likely have the most similar habits?

    a. A deer and a bear
    b. A deer and an elk
    c. A deer and a rabbit
    d. A rabbit and a bear

This item is designed to measure students' ability to apply the generalization, "Animals with similar characteristics have similar habits," to animals other than toads and frogs.

    The item has the potential weakness, however, of measuring students' knowledge of the animals, rather than their understanding of the generalization. For example, if students do not know what an elk is or where it lives, the item would be invalid. To eliminate this possibility the teacher might prepare an item such as the following:

Look at each of the following descriptions of animals. Then based on the descriptions, decide which two will have the most similar habits.

The lemu is a swift-running, four-legged animal. He stands about four feet high and weighs over 200 pounds. He has long legs, hooves, and big horns on his head. The lemu has fairly sharp teeth in the front of his mouth and large, flat ones in the back.

The habax is a muscular, four-legged animal. She has a bulky, strong body covered with thick fur. Her teeth are sharp and two of them are a bit longer than the others. The habax is about three feet high and weighs about 280 pounds.

The crandle is a short animal with a long tail. He has four short legs that are attached to the sides of his body. The crandle can move swiftly for a short distance. He can see in almost all directions with his eyes on the top of his head. His teeth are sharp and stick out a little bit even when his mouth is closed.

The viben is a beautiful animal. She stands tall and gracefully on her four slim legs. Her small hooves allow her to move swiftly if necessary. She is about five feet tall at the shoulder and weighs over 300 pounds. She is covered with short, light brown hair all over her body.

In this item the characteristics of the animals are described and students would make their interpretation on the basis of these descriptions. The need for prior knowledge of a particular animal is reduced. Notice also that any reference to food or where the animal lives is avoided in the description. If they were included, the validity of the measurement would be reduced, since the item is designed to determine students' understanding of the relationship between characteristics and habits, such as where they live and what they eat.

    An additional value in using the second item would be the potential it has for further discussion. Based on the descriptions, students could infer the habitat of each animal, the type of food they would eat, and other habits, such as how they would protect themselves. In this way, a content measure has the potential for further developing critical thinking.

Measuring Critical Thinking

Students' thinking can be measured at several levels. In the first, students can be referred to the chart used in the lesson and asked to form conclusions not developed in class. For instance, referring again to Kim's lesson, consider the following item.

> Look again at the chart involving frogs and toads. Based on the chart, which of the following would be the best conclusion?
>
>   **a.** You would be more likely to be harmed by a frog than by a toad because a frog is poisonous and a toad is not.
>   **b.** A frog would be more likely to survive in a strange place because his habitat is more varied than that of a toad.
>   **c.** A toad would win a race with a frog because he can run faster.
>   **d.** Toads get bigger than frogs because the food they eat is different.

In this item, each of the choices except (b) is directly contradicted by information in the chart. An item such as this would be an effective beginning point for helping students learn to critically assess information.

The process can also be advanced by changing the level of sophistication. For example, consider the following item.

> Look again at the information in the chart. Based on this information, which is the best conclusion?
>
>   **a.** A frog is more adaptable than is a toad.
>   **b.** A toad's diet is more varied than that of a frog.
>   **c.** A toad would probably win a race with a frog.
>   **d.** You would be in more danger holding a frog than you would be holding a toad.

In this item, the data in the chart support choice (a) more than any of the other choices, but more interpretation is required by students than with the previous item.

As we saw from the illustrations, the first level of measuring critical thinking involves asking students to extend their thinking using familiar data, as was the case with the frogs and the toads. At succeeding levels, the teacher could prepare items similar to the illustrations presented in this section, but students would have less experience with the content. In these cases, students would be presented with a chart not covered in a lesson and would then be asked to form or identify conclusions based on the information.

Consider the immigrants chart used previously as an illustration. The following are sample items designed to measure critical thinking abilities.

> Look again at the chart. Of the following, the conclusion most supported by the data in the chart is:

    a. The Chinese came primarily because of adventure while the Puerto Ricans came because of undesirable conditions at home.

    b. While the Chinese and Italians came because of agricultural problems at home, the Puerto Ricans came primarily because of population pressures.

    c. All three groups came partially because America seemed to offer more opportunities than their homelands.

    d. All three groups came because of industrial problems in their homelands.

As a final example, consider an item designed to measure students' ability to identify irrelevant information, again in a multiple-choice format.

Look at the chart. Based on the information in it, which of the following is least relevant to the issue of assimilation?

    a. The Italians were Catholics while the Chinese were Confucians.

    b. The Italians learned English more quickly than did the Chinese.

    c. The Chinese were found mostly in the western United States.

    d. The second generation of Italians tended to intermarry with other Americans.

Each sample item so far has been written in a multiple-choice format. Short essay formats can also be used equally or even more effectively. For instance, consider the following item designed to measure students' ability to assess hypotheses.

Let's think about some immigrant groups. Consider immigrants to the United States coming from Pakistan, Greece, and Kenya. Based on the information in the chart, which of the three would be likely to assimilate most rapidly, and which would be likely to assimilate least rapidly? Defend your answer based on the information in the chart and your understanding of the immigrant groups.

This item measures several outcomes:

- The students' knowledge of the immigrant groups and their cultures
- Their ability to apply generalizations about assimilation to new immigrant groups
- Their ability to make and defend an argument with evidence
- Their ability to communicate clearly

All of these are appropriate outcomes if the teacher has helped students develop these skills and abilities and the assessment is consistent with the teacher's goals.

Measuring critical thinking requires careful planning and judgment by the teacher. For instance, if items are based on a chart used in the lesson and the information related to the item has been discussed, it then measures knowledge and not thinking. This is appropriate if the teacher's goal is to measure knowledge. It is important that the teacher is clear about what he or she is trying to accomplish and consciously moves toward that goal.

A solution to the inseparability of content and critical thinking is to develop items based on content not covered in the lesson. This also requires caution to be sure that all the information needed to form the conclusions is included in the chart and that students understand the chart's content. Otherwise, the item measures students' knowledge of the content or their reading comprehension.

We do not want to suggest, however, that measuring thinking is impossible. With care and practice, you will develop the ability to write items that will not only measure student understanding and thinking but will also serve as a means to promote further student thinking.

Summary

The Integrative Model: An Overview

The Integrative Model, like the other models in this text, is grounded on cognitive views of learning, which assume that learners are active in constructing their own understanding of the topics they study.

When the model is used, teachers guide learners' developing understanding in a safe and supportive classroom environment.

Goals for the Integrative Model

The Integrative Model is designed to teach organized bodies of knowledge, which are combinations of facts, concepts, generalizations, and the relationships among them.

While developing understanding of organized bodies of knowledge, learners involved in Integrative Model lessons practice critical thinking, specifically finding patterns, generalizing, forming conclusions and hypotheses, and justifying their thinking in each case.

Planning Lessons with the Integrative Model

Planning for lessons using the Integrative Model includes identifying clear goals and then preparing displays of data to help learners reach the goals. The data displays are commonly matrices but can include graphs, maps, and charts in pictorial form.

Implementing Lessons Using the Integrative Model

Integrative Model lessons involve four phases. In the first phase, learners observe, compare, and search for patterns. In the second, they offer explanations for the similarities and differences they find. They consider hypothetical possibilities in the third phase, and they form broad generalizations in the final phase. As often as possible, they are asked to justify their thinking by offering data taken from the display of data to defend their conclusions.

Modifications of the Integrative Model

The Integrative Model can be made more effective with young children by designing data displays in pictorial form. Organizing information in this way also increases its effectiveness with students lacking experience with the topic or nonnative English speakers.

Charts, graphs, and maps from textbooks also serve as readymade data displays that can be used for analysis using the Integrative Model.

Assessing Integrative Model Activities

Learners' understanding of the topic and their abilities to think critically can be simultaneously measured by having them make and assess conclusions about information from matrices they've already studied, or with unique data displays.

IMPORTANT CONCEPTS

Organized bodies of knowledge   *(pp. 190, 193)*

EXERCISES

Look at the following dialogue, which is based on the matrix containing information about Shakespeare's *Romeo and Juliet, Hamlet,* and *Julius Caesar,* which appears on p. 217 of the chapter. Classify each teacher question as Phase 1, Phase 2, Phase 3, Phase 4, or JT—a question that asks students to justify their thinking.

1. ___   **T:** Look at the "Events" for the three plays. What similarities do you see in the events?

     S: People die or are killed in each of the plays.

2. ___   **T:** What else?

     S: There are conflicts or fighting in each.

3. ___   **T:** For instance?

     S: For *Romeo and Juliet* it says that the Montagues and Capulets were feuding, and it says that Hamlet was seeking revenge on Claudius, and in *Julius Caesar* it says that the armies of Brutus and Cassius fought with the armies of Antony and Octavius.

4. ___   **T:** We know that each of the three plays are tragedies. Suppose one or more of them were comedies instead. Do you think the patterns in the events would be different, and if so, how?

     S: I wouldn't expect to see so much conflict and death.

5. ___   **T:** What makes you say that?

     S: Conflict and death aren't all that happy, so they don't fit with comedies.

6. ___   **T:** Let's look at the second column. What similarities or differences do you see there?

S: The characters in *Hamlet* and *Julius Caesar* appear to be less likable than the characters in *Romeo and Juliet.*

7. ___   **T:** What makes you say that?

S: It says for both Romeo and Juliet that they are innocent and guileless, but in *Hamlet* it says that Claudius is deceitful and hypocritical and in *Julius Caesar* it says that Caesar is arrogant and that Cassius is quick tempered.

8. ___   **T:** Look at the themes for *Julius Caesar.* We see ambition, jealousy, and revenge as themes, which appear somewhat negative, but we also see idealism. Why do you suppose idealism appears as a theme?

S: Brutus was idealistic. He did what he did because he thought it was in the best interests of Rome and the people.

9. ___   **T:** Let's describe some general patterns in Shakespeare's tragedies if we can.

S: The themes are complex and they vary a lot.

10. __   **T:** What else?

S: The characters aren't all good or all bad; they have some characteristics of both.

S: There's a great deal of conflict between people in the plays.

S: The characters all have conflicts within themselves, too.

11. __   **T:** Can you give us an example of what you mean?

S: Hamlet is described as sentimental and sensitive, and at the same time he's ambitious.

S: Brutus is caught between his feeling of loyalty to Caesar and his fear of Caesar's ambition.

Look again at the matrix containing the information about the solar system on pages 200–201.

12. Write a minimum of two questions in each of the four phases and provide what would be an acceptable answer to the questions.

DISCUSSION QUESTIONS

1. We said that the Inductive Model is designed to teach concepts, generalizations, principles, and academic rules, and the Integrative Model is designed to teach organized bodies of knowledge. Prepare a list of topics that you have taught or you have seen taught in schools, and identify which of the two models is more appropriate for each of the topics. Are there topics that are inappropriate for either model? What are the characteristics of those topics that makes them inappropriate?

2. Phase 4 in the Integrative Model is similar to closure for the Inductive and Concept Attainment Models. Explain how it is similar. In what way or ways is it different?

3. We discussed prompting and repetition as questioning skills used with the Inductive Model. How might they be employed with the Integrative Model?

4. The Integrative Model is commonly described as an *inductive* model. What does this mean? How would the procedure for a *deductive* model be different than the procedure for an inductive model?

5. Consider using the Integrative Model in content areas such as art, music, physical education, and technology. Discuss how lessons could be designed to promote critical thinking in those areas.

6. How might data be gathered and displayed in ways other than using matrices, charts, maps, or other written materials? Provide an example in a content area of your choice.

7 Problem-Based Learning Models

In this chapter we examine **problem-based learning,** a *teaching strategy designed to teach problem-solving skills and content and develop self-directed learning.* Problem-based learning, as its name implies, uses a problem as a focal point for student investigation and inquiry (Krajcik et al., 1994). Problem-based learning is a broad family of teaching strategies that includes problem solving, inquiry, project-based teaching, case-based instruction, and anchored instruction. Common to all of these different strategies is students' active involvement in trying to solve some problem or answer some question.

When you have completed your study of this chapter, you should be able to meet the following objectives:

- Identify the characteristics of problem-based learning.
- Design problem-solving lessons that include all of its characteristics.
- Design case-based instruction lessons.
- Plan and implement inquiry lessons, including each of the elements of the inquiry process.
- Prepare assessments that validly measure learners' understanding of the problem-based process.

To introduce you to the topic of problem-based learning, let's look at three lessons based on this model.

A third-grade science class is beginning a unit on plants. As the teacher gives an overview of the unit, she holds up several packets of seeds explaining how the class would plant these to study plant growth. One student raises her hand

and asks, "Why don't seeds grow in those packets?" "Good question," replies the teacher, "That's one of the first things we're going to find out."

She divides up students into groups to investigate factors that influence seed germination. Each group is given packets of different kinds of seeds along with pots, potting soil, fertilizer, and water. Each group is responsible for designing an experiment to answer the germination question, carrying it out and reporting the results to the class.

A middle-school class has been studying area in math. One day their teacher announces that their classroom is getting new carpeting and enlists the class's assistance in figuring out how much carpet they will need. The task is made more complex by the fact that the classroom is irregularly shaped, with alcoves, nonsquare corners, and areas where linoleum is used. After the class measures the room, the teacher breaks the students into groups and asks each to devise a strategy for finding the amount of carpeting they'll need.

A high school health class has been studying how different diseases are spread. One day the teacher places the following on an overhead:

Your Mission:
Protect the Islanders from the Muscle- and Mind-Killers

The client is a health officer at a military base on a Pacific island. He knows that many of the people who have lived on the island for a long time suffer from neurological diseases. Many lose control of their muscles and become rigid and paralyzed. Others lose their memories.

What causes this? What action should he take to protect the people?

Your mission is to determine the cause of these problems and report on your findings.

Students use their computers and the internet to gather data about this problem.

How are these problem-based teaching episodes similar? What characteristics do they share, and how do these characteristics contribute to learning? What specific roles do students and teachers play in problem-based learning? We attempt to answer these questions in this chapter by analyzing three kinds of problem-based learning: problem solving, case-based instruction, and inquiry.

The Problem-Based Learning Model: An Overview

Problem-based learning strategies share the following common characteristics:

1. They all begin with a problem or question (Duffy & Cunningham, 1996; Grabinger, 1996). This problem or question serves as the focal point for student investigative efforts. In the elementary science lesson, the student's question, "Why don't seeds grow in those packets?" provided a focus for student's inquiry. The teacher in the middle-school math lesson used the carpet problem to frame her student's investigation.
2. Students assume primary responsibility for investigating problems and pursuing inquiry (Slavin et al., 1994). This responsibility is important because students in problem-based lessons literally learn by doing.
3. The teacher's role in problem-based learning is primarily facilitative (Stepien & Gallagher, 1993). As opposed to more content-oriented models, in which the teacher actively disseminates information, problem-based learning requires teachers to assist more indirectly by posing problems or questions and asking helpful but probing questions.

Goals of Problem-Based Learning

Problem-based lessons have three interrelated goals. One is to develop students' understanding and ability to investigate a question or problem systematically. By participating in structured problem-based activities, students learn how to attack similar problems in a comprehensive and systematic manner.

A second goal of problem-based learning is the development of self-directed learning. **Self-directed learning** *develops when students are aware of and take control of their learning progress.* Self directed learning is a form of metacognition, which involves knowing what we need to know, knowing what we know, knowing what we don't know, and devising strategies to bridge these gaps. Hmelo and Lin (1998) developed a model of self directed learning for problem-based learning that is shown in Figure 7.1

In this model, students first assess what they know about the problem they are facing. On the basis of this assessment, students decide what additional information they need and develop plans to address these deficiencies. As they gather new information, they use this information to solve the problem they're encountering. If the information is sufficient and their goal met, the problem is solved. If not, students, on the basis of need, reformulate new learning strategies. The teacher assists in the process by asking facilitative questions, such as:

> What do you already know?
> What additional information do you need?
> Where can you find this information?

A third, but less prominent goal for problem-based learning is content acquisition. Much of the content that students learn in problem-based lessons is implicit and incidental

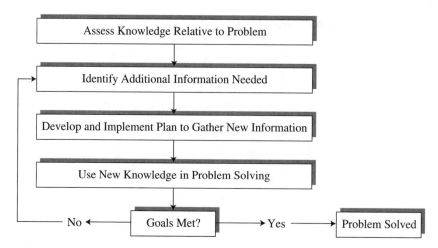

FIGURE 7.1   Model of Self-Directed Learning

in the sense that neither the teacher nor students know exactly where the investigation will proceed. Because of this, problem-based strategies are less effective for teaching content than more teacher-centered strategies such as Direct Instruction or Lecture Discussion. However, there is some evidence that information learned in this way is retained longer and transfers better (Duffy & Cunningham, 1996; Sternberg, 1998).

Theoretical and Conceptual Foundations of the Model

Problem-based learning is based upon two conceptual and theoretical foundations. One of these is the work of the educational philosopher John Dewey, who emphasized the importance of learning through experience. The second is sociocultural learning theory, a cognitive view of learning that emphasizes student participation in meaningful learning activities. Let us examine these two theories.

John Dewey.   John Dewey (1859–1952) is probably the most influential educational philosopher in America. His views about teaching and learning and the place of schools in society had a major impact on educational thinking in the early part of the twentieth century and are still influencing teaching and learning today.

Dewey basically believed that children are socially active learners who learn by exploring their environments (Dewey, 1902, 1916). Schools should take advantage of this natural curiosity by bringing the outside world into the classroom, making it available and accessible for study.

In studying the natural world, students should be active inquirers. Dewey (1916) proposed that the active inquiry should be guided by the scientific method, which has the following characteristics:

1. The learner should be involved in an authentic experience that genuinely interests him or her.

2. Within this experience, the learner should encounter a "genuine problem" that stimulates thinking.
3. In solving the problem, the learner acquires information.
4. The learner forms possible, tentative solutions that may solve the problem.
5. The learner tests these solutions by applying them to the problem. Application helps the learner validate his or her own knowledge.

Dewey believed that the knowledge students learn shouldn't be some inert information found in books or delivered in lectures. Instead, knowledge becomes useful and alive when it is applied to the solution of some problem. Dewey's work had a major influence on the progressive education movement in the United States and continues to be felt in areas such as project-based learning, thematic units, and interdisciplinary teaching.

Sociocultural Theory. **Sociocultural theory** *is a cognitive view of learning that emphasizes student participation in communities of learning.* Based upon the early works of Lev Vygotsky (1978, 1986), who was discussed in Chapter 3, sociocultural theory explains how very complex forms of learning can be facilitated through cognitive apprenticeship.

Recall from Chapter 3 that Vygotsky stressed the importance of social interaction in learning. A major way that we learn is by dealing with others, exchanging ideas and comparing our ideas with other people. More recent work in sociocultural theory emphasizes the importance of students' active participation in authentic learning tasks.

The concept of apprenticeship is central to this view of learning (Lave, 1988, 1990). Many complex learning tasks are mastered by students working alongside someone who is already good at the task. This is the way most of us learned how to drive a car, cook, or change a tire—by watching someone better than ourselves do something—and then by trying the new skill out under the direction of the expert. This is the essence of apprenticelike learning.

Sociocultural theory stresses **cognitive apprenticeship,** *in which learners learn by doing alongside an expert but also learn* why *they are performing something in a certain way.* This *why* is the cognitive aspect of cognitive apprenticeship. Through modeling, think-alouds, and questions, teachers help students not only learn how to do something, but also why to do it. Sociocultural theory also stresses the importance of participation in communities of learning. Teachers facilitate problem-based learning by making their classrooms into communities of learning where students work together toward common goals—the solution of a problem. Teacher tasks in transforming their classrooms into communities of learners include creating a positive learning environment, assigning students to productive work groups, monitoring those groups, and facilitating inquiry through questions. We discuss these roles in greater depth in the planning and implementation sections of this chapter.

The Problem-Solving Model

Laura Hunter, the middle-school math teacher we encountered earlier in the chapter, begins her problem-solving lesson by explaining that the classroom needs new carpeting and enlisting the assistance of students in finding the area of the classroom. She structures her lesson by showing the following problem-solving model to her students:

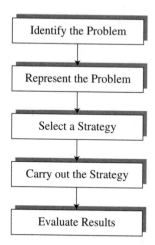

FIGURE 7.2   Problem-Solving Model

"According to our model," Laura continues, "What do we have to do first? Kara?"

"Identify the problem?" Kara answers hesitantly.

"That's right, Kara, the first thing we do is identify the problem. Do we know what our problem is? Janelle?"

"To find out how much carpet we need," Janelle replies.

"Good, Janelle, and, class, what kind of problem is this? When we try to find out how much carpet we need, what are we trying to do? Alicia?"

"Umm . . . area?"

"Excellent, Alicia, we're trying to find the area of the room. What problem did we talk about yesterday that is similar to this one? Think! Antonio?"

"Umm. . . . It's kind of like the playground problem where we had to find how many rubber tiles we needed to cover the jungle gym area."

"Does everyone remember that problem? And what were two ways that we used to solve that problem. What was one way, Shalynne?"

"We counted the squares in the box."

"Okay, first we counted the tiles in the box. Then what did we do? What was an easier way to find the area, Lynn?"

"Well, like we measured the outside, uh, the perimeter, and then we multiplied and that told us how many squares that equaled."

"Good, Lynn. We multiplied the length times the width and that gave us the area. So what do we have to do with our carpet problem? . . . Any idea? I'll give you a hint. Do we have any squares to count?" Pausing for a few moments, Laura scans the room to see if the class is with her. Then she continues.

"Not really, so what do we have to do next? Look up here." (pointing to the overhead) "It says 'Represent the problem.' How did we represent our problem yesterday? What did we have to do, Tamara?"

"We drew a picture of it on graph paper."

"Good, Tamara. Class, do you think that might work here?"

Responding to the students' nods, Laura now divides the class into groups to measure different parts of the room. As the different groups complete their task, they report back to Laura, who records the information for the next day.

At the beginning of class the next day, Laura passes out a diagram of the room with the dimensions her students gave her. After she does this, she turns on the overhead and begins, "Class, we're still working on the carpet problem. We decided it was an area problem and we measured the room to get this diagram. What's our next step? Geno?"

"I think it's select a strategy."

"Good, Geno. I'd like us to get into our regular groups, and each group is responsible for not only selecting a strategy but also carrying out the strategy. That means use it to find the area. I'll be around to answer questions.

"Any questions? Let's do that now."

Laura's class then breaks up into groups of four and each group uses the diagram and calculations to work on the problem.

As students attempt to solve the problem, they come up with two basic strategies. One is to find the area of the whole room and subtract the linoleum and odd-shaped corners; the other is to find the area of an interior rectangle in the middle of the carpeted area and then add extra, irregularly shaped carpeted areas.

As the groups complete their tasks, Laura reconvenes the class.

"Okay, let's look back up here at our diagram," Laura directs after the class again reassembles. "In the select-your-strategies part, there were several different strategies that I saw as I was walking around. Raise your hand and tell me what one of the strategies was. . . . Yashoda?"

"We measured everything first, and then we subtracted where the linoleum was. We figured out . . . we multiplied the perimeter. And then we subtracted the places where the linoleum was."

"Okay, when you multiplied the perimeter, what did you get?"

"1440 square feet."

"Okay, that's called the . . . ?"

"Area," several students respond.

"Okay, raise your hand if your team tried that strategy," Laura directs.

Students from several groups raise their hands.

"Raise your hand if you tried a different strategy."

Several more students raise their hands.

"Matt, explain what your team did," Laura directs.

"We had a different strategy. We took the middle . . . we squared it off, like covering up this," Matt responds, pointing to the diagram, "and then we multiplied the two sides, then we got the area of the middle part of the carpet, and then we put the other pieces together. . . . We added these others."

"Okay, I'm going to put 'found inside measurements and add other areas.' Is that okay?" Laura asks.

"Uh-hunh," Matt answers.

Laura then asks each group to put their findings on the board and her class discusses differences and discrepancies between the different groups' answers.

"Well, are you guys comfortable with the fact that some groups got slightly different answers?"

Several students say, "No," while a few say, "Yes."

"If you were the person purchasing the carpet, would you be comfortable with that. . . ?" Waiting for an answer, Laura pauses.

"If you were the person *estimating,* would you be comfortable with that?" Laura continues.

Most of the class say they wouldn't be comfortable if they were the person purchasing the carpet, but offer that they would be if they were merely estimating.

"If we were going to redo this tomorrow, what could we do to be more accurate? . . . Talk to your team for 2 minutes," Laura directs.

The students talk to their teammates and offer some suggestions, such as remeasuring the room, rechecking to see if the strategy makes sense, and even asking the janitor about the dimensions of the room.

Laura then looks at the clock and asks, "So, class, what did we learn about problem solving today? Think about that one for a moment and then tell me what you think. Kareem?"

"Well, like there's different ways to solve problems."

"Good, Kareem. We found out we can solve the same problem in different ways. What else? Shannon?"

"There are certain steps to follow when we solve problems—like the ones up there," Shannon replies, pointing up at the overhead.

"Right, Shannon. These steps are important because they help us organize our thinking and solve problems in a systematic way. Anything else? Sean?"

"Problem solving is hard. It really makes you think."

"That's right, Sean." Laura replies with a smile. "That's why we do it—because it makes us think."

(Adapted from Eggen & Kauchak, 1999)

The Problem-Solving Model: An Overview

Problem solving is a problem-based teaching strategy in which teachers help students learn to solve problems through hands-on learning experiences. Like all problem-based strategies, it begins with a problem, which students are responsible for solving with the assistance of the teacher.

The Problem-Solving Model has the following six steps that we saw Laura Hunter implement in her lesson:

- Identify the problem.
- Represent the problem.
- Select a strategy.
- Carry out the strategy.
- Evaluate results.
- Analyze the process.

The first five of these steps were shared on the overhead; the sixth step occurred at the end of the lesson, when Laura encouraged her students to reflect on their problem-solving experience.

Social Structure of the Model

The Problem-Solving Model presents several challenges to teachers. They need to create safe, learning-focused classrooms where students feel both challenged and secure to take risks (Eggen & Kauchak, 1999). Challenge is important because it motivates students to engage cognitively in the difficult task of solving problems. At the same time, students need to feel safe to take risks as they wrestle with problem solutions.

In addition to these classroom climate variables, teachers also assist students in their problem-solving efforts through structured input and questioning. Laura helped students understand the processes involved in problem solving through her overhead, which she used to structure this and subsequent problem-solving efforts. Laura used questioning to actively guide students through the problem-solving stages and to help them understand the logic behind each of these steps. Let us turn now to some considerations a teacher makes in planning for problem solving.

Planning for Problem-Solving Activities

Problem-solving lessons have both short- and long-term goals. In the short term, the teacher wants students to solve the problem successfully and understand the content behind the problem solution. This relates to the content component of problem-based learning that we discussed earlier. In Laura's lesson, she wanted students to understand the concept of area and relate it to different shaped geometric figures.

Laura's long-term goals were for students to understand the process of problem solving and develop her students as self-directed learners. She helped students understand the process of problem solving by concretely relating what they were doing to the Problem-Solving Model. She helped students develop as self-directed learners by providing them with opportunities to think about what they knew and what they didn't know and by encouraging them to reflect on the process of problem solving as they proceeded.

Logistical Considerations. Laura's lesson proceeded smoothly because she had attended to several logistical concerns. The first was providing a concrete problem that served as a focal point for the lesson. Laura made the problem more motivating and meaningful by using her own classroom as a focus and allowing students to measure the room and gain firsthand experience with the dimensions. She also had prepared the overhead, which provided both focus and structure for the lesson.

A second major logistical concern was grouping. Problem solving is more effective when students have opportunities to discuss their developing ideas with other students. Laura already had a group structure in place in her classroom that she was able to use in this specific lesson. Had this small group structure not been in place, she would have had to develop these, as we discussed in Chapter 3.

Implementing Problem-Solving Lessons

Effective problem-solving lessons exist on two levels, which correspond to the major goals of this model. At one level, our goal is to teach students to solve a specific kind of problem. Teachers do this though interactive questioning, which involves students in a form of cognitive apprenticeship. At another level, we want our students to understand the process of problem solving and become better self-directed learners. Let's see how we accomplish these goals in the sections that follow.

Identify the Problem.   While this step in problem solving may seem self-evident, many students experience problems with this process (Bruning et al., 1999). This outcome results from several factors, perhaps the most important of which is that students are not provided with sufficient practice with ill-defined problems—the most common kind found in everyday problems. **Ill-defined problems** *have ambiguous goals and no agreed-upon strategy for solving them* (Mayer & Wittrock, 1996). Most teaching problems are ill defined; how to motivate a student, manage a class, or teach a particular lesson all are ambiguous both in terms of goals and strategies. In a similar way, most of the problems we encounter in real life are also ill defined. The best way to teach students how to deal with problems like these is to provide them with lots of practice, including work with defining exactly what the problem is.

Other obstacles to defining the problem include lack of domain-specific knowledge and students' tendency to rush toward a solution (Eggen & Kauchak, 1999). When students lack background knowledge for a problem, they will encounter difficulties in clearly identifying what the problem requires. For example, if Laura's students hadn't possessed some knowledge of area and perimeter, they would have experienced difficulties in knowing that carpeting a room is basically an area problem. The other problem students encounter at this stage is jumping to a solution before they have considered all the complexities of a problem. Expert problem solvers take more time at the beginning of a problem, evaluating what is given and what needs to be done (Bruning et al., 1999).

Represent the Problem.   Teaching students how to represent problems gives them a strategy that bridges the conceptual gap between defining a problem and selecting a strategy. Students are often overwhelmed at this stage of problem solving, and strategies like drawing a picture diagram and listing knowns and unknowns often help. Laura did this when she had her students measure the room and come up with a diagram. This not only provided students with firsthand experience with the problem, but also resulted in a diagram they could use later when they selected a strategy.

Selecting a Strategy.   At this stage of the Problem Solving-Model, students are assisted in choosing an appropriate strategy for the problem. One problem is the tendency for students to grab onto the first solution that arises without thinking about alternate solutions. This may give them an immediate answer but fails to place this problem in a larger context. The result is that students may get the right answer but fail to understand why, or fail to relate this problem to similar ones they will encounter.

Teachers can encourage students to be more reflective at this stage of problem solving by using several heuristic strategies. **Heuristics** *are general, widely applicable problem-solving strategies* (Mayer, 1997). Two of the most widely applicable heuristic strategies are means-end analysis and drawing analogies. When we use means-end analysis, we identify our ultimate goal and then work backwards in substeps. For example, Laura could have used this strategy by encouraging her students to identify the ultimate goal (finding the area of the carpeted part of the room) and then working backwards to the subgoals of finding the area of the whole room and the area of the noncarpeted areas.

A second heuristic strategy is drawing analogies. When we draw analogies, we ask students, "What is this problem like?" Laura did this when she compared the present problem to finding the area of the playground. By thinking of the problem in terms of squares, Laura activated students' background knowledge and provided a concrete frame of reference to think from.

Carry Out the Strategy.   If the previous steps are systematically pursued, carrying out the strategy allows students to try out or reality-test the quality of their thinking. This stage is a natural extension of the previous three and provides opportunities for students to implement and experiment with their ideas.

This stage should flow smoothly from the other three, but if it does not, teachers can provide scaffolding through supportive questioning. Sometimes students get so close to a problem they'll fail to see the logical next step. Often all it takes at this stage is for students to step away from the immediate problem, understand what they're doing and why, and then return to the data at hand. Teacher support and questions are helpful here.

Evaluating Results.   In this stage of the model, teachers encourage students to judge the validity of the solution they produced. Students often have problems with this stage because they are so ego involved, not only with the problem but with the work that they put into it. Other times students are eager to complete or wrap a problem up and get on with other things, even if a solution does not make sense. For example,

> One boy, quite a good student, was working on the problem, "If you have six jugs, and you want to put two thirds of a pint of lemonade into each jug, how much lemonade will you need?" His answer was 18 pints. I [Holt] said, "How much in each jug?" "Two thirds of a pint." I said, "Is that more or less than a pint?" "Less." I said, "How many jugs are there?" "Six." I said, "But that

doesn't make any sense." He shrugged his shoulders and said, "Well, that's the way the system worked out." (Holt, 1964, p. 18)

This case illustrates a common problem in problem solving. Getting an answer, regardless of whether or not it make sense, is all too often the students' goal. Young children in particular have trouble at this stage, wanting to rush through, get on to the next problem, and finish the assignment (Schunk, 1994). This occurred in Laura's class, where several students were satisfied with discrepant answers. Laura dealt with this problem when she encouraged her students to think about how their answers would be used and the level of precision required by these different uses.

Analyzing Problem Solving.   This final step in the Problem-Solving Model may be the most important in terms of our long-term goals in using the model. A primary reason for using this model is to help students become more systematic and analytical problem solvers and more aware of their own thinking as problem solvers. Laura attempted to do this when she asked, "What did we learn about problem solving today?" Students' responses indicated several important outcomes: (1) that any problem can have more than one solution, (2) that problem solving can be pursued systematically, and (3) that problem solving is hard work. These are valuable insights and worthy outcomes for problem-solving lessons.

This concludes our discussion of implementing problem solving. In the next section we consider a second type of problem-based learning called Case-Based Problem Solving.

Case-Based Problem Solving

April Sumner teaches remedial English to a first-period class of inner-city high schoolers. Students need to pass the class to graduate from high school, but motivation and attendance are major problems.

She likes the class and, because it's small, she knows all her students well. This closeness is rewarding, but the class is also frustrating: The students refuse to bring any materials to class. *Refuse* isn't exactly the right word. On students' lists of important things to do in the morning, finding a pencil and notebook paper does not rank high. Daily reminders don't seem to help, nor do threats of failure, because many students are repeating the class for the second or third time.

April talks with other teachers. Some say, "Let them sit"; others respond, "Lend them your own," but warn of logistical nightmares and economic disaster when the pencils disappear and she runs out of paper.

April has been hired to teach English, but first she has to solve the materials problem. What would you do? (Eggen & Kauchak, 1999, pp. 10–11)

The above is an example of a case used in an educational psychology course. **Cases** or **case studies** are *a specific kind of problem-based learning that present students with a segment or sample of a professional problem or dilemma* (Duffy & Cunningham, 1996). Cases have been used as problem-based teaching aides in a number of professional disciplines ranging from medicine to business to teacher education. When used in medicine, cases present students with a realistic medical problem (a patient) that students work on in teams to diagnose and cure. In business, cases provide students with data about a particular company and its problems, and they are asked to suggest solutions to these problems. In law, students are given sample legal cases and asked to identify issues and precedents and either rule on the issue or defend a client. In education, students analyze narratives describing teachers in real-life situations. In solving these cases, teachers are encouraged to apply knowledge from personal experiences, theory, and research to make informed decisions about teaching. In doing so, teachers learn to think like professionals, practicing problem-solving behaviors that are applicable to everyday life in schools" (Kilbane & Herbert, 1998, p. 2). In each of these areas, cases have been used to:

1. Increase student involvement and motivation.
2. Help students develop problem solving and cooperative learning skills.
3. Provide concrete examples of abstract ideas embedded in realistic classroom settings (Merseth & Lacey, 1993).

The increasing popularity of case-based pedagogy can be linked to developments in cognitive psychology, which documents the importance of student involvement in problem-solving tasks that are embedded in realistic contexts (Bruning et al., 1999). Cases are one way of presenting realistic, contextualized problems (Harrington, 1996; Mostert, 1996). Cases can also effectively illustrate abstract ideas. Shulman (1993) compares cases to manipulatives in math instruction, providing concrete representations of events and abstractions, and allowing opportunities for analysis of experience.

Research supports the promise of case-based instruction. Hmelo (1995) found that students exposed to cases provided more elaborate and comprehensive explanations of problems than did students exposed to traditional, teacher-centered instruction. Morine-Dershimer (1993) found that opportunities to analyze cases in small groups led to more complex processing of information about the case and increased application of principles than did teacher-led discussions. Additional research indicates that cases can stimulate the development of expertise in teachers (Copeland & Decker, 1995). Collectively, these studies suggest that cases help students learn to process information in deep, meaningful ways and become more effective problem solvers.

Using Cases to Promote Problem-Based Learning.

Planning.   The primary planning task when using Case-Based Problem Solving is the construction or creation of a case around some relevant or important topic. The case needs to provide enough detail so that students can identify with and work with the problem. In addition, the case needs to present or pose a dilemma to students that they need to solve.

The case at the beginning of this section did both. It provided enough contextualizing information (e.g., the kind of school, the class and type of students) to provide an entry to problem solving. In addition, it ended with a specific problem to solve.

Implementing.   The general Problem-Solving Model provides a conceptual framework to direct the teacher's actions in using Case-Based Problem Solving. Teachers should first encourage students to identify what the problem is. For example, in the April Sumner case, is the problem management, instruction, or motivation (or a combination of all three)? As students attempt to represent the problem, they can rely upon resources in reference books about these topics as well as information about inner city schools and remedial classes.

Case-Based Problem Solving differs from regular problem solving in that students can select a strategy and plan for implementation but do not actually implement or evaluate the results. Student presentations to the whole group about proposed strategies together with discussion and analysis serve the same functions here.

This concludes our discussion of Case-Based Problem Solving. In the next section we examine *inquiry,* a third kind of problem-based learning.

The Inquiry Model

Inquiry is both a teaching strategy and a way of discovering how the world works. The process of the Inquiry Model sounds somewhat scientific and remote, but in fact it is very much a part of our everyday lives. The investigation of disease and other health-related matters along with conclusions suggesting that smoking, high cholesterol foods, and lack of exercise are detrimental to health are all results of inquiry processes. These conclusions originate in studies that ask questions such as, "Why does one group of people have a higher incidence of heart disease than another?" The research studies cited in Chapter 2 of this text were all based on inquiry problems, which attempted to answer questions such as, "Why do students in one kind of classroom learn more than those in another?"

Involving students in inquiry problems is one of the most effective ways there is to help them develop higher-order thinking skills, develop as self-directed learners, and learn content. The Inquiry Model described in this section is designed to give students systematic practice with these processes. The Inquiry Model is similar to the Problem-Solving Model in that both are types of problem-based learning. It differs from the Problem-Solving Model in that it focuses on general, causal relationships about how the world works rather than a context-specific problem. To begin our discussion, let us take a look at a home economics teacher using the inquiry process with her students.

Karen Hill, a middle-school life skills/home economics teacher, is beginning a unit on baking breads and baking in general. As she is discussing general baking procedures at the beginning of a lesson on breadmaking, she begins to explain the importance of kneading the dough thoroughly.

Partway through her explanation, José raises his hand and asks, "Why do you have to knead it so long?"

"That's a good question, José. Why do you think so? . . . Anyone?"

". . . Maybe it's to mix the ingredients together well," Jill offers.

Ed adds, "Yeah. If the stuff isn't mixed well enough, it might affect the way the yeast works. If you don't knead the dough enough, it won't rise."

Seizing on the chance to expand her goals for the lesson, Karen writes the students' ideas on the board, and then says, "What Jill and Ed have offered is a tentative answer to Jose's question. When people offer tentative answers to questions or tentative solutions to problems, we call them *hypotheses*. They suggested that thorough mixing affects the yeast, which affects how well the bread will rise.

"Now," she continues. "Does anybody have an idea of how we could check to see if this idea is correct?"

". . . We could take a batch of dough and separate it into about . . . maybe . . . three parts . . . and then knead them for different amounts of time," Chris suggests tentatively after thinking for several seconds.

"Excellent thinking, Chris," Karen smiles. "What do you say, everyone? Should we try it?"

Amid, "Sure," "Okay," "Why not?" and a number of nods at a unique idea, Karen continues, "How long should we knead each? Our book recommends about 10 minutes."

". . . How about 5 minutes for one, 10 for the second one, and 15 for the third," Naomi suggested."

"Then we'll bake them all the same way," Natasha added.

"To be sure that we're getting a good test of Jill's *hypothesis*," Karen continues, "what else do we need to take into account?"

". . . Well, we'd have to use the same dough," Jeremy suggested, "and we'd have to have the same amount of dough, wouldn't we?"

"And we'd have to knead them the same way," Andrea adds, beginning to see the point in the activity. "If people's kneading was different, it could affect the mixing, and that's what we're trying to test, isn't it?"

"Very good thinking, Andrea," Karen nods. "Anything else, anyone?"

". . . I think one more thing," Mandy adds. "You said that the ovens in here are different. We need to bake them all in the same oven, won't we, or won't that throw us off?"

"That's excellent thinking, everyone. . . . Now let's think back for a minute. . . . We talked about having the same dough, kneading them all the same way, and baking them all in the same oven. . . . Why do we want to do that?"

". . . Well, if we . . . like . . . had different dough, and they came out different . . . we wouldn't know if it was the amount of time we kneaded them or if it was the dough, would we?" Talitha offers uncertainly.

"Excellent thinking, Talitha. What we're doing is keeping each of those constant, and the only thing we're changing is the amount of time we knead each piece of dough. When we keep them the same, we say that we've controlled those variables. . . . So let's review for a minute and write down the variables we're controlling. . . . Someone?"

". . . Type of dough," Adam offers.

"Good, . . . what else?"

"The way we do the kneading."

"Excellent. . . . What else?"

"The oven."

"Good, everyone. That's excellent thinking."

The students then follow the suggestions they made, separating a piece of dough into three equal parts, carefully kneading each piece in the same way, and baking them in the same oven, but kneading one part for 5 minutes, the second for 10, and the third for 15. Then they check to see if there are differences in the way the different pieces look. They discuss their results and relate them to the hypothesis. They have found that the pieces kneaded for both 10 and 15 minutes are the same height but taller than the piece kneaded for only 5 minutes. There is a considerable amount of uncertainty about what those results actually mean, but they tentatively conclude that bread must be kneaded an adequate amount, but kneading beyond that amount doesn't matter.

"Before our time is all gone, I'd like us to think a little about what we did and why. How did we get started on this problem? Who remembers? Anthony?"

"José asked why we had to knead the bread so long?"

"Good memory, Anthony. That's correct. Our inquiry started with a question. Then we had some tentative ideas or guesses. Who remembers what we call these tentative ideas? Shanda?"

"Hypotheses?"

"Fine, Shanda. Hypotheses are our best guesses about how the world works. And why was it important to cook all of the loaves. . . ."

Just then the bell rings and Karen dismisses her class with smile and, "Let's stop here. Good work, class. See you tomorrow."

The Inquiry Model: An Overview

Inquiry *at the most fundamental level can be viewed as a systematic process for answering questions based on facts and observations.* One of our goals in including a discussion of inquiry in this text is to increase your awareness of the powerful role this process plays in our lives.

Instructionally, the **Inquiry Model** *is a teaching strategy designed to teach students how to investigate questions through the systematic gathering of facts. The Inquiry Model is implemented in six steps, which are:*

1. *Identifying a question*
2. *Making hypotheses*
3. *Gathering data*
4. *Assessing hypotheses*
5. *Generalizing*
6. *Analysis of the inquiry process*

When teachers use the Inquiry Model, they guide students through these six steps as students work toward a solution to a question or issue. For example, a *question* was identified in Karen's class when José asked about the length of time the dough had to be kneaded. This was followed by Jill's and Ed's suggestion that the kneading affected the way the dough would rise—the process of *making a hypothesis*. The class then discussed ways of controlling their investigation so that the information they got would be valid. Then they baked the pieces and observed the results. This is all part of *data gathering*. Finally, students discussed the results and concluded that an optimum amount of kneading is necessary, which partially supports their hypothesis. This discussion and their tentative conclusion are all part of the *assessing hypothesis* phase. They then formed the generalization—also tentative—relating the optimum amount of kneading to the amount the bread rose. Finally, Karen encouraged them to think about the inquiry process, making them more cognitively aware of the steps they had been following.

Social Structure of the Model

Like the other problem-based learning models discussed in this chapter, the Inquiry Model requires a classroom environment in which students feel free to take personal risks and feel free to offer their conclusions, conjectures, and evidence without fear of criticism or embarrassment. This supportive atmosphere is particularly important because the success of the lessons depends on students' willingness to take risks. If students are fearful or unwilling to participate, the effectiveness of the lesson is limited. The teacher plays a critical role in developing this atmosphere.

The Teacher's Role. In the Inquiry Model, both Karen's and the students' roles were quite different from the roles they play in traditional instruction. First, Karen became a facilitator of the process rather than merely lecturing and presenting information to the students. For example, she could have answered José's question directly and then moved along with the lesson. Her choosing to respond the way she did was related to her goals—both long-range and immediate. Development of students' inquiry skills and self-directed learning was important for her in her instruction, so she chose to seize on the opportunity to develop these thinking skills whenever opportunities came up.

Doyle (1983), in a review of research investigating the types of tasks students are asked to perform in school, makes a persuasive argument that students learn what they do. If they spend their time passively learning facts, they not only develop misconceptions about how and where knowledge originates but also fail to develop the skills necessary to generate their own knowledge. In contrast, if they experience processes such as inquiry, over time they develop important "life skills," such as the inclination to make conclusions based on evidence, to consider others' points of view, to reserve judgment, and maintain a healthy skepticism. Obviously, these inclinations don't develop quickly, but with time and effort on the part of the teacher, significant progress can be made. It is the teacher who determines whether or not students are given these opportunities.

Let us turn now to some considerations a teacher must make in planning for inquiry activities in the classroom.

Planning for Inquiry Activities

Planning for the Inquiry Model is different from using the models in other chapters in several important ways. First, since inquiry problems, hypotheses, and the data used to test them ideally come from the students, teachers must plan carefully so that they can provide enough guidance to keep the process moving—but not so much guidance that they intrude on students' initiative and experience. Keeping this balance requires skill and sensitivity. Second, most inquiry lessons are ongoing, i.e., they usually require more than a single class period, and the teacher must also take this factor into account when planning. Finally, and most importantly, inquiry lessons are designed to achieve certain goals—the development of inquiry skills and self-directed learning. We consider these goals in the next section.

Identifying Goals. As with all models described in this text, the planning process begins with careful consideration of goals. We also suggested that content goals and goals for teaching thinking are inextricably interrelated. The emphasis placed on content compared to thinking varies among the models, but in all cases both kinds of goals coexist. The Inquiry Model described in this chapter follows this pattern.

Content Goals. When inquiry models are used, content primarily serves as the context for practicing higher-order thinking skills. However, inquiry models also help students reach an important content goal, which is finding relationships between different ideas. In Karen's lesson, for example, students looked for a relationship between the amount of time bread was kneaded and the amount it rose.

Most content areas have topics that contain cause-and-effect relationships. Table 7.1 includes some examples.

As a result of inquiry lessons, students construct generalizations, such as, "The higher the level of aerobic exercise, the greater the cardiovascular fitness," or "Many wars are the result of economic problems." As students' thinking improves, they develop their ability to assess these generalizations based on facts and observations. This illustrates the close relationship between content and thinking.

Higher-Order and Critical Thinking. A teacher conducting inquiry lessons has as a primary goal the development of students' ability to recognize problems, suggest tentative answers, identify and gather relevant facts, and critically assess tentative solutions. These

TABLE 7.1 Relationships in Different Content Areas

Content Area	Relationship
English/Language arts	Authors' lives compared to the content of their writing
Science	Plant germination related to the amount of sunlight, water, or type of soil
Social studies	Wars related to economics, political problems, repression, or religion
Building technology	Type of building material compared to durability
Health	Type of exercise related to level of fitness

are the thinking skills of inquiry, and the development of these skills is an explicit process goal when inquiry models are used.

While students are the primary investigators in an inquiry lesson, a teacher must carefully plan in order to facilitate the process. To conduct inquiry lessons, students need a focal problem or question to examine and must have access to data that allow investigation of the problem. Both of these prerequisites require careful planning.

Identifying Questions.   Having identified a topic or content area that can be investigated, next the teacher must prepare a focal question. For instance, a question in the English example could be, "What factors in Poe's life may have impacted the style of his writing?" In the science class a question could be, "What factors affect plant growth?" Ideally, these problems grow spontaneously out of class discussions, as occurred in Karen's lesson, but they often have to be planned by the teacher in advance.

Preplanning can assist the teacher in guiding a class toward inquiry problems. For example, as students discuss different American authors, the teacher could introduce facts about one or two authors' lives. As these authors' works are discussed, the teacher could then raise a question, such as, "What impact do you think authors' lives in general have on their work?" Study of additional authors, their works, and their lives could then serve as the data-gathering phase for the inquiry problem.

As another example, the science teacher could embed an inquiry lesson on plant germination in a larger unit on plant growth in general. As the unit develops, the teacher could relate the investigation of plant germination, characteristics of different plants, plant growth and the environment, and plant nutrition.

Planning for Data Gathering.   Once the teacher has planned for problem identification, she must then consider how students will gather information to be used in assessing hypotheses. As with the process of identifying problems, successful inquiry lessons require the teacher to plan in advance for data gathering. While procedures for data gathering should come from students to the extent possible, the teacher often needs to guide and facilitate the process. This requires planning.

The number of data-gathering options are as broad and diverse as the subject areas themselves. Table 7.2 presents several examples of questions and potential data-gathering procedures.

Primary and Secondary Data Sources.   For older learners and for goals that focus on critical thinking, the distinction between primary and secondary sources of data can be important. **Primary data sources** *are individuals' direct observations of the events being studied*. Karen's students' observations of the baked bread, the observations of the pendulum swinging under different conditions, or interviews with people are primary sources. **Secondary data sources** *are other individuals' interpretations of primary sources*. Textbooks, encyclopedias, biographies, and other reference books are all secondary sources.

Because secondary sources have been screened through the perceptions and potential biases of others, primary sources are preferred if possible. In some cases, such as Karen's lesson or the lessons on pendulums or plant growth, using primary sources is quite easy. Karen could have referred the class to reference books on baking, but the

TABLE 7.2   Questions and Procedures for Gathering Data

Questions	Possible Data Sources
How are authors' works related to their to their personal lives? (English)	Author biographies and samples of their works
How is the road system in a city related to the city's traffic patterns? (Social studies)	Observations of traffic flow at different times of the day, city traffic reports
How is the type of shingle related to its durability? (Industrial technology)	Shingles subjected to different kinds of wear
What factors impact the growth rate of cities? (Social studies)	Geographical information, census data, and historical events
What factors influence the frequency of a simple pendulum? (Science/math)	Pendulums of different weights and lengths

students would have had less opportunity to learn how to form hypotheses, control variables, and analyze data. In her lesson, using primary sources resulted in a better quality learning experience. In other cases, such as the lesson on authors and their works, using primary sources is nearly impossible and secondary sources are almost a must. On the other hand, an analysis of secondary sources for potential bias is, in itself, a valuable learning experience.

Time.   In many instances, inquiry lessons usually take more than a single class period. Because of the time required, teachers must consider how the lesson will be integrated with other activities. For example, the English teacher might pose the question about authors' lives and their works. Discussion would then result in one or more hypotheses, such as "Authors' personal lifestyles are reflected in their works," or "Authors' works reflect their personal beliefs and needs." Individuals or teams of students could then be assigned to gather personal information about different authors and report this information to the class. As students complete their assignments, class time could be spent in discussing different authors' works, or some other aspect of the curriculum, such as writing, or even grammar. As students report, the class would revisit the problem, discuss the hypotheses, and form tentative conclusions about their validity. In the science example, the teacher could guide students through a process where plants would be grown under different sets of conditions, and their growth would be monitored over a period of weeks. Again, while this is occurring, the teacher could continue with other topics in the unit or even move on to other topics, returning to plant growth when data become available.

Having determined how students will be guided into identifying meaningful problems, how data will be gathered, and how the lesson will be integrated within the regular curriculum, the teacher is ready to implement inquiry lessons.

Implementing Inquiry Lessons

Inquiry lessons begin with a question or issue, which is followed by a tentative answer or solution (hypothesis). Data are gathered to help determine the validity of the hypothesis, and once an assessment has been made, generalizations are constructed. Finally, students are encouraged to reflect upon the inquiry process. We discuss implementing these steps in the sections that follow.

Presenting a Question. An inquiry investigation begins when a question is identified. As we saw in Karen Hill's lesson, the question can grow naturally out of a class discussion or, as we discussed in the last section, the teacher can plan for and guide the students into identifying the question or issue.

To ensure that the question is clear, the teacher should write it on the board or display it on an overhead and check to be sure that the students understand the language and concepts in it. Asking students to explain the question in their own words or relate it to prior discussions can help determine whether or not it is clear. An even better indicator of whether or not a problem is clear to students results from asking them to form hypotheses that answer or address the question.

Forming Hypotheses. Once a question has been clarified, the class is ready to try to answer it. In providing a tentative answer, students are involved in the process of hypothesizing. A **hypothesis** *is a tentative answer to a question or solution to a problem that can be verified with data.* Often a hypothesis is a tentative generalization, and for young children it can be presented as a "hunch" or "educated guess."

To facilitate the process, you may ask students to brainstorm possible hypotheses. Initially, all ideas should be accepted and listed. Later, students can be asked to determine if each is relevant to the question or problem.

After students have developed a list of hypotheses, the hypotheses should be prioritized for the purposes of investigation. For example, suppose a science class is investigating the problem: "What factors determine the frequency of a simple pendulum?" and students suggest hypotheses, such as:

"The shorter the pendulum, the greater the frequency."
"The heavier the weight, the greater the frequency."
"The greater the initial angle, the greater the frequency."

Students need to be clear about which hypothesis they are investigating in order to know which variables they must control and how they will gather the data. This means they need to be clear about which hypothesis they're initially investigating. After having investigated the first one, they can move to the second and then the third, but this must be done systematically.

Once hypotheses have been stated and prioritized, the class is ready to gather data.

Data Gathering. However generated, hypotheses are then used to guide the data-gathering process. The complexity of this process depends on the problem. For example, in the investigation of plant growth, students could plant seeds, such as beans or radishes;

systematically vary the growing conditions; and measure germination time and growth. To investigate the first hypothesis in the pendulum problem, students would systematically vary the pendulum length, keeping the weight and angle constant, and measure the number of swings in a specified amount of time for each length. To investigate the second hypothesis, they would systematically vary the weight and keep the length and angle constant, and for the third they would vary the angle, keeping the length and weight constant.

For the lesson on authors' lives compared to their works, gathering data would be more complex and demanding, requiring older and more advanced learners. They would have to go to libraries or get on the Internet to get biographical information about the authors, study a variety of sources to get insight into the authors' lives, and carefully study the authors' works. In this case the teacher might have to provide considerable assistance in gathering the information.

While it is demanding, the experience would help students develop skills far beyond the inquiry problem. For example, they would learn library research techniques, would learn to critically assess secondary sources, would learn to decide what information was important and what should be ignored, and would develop tolerance for ambiguity when information in different sources was inconsistent. These are valuable experiences for students.

Displaying Data.   A major task facing students during this phase is how to organize and present data. The best way to develop data-gathering skills is to involve students in the process, helping them display their results and discussing the strategies used. With experience, their abilities to display and explain the most valid and reliable data possible will improve.

A variety of displays, such as tables, matrices, or graphs can be used. Table 7.3 shows a display of data gathered for the pendulum problem.

Teacher questioning can help students think more analytically about what they're doing. For instance, we see that the students made three trials for each length and averaged the number of swings. The teacher could ask them to consider what they might do if two

TABLE 7.3   Data Gathered for the Pendulum Problem

Weight: two large paper clips
Time: 15 seconds
Angle: 45°

Length	Average Number of Swings for Three Trials
30 cm	12
40 cm	11
50 cm	10
60 cm	9
70 cm	8.5
80 cm	8
90 cm	7.5
100 cm	7

of the trials were identical and a third was very different (suggesting experimenter error in the third trial), why they chose a 15-second time trial, two paper clips, a 45° angle, and variations in length of 10 cm (probably arbitrary). The teacher might also ask if varying the length by the same amount (10 cm in this case) each time is necessary. Students could also be asked what improvements might be made in their data-gathering techniques.

In the lesson on authors and their works, the data might be displayed in a matrix similar to those we saw in Chapter 6 when we discussed the Integrative Model. A skeleton of the matrix could appear as follows:

Author	Personal Characteristics	Experiences	Samples from Works
Poe			
Faulkner			
Hemingway			
Fitzgerald			

As with the pendulum problem, a discussion of why certain information was included and other information was ignored and why the matrix was organized the way it was helps students think about the logic behind their thinking. This process is valuable because it helps students understand the kinds of decisions journalists, historians, and scientists make when they attempt to study something systematically.

Data Analysis.   In this phase of the lesson, students are responsible for assessing their hypotheses on the basis of the data. In some instances, the analysis is fairly simple. For example, a casual glance at the table comparing lengths of pendulums to the number of swings indicates that frequency decreases as length increases. Assessment of the other hypotheses in the case of the pendulum problem and in the case of plant growth would also be straightforward.

In other cases, such as the problem with authors, the process will be more complex. Clear and distinct patterns, such as the relationship between frequency and length of a pendulum, won't exist. Trends that do exist will be much more problematic and arguable. The fact that the data are inconsistent is, in itself, a valuable experience for students. Little in life is clear and unambiguous, and the more experience students have in dealing with ambiguity—which requires tentative rather than dogmatic conclusions—the better prepared they are for the "real world." Discussing the data as they relate to the hypothesis may be the most valuable part of the inquiry process.

Generalizing.   Content closure occurs in an inquiry lesson when students tentatively generalize—if possible—about the results, on the basis of the data. For example, in investigating the relationship between the frequency of a pendulum and its weight, the data indicate that weight does not impact the frequency. Students would reject the hypothesis,

"The heavier the pendulum the greater its frequency," and would conclude, "The weight of a pendulum doesn't affect its frequency." Since the data are consistent, generalizing would be straightforward.

In other cases, such as the problem with authors and their works, patterns in the data will be much less apparent, accepting or rejecting the hypothesis will be much less certain, and so generalizing will be much more tentative. In fact, generalizing may then lead to additional questions, setting the stage for new inquiry problems. This process goes on continually in science and the world at large. In learning to generalize tentatively, students learn an important lesson about living. They begin to realize that the tidy, structured answers we all strive for often do not exist. Over time, they develop tolerance for complexity and ambiguity, which is a powerful aid in helping them understand and cope with life.

Analyzing the Inquiry Process.   In the final stage of the Inquiry Model, the teacher asks students to analyze and reflect upon the inquiry process. Karen Hill initiated this stage when she said, "Before our time is all gone, I'd like us to think a little about what we did and why." In response to this request, students identified how inquiry began and how hypotheses guided the inquiry process. By talking about inquiry processes in the context of lessons, teachers make abstract ideas become real and help students see how inquiry plays out in real life.

Spontaneous Inquiry.   So far we have focused on carefully planned and systematic approaches to inquiry lessons. However, one of the greatest benefits of studying inquiry is an increased awareness of the fact that inquiry activities can begin from questions that occur spontaneously. This was the case in Karen Hill's lesson earlier in the chapter. The investigation in that case developed on the spot. A question came from the class, and Karen was alert and sensitive to capitalize on the opportunity when it occurred. A full-scale inquiry lesson was the result.

Other opportunities abound if teachers are aware of the possibilities. In some ways, this process is like learning a new word. Once learned, it begins to "appear" in everything we read. One of our goals in writing this chapter is for you to increase your awareness so that you will seize on these opportunities when they present themselves.

Opportunities for spontaneous inquiry commonly occur when students encounter situations that have no clear answers. For instance, consider the following simple science demonstration, in which students see an inverted cup of water covered by a card, and the card stays on the cup, preventing the water from spilling as shown in Figure 7.3. We have seen this lesson being taught to elementary students and have heard students ask questions, such as:

"What if the cup wasn't completely full?"
"What if the cup only had a small amount of water in it?"
"What if the cup were turned 90 degrees?"
"What if we used a liquid other than water?"

Each of these is a question that could be a starting point for an inquiry minilesson. Students could be asked to conjecture answers to the questions and explain why they believed

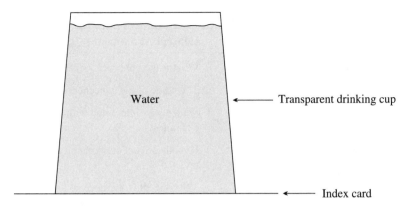

FIGURE 7.3   Simple Science Demonstration

that way. Then each could be systematically investigated. For example, the class could vary the amount of water to see if this variable makes a difference (it doesn't). Finding that the card stayed against the cup in each case, the class would eliminate "amount of water" as a variable causing the card to stay against the cup and would then pursue other variables.

Spontaneous inquiry lessons have several advantages. First, motivation is high. Students can see that the investigation results directly from a question they (rather than the teacher) ask. Often, students suggest creative ways to investigate a problem, and a classroom climate of teamwork and cooperation develops. Second, the spirit of inquiry is captured, yet very little time and effort are required from the teacher except to guide students toward thinking about the question and how it could be investigated rather than instantly responding, "It wouldn't make any difference," when a student asks, "What if the cup were only half full?"

Another advantage of inquiry lessons that occur spontaneously is that students see how the process directly relates to the subjects they study. The distinction between teacher-generated and student-generated questions is a subtle but powerful one. When students only pursue questions generated by others, they learn that knowledge is external and impersonal rather than functional and integrated. Our view, which is corroborated by others (Goodlad, 1984), is that content is too often presented as pre-established truths to be memorized and repeated. Students are seldom asked to investigate or generate their own problems. The use of spontaneously generated student investigations can do much to help them understand how knowledge is produced and the relationship of that knowledge to themselves.

Inquiry and Concept Attainment.   When we discussed the Concept-Attainment Model in Chapter 5, we suggested that it also could be used to help students understand the process of inquiry and the scientific method. Based on the first positive and negative example, students hypothesize possible labels for the concept, and these hypotheses are analyzed based on additional examples. The examples and nonexamples then serve as the

TABLE 7.4   A Comparison of Inquiry and Concept Attainment Processes

Inquiry	Concept Attainment
1. Problem or question	What is the concept?
2. Hypothesizing	The name of the concept could be. . . .
3. Data gathering	Students are presented with positive and negative examples.
4. Analysis of hypotheses	Hypotheses not supported by the examples are rejected.
5. Generalizing	The concept is defined.

data used to analyze the hypotheses. Table 7.4 provides a comparison of Inquiry and Concept Attainment activities.

Concept Attainment can be an effective tool to introduce students to the processes of inquiry. It doesn't take a great deal of time to complete a lesson, and the teacher needs only to prepare examples and nonexamples. It doesn't give students a totally valid notion of the process of inquiry, since the teacher provides them with all the data—the examples and nonexamples. However, it can be an effective way to help students develop an idea of what inquiry is all about before they conduct "full-blown" inquiry investigations on their own.

Using Technology to Support Problem-Based Learning

The success of problem-based learning is dependent upon its ability to present realistic, motivating problems to learners. Our goal in using this model is to bring the real world into the classroom for application, analysis, and reflection. Technology has the unique potential to accomplish this goal.

Problem-Based Learning in Math: The Jasper Series

The mathematics curriculum is full of opportunities to promote problem solving, and recent reform efforts in math have targeted problem solving as a major vehicle to promote mathematical thinking (National Council of Teachers of Mathematics, 1989, 1991). Unfortunately, many of the math problems we give our students fail to capture the realism and complexity of actual life-related math applications (Williams et al., 1996). To remedy the problem, researchers have developed a video-based math series called *The Adventures of Jasper Woodbury*. Each problem begins with a 15–20 minute video scenario that reveals a challenge to the major characters or actors in the segment. The following condensed version gives us some idea of the types of problems found in these scenarios.

Jasper has just purchased a new boat and is planning to drive it home. The boat consumes 5 gallons of fuel per hour and travels at 8 mph. The gas tank holds 12 gallons of gas. The boat is currently located at mile marker 156. Jasper's home dock is at mile marker 132. There are two gas stations on the way home. One is at mile marker 140.3 and the other is at mile marker 133. They charge $1.109 and $1.25 per gallon, respectively. They don't take credit cards. Jasper started the day with $20. He bought 5 gallons of gas at $1.25 per gallon (not including a discount of 4 cents per gallon for paying cash) and paid $8.25 for repairs to his boat. It's 2:35. Sundown is at 7:52. Can Jasper make it home before sunset without running out of fuel? (Williams et al., 1996, p. 2)

The problem is purposefully left open ended to provide students with opportunities to solve the problem by first defining the problem, identifying subgoals (e.g., finding out how much money he has left), separating relevant from irrelevant data (e.g., is the time of day important?), and solving for the final solution. Students are given an extended period of time, three to four days, to work on each problem, and they must solve it before they can see how the characters in the video solved the challenge.

Research on the series has been positive. Middle-school students using the Jasper series did as well as control students on basic math concepts, performed better on math verbal problems, and were better at planning for problem solving and generating subgoals. They also had more positive attitudes toward math (Cognition and Technology Group at Vanderbilt, 1992). Teachers' comments confirmed these positive results: "The kids would go home so excited and [the parents would say] 'I've got to find out about this Jasper. It is all my kids would talk about. . . .'" and "If you have any way of getting to (my) kids in high school, you'll find that they remember those four Jasper episodes. They may not remember anything else that we did that year but they'll remember . . . those episodes because it did hit them and it did make an impact on them this year" (Cognition and Technology Group at Vanderbilt, 1992, p. 308).

For additional information about the Jasper series, consult the following World Wide Web site:

http://peabody.vanderbilt.edu/projects/funded/jasper/preview/AdvJW.html

Computer-Supported Collaborative Learning

A second use of technology in problem-based learning is the use of computers to support group problem solving in the sciences (Suthers, 1998). A group of researchers out of the Learning and Research Development Center at the University of Pittsburgh designed the Belvedere Software Environment to support students in their problem solving. The goals of the program are:

1. To facilitate students acquisition of content knowledge.
2. To develop an understanding of how scientists' data gathering efforts are guided by theories.
3. To develop students' inquiry and collaborative problem solving skills (Suthers, 1998).

The Belvedere Computer Software series is designed to provide representational and coaching support to students engaged in collaborative problem solving. The series facilitates gathering data through a branching series of choices included in the program. To see how this works, let's return to the problem at the beginning of the chapter, where a health official is trying to find the source of a mysterious neurological disease that causes people to lose control of their muscles, become rigid and paralyzed, and lose their memories. Faced with this problem, students can pursue the following courses of action, which appear as a menu on their computers:

- Define the questions in detail.
- Consider several working *hypotheses.*
- Gather data from several types of sources.
- Consider *analogues.*
- Search for physical evidence.
- Use scientific methods to understand the relationships and predict the effects.
- Look for *data* that can confirm or rule out each of the hypotheses.
- Report what hypotheses you have ruled out and how you know. (http://advlearn/lrdc.pitt.edu/belvedere/materials/Chamorro/Mission.htm/p.1)

If students decide to search for physical evidence, one of their options is to go to Guam, where the disease is actually occurring. Once on Guam, they are faced with the choices shown in the box on the following page. Through a series of choices like these students are provided with a simulated exposure to problem solving.

Let's analyze this program in terms of its strengths and weaknesses. In terms of strengths, it does an excellent job of providing students with realistic problems combined with access to a multitude of data sources. Using the computer, students can pursue realistic problems, bypassing logistical problems such as travel and materials. This strength is also the program's greatest weakness. By pursuing problem solving on a computer, students may get the mistaken idea that problem solving is only something that is done through technology. Also, though the program makes every effort to be open ended, students are still limited to the options available. Despite these potential problems, software such as this has great potential to make problem solving in the classroom more realistic, motivational, and challenging.

This concludes our discussion of using technology to support problem-based instruction. We turn now to a discussion of motivational factors in problem-based lessons.

Increasing Motivation in Problem-Based Learning

Increasing motivation in problem-based learning is relatively easy because the instructional strategies within this family of models are based upon sound motivational principles. Current theories stress the central role of curiosity, authentic tasks, and autonomy in increasing students' motivation to learn (Pintrich & Schunk, 1996)). In this section of the chapter we examine how teachers can use these concepts to increase learning and motivation in the classroom.

Problem-Solving Options

Okay, you're in Guam. What's your next step?

Get Information about Guam

       —General description

       —Map the distribution of Guam diseases

Talk to People

       —Interview the husband of a disease victim

       —Interview some unaffected Chamorro people

       —Consult others

Test the Environment

       —Test the water in a stream where there are most victims

       —Test other streams

Do Medical Tests on Patients

       —Test blood for microbes

       —Study brains after death

Look at Records

       —Before 1900

       —1900–1920

       —1921–1940

       —1941–1960

       —1960–1980

       —Now

       —Records of illness in non-Chamorros on Guam

Curiosity appears to be an innate human quality and can be used to increase learning in the classroom (Lepper & Hodell, 1989). Curiosity induces arousal, which can energize student efforts as they try to satisfy this urge to know. Teachers can capitalize on curiosity motivation in problem-based models by posing problems that stimulate students' need to know. The science teacher did this when she based her inquiry lesson on a student's question about seed germination. The health teacher also capitalized on curiosity motivation when she asked her students to solve the neurological and disease problem. Teachers can use curiosity motivation in their classroom by framing new content as concrete problems to be solved rather than abstract content to be learned.

A second way that teachers can use problem-based learning activities to increase student motivation is through authentic learning tasks. Authentic tasks are learning activities that require understanding that can be used in the world outside the classroom. (Eggen & Kauchak, 1999). Authentic tasks are motivating because they help students see how abstract concepts and processes relate to the real world. Laura Hunter used an authentic task—finding the area of carpet in a classroom—to motivate her students to learn about area. Effective teachers make real-world linkages like this all the time in their instruction (Strong et al., 1995).

A third way that problem-based activities can be used to increase motivation is through autonomy. Student autonomy increases when students have choices in deciding what to do and how to do it (Rosenholtz & Simpson, 1984). All too often, classrooms present unidimensional learning environments where student choice is minimized and everyone does the same thing at the same time. Teachers can increase student autonomy during problem-based activities by giving students choices about:

- What problem to pursue
- How to investigate the problem
- How to report results

In addition to increasing motivation, student autonomy also increases students' ability to direct their own learning, the essence of self-regulation.

Assessing Learning in Problem-Based Learning

As with all instructional models, the form that assessment takes should be determined by the goals of the lesson. Problem-based learning has three interrelated goals:

- An increased understanding of the processes involved in problem-based learning
- Development of students' self-directed learning
- Content acquisition

The assessment of content acquisition in this model is similar to assessment processes for other models, so we won't discuss this aspect of evaluation further. Instead, we will focus our discussion on how to assess the first two goals in the model.

Authentic Assessment and Problem-Based Learning

Traditional assessments, most commonly in the form of multiple-choice tests, have come under increasing criticism over the past several years (Kilbane & Herbert, 1998; Reckase, 1997). In response to these criticisms, the use of authentic assessments, or "direct examination of student performance on significant tasks that are relevant to life outside of school" (Worthen, 1993, p. 445), is growing in importance. The term **authentic assessment** is used to describe *assessments that directly measure student performance through* *"real life" tasks* (Wiggins, 1996/97; Worthen, 1993). Examples include assessing students' abilities to:

- Solve a problem
- Conduct an inquiry investigation
- Work collaboratively in a group to solve a problem-based case

In addition to products, such as the answer or a solution to a problem, teachers using authentic assessments are also interested in the processes students use to prepare the products, which emphasize higher-order thinking (Gronlund, 1993). Insights into these processes provide teachers with opportunities to assess student knowledge and correct student misconceptions (Parke & Lane, 1996/97). For example, a structured interview might be used to gain insight into students' thinking as they design science experiments.

Performance Assessments. **Performance assessments** are tasks on which *"students are required to demonstrate their level of competence or knowledge by creating a product or a response"* (Valencia et al., 1994, p. 11). They attempt to increase validity by placing students in as lifelike a situation as possible and evaluating their performance against preset criteria (Feuer & Fulton, 1993). The label *performance assessment* originated in content areas such as science, where students were required to demonstrate a skill in a hands-on situation rather than recognizing a correct answer on a teacher-made or standardized test (Hiebert & Raphael, 1996).

For example, a middle-school science teacher notices that her students have difficulty applying scientific principles to everyday events. In an attempt to improve this ability, she focuses on everyday problems (e.g., why an ice cube floats in one cup of clear liquid but sinks in another), which students have to solve in groups and discuss as a class. On Fridays, she presents another problem (e.g., why two clear liquids of the same volume, when put on a balance, don't have the same mass), and the students have to solve it in groups. As they work, she circulates among them, taking notes that will be used for assessment and feedback (Eggen & Kauchak, 1999, p. 595). Performance assessments allow teachers to assess their students' work while engaged in realistic problem-solving situations.

Systematic Observation. One way to evaluate the processes students utilize when they are engaged in problem-based learning is through systematic observation. **Systematic observations** *require teachers to specify criteria in terms of the processes they are assessing and take notes based on the criteria.* For example, a science teacher attempting to teach her students scientific problem solving might establish the following criteria.

1. States problem or question.
2. States hypotheses.
3. Identifies independent, dependent, and controlled variables.
4. Describes the way data will be gathered.
5. Orders and displays data.
6. Evaluates hypotheses based on the data.

By gathering data systematically while students are engaged in authentic learning activities, teachers are in a better position to assess students' strengths and weaknesses, and provide feedback.

Checklists.   Teachers can make their assessments of students' thinking more systematic by using checklists. **Checklists** *are written descriptions of dimensions that must be present in an acceptable performance.* When checklists are used, the desired performances are typically "checked off" rather than described in notes, as they would be with a systematic observation. For example, the science teacher wanting to assess scientific problem-solving ability might use a checklist such as the one shown in Figure 7.4. Notes could be added to each dimension to combine the best of checklists and systematic observations.

Rating Scales.   One of the limitations of checklists is they require a yes/no response from the evaluator and do not take into account degrees of success. Rating scales address this problem. **Rating scales** *are written descriptions of evaluative dimensions and contain scales of values on which each dimension is rated.* Rating scales such as the one as shown in Figure 7.5 can be used to evaluate the processes students used during problem solving or inquiry.

Rating scales can be designed to provide even more information to students by providing anchors for each of the numerical values. For example, how do we know whether "States problem or question clearly and accurately" warrants a rating of 4 or 3? To provide better feedback, definitions of values, such as the following, could be included.

Rating = 4

Problem is stated in clear, complete, and observable language; communicates clearly with reader; indicates understanding of content by specifying significance and importance of problem; provides a clear basis for hypothesizing solution.

Anchors such as these help teachers assess more systematically and also provide students with better feedback about their performance.

DIRECTIONS: Place a check in the blank for each step performed.

_____ **1.** Writes problem at the top of the report.

_____ **2.** States hypothesis(es).

_____ **3.** Specifies values for controlled variables.

_____ **4.** Makes at least two measurements of each value of the dependent variable.

_____ **5.** Presents data in a chart.

_____ **6.** Draws conclusions consistent with the data in the chart.

FIGURE 7.4   Checklist to Evaluate Scientific Problem Solving

DIRECTIONS: Rate each of the following items by circling 4 for an excellent performance, 3 for a good performance, 2 for fair, 1 for poor, and 0 for nonexistent.

4 3 2 1 0   **1.** States problem or question clearly and accurately.

4 3 2 1 0   **2.** States hypothesis that clearly answers the question.

4 3 2 1 0   **3.** Controls variables.

4 3 2 1 0   **4.** Uses appropriate data-gathering procedures.

4 3 2 1 0   **5.** Displays gathered data accurately and clearly.

4 3 2 1 0   **6.** Draws appropriate conclusions.

FIGURE 7.5   Rating Scale for Evaluating Experimental Technique

Group Versus Individual Assessment.   Throughout the text, we have encouraged teachers to utilize student interaction as a learning tool. However, groupwork presents special challenges in the area of assessment. Research shows that group composition during collaborative group assessment can significantly influence both the quality of the products as well as the processes (Webb et al., 1998). As expected, high-ability students tend to increase performance of the group, while low-ability students tend to depress performance. This outcome is problematic not only because it provides a distorted picture of individual performance, but also because it fails to provide helpful and informative corrective feedback that specific individuals can use to improve their performance.

This suggests that teachers should combine both group and individual assessments in evaluating problem-based learning. Group-based assessments provide the teacher with information about how well students and groups collaboratively work together. Individual assessments provide the teacher with information about individual student growth and progress.

Using Cases to Assess Student Understanding in Inquiry Lessons

Inquiry lessons provide unique assessment challenges to teachers. One of the most important aspects of assessment in inquiry lessons is determining whether or not students can form hypotheses and relate data to explanations. Case studies provide one way of accomplishing this. When case studies are used, students are given a problem and are asked to provide relevant hypotheses, data-gathering questions, and observations or data from the problem itself.

As an example, consider the following item:

> For the following situation, develop a hypothesis for Joe's behavior, write two data-gathering questions that could be used to test this hypothesis, and list three observations that can be made from reading the passage.

Two boys had been good friends throughout their childhood. One day the boys were diving from a tree into a swimming hole. As Lionel crawled out to the end of the tree branch and prepared to dive, Joe shook the branch and Lionel fell to the ground, suffering a permanent injury to his hip. Why did this happen?

    a. Hypothesis:
    b. Data-gathering questions:
    c. Observations:

The following might be responses to the questions.

    a. Hypothesis: Joe was jealous of Lionel's athletic ability.
    b. Data-gathering questions:
        1) Is Joe the smaller of the two boys?
        2) Are Lionel and Joe on an athletic team together?
    c. Observations:
        1) The boys were good friends.
        2) The boys went swimming together.
        3) Joe shook the branch.

[This problem was adapted from John Knowles' novel, *A Separate Peace* (1959).]

An alternate way of measuring students' inquiry skills is to provide them with the script from an inquiry session together with a possible explanation and ask them to determine the relationship of data to that explanation. As an example of this format, consider the following example based on a social studies problem concerning the unequal growth of two cities.

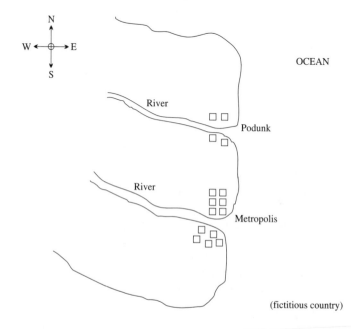

Both cities are on the coast and exist at the mouth of rivers. However, Metropolis is large and a busy transportation center while Podunk is small and insignificant.

The following is a proposed explanation for why there should be so much difference in size and significance:

> While both Podunk and Metropolis are on the coast and are at the mouth of rivers, the entrance to Podunk's harbor is quite small, and the prevailing winds and tricky currents made entrance dangerous in the early years when sailing ships were used. Further, a coast range of mountains isolated Podunk by land but became foothills by the time they reached Metropolis, leaving it freely accessible to overland shipping.

The following data were gathered in the form of questions with the responding answer in parentheses. In the blank by each question, write Support (S), Not Support (NS), or Unrelated (U) if the data respectively support the explanation, do not support the explanation, or are not related to the explanation.

a. Does the current along the coast run from north to south? (Yes)
b. Is Metropolis's harbor larger than Podunk's? (Yes)
c. Are Metropolis and Podunk over 100 miles apart? (Yes)
d. Did approximately as many ships run aground near Metropolis as near Podunk in the sailing days? (Yes)
e. Is the river near Metropolis capable of carrying heavier ships than the river near Podunk? (Yes)
f. Are the mountains around Podunk more rugged than the mountains around Metropolis? (Yes)
g. Are Metropolis and Podunk both in the meteorological belt of the prevailing westerly winds? (Yes)
h. Are the local winds more variable around Podunk than they are around Metropolis? (Yes)

As an additional measure of students' inquiry skills, the teacher may also choose to expand the measurement process by asking students to rewrite the explanation (hypothesis) in keeping with the additional data.

With any type of format for measuring higher-order and critical thinking, the teacher should be certain that the situation used in the measurement is one not previously presented. Otherwise, students may be merely recalling previous information.

Summary

Problem-Based Learning: An Overview

Problem-based learning models are designed to teach students how to pursue problems in a systematic fashion, develop as independent learners, and acquire content in the process. The models in this family are based upon Dewey's views of meaningful learning as well as sociocultural views of how language and interaction facilitate learning. In addition, each of the models in this family begins with a problem and asks students to solve the problem using different strategies.

Problem Solving

The Problem-Solving Model has six sequential stages. In the first, students identify the problem, differentiating relevant from irrelevant information. In the second step, students represent the problem, which helps them conceptualize different relationships within the problem. This leads to selecting a strategy, the third step, which leads naturally to the next, which is carrying out the strategy. In the final two steps of the model, students evaluate results and analyze the process.

Inquiry

Inquiry is a process of systematically answering questions based on evidence. The inquiry process typically begins with a question about a causal relationship. Tentative solutions or answers (hypotheses) to the question are offered, and data are then gathered, which allows an assessment of these solutions and answers. Then the hypotheses are assessed based on the available data and generalizations are made about the conclusions. Finally, students are asked to reflect about their cognitive processes during inquiry.

Using Technology to Support Problem-Based Learning

Technology provides opportunities for teachers to bring aspects of the real world into the classroom for analysis and study. The Jasper Series presents students with a number of realistic, complex problems to solve. The Belvedere Software Environment places students into problem-solving situations and provides them with ways to explore solutions through branching choices.

Increasing Motivation in Problem-Based Learning

Motivation in problem-based learning models can be increased in several ways. One is to capitalize on student curiosity by introducing problems to solve. Authentic tasks also increase motivation by linking abstract content to the real world. Motivation can also be increased by increasing student autonomy and choices.

Assessing Learning in the Problem-Based Learning Model

Authentic assessments are especially valuable in evaluating problem-based learning because they provide teachers with ways of assessing process outcomes. Performance assessments, systematic observation, checklists, and rating scales provide both teachers and students with informative feedback about learning progress.

Case studies provide an additional way to assess learning in inquiry lessons. By providing students with inquiry-based cases, teachers can assess the different component processes in inquiry.

IMPORTANT CONCEPTS

Authentic assessment *(p. 256)*

Cases *(p. 238)*

Checklists *(p. 258)*

Cognitive apprenticeship *(p. 231)*

Heuristics *(p. 237)*

Hypothesis *(p. 247)*

Ill-defined problems *(p. 236)*

Inquiry *(p. 242)*

Inquiry Model *(p. 242)*

Performance assessments *(p. 257)*

Primary data sources *(p. 245)*

Problem-based learning *(p. 227)*

Rating scales *(p. 258)*

Secondary data sources *(p. 245)*

Self-directed learning *(p. 229)*

Sociocultural theory *(p. 231)*

Systematic observation *(p. 257)*

EXERCISES

1. Examine the following teaching episode and identify where the following problem-solving steps occur:

   a. Identify the problem.

   b. Represent the problem.

   c. Select a strategy.

   d. Carry out the strategy.

   e. Evaluate results.

   f. Analyze the process.

   The stray dog has been seen around the school for several days and children feed it scraps of food left over from their lunches. The situation comes to a head one cold, rainy day when the dog walks into Sherry Myers's fourth-grade social studies class.

   "Can we keep him for a pet?"

   "Can he be our class mascot?"

   After the class settles down, Sherry and the students talk about alternatives with the dog curled up quietly in a corner of the room. The class concludes that he is a stray because he has no tags. After determining that the school cannot become a permanent home for the dog, the class considers the following alternatives: find the original owner, find a new one, seek outside help.

   The names Humane Society and Animal Control Division come up, and students are not quite sure what they mean.

   In the next few days, a temporary home is found for the dog, but the problem of stray and unwanted animals is still a topic of interest to the class. To research the problem, the class divides up into groups of four or five. One group focuses on the general topic of pets in America. Another does research on the Humane Society, using printed information from the organization as a major source. A third group attacks the problem from a government perspective and arranges to have a speaker from the County Animal Control Division come and visit. Sherry assists by coordinating the various groups and helping them in their group tasks. After several weeks, the different groups report back to the class, which analyzes the recommendations in a whole-class discussion. Out of this discussion students decide to launch a public information campaign about the plight and problem of unwanted and stray pets.

2. Examine the following list of objectives and describe a problem that would allow the objective to be met using an inquiry activity.

   a. A music teacher wants students to understand the reasons that some sounds are considered music and others are considered noise.

   b. A teacher of literature wants to study the nature of traditions and has chosen the story "The Lottery" as a vehicle for study.

   c. A social studies teacher wants students to know factors affecting the decision to drop the first atomic bomb on Hiroshima.

   d. A social studies teacher wants students to understand the factors involved in the astounding victory of Truman over Dewey in 1948.

   e. A science teacher wants students to understand that objects will float on a fluid if they are less dense than the fluid.

   f. An art teacher wants students to understand the factors that will affect the price of a commercial painting.

3. Read the following teaching episode, which describes a teacher using the Inquiry Model, and answer the questions that follow.

   Renee Stanley is beginning a unit on the newspaper in her high school journalism class. She wants students to understand factors that shape the form that newspapers take and the role that newspapers play in the total context of journalism. She begins her lesson by saying: "Class, today we are going to begin our unit on the newspaper. As an introductory activity, I'd like us to take a look at some newspapers that I've saved from the past week and see what we can discover." With that, she places newspapers from each day of the previous week on a table in front of the class and puts a little sign on each indicating the day of the week.
   "Class, what do you notice about these newspapers? Jill?"
   "The ones toward the end of the week are fatter than the ones toward the beginning."
   "Okay, Anything else, Tod?"
   "Sunday looks to be the fattest and seems to have the most color photographs."
   "Does everyone agree? Any other observations, Mary?"
   "There seem to be more inserts in Wednesday and Thursday's papers."
   "Those are all good observations, class. Now I'd like us to go one step farther with one of those, which is the size of the newspaper. I'd like us to investigate factors that influence the size and composition of our daily newspaper."
   Saying that, she proceeds to write the following on the board:
   "What factors influence the size and composition of the daily newspaper?"

She continues, "Any ideas, class? How about you, Rob? Do you have a hypothesis?"

"It might be feature articles, like things to do on the weekend or travel stuff. Maybe that's what makes some days fatter than others."

"Okay, let's put that on the board under hypotheses. Any other ideas, Sally?"

"It could also be advertising. People have more time to shop for things on the weekend."

"All right, let's put advertising up there, too. Any others, Dave?"

"Another factor could also be sports. There are more sports events on weekends, so that might be one reason why Sunday is so fat."

"That's a good idea, too. Let's stop there in terms of working on hypotheses, and let's spend a moment trying to figure out how we could gather some data related to our hypotheses. Any ideas, Susan?"

"I'm not sure if this will work, but we could count the number of pages that have these different topics on them."

"Interesting idea. Jim, did you have a comment?"

"What about pages that have more than one thing on it? What would we do there?"

The class continues to discuss the procedures they will use to analyze the newspapers and finally arrives at the following table.

National and International News, Local News
No. of Pages
Features
Sports
Advertising
% OF TOTAL

Now Renee assigns students to seven groups, with each group responsible for analyzing a newspaper from a given day of the week. As each group completes its task, it puts its information in the form of a table on the board to share with others. When all the groups are finished, Renee continues.

"Well, class, what do we have here? That sure is an awful lot of data. To make our job a little bit easier, I think we ought to analyze the data systematically. Let's take our hypotheses one by one and see what we find out. Can we look at the 'features' hypothesis first? What patterns do you see? Jackie?"

"It looks like in terms of pages there are the most feature articles on Sunday."

"Does everyone agree? Why do you think we see that pattern, Sam?"
"I think it's because people have more leisure time on Sunday to
read feature stuff."

"Everyone agree? Joe, did you have a comment?"

"But look at the percentage column for features on Sunday. It's no higher than any of the others. I can't figure that out."

"Any ideas, class? I see that the bell is going to ring in a few minutes. Let's save the information on the board and continue our discussion tomorrow, beginning with Joe's question."

Answer the following questions based on the information in the scenario.

    a. Was Ms. Stanley's inquiry lesson spontaneous or preplanned?

    b. Were the data sources that students used to investigate their problem primary or secondary? Explain.

    c. Identify in the teaching lesson where each of these phases occurred.

        1) Question or problem definition

        2) Hypothesis generation

        3) Data gathering

        4) Investigation of hypotheses through data analysis

        5) Generalizing

4. David Smith wants to measure his students' process inquiry skills, so he prepares a case study for students. The case study is composed of (a) a problem, (b) hypotheses suggested as an explanation for the problem, and (c) data gathered to test the hypotheses. He then prepares several questions for his students. Your task is to analyze the quality and appropriateness of David Smith's questions. The case study appears as follows:

> There is a country that is shaped as it appears on the map below. This country is unusual in that most of the population lives on the eastern coast. Why did this unequal distribution of population occur?

The following hypotheses are included with the case study.

    1. There are more natural seaports on the east coast that promote shipping to that area, thus leading to a buildup in population.

    2. A mountain range exists on the west coast, preventing the area from being developed.

    3. A railroad extends from the country to the north down the east coast, promoting immigration and commerce between the two countries and leading to a buildup in the population in the east.

The data relating to the problem are as follows:

    1. The number of seaports on the east and west coasts are approximately the same.

    2. The country is flat throughout its area.

    3. The climate conditions in all parts of the country are similar.

    4. The ocean currents along the east coast run from south to north.

    5. Railroads run north and south in the country on both coasts.

    6. The first railroad was built on the east coast.

    7. A mountain range runs from north to south in the country above the country in question, about 200 miles in from the coast.

Next David prepares the three questions that follow. Your task as a reader is to analyze each question and determine if each is appropriate for measuring the processing abilities of David's students.

a. Which of the following factors can influence the location of cities?

    1) Rail line

    2) Currents

    3) Mountains

    4) Harbors

b. On the basis of the data, decide which of the three hypotheses can be accepted and which must be rejected, and explain the basis for the decision.

c. On the basis of the data, revise the hypotheses to form a final explanation for the problem.

5. Read the following anecdote and answer the questions that follow.

> Two teachers, Susan and Bill, are sitting in the lounge one day discussing an incident between two other teachers.
>   "I've never seen Joan flare up that way," Susan says to Bill.
>   "Why do you suppose she jumped all over Mary that way?"
>   "I don't know for sure," Bill responds. "But I think she's having some trouble at home. I notice that she's edgy when she first comes in in the morning but settles down as the day goes on. Also, she made some snide remark about her husband yesterday morning."
>   "Yes, I heard that, too," Susan nods. "But I think it was all in fun. Also, she commented only last week how happy she was and how well things were going both at home and at school. I really don't think her home life would cause her to jump on Mary that way."
>   Joe was also in the lounge, saw the incident, and has been listening to Susan and Bill talking. "I think," he says, "that she's simply exhausted and her nerves are on edge. She's taking two classes at the university in addition to teaching, she's the annual and school paper advisor, and now that it's spring she's trying to help with the girls' tennis team. It's just too much."
>   "That's probably it," Susan agrees.
>   "She commented that she's averaged five hours of sleep since she started with the coaching. That's been three weeks, and she's probably exhausted."
>   "Also, her husband sells," Bill adds, "and they do an awful lot of entertaining of prospective buyers."

a. Identify the inquiry problem/question in the anecdote.

b. Identify two hypotheses that were offered to answer the question.

c. Identify at least four comments in the anecdote that could be called items of data. (Some of the items are inferential and therefore not as valid as observations, but include them anyway.)

d. For each item of data, identify to which hypothesis it relates, and whether it supports the hypothesis or detracts from it.

DISCUSSION QUESTIONS

1. Identify at least two areas of the curriculum that are well suited to problem-based learning activities. Identify at least two areas of the curriculum in which it is difficult to implement problem-based learning activities. Explain why you offered the choices you did.

2. Are problem-based learning activities more effectively taught at the beginning or end of a unit? Why?

3. From a developmental perspective, what would be an optimal sequence for introducing the Inquiry Model, Case-Based Problem-Solving Model, and Concept Attainment I, II, and III?

4. What would be the advantages and disadvantages of asking students to *independently* pursue a research topic using the Inquiry Model? If you did this, what would have to precede individual inquiry?

5. List as many primary data sources as you can in your area of the curriculum. Do the same with secondary data sources. Compare your answers with those of others in your class.

CHAPTER

8

The Direct-Instruction Model

The Direct-Instruction Model is a widely applicable strategy that can be used, to teach both concepts and skills. Based on the effective teaching research, this model places the teacher at the center of instruction. When direct instruction is used, the teacher structures the topic, explains it to students, provides them with opportunities to practice, and gives feedback. Direct instruction, also called *explicit instruction* (Pearson & Dole, 1987), derives from hundreds of studies that have attempted to identify links between teacher actions and student learning (Brophy & Good, 1986; Rosenshine & Stevens, 1986).

When you have completed your study of this chapter, you should be able to meet the following objectives:

- Identify topics most effectively taught with the Direct-Instruction Model.
- Plan for lessons using the Direct-Instruction Model.
- Implement the Direct-Instruction Model, including all four phases in the lessons.
- Assess learner understanding in lessons using the Direct-Instruction Model.

To begin our discussion, let's look at two teachers using the Direct-Instruction Model in their classrooms.

Tim Hardaway, a first-grade teacher, looks up from his planning book and stares out the window. "I wonder if they are ready?" he thinks. "We've been working on addition for weeks now. They understand the process and most even know their math facts, but is transition to addition with two-digit numbers going to be tough? I've got to make sure that we review place value before we begin. If they don't understand that, I'll lose them."

The next Monday Tim begins his math class by saying, "Please put away your reading books and take out your math pieces. Today we are going to learn a new way to add. This new way to add will help us solve problems like this one." With that, he displays the following problem.

> Sonya and Willy are working together to save soft drink cans, so they can get a free soccer ball. Sonya has 13 cans and Willy has 14. How many do they have together?

After giving the children a few seconds to read the problem, Tim continues, "Problems like this are important in math because they help us in our everyday lives. When we're done with today's lesson, you'll be able to solve problems like this.

"Now let's review for a few minutes. Everyone do this problem." He writes the following problem on the board.

$$\begin{array}{r} 5 \\ +\ \underline{4} \end{array}$$

Tim quickly circulates around the room, then comments, "Great! We really know how to do that. . . . Now, I want you to try a slightly harder one, and I want you to use your math pieces for this one," as he writes the following problem on the board.

$$\begin{array}{r} 6 \\ +\ \underline{7} \end{array}$$

Again, Tim circulates around the room, offering brief suggestions and comments.

Then he moves back to the front of the room and says, "Who would like to come to the flannel board to show us how they did this problem? . . . Antonio? . . . Good! Come on up here and use the same color pieces as you used at your desk."

Antonio walks up to the front of the room and starts arranging the pieces on the flannel board.

"Antonio, talk out loud while you're doing it and explain what you're doing so everyone can understand."

". . . Well, you take 6 of these . . . [unit pieces] here, and . . . you . . . add these . . . these 7 . . . and 13, you get 13. . . . That's the answer."

"Excellent, Antonio. Does everyone see how he did that? Now, Antonio, do you remember what we can do when we have ten unit pieces? How can we make the answer simpler?"

". . . We can . . . trade 10, . . . 10 of these for that one" [a 10s piece].

"Okay, go ahead and do that. Class, if you haven't already done that, do that at your desk."

Tim pauses for a few seconds while the class rearranges their counting pieces so that they have one 10 piece and three unit pieces.

"Does everyone see how Antonio did that? He traded 10 of his unit pieces for one of his 10 pieces and still got 13. Good thinking, Antonio.

"Now, class, we are ready to learn something new today. Today we're going to learn how to add numbers that have 10s in them. We already know how to add smaller numbers, and we know how to convert units to 10s, so this shouldn't be too difficult if we all work hard. When we add numbers with 10s and units, we just have to remember to add the units with units and the 10s with 10s. Let's begin by looking at our problem."

Again he displays the problem:

Sonya and Willy are working together to save soft drink cans, so they can get a free soccer ball. Sonya has 13 cans and Willy has 14. How many do they have together?

"Everyone look up here at the overhead. Good. Now what does the problem ask us? Shalinda?"

"How . . . many they have . . . together?" Shalinda responds hesitantly.

"Good. . . . So how might we solve this problem? . . . Lakea?"

"I . . . I . . . think we could add them up."

"Good," Tim smiles. "Why do you think so?"

"It . . . says . . . how many do they have together, so if we added, we . . . would know that."

"Excellent," Tim nods. "Now let's put the problem on the board. What is one number that we add? Carlos?"

"13."

"Good, Carlos. And what's the other number we add, Cheryl?"

"14."

"Fine, so let's put the problem on the board like this," Tim continues, writing the following on the board.

    14
  + 13
  ‾‾

"Now, what is this 14?" Tim asks, pointing to the 14 on the board.

". . . How many cans . . . Willy has," Leroy answers.

"Now I'd like everyone to show me how to make a 14 at your desk using both 10 and unit pieces."

Tim pauses as the class works at their desks.

"Does everyone's look like this?" Tim asks as he does the same at the flannel board.

"Now I'd like you to do the same with 13. Everyone do that at your desk," Tim adds, then pauses for them to work.

"Here's what my 13 looks like. Is that right? Good. Now we're ready to add them. When I add 3 and 4, what do I get? . . . Hmm, let me think about that . . . 3 and 4 are 7. Let's put a 7 up on the board," Tim says as he walks to the board and adds a 7.

    14
  + 13
  ‾‾
     7

"Now we still have to add the 10s. What do we get when we add two 10s? Hmm, that should be easy. One 10 and one 10 is two 10s. Class, look where I have to put the 2 up here. It is under the "10s" column because the 2 means two 10s." With that, he writes the following on the board:

$$\begin{array}{r} 14 \\ + \underline{13} \\ 27 \end{array}$$

"So how many cans did Sonya and Willy have together? Alesha?"

"27?"

"Good, Alesha. They had 27 all together. . . . Show me the number with your pieces."

Tim watches as the children put seven of their units pieces in a group and place two of their 10s pieces beside them. A few of the children are uncertain about how to represent the number, and Tim gives them enough help so that they are also able to correctly represent the number with their pieces.

Then he continues, "Let's try another one."

Let us leave Tim and his children now and visit Karen Hendricks, a middle-school science teacher who is beginning a unit on plants.

"Class, that was the bell, so I need to have everyone's eyes up here," Karen announces loudly as she scans the room for silence.

"Thank you. Billy . . . Thank you. Sandra, we're waiting."

After a short pause, Karen continues, "As you'll recall, we've been studying different kinds of plants for the past several weeks. We talked about one-celled plants, algae, mosses and ferns, and last week we talked about gymnosperms. Who can remember some plants that are gymnosperms? . . . Becky."

". . . Pine . . . trees and that funny one from China . . . Gink . . . Gingko."

"Good, Becky. Also last week we learned about angiosperms or flowering plants. Who can remember some examples of angiosperms? Wade?"

". . . Umm, roses and . . . maple . . . maple trees."

"Good, Wade. Today, class, we are going to learn about two kinds of angiosperms—monocotyledons and dicotyledons, or monocots and dicots for short. These are important members of the plant family because most of the food we eat comes from them. When we're all done, you'll be able to tell the difference between monocots and dicots and explain how they're related to angiosperms. Look up here on the overhead and you'll see these terms defined."

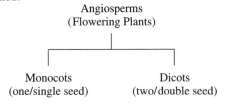

Angiosperms
(Flowering Plants)

Monocots   Dicots
(one/single seed) (two/double seed)

"Now first I'd like to focus on monocots. Look up here [holding up a grass plant]. This is monocot that I found on our playground. Monocots are flowering plants that produce seeds with a single cotyledon. That's why we call them monocots—because *mono* means one. If you will look up here at the overhead, you will see a cross-section of a corn seed. Note that it has a unitary construction—it isn't in halves, and there is only one leaf coming out of the seed. Corn and this grass plant are examples of monocots."

"The second type of angiosperm we are going to learn about today is dicots or dicotyledons. Who knows what *di* means? Maria?"

". . . If . . . the other stuff meant one . . . it must mean two," Maria replies.

"Excellent, Maria. So dicots have two seed leaves. Look up here at a cross-section of a bean plant." Karen continues, pointing up at the overhead, "Can you see the two halves of the seed and the two seed leaves coming out? . . . Good."

"Now, besides the seeds, there is a second difference between monocots and dicots. Look at the leaves of this grass plant and this bean plant and see if you can tell. Clarice?"

". . . Well, the grass leaves are long and thin and the bean leaves are kind of round."

"Good, Clarice. And what about the leaf veins? Take a closer look. Alfredo, what do you see?" Karen asks, holding the plants close for Alfredo to see.

". . . The veins in the grass plant are long and narrow; the veins in the bean plant go all over and are hooked to each other."

"Good, Alfredo. So a second difference is in the shape of the leaves and the veins in the leaves. Let's add these to our diagram."

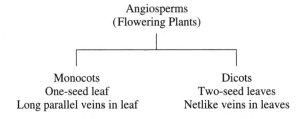

Angiosperms
(Flowering Plants)

Monocots	Dicots
One-seed leaf	Two-seed leaves
Long parallel veins in leaf	Netlike veins in leaves

"Let's try another plant and see if these characteristics make sense," Karen continues, taking out a green onion and holding it in front of the class. "What kind of angiosperm do we have here and why?"

The class continues as Karen presents pictures and overheads of rice, corn, daffodil, rose, and sunflower plants. In each instance, they talk about the plant structure and analyze the seeds, when available.

Finally, Karen brings the lesson to a close by saying, "Class, let's summarize what we learned today. . . . Cheryl, what is one thing you learned today?"

". . . About angiosperms and how they . . . like . . . have two families," Cheryl replies, pointing to the board.

"Good, what else? . . . Kenny?"

"We learned about monocots and dicots and how they're different," replies Kenny.

"Fine, and what is one difference between them? Trang?"

"Monocots have one seed leaf and they have long, parallel veins."

"Excellent, Trang. You were listening. And what about dicots? Kaylynne?"

". . . Ummmm, dicots have two seed leaves and their leaves are rounder and have lots of veins that go every which way."

"Good, Kaylynne. Class, it seems like you are understanding the differences between these two types of plants. What I would like you to do now is work on this handout that has some additional examples of plants. Your job is to classify them as monocots or dicots and explain why."

After Karen passes the worksheet to the students, she circulates around the class, answering questions. Toward the end of the class, Karen begins again. "Class, I have an assignment for each of you. I want you to go home tonight and look in your yards, or in your refrigerator or even a park and find one more example of a monocot or dicot. Bring it in if you can, but don't pull up somebody's flowers." She pauses as the class giggles and exchanges glances. "Make sure you write that assignment down and we'll discuss what you find first thing tomorrow morning."

The Direct-Instruction Model: An Overview

The **Direct-Instruction Model** *is a teacher-centered strategy that uses teacher explanation and modeling combined with student practice and feedback to teach concepts and skills.* It is teacher centered in the sense that the teacher identifies lesson goals and initially explains the content and models skills for the students. Students are actively involved in developing initial understanding and practicing to mastery.

The Direct-Instruction Model occurs in four phases.

- *Introduction:* The teacher reviews and describes lesson goals and reasons for the goals.
- *Presentation:* The teacher explains the new concept or models the skill.
- *Guided practice:* The students practice the skill or categorize examples of the concept.
- *Independent practice:* The students practice the skill or concept on their own. These phases are summarized in Table 8.1.

The Direct-Instruction Model is a research-based model that is applicable in a number of content areas (Gersten et al., 1999). One of the distinguishing characteristics of the model is the pattern of interaction between the teacher and students. Let's look at this pattern.

TABLE 8.1   Phases and Examples of the Direct-Instruction Model

Phase	Purpose	Example
Introduction	Provides an overview of new content, explores connections with students' background knowledge, and helps students understand the value of the new content.	Karen reviewed gymnosperms and angiosperms. She explained that monocots and dicots were important food sources.
Presentation	New content is explained and modeled by the teacher in an interactive format.	Karen displayed a hierarchy explaining monocots and dicots and provided examples of each.
Guided Practice	Students are provided with opportunities to try out the new content.	Karen had students classify examples of monocots orally and on a worksheet.
Independent Practice	Retention and transfer are promoted by students practicing the concept or skill on their own.	Karen had the students find additional examples and bring them to class.

Social Structure of the Model

The Direct-Instruction Model is teacher centered, meaning the teacher plays a primary role in structuring and explaining the topic, using examples to develop student understanding, and providing feedback. *Teacher centered,* however, does not imply that students are passive. In effective direct-instruction lessons, students are very active in responding to teacher questions, examining examples, and practicing.

Transfer of responsibility, *which gradually shifts control of learning from teacher to students,* is an important concept that guides interaction when the Direct-Instruction Model is used. Initially, the teacher assumes major responsibility for explaining and describing content. Then, as the students' understanding develops, they assume more responsibility for solving problems and analyzing examples.

The patterns of interaction correspond to this transfer of responsibility. Initially, teachers talk more than students as they present and explain the content. As the lesson progresses, the pattern shifts from explaining to questioning, and student talk increases as they describe and explain their answers. These transitions, in both responsibility and talk, are characteristic of successful Direct-Instruction lessons.

The Direct-Instruction Model: Theoretical Perspectives

The Direct-Instructional Model is based on research from three areas. They are:

■ Teacher-effectiveness research, which was described in Chapters 1 and 2

- Observational learning, based on the work of Albert Bandura (1989, 1986), which emphasizes the role of modeling on learning skills
- The influence of interaction in learning, based on the work of Lev Vygotsky (1978)

Let us look at these three areas in turn.

Teacher-Effectiveness Research

We examined the teacher-effectiveness research in Chapters 1 and 2. There we saw that teachers who are well organized, use clear language, provide effective feedback, and are skilled in questioning increase achievement more than teachers who have less expertise in these areas.

In addition, researchers found that effective teachers tended to follow a general pattern of instruction that increased learning. Different labels were used for this pattern, one of which was *direct instruction,* which Rosenshine described as follows:

> Direct instruction refers to academically focused, teacher-directed classrooms using sequenced and structured materials. It refers to teaching activities where goals are clear to students, time allocated for instruction is sufficient and continuous, coverage of content is extensive, the performance of students is monitored . . . and feedback to students is immediate and academically oriented. In direct instruction the teacher controls instructional goals, chooses materials appropriate for the student's ability, and paces the instructional episode. Interaction is . . . structured, but not authoritarian. Learning takes place in a convivial academic atmosphere (1979, p. 38).

Direct instruction has six characteristics that are effective across grade levels and content areas. They are:

- Reviewing the previous day's work
- Presenting new material in clear and logical steps
- Providing guided practice
- Giving feedback with correctives
- Providing independent practice
- Reviewing to consolidate learning (Rosenshine & Stevens, 1986)

These characteristics provide the structure for the Direct-Instruction Model.

Modeling: Learning by Observing Others

Observational learning, *which describes changes in behavior, thinking or emotions that result from observing the behavior of another person* is a second foundation for the Direct-Instruction Model. Based on the work of Albert Bandura (1986, 1989), **modeling** explains how people learn by imitating behaviors they observe in others. We have all seen little children imitate sounds and actions of their parents, and the tendency of teenagers to imitate the hair and fashion styles of rock and movie stars forms the basis for a multimillion dollar fashion industry.

The Direct-Instruction Model incorporates the benefits of modeling by having teachers demonstrate (model) the steps involved in learning a skill or the thinking involved in classifying examples of concepts. Tim Hardaway used modeling when he demonstrated adding with two-digit numbers. Tim also used Antonio as a model when he asked Antonio to come to the flannel board and demonstrate the skill.

As Tim was modeling the process for adding two-digit numbers to each other, he also said, "Here's what my 13 looks like. . . . Now we're ready to add them. When I add 3 and 4, what do I get? . . . Hmm, let me think about that . . . 3 and 4 are 7. Let's put a 7 up on the board. . . . Now we still have to add the 10s. What do we get when we add two 10s? Hmm, that should be easy. One 10 and one 10 is two 10s. Class, look where I have to put the 2 up here. It is under the '10s' column because the 2 means two 10s." In talking as he did, Tim was attempting to capitalize on the process of **cognitive modeling,** *which is verbalizing thinking as a person solves a problem.* Just as direct modeling is the display of behaviors intended to be imitated, cognitive modeling is the display of thinking also intended to be imitated, or approximated. He also attempted to use cognitive modeling when he said, "Antonio, talk out loud while you're doing it (solving the problem) and explain what you're doing so everyone can understand."

Vygotsky: The Social Side of Skill Learning

Research on the social aspects of learning emphasizes the importance of verbal interaction in helping students learn (Cohen & Lotan, 1997; Wertsch, 1991), and while the Direct-Instruction Model is teacher centered, much of its effectiveness results from the interaction between the teacher and students.

Two concepts from the work of Lev Vygotsky (1978) capitalize on this interaction. The first is **scaffolding** *which is the instructional support teachers provide as students learn skills.* Teachers can provide instructional scaffolding in a variety of ways, including breaking complex skills into subskills, asking questions and adjusting their difficulty, presenting examples, modeling the steps in solving problems, and providing prompts and cues.

The second is the **zone of proximal development,** *which is the state of learning in which a student cannot solve a problem or perform a skill alone but can be successful with the help of a teacher.* The zone of proximal development is instructional paydirt; it is within the zone that teachers are most effective in aiding learning. Outside the zone, students either don't need help (they have already mastered a new skill) or lack the prerequisite skills or background knowledge to benefit from instruction.

In using the Direct-Instruction Model, we attempt to implement lessons within students' zone of proximal development. For example, when Tim first introduced adding with two-digit numbers, most of his students were not able to perform this skill by themselves. However, by the end of the lesson, with his help, most of his students were able to perform the skill on their own. Tim had successfully helped his students proceed through the zone of proximal development.

In summary, three lines of research provide the conceptual framework for the Direct-Instruction Model.

- The teacher-effectiveness research, which summarizes the strategies teachers use to promote learning
- Observational learning, which focuses on the importance of modeling in learning complex behaviors
- Vygotsky's work, which stresses the importance of learning from others through verbal interaction

Planning Lessons with the Direct-Instruction Model

Planning for the Direct-Instruction Model is a three-step process that begins by specifying goals, continues by identifying prerequisite knowledge, and concludes when sample problems are selected or prepared. We describe each of these steps in the sections that follow.

Specifying Goals

If a teacher's goal is for students to understand a specific concept or learn a specific skill, the Direct-Instruction Model can be effectively used.

Let us review these forms of content.

Concepts.   Concepts form a major content focus of the Direct-Instructional Model. As we saw in Chapter 3, students learn concepts, how they relate to other concepts, and their characteristics by examining positive and negative examples.

Karen taught two closely related concepts—*monocots* and *dicots*—in her science lesson. She first reviewed the superordinate concept, *angiosperm,* and then related dicots and monocots to it. In teaching the concepts, Karen used both real plants and pictures displayed on overheads as her examples.

In this lesson Karen actually taught two concepts at one time, and examples of one served as nonexamples for the other. There are a number of teaching situations where presenting two related concepts is both time efficient and effective for increasing understanding (Tennyson & Cocchiarella, 1986). Some cases include *antonyms* and *synonyms* or *simile* and *metaphor* in language arts, *longitude* and *latitude* in geography, and *acid* and *base* in science. In each case, teaching the two simultaneously helps students see the differences between two closely related and often confused concepts. In instances where there is no closely related coordinate concept, an array of negative examples can be used to help clarify the boundaries of the concept.

Skills.   To begin this section, we would like to pose this problem to you:

987
−788

Solving it is easy for most of us, but now let us consider how we would attempt to teach its solution to a child who understands simple subtraction but hasn't yet been introduced to regrouping. We need to explain the process so that children understand what they are doing and why. Ultimately they need to be able to perform the operations essentially automatically.

Solving problems such as this is a skill, and the Direct-Instruction Model is an effective way to teach skills.

Skills are cognitive operations that:

- Have a specific set of identifiable operations or procedures.
- Can be illustrated with a large and varied number of examples.
- Are developed through practice (Doyle, 1983).

These characteristics are interrelated; the operations are illustrated through examples or sample problems, which provide practice for students.

Skills are found across the curriculum and at virtually every grade level. For example, the language arts curriculum contains writing skills, including general organizational strategies, as well as specific skills such as capitalization, grammar, and punctuation. As we saw in Tim's lesson, math is replete with skills, ranging from basics, such as addition and subtraction, to those more complex, such as factoring and solving quadratic equations. Social studies and science also contain many skill areas. For example, students are asked to read maps and read and display information in charts and graphs in social studies, and science students measure and operate scientific equipment, form and test hypotheses, and conduct experiments.

We have two long-range goals when we teach skills—automaticity and transfer. As we saw in Chapter 2, **automaticity** *results from overlearning a skill to the point that it can be performed with little conscious effort,* and it is important because it reduces the demand on our limited working memories. Word processing is an example. Once we achieve automaticity in this skill, we spend virtually no effort thinking about what keys we will press; rather, we devote our working memory spaces to composing the document we're preparing. Similarly, in order to solve word problems in math, automaticity in basic operations— such as addition and multiplication—is important because it allows us to devote all of our limited working memories to solving the problem (Sweller et al., 1998).

Teachers promote automaticity by providing practice to the point of overlearning. This practice can occur under the guidance of the teacher or independently, and both are important.

A second goal of skills instruction is transfer. **Transfer** *occurs when a skill or understanding acquired in one setting can be applied in a different setting.* For example, transfer occurs when students apply algebra to solve physics problems or when students use math skills to determine which of two products is a better buy.

Teachers teach for transfer in at least three ways. The first is by ensuring that students understand the skill. Tim had his students use their counting pieces to help reach this goal. The second is by providing a variety of problems or examples in which the skill is required, and the third is by giving students a chance to practice the skill on practical problems.

Having identified the concept or skill you want the students to learn, you are ready to identify prerequisite knowledge.

Identifying Prerequisite Knowledge

The Direct-Instructional Model focuses on teaching and learning specific concepts or skills. However, research on learning indicates that all new learning depends on what students already know—their background knowledge (Eggen & Kauchak, 1999). Background knowledge provides "hooks" for new learning. In planning for direct instruction lessons, teachers need to plan for how the concept or skill will be introduced and connected to what students already know.

Planning for accessing prerequisite knowledge is slightly different for teaching a concept compared to a skill. For concepts, the task usually involves identifying a superordinate concept to which the concept can be linked. Karen used the superordinate concept *angiosperm* because she had taught the concept and it was meaningful to students. Though the goal in a direct instruction may be to understand a specific concept (or concepts), such as *monocot* and *dicot* in Karen's lesson, a broader goal is for students to understand how the concept relates to other ideas.

Identifying prerequisites for a skills-oriented lesson is slightly more complicated because it involves identifying subskills that lay the foundation for the new skill. **Task analysis,** *or the process of breaking a skill into its component subparts,* can be helpful here. Tim did this when he determined that students first needed to understand place value before they could learn to do two-column addition.

Consider a second example from the area of writing or language arts. Our ultimate goal is to teach students to write well. What knowledge or skills are required to accomplish this goal? Among them are understanding what a sentence is, knowing the difference between sentence fragments and complete sentences, punctuating sentences correctly, and being able to use the specific symbols that are used with each sentence type. Once learned, these prerequisite skills provide a foundation that allows students to focus on the skill at hand.

Selecting Examples and Problems

The final phase in planning for Direct-Instruction lessons is selecting examples or problems. A strength of Direct Instruction is the opportunities it provides for practice. In learning a concept, students can relate the definition to examples and can categorize examples themselves. In learning a skill, students are helped both to understand the procedures and to practice the skill on their own by working sample problems. In both instances—concept and skill learning—selecting concrete examples and problems is essential to the success of the lesson.

In teaching concepts with the Direct-Instruction Model, the teacher has two tasks—selecting and sequencing the examples. Examples are selected based on the extent to which they illustrate the concept's essential characteristics. In Karen's lesson, these characteristics included the number of seed leaves and the type of venation. Karen used a combination of real examples and pictures on overheads to help illustrate these characteristics.

After selecting examples, the next task is to sequence them. Usually, the clearest and most obvious ones are presented first. For example, in teaching a simple concept, such as *mammal,* we would first use obvious examples like *dog, cat, cow,* or *zebra* rather than *whale, seal,* or *bat.* Once learners begin to understand the concept, additional examples can be used to enrich their understanding.

The extent to which examples illustrate the essential characteristics is a second way to think about sequencing. Again, in a lesson on mammals, *dog* and *cat* are good examples because they clearly illustrate characteristics such as being furry, warm blooded, and milk producers. Further, most students have had direct experiences with these mammals, which makes them more meaningful.

In selecting and sequencing examples and problems for skill acquisition, student success is important. One reason for using the Direct-Instruction Model is to help students acquire proficiency with the skill as efficiently as possible. This suggests that problems should be selected and sequenced so that students can develop both the skill and confidence through successful practice.

Tim helped accomplish this goal by providing the easiest problems first. He first used problems that involved single-digit addition without regrouping, then moved to single-digit addition with regrouping, proceeded to double-digit addition without regrouping, and finally arrived at double-digit addition with regrouping. By sequencing from simple to complex, Tim provided instructional scaffolding that ensured high success rates and minimized frustration and confusion.

Having identified goals, determined prerequisite knowledge and skills, and selected and sequenced examples and problems, the teacher is ready to put these planning steps into action.

Implementing Lessons Using the Direct-Instruction Model

Implementing lessons using the Direct-Instruction Model occurs in four phases. They are:

- Introduction, including a lesson overview an attempt to motivate students
- Presentation, in which the concept or skill is explained and illustrated
- Guided practice, where learners practice with the concept or skill under the guidance of the teacher
- Independent practice, where learners practice on their own

Let us look at these phases in turn.

Introduction

The *introductory phase* of a Direct-Instruction lesson performs several functions. First, it draws students into the activity; without student attention, the teacher's best efforts are wasted. In addition, the introduction provides an overview of the content to follow, allowing students to see where the lesson is going, and how it relates to content already learned (Gersten et al., 1999). The introduction also provides opportunities for the teacher to motivate students, to explain how the new content will be beneficial to them in the future. Let's examine each of these functions.

Introductory Focus. In Chapter 2 we defined *introductory focus* as "teacher actions at the beginning of a lesson designed to attract students' attention and pull them into the lesson." It is important to draw students into any lesson and to focus their attention on the learning task. However, research indicates that teachers often neglect this essential attention-getting function; in one study of skills instruction, researchers found that only 5 percent of the teachers made a conscious attempt to draw students into the lesson (Anderson et al., 1985).

This part of the lesson is also called *anticipatory set,* a term which emphasizes the task of getting students ready to learn (Hunter, 1984). Tim provided introductory focus by presenting his students with the word problem that he returned to later in the lesson, and Karen used the transparency showing the relationship of dicots and monocots to angiosperms as her introductory focus.

Lesson Overview. A second function of the introduction is to provide students with an orientation to the lesson's content. The lesson overview often includes objectives, a brief summary of the new content, and what will occur in the lesson (Gersten et al., 1999). Tim presented a sample problem on the overhead as his lesson overview and explained that students would be able to do these when the lesson was completed. Karen structured her lesson with the transparency by explaining that students would be able to differentiate between monocots and dicots when the lesson was over.

Motivating Students. Motivation is a third function performed by the introduction. Teachers do this by explaining how and why new content should be learned. Tim attempted to motivate his students by emphasizing that the new math skill would help them solve common, everyday problems. Karen addressed motivation when she explained how monocots and dicots formed an important food source. The motivational component builds on introductory focus by helping to sustain attention.

Presentation

During the *presentation phase* of a direct-instruction lesson, the teacher explains and illustrates the concept or explains and models the skill being taught. Sometimes called the *development* phase (Murphy et al., 1986) or *input and modeling* (Hunter, 1984), it is during this phase that the teacher uses examples, demonstrations, and modeling to help make the topic meaningful to students.

While this phase of the model appears simple and straightforward, research indicates that implementing it can be challenging for teachers. One of the problems is being able to think like a student and conceptualize the new content in a way that is simple and makes sense to students. Teachers describe the problem in this way:

"I've never thought through [how to teach a cognitive skill]. The most difficult thing is to think it through. . . . Figuring out how to model [the skill] is a
hard thing for me. . . . I have to really sit down and write it out. I mean, I am
still doing that pretty much, like every day with that group" (Duffy et al.,
1985, p. 6).

One explanation for this problem relates to internalization and automaticity. The concepts
and skills that we teach often become so automatic for us that we perform them nearly
unconsciously. As a result, we encounter difficulty when we try to verbalize—or even
model—them for our students. For example, stop for a second and think about how you
would explain and model tying a shoelace for a youngster. Our explanation might be
somewhat vague, such as, "Well, first you do this, and then you put one lace over the other
. . ." and our modeling might be rushed and confusing. The difficulty you experience is
similar to the one teachers encounter when they try to explain skills.

In reaction to this problem, teachers often rush through this phase of the lesson, providing too little explanation and modeling, asking students to try the skill before they are
ready. A partial solution to this problem is to use task analysis to break complex skills into
more specific parts.

The most effective presentations are clear and interactive, and they contain enough
examples and modeling to develop student comprehension. Both Tim and Karen effectively implemented this phase in their teaching. For example, Tim modeled problem-
solving processes himself, and then he asked Antonio to demonstrate and explain how he
solved his problem. Also, both Tim and Antonio used cognitive modeling while they were
involved in problem solving, allowing others to share in their thinking.

Karen used several examples to make her presentation effective. As she introduced
monocots and dicots, she shared examples of each plant type with students, and as she
discussed the concepts' essential characteristics, she related them to both examples and
overheads. She also wrote the characteristics and important information on the board.
Both Tim and Karen also actively involved students through questioning during the presentation phases of their lessons.

Guided Practice

During guided practice, students try out new content as the teacher carefully monitors
their progress and provides feedback. During the guided practice phase of a Direct-
Instruction lesson, both teacher and student roles change. The teacher moves from
information giver and model to coach, and the students move from receiving information
to testing their understanding with examples and problems provided by the teacher.

During the early phases of guided practice, the teacher provides instructional scaffolding to ensure that students experience success when they try new skills. Gradually,
teachers reduce the number of these prompts and transfer more responsibility to students.

The kind and amount of teacher talk also shifts during this phase. Initially,
the teacher gives cues and prompts that provide instructional scaffolding. Later, as students assume more responsibility for explaining problems and classifying examples,

teachers' talk will be more probing, designed to raise the level of student thinking and application.

Guided practice occurred in Tim's lesson when he assisted his students in solving problems using their counting pieces and the flannel board. Karen provided guided practice when she presented pictures and overheads of plants like rice and corn and asked students to classify them and explain their answers.

During guided practice, teachers must decide when to make the transition to independent practice—when students try out the new skill on their own. Effective independent practice requires that students have enough expertise to be successful with little teacher assistance (Gersten et al., 1999).

There are several ways to gauge whether students are ready for this transition. One is student success rates; when 80 percent to 90 percent of students' responses during guided practice are correct, the class is probably ready for independent practice. A second gauge is the quality of student answers. Confident and quick answers signal that students are ready; hesitant or partially correct answers suggest the need for more practice under the guidance of the teacher.

A high level of interaction between teacher and student is essential during this phase of the model. Teachers need to ask clarifying and probing questions to determine if students actually understand the new content or are following a set of memorized procedures. Research indicates that more effective teachers ask three times as many questions during this phase of direct instruction than do their less effective counterparts (Evertson et al., 1980). Teacher-student interaction also provides teachers with access to student thinking, allowing them to understand and "debug" student errors and misconceptions.

To this point the topic has been introduced, explained, and modeled, and students have had a chance to practice with the teacher's guidance. They should now be ready for independent practice.

Independent Practice

Independent practice is the final phase of Direct-Instruction lessons. During this phase, students practice the new skill or concept on their own, developing both automaticity and the ability to transfer (Gersten et al., 1999).

Ideally, independent practice occurs in two stages. During the first, students practice in class under the supportive umbrella of the teacher. Later, students work on their own in a homework assignment.

Independent practice in the classroom is important because it allows the teacher to monitor learning progress and provide assistance if needed. Student success rates and the learning problems the students encounter both help the teacher in diagnosing learner problems. If few students are having problems, the teacher can work with individuals. If a number of students are having the same problems, it may be necessary to pull the class back together and reteach the parts of the topic that students don't understand (Brophy & Good, 1986).

The students began independent practice in Karen's lesson when she passed out a worksheet and had each student classify additional examples of monocots and dicots. We left Tim's lesson before it progressed to independent practice.

Increasing Motivation in the Direct-Instruction Model

Even though it's teacher centered, the Direct-Instruction Model provides many opportunities to increase student motivation. This increased motivation can result in improved learning when the model is being used as well as improved attitudes about learning in general.

Central to motivation strategies within this model is the concept of **competence motivation,** *which is an innate need in people to master tasks and skills* (White, 1959). Competence motivation helps explain why young children practice a developing skill like tying a shoe or zipping a coat over and over. It also helps explain why adults will work countess hours getting better at sports like tennis and golf or struggle to improve their times when running. People feel a sense of accomplishment when they get better at something (Deci et al., 1991).

Research supports the link between increased competence and attitudes toward learning; when students become better at something, they not only feel better about themselves but also about the content they're learning (McLeod, 1989; Kloostermann & Cougan, 1994). Teachers can assist in this process in at least three ways. First, they can design instruction that ensures that students make learning progress. Second, as learners improve, teachers make this progress visible and tangible, and third, teachers need to develop in students the belief that their learning progress results from personal effort and hard work (Weiner, 1994a, 1994b). Let's see how teachers can employ these motivational strategies in their instruction.

For motivation to increase when the Direct-Instruction Model is used, learning progress needs to occur. Students need to get better at the skill they're learning or understand the new concept in deeper and richer ways. Teachers ensure that this happens through careful planning that breaks complex, difficult tasks into simpler, more manageable ones and by providing practice and feedback along the way.

As learning progresses, teachers can improve motivation by consciously calling attention to this growth, such as doing timed trials in math or charting learning progress in all content areas (Alberto & Troutman, 1999). For example, when using timed trials in math, teachers put basic math facts on a sheet of paper and give students a time period, such as 1 minute, to do as many as they can. These trials are repeated daily; with practice and feedback, students' ability to do the problems increases. Teachers can call students' attention to this increase by having students chart their learning progress, a strategy that works in other content areas as well.

Teachers should emphasize individual learning progress rather than competition with others; research suggests that competition can have negative effects on learning, especially for low-ability students or students who don't fare well in competitive situations (Pintrich & Schunk, 1996).

A final way that teachers can increase motivation when the Direct-Instruction Model is used is to emphasize the influence of effort over other success factors such as luck or innate abilities. Comments like, "Nice job, your hard work paid off," and, "I can really tell you're trying hard, your scores are improving," on written work as well as in verbal interactions helps students attribute their success to their personal efforts.

The Direct-Instruction Model: Variations

To this point in the chapter, we have described the Direct-Instruction Model as a strategy for teaching concepts and skills. However, the model can also be used to teach other forms of content such as generalizations, principles and academic rules.

In Chapter 2, we said that generalizations, principles, and rules are similar in that each uses concepts to describes trends or patterns in the world. Some examples include:

- People immigrate for economic reasons. (generalization)
- A diet high in saturated fat raises a person's cholesterol level. (generalization)
- The greater the unbalanced force on an object, the greater the object's acceleration. (principle)
- A pronoun must agree with its antecedent in number and gender. (academic rule)
- In rounding off a number, if the last digit is 5 or more, you round up; if it is 4 or less, you round down. (academic rule)

Generalizations, principles, and rules are similar to concepts in that they can be illustrated with examples, and high-quality examples are the key to successful learning in all cases. In this section we discuss using the Direct-Instruction Model to teach these different forms of content.

Planning

Planning to teach generalizations, principles, and rules with the Direct-Instruction Model is very similar to the planning process when concepts are being taught. Goals need to be clearly identified, prerequisite knowledge determined, and examples constructed or selected and sequenced. As with teaching concepts, a clear idea of teaching goals and a thorough understanding of the abstraction are essential.

Implementation

Implementation of the Direct-Instruction Model to teach generalizations, principles, and rules is similar to using the model to teach concepts. During the introductory phase, the teacher provides an overview of new content, establishes links with students' background knowledge, and helps students understand the value of the new content. During the presentation phase, the teacher describes the topic, explains the concepts embedded in the abstraction, and uses examples to help students understand the relationships described in it. Guided practice allows students to experiment with the topic, and independent practice provides additional examples to develop automaticity and transfer. Look for these phases in the following case study.

> Tamra Evans, a high school social studies teacher, wants to teach her students the generalization, "If demand stays constant, price is inversely related to supply."

She begins her lesson by stating, "We have been studying the economics of different countries for several lessons, so let's review what we've done so far. What do we mean by economics? . . . Jerry?"

"Economics sort of deals with money," he responds.

"Good, and what particular aspects of money? Tim?"

" . . . Well, it tells how money is made and how it is spread around," Tim answers.

"Excellent, Tim," Tamra smiles. "Now, everyone, today we're going to deal with a particular law in economics. This law states that 'when demand stays constant, price and supply are inversely related.'" As she states the generalization, Tamra writes it on the chalkboard.

"This law is important," she continues, "because it will help us understand why the prices of things we buy in stores go up or down. Supply, as we'll see in today's lesson, is a major factor influencing price."

"Now . . . how do supply, demand, and price relate to the larger topic of economics? . . . Cheryl?"

". . . I think . . . price relates to money and . . . how someone would make money," Cheryl answers hesitantly.

"Yes! Very good, Cheryl. Now let's look at the terms *supply, demand, price,* and *inversely*. What does the word *inversely* mean? . . . Mike?"

". . . It means something like when one thing gets bigger, another gets smaller," Mike responds.

Tamra continues the discussion of each term until she is satisfied that students' understanding of each is correct. At this point, she continues: "Look up at the overhead. The paragraph on it illustrates the generalization." She shows the students the following example.

As I drove into a city of approximately a half million people in August of 1999, I filled my car with gas at an independent station for 94.9 cents per gallon. In March of 2000, I made a trip into the same city. I looked at a pump which said $1.249 for unleaded. When I asked the attendant about the big price jump he explained that a strike at local refineries had made gas hard to get.

After allowing the students time to read the anecdote, Tamra asks, "How does the example relate to our generalization? . . . Judy?"

". . . The strike would mean that the supply was reduced, I guess."

"Yes, good, you've identified a key variable in the example, Judy. What else? . . . David?"

"The price shot way up," David answers quickly.

"And what do we call that kind of relationship?"

" . . . Oh. That's what inverse means," David answers after thinking a moment.

"And the amount people wanted to buy stayed about the same," Anna volunteers.

"Very well done," Tamra smiles. "We see how the example illustrates that the price and supply are inversely related if the demand stays the same.

"Now look at another example and tell me if it illustrates the law," she goes on. She shows them the following example:

Jimmy decided to put up a lemonade stand. He charged 4 cents a cup, and people were buying lemonade at the corner of his father's lot faster than he could make it. Jimmy decided, "I'll bet they'll still buy my lemonade if I charge five cents a glass." So he did.

Two days later Joey, who saw how well Jimmy was making out, decided to open up his own lemonade stand across the street from Jimmy's. He charged 3 cents a glass, and soon most of the people who had been stopping at Jimmy's stand were going to Joey's instead. Jimmy then lowered his price to 3 cents a glass, and both the boys sold lemonade.

"Does this example illustrate the principle we've been discussing?" Tamra asks. "How is the demand affected by Joey opening his stand? . . . Jason?"

"I guess it isn't. It should be about the same."

"Very good, Jason. There is no reason to think that Joey's stand would have any effect on the amount people wanted to buy."

"Yes, Kristy," Tamra smiles in response to Kristy's waving hand.

"I've got it," Kristy says excitedly. "Since the demand was the same and Joey's stand increased the supply, the price had to go down, which is an inverse relationship."

"Excellent analysis, Kristy. So does the example illustrate the principle?"

"Yes," Kristy replies confidently.

"Let me show you one more," Tamra says, and she displays the following example on the screen.

In the early 1990s, with the boom in Asian trade, many universities dramatically expanded their international trade preparation programs and a campaign was on to try and maintain a lead over other industrialized countries, such as Germany and Japan. At that time, PhDs in Asian business trade could virtually name their salaries at most universities.

As the country moved into the late 1990s, a great many students still took majors in Asian business trade, but with the slump in the economies of many Asian countries, the emphasis on this aspect of international trade was reduced somewhat.

In the late 1990s, many business majors in Asian trade were unable to get jobs, and those that were employed received lower comparative salaries than those trained ten years earlier.

"Does this example illustrate the law we're discussing?" Tamra queries. "Karen?"

". . . I'm . . . I'm not sure," Karen answers.

"Let's look carefully," Tamra suggested. "What has happened to the price?"

"... Their salaries were lower," Karen tentatively suggests.

"Yes they were. That's good, Karen. Now, how about the supply? ... Jan?"

"It doesn't look to me as if it's changed that much."

"Aha! But the demand has gone down!" John adds with a look of insight on his face. "The example doesn't illustrate the idea we're discussing, because our generalization says the demand stays constant."

"Excellent, everyone!" Tamra praises. "That is a real good analysis. Since you've done so well, think now and see if you can create some more examples that illustrate the generalization."

The students, with Tamra's help, generate additional examples that they analyze as they did the first three.

She continues, "Class, I have some additional cases that I'd like you to do now. In each case if it does illustrate the generalization, explain *how* it's illustrated by identifying each part—supply, demand, and price—in the generalization, and if it doesn't illustrate it, explain why. I'd like you to start on these with the time remaining, and I'll come around to see if you have any questions. Whatever you don't finish, take home for homework and we'll discuss them tomorrow."

As we can see, using the Direct-Instruction Model to teach generalizations, principles, and rules is very similar to procedures used in teaching concepts. In the introductory phase, the teacher still outlines the lesson and explains how the new content relates to students' lives. During the presentation phase, the teacher describes the generalization and makes sure that concepts contained within it are understood by students. Tamra used case studies to illustrate the generalization and to help students see how it related to the real world. During independent practice, students analyzed additional examples as both an in-class assignment and homework.

In summary, the Direct-Instruction Model provides an effective and time-efficient way to teach generalization principles and rules. As with concept teaching, the essential ingredients for successful lessons are the liberal use of examples and teacher-student and student-student interaction that involves learners in making sense of these examples.

Direct Instruction and Diversity

While research has shown direct instruction to be effective with students in general, additional research indicates that direct instruction is especially effective with students from diverse backgrounds (Gersten et al., 1999). This explicit approach to teaching concepts and skills provides culturally and linguistically diverse students with additional structure, which facilitates learning. In addition, the interactive nature of the model provides opportunities for teachers to link new ideas to students' diverse content backgrounds. Let's examine how the Direct-Instruction Model does this.

Structure is important for all students. It organizes ideas and procedures, making them understandable and predictable. Structure seems to be especially important to culturally and linguistically diverse students, because school can be confusing and chaotic for them. Research in the basic skills areas of reading and math suggest that a structured approach such as direct instruction facilitates learning in these areas.

A second reason that direct instruction is effective with minority students is that it provides opportunities for academically focused interaction between teacher and students. These interactions are important because they help cross cultural and linguistic boundaries (Gersten et al., 1999). Often problems and examples make sense to teachers; that is why they chose them. Unfortunately, these same problems and examples may not be meaningful to students. Interactions within the Direct-Instruction Model provide opportunities to clarify examples and elicit culturally relevant examples from students.

Direct instruction can also be effective with English as a second language (ESL) students and in sheltered English instruction. In these classes teachers have the dual goals of teaching content while building upon students' developing English skills. Experts in the area (Gersten et al., 1999) recommend the following elements of effective ESL instruction:

- Specific targeting of key concepts or skills
- Activation of students' prior knowledge
- Extensive use of demonstrations and modeling
- Emphasis on students' active involvement
- Opportunities for extensive practice

Each of these recommendations is an integral component of direct instruction. Direct instruction is optimally suited for linguistically diverse students.

Assessing Student Understanding

The assessment of content outcomes in a Direct-Instruction lesson is similar to the process with the Inductive Model and the Concept-Attainment Model. This process was discussed in detail in Chapter 4 and reinforced in Chapter 5. You may want to review those sections at this time.

To further examine the assessment process, let us look again at Karen's lesson. She has several options to choose from in assessing her students. For example, she could:

1. Have the students define monocots and dicots.
2. Give them pictures of monocots and dicots and ask them to identify each.
3. Give them actual examples of monocots and dicots and ask them to classify and explain their classification.
4. Have them bring in their own examples of monocots and dicots and explain the examples in each case.

Having the students define these concepts is a very superficial measure of their understanding of the concept because it basically involves memorizing a string of words—something that may or may not involve meaningful learning. However, each of the others would be a valid indicator of their understanding, with the demands on the students being progressively greater in each case.

An effective measure of concept learning in general is to have students classify examples and nonexamples of the concept. For example, in a lesson on adjectives, the teacher could present students with an item such as the following:

Circle each of the following words that could be adjectives.

 a. pretty
 b. go
 c. ball
 d. early
 e. big
 f. crazily
 g. event

An item such as this is easy to prepare and score. However, this efficiency comes at a price. In the real world, we want students to be able to write using adjectives appropriately. A more valid item would require students to write a paragraph and identify the adjectives within it. Authentic assessments such as these attempt to place students in more realistic and lifelike settings to make the assessment process as similar as possible to real-life situations (Airasian, 1997; Stiggins, 1997).

However, scoring such an item can be time consuming. A reasonable compromise could be to present the students with an already prepared passage and have them identify the adjectives within it. While this is not as effective a strategy as having them write their own, the passage could be scored efficiently. Determining the appropriate compromise between the validity of the assessment and the demand on the teacher is a matter of professional judgment. Only you, the teacher, can make that decision.

Summary

The Direct-Instruction Model: An Overview

The Direct-Instruction Model is a teacher-directed strategy that can be used to teach concepts and skills. It does this through strategic use of problems and examples and through structured interaction between teacher and student.

Direct Instruction: Theoretical Perspectives

The Direct-Instruction Model is derived from several sources including the teacher-effectiveness research, which looked into actual classrooms to document the strategies of effective teachers. It is also based upon observational learning theory, which emphasizes the importance of modeling for the acquisition of complex behaviors. In addition, Direct Instruction is based upon the work of Lev Vygotsky, who pointed out the importance of dialogue in learning.

Planning Lessons with the Direct-Instruction Model

Planning with this model begins with the identification of a specific concept or skill. This is followed by identifying prerequisite knowledge that serves as the conceptual foundation for new learning. Finally, teachers need to carefully select examples and problems to illustrate important ideas.

Implementing Lessons Using the Direct-Instruction Model

The model exists in four sequential phases—introduction, presentation, guided practice, and independent practice. The use of well-thought out examples and problems is the key to the success of learning activities in which the model is used.

Though it is strongly teacher directed, effective use of the Direct-Instruction Model requires high levels of interaction between the teacher and students. The patterns in this interaction shift as a lesson develops. Initially, the teacher presents information and strongly guides students as they work with examples and problems. Later, students work more and more independently until they are able to analyze examples and solve problems without the teacher's help.

The Direct-Instruction Model: Variations

While the model is designed specifically to teach skills and concepts, it can be easily modified to teach principles, generalizations, and academic rules as well.

The model is especially effective in teaching students of diversity because of its structure and opportunities for interaction. The structure provides a familiar learning landscape for students; the interaction provides opportunities for teachers and students to identify mutually meaningful examples.

Assessing Student Understanding

The key to effective assessment with this model is to ensure that students learn content at a meaningful level. This requires that students work actively with examples and concepts, linking them to the abstraction being taught.

IMPORTANT CONCEPTS

Automaticity   (p. 280)
Cognitive Modeling   (p. 278)
Competence Motivation   (p. 286)
Direct-Instruction Model   (p. 275)
Modeling   (p. 277)
Observational learning   (p. 277)

Scaffolding   (p. 278)
Skills   (p. 280)
Task analysis   (p. 281)
Transfer   (p. 280)
Transfer of responsibility   (p. 276)
Zone of proximal development   (p. 278)

E X E R C I S E S

1. Consider the following list of goals. Identify those most appropriately reached using the Direct-Instruction Model.

   a. To understand *prime number.*

   b. To simplify arithmetic expressions that follow the rule: Multiply and divide left to right and then add and subtract left to right.

   c. To understand *square.*

   d. To understand *major scale.*

   e. To understand "For substances that don't mix, less dense materials float on more dense materials."

   f. To understand *gerund.*

   g. To identify the relationships between the economy and geography of the North and South prior to the Civil War and how these factors impacted the outcome of the war.

2. Select a topic in your teaching area. Then prepare a set of examples that could be used to effectively teach the topic.

3. Read the following description of a teacher using the Direct-Instruction Model and then answer the questions that follow.

   Kathy Lake begins her language arts class with, "Today, class, we're going to talk about a different kind of word pair. Who remembers what other word pairs we've been studying? . . . John?"

   ". . . Synonyms," John answers.

   "Good, and who knows what a synonym is? . . . Maria?"

   ". . . They . . . like . . . mean the same, their meanings are the same, like . . . big and large."

   "Very good, Maria. How about another example? . . . Toni?"

   " . . . Fast and speedy."

   "Super! And one more? Roberto?"

   ". . . Skinny . . . and thin?"

   "Yes, very good example, Roberto. Well, today we're going to study a different kind of word pair called *antonyms.* When we are all done with the lesson today, you will be able to give me some examples of antonyms. Also, when I give you a word you will be able to give me an antonym for it."

   She writes the following on the board.

Synonyms	*Antonyms*
(Same Meaning)	(Opposite Meaning)

   "Antonyms are word pairs that have opposite meaning. What do we mean by word pairs?" Kathy asks.

   Susan hesitates and then says, "Like . . . two words."

   "Good, Susan," Kathy nods with a smile. "So *word pair* means two words. Now, what does *opposite* mean?"

   "Not . . . the same," Joe volunteers.

"That's very close, Joe," Kathy. She continues, "Let me give you an example. Big and small have opposite meanings and they're two words, so they're antonyms. *Opposite* means having a different or almost a reversed meaning, like *big* and *small*."

With that, she writes *big* and *small* under the term *antonym*.

"Another example of antonyms is *up* and *down*. They are antonyms because they're pairs of words whose meanings are opposite. So let's put them up here under the Antonym column. Let me try another one. Are *happy* and *glad* antonyms? Antonio?"

". . . No," replies Antonio.

"Why not?" Kathy asks.

"Because . . . because their meanings are the same . . . not opposite."

"So what are they, Antonio?"

". . . Synonyms."

"Fine, Antonio. Let's put them under the Synonym column. Now let's try another one. Are *cold* and *hot* antonyms? Ted?"

". . . Yeah . . . they're a word pair, and the words have opposite meanings."

"So let's put them over here on the board. And what about *alive* and *dead?* . . . Pat?"

"Those . . . are antonyms, too, they're the opposite."

"Fine. Now I want to see if you can give me some examples of antonyms. Think real hard. . . . Anyone? . . . Lynne?"

"How about *in* and *out?*"

"Good. Anyone else? . . . Clarissa?"

"How about *high* and *low?*"

"And why are those antonyms?" Kathy probes.

". . . 'Cuz . . . they're . . . word pairs that are opposite . . . have opposite meanings."

"Real fine. Now one last test. Remember we had the word pair *happy* and *glad* and you said that they weren't antonyms? Can anyone make antonyms from these words? . . . Juan?"

". . . How about . . . *happy* and *sad?*"

"Good, Sam, do you have another one?"

"*Glad* and *upset.*"

"Those are both excellent antonyms. I think you've all done a good job today in learning about this new kind of word pair. Now someone tell me what we learned today. . . . Susan?"

" . . . Well, we learned about antonyms."

"Good. Go on," Kathy smiles.

"Antonyms . . . mean . . . opposite."

"Yes, excellent! And one more thing. . . . Brad?"

"They're word pairs."

"Exactly. Very good, Brad."

She closes the lesson by saying, "Remember, word pairs that mean the same are . . . class?"

"Synonyms!" they all responds in unison.

"Fine, and word pairs that are opposite are . . . ?"

"Antonyms!" they answer.

"Excellent. Now I have some exercises that I would like you to do individually." She distributes a worksheet among the students and circulates as they begin working on it.

A. Identify each of the phases of the Direct-Instruction Model in Kathy Lake's lesson.

B. Consider assessing the concepts Kathy taught. Prepare a test item that could be used to evaluate students' understanding of the concepts.

C. While Kathy's instruction technically followed the Direct-Instruction Model, we might criticize it on one important basis. Offer that criticism. (*Hint:* Think about the idea of meaningfulness.)

DISCUSSION QUESTIONS

1. Compare the Direct-Instruction Model to the Inductive and Concept-Attainment Models. What similarities and differences do they share? What are advantages and disadvantages of each?

2. How does the Direct-Instruction Model differ from typical lecture? What are its advantages and disadvantages compared to the lecture method?

3. The Direct-Instruction Model is heavily teacher centered. What advantages are there to this? Disadvantages?

4. Consider content goals again. How do these goals affect the decision to select the Inductive or Direct-Instruction Model? Discuss this question in terms of the abstraction of the concept or generalization, how "vague" the topic is, and the background of the students.

5. What alternative does the teacher have if he or she reaches the end of a Direct-Instruction lesson and the students still do not understand the abstraction? How would this compare to an Inductive lesson?

6. Compare the amount of teacher talk and student talk in a Direct-Instruction compared to an Inductive lesson. What conditions could cause these amounts to vary?

The Lecture-Discussion Model

As we saw in Chapter 8, the Direct-Instruction Model is designed to teach concepts and skills, with emphasis on active teaching and high levels of student involvement. However, as we saw in Chapter 6, teachers often have goals such as understanding the Revolutionary War in social studies or the respiratory system in health, which involve understanding organized bodies of knowledge. In Chapter 6 we discussed the Integrative Model, a learner-centered approach to teaching these topics, and in this chapter we examine the Lecture-Discussion Model, a teacher-centered approach to helping students understand organized bodies of knowledge.

When you have completed your study of this chapter, you should be able to meet the following goals:

- Describe the theoretical foundation of the Lecture-Discussion Model.
- Use the Lecture-Discussion Model to plan for teaching organized bodies of information.
- Construct different kinds of advance organizers.
- Implement effective Lecture-Discussion lessons.
- Assess content acquisition in Lecture-Discussion lessons.

Let us begin our study of the Lecture-Discussion Model by looking at a teacher using this model to teach a lesson from a unit on *behaviorism* in a high school psychology class.

Lorrie Martello begins her class by saying, "Class, today we are going to continue our discussion of operant conditioning by looking at different reinforcement schedules. I've got a problem I'd like you to think about. There was a woman with a dog named Paxie. She wanted to train Paxie to get the newspaper from the lawn and put it on the porch every morning to keep it from getting wet and soggy. Now, she knew that some mornings she wouldn't be home to reward Paxie, but she wanted Paxie to get the paper anyway. What could she do to train her dog? . . . Stop and think about that one for a moment."

Lorrie pauses briefly and then continues, "Let's keep that problem in mind and we'll return to it in a moment. For right now, let's review some points that we discussed yesterday. Who can give us an example of operant conditioning and explain why it's a form of behavioral learning? . . . Bill?"

". . . I . . . I think it's because in operant conditioning we focus on behaviors and rewards that we can see."

"Good, Bill. Now who can describe how it differs from classical conditioning? . . . Jack?"

". . . Well, in classical conditioning the response that the . . . the . . . whoever makes is out of their control, like the dog salivating. In operant conditioning the response is voluntary."

"Can you give us an example of that?" Lorrie probes.

" . . . Well, my mother always thanks my dad when he helps pick up the kitchen and living room, so he does it more now," Sherry responds hesitantly.

"Also, in classical conditioning the behavior follows the stimulus that influences it, and in operant conditioning the behavior comes before the stimulus, like in . . . reinforcement or punishment," Hakeem volunteers.

"Very good! Now today we're going to focus on one aspect of operant conditioning, which is the system of reinforcers that follow the desired behaviors."

With that she displays the following statement on the overhead.

Reinforcement schedules are applications of operant conditioning in which the frequency of rewards is specified. When we reinforce behaviors, we can reinforce every time, not at all, or somewhere in between. The somewhere in between can be based on number of responses or time. When we periodically compliment our brother or sister for helping us clean up around the house, we are using a reinforcement schedule.

Then Lorrie put the following outline on the board.

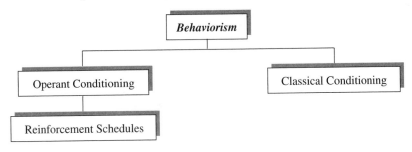

"Before we go on, I'd like to talk a little about the statement on the overhead. If it makes sense to us, it will help us understand the rest of the material to follow. The first concept we should focus on is *reinforcement*. Remember we said that reinforcement results in an increase in behavior due to some desired consequence, such as a compliment for a person or a doggy treat for a dog.

"Now we can decide to reinforce a behavior every time it occurs or only part of the time. That's what we mean by frequency or interval. So if we're trying to train our dog to shake hands, we can reward him every time he does this or every other time or even some sort of random pattern. That's what we mean by frequency.

"Another way to reinforce is by time. Let's say we want to train our dog to stay on the porch. We could reward him every 15 seconds, every 30 seconds, or every minute he stays on the porch. That's what we mean by interval.

"Now let's focus on this outline. What can you conclude based on it? . . . Jim?"

". . . Well . . . reinforcement schedules mainly apply to operant conditioning," Jim responds, ". . . because we only see them under it and not under classical conditioning."

"Excellent, Jim. That's exactly right. Now look at the statement on the overhead again. It talks about rewards for desired behavior. This means that the reward comes after the organism has responded, so it's operant conditioning.

"Now, let's go on and focus on the rewards. What does the statement suggest about reinforcement schedules? . . . Juan?"

". . . They describe how often the person or I guess even other animals get rewarded."

"Good, Juan, and what would continuous reinforcement mean? . . . Sandy?"

". . . I guess when they get a reward every time they did what you wanted," Sandy replies after thinking a moment.

"Excellent, Sandy. Now give us an example of that . . . Susan?"

". . . I guess it would be like every time Paxie brought the paper, it would get a doggy biscuit."

"Fine, Susan, and so now you can draw in your notes this outline:

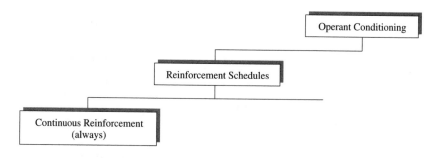

"And what do we have at the other end of the continuum? What happens when a behavior is never reinforced? Shanelle?"

". . . The dog or person or whatever would stop doing the behavior after a while."

"Excellent, Shanelle. That's called extinction. Let's put that up on our outline, too."

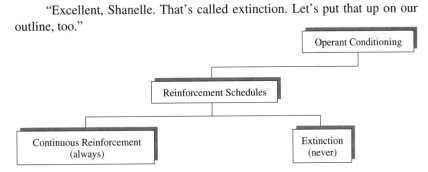

Lorrie continues, "How do continuous reinforcement and extinction compare?"

"They're . . . like opposite of each other," Judy volunteers. "At one end you get reinforced for everything, and at the other, you don't get reinforced for anything."

"Let's look again at our statement," Lorie goes on. "It said that a reinforcement schedule is the frequency or interval of rewards. How do the two items on our outline relate to the statement? . . . Nikki?"

". . . In the first case the frequency is high and in the second, it's low. . . actually doesn't exist," Nikki responds.

"Excellent, Nikki. So we see that both are forms of reinforcement schedules because they both describe a frequency of rewards. Now let's add *intermittent reinforcement* to our outline and define it as a schedule in which behavior is reinforced some of the time."

After writing the definition on the board, she continues, "There are two main kinds of intermittent reinforcement schedules that depend upon how the reinforcer is delivered. These are called ratio or interval schedules. Let's talk about ratio schedules first. In a ratio schedule the organism has to produce a certain number of responses before it is reinforced. It's like piecework in a factory. Who knows how that works? . . . Gerry?"

". . . Well, my dad works in a factory that has piecework, and he gets paid based on how many cars they make in a day."

"Good, Gerry. That's a good example of a ratio schedule. Now I'd like us to break into our groups and come up with some additional examples of ratio schedules. Each group should think of two. You've got 5 minutes." As the groups works, Lorrie circulates, answering questions and monitoring each group's progress. At the end of 5 minutes, she calls the groups back together.

"Okay, who's got another example of a ratio schedule of reinforcement? . . . Latinda?"

". . . It would be like having the cat in the Skinner box in the movie we saw get rewarded for some number of times it pressed the bar."

"Fine, Latinda. How about another one? . . . Zack?"

"We thought about delivering circulars from door to door 'cause you get paid for how many you deliver."

"Good, Zack. Anyone else? Another one?"

The class discusses other examples and then Lorie says, "Now let's compare intermittent and continuous reinforcement. Kathy?"

"I think it's kinda simple," Kathy answers. "Every behavior is rewarded with continuous reinforcement, but only some are with intermittent reinforcement."

"Good, Kathy. And, class, how does this type of reinforcement influence behavior? . . . Kwan?"

Kwan does not respond.

"Let's compare it to continuous," Lorrie prompts. "Do you think the rate of response would be greater or less?"

". . . Greater."

"Why?"

". . . Because the rat would have to press faster or more times to get the reward and wouldn't take as much time off to eat it."

"Good answer, Kwan. And what would happen if we stopped reinforcing with an intermittent schedule? Would the behavior stop quicker or slower than with continuous reinforcement and why? . . . Dan?"

". . . I think . . . faster because the behavior isn't as firmly established."

"Sarah? You have your hand up."

"I think slower because the cat is used to not being reinforced."

"Interesting. We have two different predictions. What about our work with classical conditioning? Does that help us out any? Let's break out in our groups and see if we can figure that one out. Quickly now, you've got 3 minutes."

The lesson continues as the students discuss the question of whether or not a continuous or an intermittent schedule would result in the most enduring behaviors. Now Lorrie moves to the topics of variable- and fixed-ratio schedules and finally ends with a discussion of fixed- and variable-interval schedules. The period ends as Lorrie uses the following outline to review the major concepts discussed during the period.

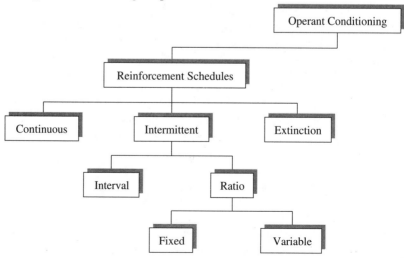

The Lecture-Discussion Model: An Overview

In the lesson we just saw, Lorrie Martello uses the Lecture-Discussion Model to help her students understand connections among ideas within the topic *behaviorism*. In implementing the model she first provided an overview that served as a framework for new information. Then she introduced new concepts and helped students link them to each other and to the content they already understood. Throughout the lesson, Lorrie used questioning to monitor students' understanding and to prevent them from learning the concepts as isolated ideas. In addition, she used groupwork to actively involve as many students as possible. At the end of the lesson, she further integrated the topics with a careful review and closure. These stages of the Lecture-Discussion Model are summarized in Table 9.1.

The Lecture-Discussion Model: Theoretical Perspectives

The effectiveness of the Lecture-Discussion model is based on three theoretical sources. First, it is intended to utilize what students already know by building on their existing background knowledge. Second, based on the work of David Ausubel (1963, 1968), teachers using the model present information in a systematic way, which helps students construct an organized understanding of the topic. Finally, it uses teacher questioning to actively involve students in the learning process. We examine each of these underpinnings in the sections that follow.

Schema Theory: Building on Students' Background Knowledge

Schema theory *is a view of knowledge construction which says that the information people store in memory consists of networks of organized and interconnected ideas, relationships, and procedures* (Good & Brophy, 1997). *The interconnected ideas,*

TABLE 9.1   Structure of the Lecture-Discussion Model

Stage	Function
Introduction	The purpose of the lesson is described, objectives are shared, and an overview helps students see the organization of the lesson.
Presentation	Major ideas are defined and explained.
Comprehension Monitoring	The teacher determines whether or not students understand concepts and ideas.
Integration	Connections between important ideas are explored.
Review and Closure	The lesson is carefully summarized.

relationships, and procedures are called **schemas** (Anderson, 1990). For example, let's take our schema for the process of learning. This schema has information in it about learning in general and other more specific information about learning in school. It helps us understand how to dress, when to go to school, what to do when we get there, and how to act toward the teacher and the other students. Within it, even more specific concepts and procedures for specific learning situations, such as discussion or small groupwork, are embedded.

Contemporary interest in the concept of schemas goes back to the 1920s and the work of the psychologist F. Bartlett (1932). Bartlett was interested in the processes involved in remembering information from written passages. To examine these processes, he asked subjects to read passages about Native American folklore and to recall information from them at different times. His results were unexpected. First, he found that even with immediate recall, different individuals remembered different parts of the stories. Also, because they interpreted the stories from their own frames of reference, they changed the facts to make them fit these reference frames. As time went on, subjects' distortions of the stories increased, but the distortions invariably were linked in such a way that the information was meaningful to the subjects themselves.

From these results, Bartlett concluded that a strong drive exists in people to make sense of what they encounter. In addition, he accounted for the personal and idiosyncratic nature of the distortions through the idea of individual schemas; each person was making sense of the passages based on the way their prior experiences were mentally organized. Let's see how this works. Read the following passage and answer the questions that follow.

> In 1367 Marain and the settlements ended a seven-year war with the Languri-ans and Pitoks. As a result of this war Languria was driven out of East Bacol. Marain would now rule Laman and other lands that had belonged to Languria. This brought peace to the Bacolian settlements. The settlers no longer had to fear attacks from Laman. The Bacolians were happy to be part of Marain in 1367. Yet a dozen years later, these same people would be fighting the Marish for independence, or freedom from United Marian's rule (Beck & McKeown, 1993, p. 2).

What is happening here? How much sense does the passage make? Let's try another passage.

> In 1763 Britain and the colonies ended a seven-year war with the French and Indians. As a result of this war France was driven out of North America. Britain would now rule Canada and other lands that had belonged to France. This brought peace to the American colonies. The colonists no longer had to fear attacks from Canada. The Americans were happy to be a part of Britain in 1763. Yet a dozen years later, these same people would be fighting the British for independence, or freedom from Great Britain's rule (Beck & McKeown, 1993, p. 2).

If you're like most other readers, the second passage made much more sense than the first, even though both were almost identical in their length, structure, and amount of detail. The second was more meaningful because you were able to bring your background knowledge, or schema, about American history and the Revolutionary War to bear to help integrate the separate facts.

A parallel situation exists in every classroom. As students enter classes with widely varying beliefs, attitudes, and background knowledge, they bring with them diverse schemas. They read the same account of the Vietnam War and some go away convinced of the need at that time for a strong stand against communism, while others interpret the passage as an example of a superpower's trying to exercise control over a basically internal struggle.

From these examples, we can see that schemas have three major characteristics (Rumelhart & Ortony, 1977).

- Each contains material based upon the person's past experience. What you know about soccer, for example, is an indicator of your past experiences with soccer.
- Each schema is embedded in other larger schemas and has other schemas embedded within it, such as schemas for learning in school embedded in larger schemas for learning in general.
- Schemas are dynamic. They are active and changing, based on their ability to explain the way the world works. When they make sense, they don't need to change; when they don't, we are motivated to adjust them (Eggen & Kauchak, 1999).

For example, when we blow between two pieces of paper held parallel to each other, we expect the bottoms to fly apart; this would be consistent with our past experiences. Instead, they come together. For most people, this event can't be explained with existing schemas, and we are motivated to understand why. With additional experience, we adapt our schemas to accommodate the principle, "Increasing the speed of air (or other fluids) over a surface decreases the force on that surface." This makes our schemas richer and more powerful because we can now explain events such as how airplanes can fly, why tornados are so destructive, how atomizers work, and why shower curtains wrap around our legs.

The process of learning can be thought of as the development of schemas that allow individuals to understand and function in their world. We can view teaching as a deliberate attempt to influence the content and structure of student schemas. In doing so, we must keep in mind that students' preexisting schemas can either be liabilities or assets; they can either assist or hinder new learning.

Let us see how Lorrie applied schema theory in her lesson on reinforcement schedules. She was attempting to aid her students in their development of organized schemas about operant conditioning by systematically introducing the subordinate concepts related to reinforcement schedules and displaying them in a hierarchy. She began by having them compare operant and classical conditioning to take advantage of a larger schema into which the present one would fit. Seeing reinforcement schedules under operant conditioning helped students avoid confusing operant and classical conditioning. Further, she called for and got examples of classical and operant conditioning to ensure that learners' backgrounds were developed enough to allow the lesson to move toward a discussion of reinforcement schedules.

As she introduced new concepts, Lorrie used the outline and examples to help students link them to their developing schemas. She also compared each concept to others to be sure that they were connected.

Meaningful Verbal Learning: The Work of David Ausubel

One of the most influential people in bringing the ideas behind schema theory to classrooms was a psychologist named David Ausubel. Beginning with studies done in the early 1960s and captured in his book, *The Psychology of Meaningful Verbal Learning* (1963), Ausubel stressed the importance of cognitive structures on learning.

Ausubel placed heavy emphasis on **meaningful verbal learning,** that is, *the acquisition of ideas that are linked to other ideas.* In contrast, **rote learning** *emphasizes the memorization of specific items of information rather than exploring relationships within the material.* Meaningful learning occurs when the ideas in a new schema are connected not only to each other but also to previously established schemas.

One other aspect of Ausubel's theory should be stressed. Though he favored teacher-centered, deductively sequenced teaching, he was adamantly opposed to passive learning on the part of students. An important task for teachers is to involve students in finding relationships between old and new content and among the different parts of the new topic.

One of the most prominent ideas to have emerged from Ausubel's work is the concept of *advance organizers.* Let's look at this concept now.

Advance Organizers. **Advance organizers** *are verbal statements at the beginning of a lesson that preview and structure new material and link it to the students' existing schemas.* Advance organizers are like cognitive roadmaps; they allow students to see where they have been and where they are going. Effective advance organizers are:

- Presented prior to learning a larger body of information.
- Written in paragraph form.
- Presented in concrete fashion.
- Include an example that helps learners identify the relationship between the ideas in the organizer and the information to follow (Corkill, 1992).

To illustrate how advance organizers work, let's look at two that have been used at different school levels. The first is from an elementary social studies lesson on governments:

> The organization of a government is like a family. Different people in the government have different responsibilities and roles. When all the people work together, both families and governments operate efficiently.

The second is aimed at college students who are studying linguistics:

> We all use language every day. And yet, unless we are writing papers for a course or completing an assignment in English class, we generally give language very little thought. There are people who study language, much as there are scholars who study other important areas of life. These students of language analyze our language in ways that are far more complex than the sentence diagramming most of us have done. Not only do they study how the written language works, they also examine how it is generated. These language scholars also study spoken language—how it is learned, how people use it to share meaning with other people, and what the various parts of the spoken language are. In addition, the study of language relates what is known about spoken and written language.
>
> Another point of interest in the study of language comes from comparing different languages (e.g., English and Spanish). Just as sociologists compare life in different cultures and anthropologists study the origin of cultures, the scholars of language compare different languages in terms of how they evolved and how they are now written and spoken. The scholars you will read about believe that the study of language can shed light on how people think and how human ideas have evolved. As is the case in any field such as law, education, or science, there are some basic conventions or rules that all who study language agree on. The chapter you are about to read explains the study of language and the rules followed by people in this profession (Dinnel & Glover, 1985, p. 521).

Both of these advance organizers attempted to provide a framework for new content. The second one is obviously longer because it was designed for college students.

Differences between these advance organizers illustrate one other important feature; to be effective, they must be tailored to the learner (Ausubel, 1978). The exact form that an advance organizer takes depends on (1) the type of content, (2) the age of the learner, and (3) how familiar students are with the learning material. Ways of constructing effective advance organizers are discussed in the planning section of this chapter.

Active Learner Involvement

A third principle undergirding the effectiveness of the Lecture-Discussion Model is the way it involves students through teacher questioning. As the name implies, lecture discussions are based on the strengths of lectures but build on these strengths by adding some of the positive features of discussions. In this section we'll examine the strengths and weaknesses of lectures and see how the Lecture-Discussion Model builds upon and accommodates these features.

Lectures: Teacher Monologues. A **lecture** *is a form of instruction in which students passively receive information delivered in a verbal and (presumably) organized way by teachers.* Lectures have been a mainstay of instruction over the years, and they continue to be one of the most widely used instructional strategies in classrooms (Cuban, 1984). The popularity of lectures can be traced to three factors (Eggen & Kauchak, 1999):

- Lectures are economical in terms of planning; energy can be devoted to organizing content.
- Lectures are flexible; they can be applied to virtually all content areas.
- Lectures are relatively simple to implement; at their most basic level they involve presentation of content.

Despite these advantages, lectures have two important problems, which make them ineffective for many, if not most students. First, they promote passive learning, encouraging students to merely listen and absorb information, but not necessarily interrelate ideas. Lectures are essentially monologues in which the teacher talks and students listen.

Research on young (Berk, 1997) and poorly motivated students (Brophy, 1986) indicates that passive listening is one of the poorest ways to transmit information. Watch a class of six- or seven-year-olds during any kind of presentation where they're expected to be passive. At first they sit quietly, but soon they start to fidget and look around. If the monologue continues, they not only tune out but start talking and poking each other, seeking some type of activity.

Older, poorly motivated students are often less disruptive during lectures than are younger students, but little learning takes place. Because they've learned that fidgeting and talking can get them into trouble, they may feign interest by propping their heads on their hands and attempting to make eye contact. Harder cases give up completely and work on homework for other classes, read, or put their heads down on their desks. Unfortunately, we've seen a number of teachers continue lecturing in spite of these nonverbal signals, and despite clear signs that few are listening or learning.

The second problem with lectures is that they do not allow teachers to assess student understanding or learning. During interactive lessons, teachers informally assess student understanding by asking questions. Because communication is one way in lectures, teachers have no way of making these assessments and adjusting accordingly.

The ineffectiveness of lecture as a teaching method is well documented. In seven comparisons of lecture to discussion, discussion was superior in all seven on measures of retention and higher-order thinking. In addition, discussion was superior in seven of nine studies in terms of student attitude and motivation (McKeachie & Kulik, 1975). The fact that lectures require students to be passive is the major reason for these differences.

The Lecture-Discussion Model is designed to overcome these deficiencies by requiring the active involvement of learners. This involvement requires them to build on their existing schemas and integrate new knowledge with old. Through questioning, teachers not only encourage student involvement but also monitor learning progress, allowing them to adapt their presentations if necessary.

We turn now to planning for lecture-discussion lessons.

Planning for Lecture-Discussion Lessons

In this section we discuss how to plan for lecture-discussion lessons to ensure that the content of that lesson is incorporated into existing schemas. In addition, we discuss how to construct advance organizers, structure content, and plan for the use of questioning during the lesson.

Identifying Goals

In initial planning for lecture-discussion lessons, as with any lesson, the teacher first considers goals. The Lecture-Discussion Model is designed to teach organized bodies of knowledge rather than specific concepts or skills.

The model can be effectively used in classrooms in two ways. First, it can be used to organize content for an entire course, or a unit within a course. Teachers can use it to help them decide on the scope and sequence of the content, and it can guide students in their progress throughout the material over an extended period of time.

The second use of the model is to structure content within a lesson. Lorrie used the model in this way to teach about reinforcement schedules. Used in this way, the model provides direction in beginning, developing, and ending lessons.

The same dual levels of organization—at the macro and lesson level—apply in other content areas. How this might look in a geography class is shown in Figure 9.1.

From the diagram we see the Lecture-Discussion Model's two planning functions illustrated. First, it was used as a guide for long-range planning for the year's work on geography and a smaller unit on elements of the physical environment. Second, it was used to relate concepts in a single lesson focusing on landforms. The focus of this lesson was to understand the characteristics of the different landforms and form an overall

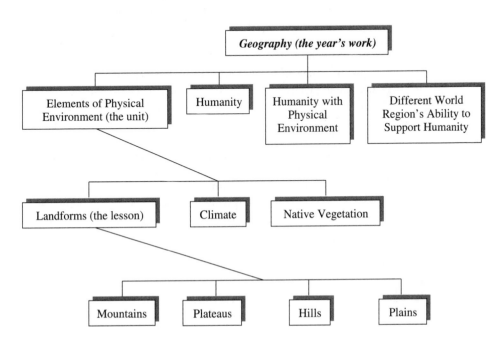

FIGURE 9.1 Organization of Content in Geography

structure of these landforms. The model was used both to organize a large body of content and to teach specific topics.

Diagnosing Students' Backgrounds

In planning for a lecture-discussion lesson, it is essential to consider what students already know. Their backgrounds provide the foundation for new learning and provide links or hooks to which new knowledge is connected.

Pretesting students is an obvious way to assess their background knowledge. However, preparing frequent pretests is demanding and time consuming, and most teachers look for simpler and more efficient ways of learning about students' content backgrounds.

A second way of informally assessing students is to ask them to list, group, and label ideas related to a concept (Taba, 1966, 1967). Using this strategy, the teacher would first ask, "What comes to mind when I say the word. . . ? Let's write down everything we can think of when we see the word." This target concept would be the focus of an upcoming unit or lesson (e.g., landforms, reptiles, novels, etc.). The responses students make give the teacher insights into their understanding of the topic.

The process can be extended by asking students to group the ideas they've listed and attach a label to the categories. Again, quality of classifications provides the teacher with information about students' background knowledge.

A slightly more complicated process for assessing students' backgrounds asks students first to define as many of the terms that the teacher has placed on the board as they can (Champagne et al., 1980). Then students are asked to explain the relationships among the terms. The combination of the two tasks provides a comprehensive description of their backgrounds. While conducting the exercise in writing is demanding, because the teacher must collect the papers and give students some form of feedback, having students first complete it and then discuss orally would be reasonably efficient.

Perhaps the simplest way to informally assess students' backgrounds is by reviewing the background material. (Remember that in Chapter 2 we identified review as one of the essential teaching skills.) The process takes little time and, if the teacher gets responses from a variety of students, it is a reasonably accurate assessment of their backgrounds. This is the process Lorrie used in her lesson. As another example, a teacher in the lesson on landforms might list the concepts on the board and ask the students to give examples or describe them in their own words.

One disadvantage of these informal assessments is that more knowledgeable and outspoken students may dominate, giving the teacher an overly optimistic impression of the overall knowledge of the class. To guard against this outcome, the teacher should attempt to get responses from enough students to be as sure as possible that the information she is getting is representative of the class as a whole.

The results of this diagnosis help teachers decide which topics should receive the most time and effort, how rapidly the material can be covered, and how the content must be structured to make it as meaningful as possible. These are the topics of the next sections.

Structuring Content

After goals for the unit or lesson have been identified and the students' background has been assessed, the next planning step is to structure content so that it is as meaningful as possible for the students. Research shows that organization promotes learning (Durso & Coggins, 1991; Van Patten et al., 1986).

One effective way to structure content is to use hierarchies. Preparing hierarchies is fairly simple, and the relationships within them are clear. For these reasons, we examine hierarchies first. For example, a lesson on mammals could be structured according to taxonomic description. The structure of such a lesson might appear as shown in Figure 9.2.

The real number system is also hierarchically structured, as illustrated in Figure 9.3.

In cases where the material does not have a natural structure, the teacher can impose structure on it. For example, a social studies topic on community helpers might be structured as shown in Figure 9.4. Structuring content in this way allows students to see the relationship of specific community helpers to each other as well as their relationship to the general idea of community helpers.

Another way of imposing a hierarchy on the content is through the use of interrelated generalizations. An example would be to structure a lesson around the following generalization: "America has expanded because of natural resources, form of government, and a unique mixture of people." The structure that evolved from this generalization might appear as shown in Figure 9.5. In this form of structure the generalization is broken down into narrower topics, which are either illustrated with examples or further broken down into subordinate concepts.

An extended analogy is a third way of using hierarchies. For example, the structure for a lesson using the solar system as an analogy for the structure of an atom might appear

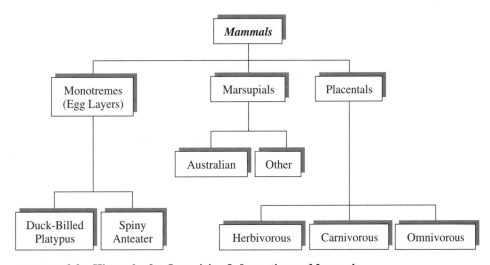

FIGURE 9.2 Hierarchy for Organizing Information on Mammals

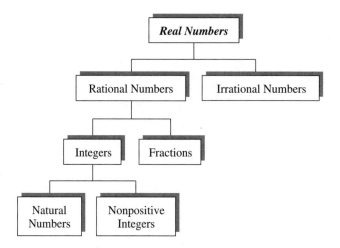

FIGURE 9.3   Hierarchy for Organizing the Real Number System

as shown in Figure 9.6. We discuss the use of analogies in more detail when we discuss the construction of advance organizers.

In each of these cases, hierarchies have been used to structure content. Structure can be imposed in a variety of other ways as well. Outlines, concept webs, models, graphs, maps, and matrices all impose structure on content. For example, the outlines that we have included at the beginning of each chapter of this book are attempts to structure the content of each chapter to make it as meaningful as possible for you. The matrices you encountered in Chapter 6 are also forms of structuring content.

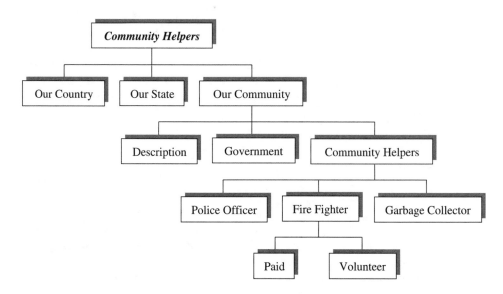

FIGURE 9.4   Hierarchy for Organizing Community Helpers

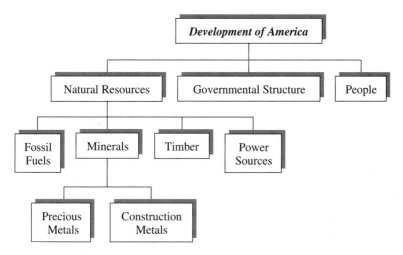

FIGURE 9.5   Hierarchy for Organizing Generalizations

In many cases, teachers combine different forms of structure to help organize their lessons. For instance, a teacher doing a unit on the Civil War might use a hierarchy to structure the content for the unit. The hierarchy would include elements such as causes of the war, significant battles and events during the war, outcomes from the war, and how the

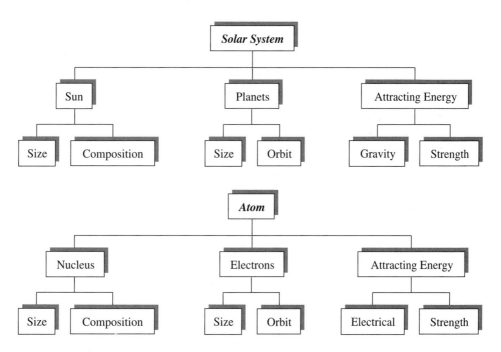

FIGURE 9.6   Analogy for the Structure of the Atom

war still affects us today. A lesson or lessons on the causes of the war could include a map that showed the northern and southern colonies together with a matrix or outline that examined the geography and economics of the North and the South. Significant battles and events could be structured with a matrix, and outcomes might be structured with a matrix, outline, or some other organizer. There is no single best way to structure content, and the form used is a matter of professional judgment. The key in structuring the content is to make the relationships between ideas as clear as possible, which in turn makes the topic meaningful for the students.

In all cases, when teachers structure their material, they should keep students' backgrounds in mind. For example, if "modern capitalist democratic countries" is part of the content, and the students don't understand terms such as *capitalist* and *democratic,* the teacher's planning must include ways of illustrating these concepts. Otherwise, the entire lesson or unit will be less meaningful to students.

Preparing Advance Organizers

An additional way to promote learning in lecture-discussions is through advance organizers. We discussed the concept of advance organizers in terms of Ausubel's theory of meaningful verbal learning. We now want to describe advance organizers in more detail and apply their use to classrooms.

As we saw earlier in the chapter, an advance organizer is a statement preceding a lesson that is designed to preview the material and link it to content learners already understand. It is more general and abstract than the content to be structured and subsumes the material that follows.

For example, Lorrie's advance organizer was:

> Reinforcement schedules are applications of operant conditioning in which the frequency of rewards is specified. When we reinforce behaviors, we can reinforce every time, not at all or somewhere in between. The somewhere in between can be based on number of responses or time. When we periodically compliment our brother or sister for helping us clean up around the house, we are using a reinforcement schedule.

Notice that this organizer was presented at the beginning of the lesson, it was more general than the content that followed, it was written in paragraph form, and it contained a concrete example—complimenting a brother or sister—that helped students identify the relationship between the ideas in the organizer and the information in the lesson. These characteristics of effective organizers help students learn new information in a meaningful fashion.

Implementing Lecture-Discussion Lessons

Having identified goals, diagnosed students' background knowledge, structured content, and prepared an advance organizer, the teacher is prepared to implement the lesson.

As described earlier, the Lecture-Discussion Model has five steps:

1. Introduction
2. Presentation
3. Comprehension monitoring
4. Integration
5. Review and closure

We discuss each of these individual steps in the sections that follow.

Introduction

The introduction phase of a Lecture-Discussion lesson includes three elements, which are:

- Introductory focus
- Lesson objectives
- Overview

These elements are outlined in Table 9.2.

Introductory Focus. When we begin lessons or make transitions from one lesson to another, we often incorrectly assume that students have the ability or inclination to refocus or reorient their attention to the topic at hand. In one study of elementary classrooms, researchers found that only 5 percent of the teachers being observed made an explicit effort to draw students into the lesson (Anderson et al., 1985).

To draw students into a lesson, teachers use the essential teaching skill **introductory focus,** which we described in Chapter 2 as *the set of teacher actions at the beginning of lessons that attract students' attention and pull them into the lesson.* Also called *anticipatory set* (Hunter, 1984), introductory focus alerts students that a transition is taking place and provides something tangible and interesting to attend to. Lorrie did this when she posed the problem about the woman training her dog to get the newspaper. Other forms of introductory focus are described in Table 9.3. Common to each of these

TABLE 9.2   Components of the Introduction to Lecture-Discussion Lessons

Component	Function
Introductory focus	Draws students into the lesson
Objectives	Identify important learning goals
Overview	Provides overview of topic and shows how major concepts are interrelated

TABLE 9.3   Types of Introductory Focus

Type of Introductory Focus	Example
Discrepant (Counter-Intuitive Events)	An ice cube is placed in a glass of water and floats, and a second cube is dropped in pure alcohol (which, because it is a clear liquid, students believe is water) and it sinks.
Personalization	A lesson on genetics begins with the teacher identifying a student with blue eyes and "guessing" the eye color of the parents (blue).
Examples	A lesson on adverbs begins with an overhead with sentences containing colorful adverbs.
Demonstration	A teacher begins a lesson on electromagnetism by showing how a magnet can penetrate certain substances (e.g., paper) and not others (e.g., a sheet of metal).

strategies is that the teacher makes a conscious attempt at the beginning of the lesson to attract and maintain students' attention.

While introductory focus is important for any teaching strategy, it is particularly important when the Lecture-Discussion Model is used because, unlike the Inductive, Concept-Attainment, and Integrative Models, which begin with something for students to do, the learning activity begins with the teacher's presenting information. If the students are not focused on the topic at the beginning of the lesson, the information that follows will be much less meaningful.

Objectives.   As we saw with the Direct-Instruction Model, objectives help students identify the important points in a lesson and what they should know and be able to do when the lesson is over. Sharing objectives is especially important because the content taught with the Lecture-Discussion Model focuses on organized bodies of knowledge, which by their nature are more global and less precise than concepts, generalizations, principles, and rules. Research indicates that objectives help learners focus on important ideas that are part of large bodies of information (Klauer, 1984).

Overview.   The overview in a lecture-discussion lesson takes two forms. The lesson structure—hierarchy, model, outline, matrix, and so on—provides a means for identifying relationships among the major ideas; the advance organizer provides a link between old and new content. Some type of visual organization is important because research shows that visual representations are remembered longer than is information only heard (Hiebert et al., 1991; Mayer & Gallini, 1990).

A common mistake teachers make is to present the lesson structure and advance organizer and then ignore it as the lesson develops. If our goal is to have students understand relationships among ideas, these relationships should be emphasized throughout the lesson. Putting the hierarchy, or model, and advance organizer on an overhead or on the board at the beginning of the lesson and periodically referring to them can help meet this goal. Lorrie displayed her hierarchy and advance organizer at the beginning of the lesson, and through questioning she kept them in front of students throughout.

Presentation

After the introduction, the teacher develops the lesson by using the advance organizer and hierarchy or other form of structure as reference points. Lorrie displayed her advance organizer and the first part of her hierarchy and then carefully described the content, dividing behaviorism into operant and classical conditioning. She then moved to reinforcement schedules as a part of operant conditioning and divided reinforcement schedules into continuous reinforcement, intermittent reinforcement, and extinction. As she presented ideas, she added concepts to the hierarchy to structure her content. All of her descriptions followed the hierarchy, and each concept was linked to her advance organizer.

The value of this presentation format relates to schema theory and the relationships among ideas. Broader concepts are used as the foundations for new concepts; as students learn the new concepts, they are connected to the broader, more general ones. Most important, ideas are not learned in isolation. Knowledge is cumulative and the outcome should be an interconnected set of ideas.

How long should this presenting of information last before the teacher uses questions to check students' comprehension? Experience suggests that it should be short—literally, a few minutes.

Teachers continually overestimate the listening capacities of their students. Before a recent Superbowl football game, advertisers were concerned whether 90-second commercials would be too long to hold viewers' attention. Ninety seconds! Compare this with the length of some lectures. Research indicates that retention rates drop sharply after the beginning of a lecture (Gage & Berliner, 1992). Student inattention and information overload are likely explanations. (Remember Chapter 2, where we said that the capacity of working memory is limited. It is easy to overload learners' working memories, and when this happens information is lost rather than encoded into long-term memory.) Comprehension monitoring through teacher questioning is one way to prevent or minimize this problem.

Comprehension Monitoring

Comprehension monitoring *is the process of informally assessing student understanding in lecture-discussion lessons,* and it is usually accomplished through teacher questioning. Such monitoring is critical because it promotes student involvement and provides students with feedback about their understanding.

How often should comprehension monitoring occur? While technically the answer depends on the difficulty of the content and the development of the students, *it almost cannot be overdone*. First, there is a tendency for lecture-discussion lessons to disintegrate into teacher monologues. Second, it's virtually impossible for students to be too involved in a lesson, and third, students need constant feedback and teachers need to continually assess their students' understanding.

To see how quickly Lorrie moved to the comprehension-monitoring phase of the lesson, let us look again at her initial presentation:

> The first concept we should focus on is reinforcement. Remember we said that reinforcement results in an increase in behavior due to some desired consequence, such as a compliment for a person or a doggy treat for a dog.
>
> Now we can decide to reinforce a behavior every time it occurs or only part of the time. That's what we mean by frequency or interval. So if we're trying to train our dog to shake hands, we can reward him every time he does this or every other time or even some sort of random pattern. That's what we mean by frequency.
>
> Another way to reinforce is by time. Let's say we want to train our dog to stay on the porch. We could reward him every 15 seconds, every 30 seconds, or every minute he stays on the porch. That's what we mean by interval.
>
> Now let's focus on this outline. What can you conclude based on the outline? . . . Jim?

Note that immediately after this presentation, Lorrie asked a question. In an actual classroom, this description would have taken no more than a couple of minutes. This is, indeed, a very short presentation time compared to some of the teacher monologues that we've all experienced.

The importance of the comprehension-monitoring phase is based on schema theory. Since learners bring with them diverse schemas and all new learning will be interpreted in the context of prior understanding, different students will interpret the information teachers present in a variety of ways. If their interpretations are invalid, their entire new schemas will be distorted or inaccurate. To determine whether or not students are interpreting new information accurately, teachers must continually check students' understanding of the information.

Alternate ways to check comprehension and involve students in the lesson include:

- *Question/Write:* Pose a question, ask all students to write down an answer, and then ask for volunteers to share.
- *Examples:* Lorrie did this when she broke the students into groups to identify additional examples of ratio schedules of reinforcement.
- *Think-pair-share:* Pose a question, ask students to individually come up with an answer, then share with a partner, and finally share with the class.
- *Voting:* When questions are controversial or require a judgment call, ask students to form an opinion and then vote with their hands and share their thinking with the group.
- *Choral response:* When a question has a single right answer choral responses can be used to involve the whole class (Harmin, 1994).

These response variations provide not only variety but also encourage students to become more actively involved in lessons.

Integration

Questions perform another important function in the Lecture-Discussion Model. Remember that the model is designed to teach interrelationships in organized bodies of knowledge. The way teachers accomplish this goal is first to present information in a systematic way and then to check students' comprehension of the information.

Simple monitoring of comprehension isn't enough however; integration is required. **Integration** *is the process of linking new information to prior learning and linking different parts of new learning to each other.* If new knowledge isn't integrated with old, and the parts of the new information aren't integrated with each other, the goal of understanding interrelationships won't be reached.

Like monitoring comprehension, questioning is an effective strategy to encourage integration. Questions can encourage vertical integration when teachers ask students to link superordinate with subordinate concepts, such as Lorrie's asking students to explain why operant conditioning is a form of behaviorism. (Her vertical integration would have been more complete if she had also asked why classical conditioning was a form of behaviorism.)

Questions can also encourage horizontal integration—most commonly by asking students to describe *similarities* and *differences* among coordinate ideas, or by asking students to describe how different ideas relate to each other. Identifying differences helps specify what makes each idea distinct, such as knowing that the behavior is involuntary in classical conditioning but is voluntary in the case of operant conditioning. Identifying similarities helps specify important relationships, such as the fact that both classical and operant conditioning illustrate a relationship between behavior and the influence of the environment.

Lorrie encouraged horizontal integration in two important places. In addition to having students compare classical and operant conditioning, later in the lesson she had them describe similarities and differences among the reinforcement schedules.

We saw the process of integration at two different points in Lorrie's lesson. In classrooms it should take place whenever new ideas are introduced. As teachers become comfortable with the model, knowing when to check for comprehension and promote integration by asking for similarities and differences will become more automatic.

Review and Closure

Review and closure are essential for any lesson, as we saw in Chapter 2. They are particularly important when the Lecture-Discussion Model is used, because they further promote integration. **Review** *summarizes the topic, emphasizes important points, and provides a link to new learning.* Although it is appropriate at any point in a learning activity, it is most effective at the beginnings and ends of lessons. Lorrie reviewed at the beginning of her lesson to remind students of the larger topic of behaviorism and to ensure that new information was embedded in that content.

As we saw in Chapter 2, closure is a form of review that occurs at the end of a lesson; it summarizes, structures, and completes the topic. Lorrie brought her lesson to closure when she used her outline to provide an overview of the major concepts studied.

Variations of the Model

In the preceding sections, we described the primary purpose of the Lecture-Discussion Model as helping learners form coherent schemas by finding relationships between old and new learning and among the different parts of an organized body of knowledge—such as reinforcement schedules in Lorrie's lesson.

Alternate Ways of Representing Content

Within the general framework of the Lecture-Discussion Model, content can be organized in a number of ways. One of these is the use of *minihierarchies* to supplement other models. For example, recall Jim Rooney's lesson on the rules for forming singular and plural possessives in Chapter 4. At some point in the lesson, a hierarchy identifying the relationships among the different parts of the rules would have made the material more meaningful for the students. The hierarchy might appear as shown in Figure 9.7. This hierarchy would help students see the relationships among the different parts of the rule. It gives a visual illustration of when the apostrophe appears before the *s*, when it is used after the *s*, and why no apostrophe is used in some cases.

As another example, consider a teacher discussing the topic of closure in mathematics. (An operation is considered to be closed if the outcome of the operation produces a number that belongs to the same set as the numbers combined in the operation.) A discussion of the topic could be supplemented with a brief hierarchy such as the one shown in Figure 9.8.

This outline is also effective it implies a pattern; the number of closed operations increases as we go from counting to rational numbers. Students could then be encouraged to hypothesize on the basis of the pattern and test their hypotheses with other numbers and sets. In addition to helping make the concepts more meaningful, the hierarchy could provide an avenue for promoting deeper understanding of the ideas being discussed.

As teachers use hierarchies to supplement other lessons, they uncover other opportunities to enhance their students' learning. We present these examples in the hope that they might further stimulate your thinking about additional uses of the Lecture-Discussion Model.

A second option that takes advantage of the organizing powers of the Lecture-Discussion Model uses hierarchies in conjunction with matrices. (Recall some of the matrices we saw in Chapter 6.) As an example, consider the outline in Figure 9.9 used with a unit of study on the novel.

The advantage of an outline such as this is that it shows at a glance the superordinate, coordinate, and subordinate relationships contained in the content. However,

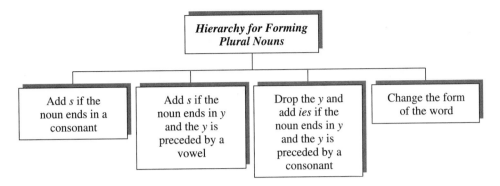

FIGURE 9.7   Hierarchy for Rules in Forming Singular and Plural Possessives

diagrams can become cluttered, and when they do, the information in them is harder to use. In this case a matrix, such as the one shown in Figure 9.10 could be used as a supplement. Matrices illustrating salient aspects of closely related concepts can help students organize similarities and differences in their minds.

The use of a data retrieval chart as a supplement to a hierarchy has two advantages. One is that a chart allows the teacher to include and organize data for a lesson; the second is that it helps promote thorough integration of ideas. The structural outline graphically illustrates how the concepts are differentiated; the chart, in turn, ensures their integration through an analysis of the data in it.

As another example of a chart used to organize content for a lecture-discussion lesson, look at Figure 9.11. Here protozoans (one-celled animals) and metazoans (many-celled animals) are compared.

A chart such as this could be used to supplement the hierarchy shown in Figure 9.12. We have shown how hierarchies can be used in conjunction with matrices to help organize information for students. Maps, graphs, models, and outlines can be used equally effectively. Remember that all are means toward ends—that students understand organized bodies of information.

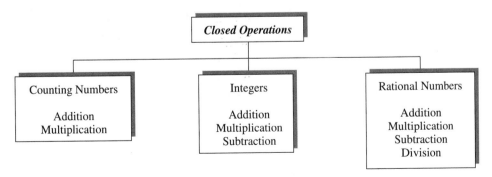

FIGURE 9.8   Hierarchy for Representing Closure in Mathematical Operations

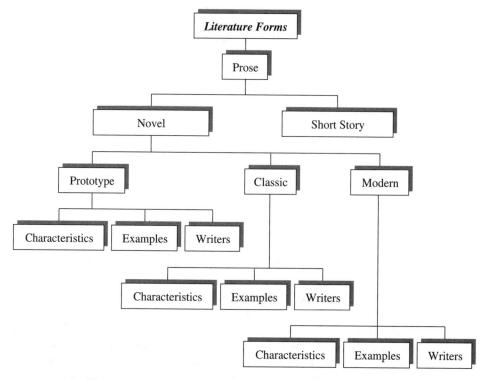

FIGURE 9.9 **Hierarchy for Organizing Information on the Novel**

Increasing Motivation and Learning
through Group Interaction

A theme of this chapter has been the need for teachers to involve students in lecture-discussion lessons. Questioning is one way of accomplishing this. In this section of the chapter, we examine an alternative way of involving students—through group interaction.

Earlier in the text we examined how group processes could be used to facilitate learning. Group interaction provides students with opportunities to think about and clarify

TYPES OF NOVELS

	Characteristics	Examples	Writers
Prototypes			
Classic			
Modern			

FIGURE 9.10 **Matrix Used as a Supplement for Organizing Content**

	Cells	Method of Reproduction	Systems	Life Span
Protozoan				
Metazoan				

FIGURE 9.11   Matrix Used to Organize Information on Protozoans and Metazoans

their own ideas about a topic, articulate these to others, compare their views with those of other students, and generate new ideas through dialogue and verbal give and take. Group interaction also provides ways to make lecture discussions more motivating. This can occur through think-pair-share, informal small groupwork, or structured cooperative learning groups.

Research supports the effectiveness of group interaction as a major motivational tool. In a study of elementary and secondary teachers' motivational practices, group tasks were reported as a major motivational strategy by 55 percent of the teachers (Zahorik, 1996). This same group of teachers recommended avoiding sedentary activities, including lectures, passive listening, and taking notes. Observations in classrooms also support the motivational effectiveness of groupwork; researchers found engagement rates above 90 percent in the majority of small groups they studied (Emmer & Gerwels, 1998). Teachers attributed these high engagement rates to high student active involvement in groupwork learning tasks.

Teachers can utilize the motivational benefits of groupwork at each of the different phases of the Lecture-Discussion Model. The introduction of a lecture-discussion lesson is designed to draw students into the lesson and provide an overview of the content. One way of drawing students into the lesson is to place students in groups and ask them to review

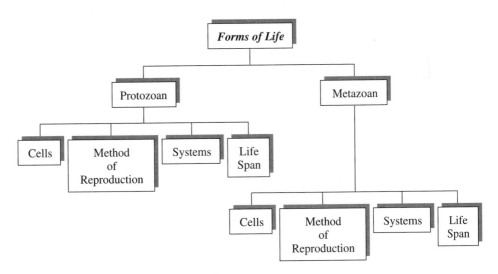

FIGURE 9.12   Hierarchy Used to Organize Information on Protozoans and Metazoans

and define major points previously covered. Teachers can circulate among the groups and informally assess student understanding. This small-group activity performs several functions It not only activates students' prior knowledge but also provides teachers with insights into what students do and do not know. In addition, it actively involves students in the background content of the lesson.

During the presentation phase, groupwork can be used to actively involve students in the development of ideas. Lorrie Martello did this when she divided her class into groups to think about additional examples of ratio schedules. This strategy not only involved all students, but also resulted in a greater variety of examples, including examples that were especially meaningful to students.

Group interaction can also be used to monitor students' comprehension. The typical way of doing this is through a question posed to the whole class. The same question(s) can be posed to groups; while the groups are discussing the answer, the teacher can circulate around the room, listening for areas of confusion. This way of checking comprehension not only involves all students but also provides a more comprehensive assessment of student understanding.

During the final two phases of the model—integration and review and closure—teachers can ask learning groups to relate concepts and present their ideas to the class as a whole. When we have done this in our classes, groups often come up with different relationships and conclusions, and these provide opportunities to compare perspectives and clarify differences. Asking students to summarize ideas also has motivational benefits because students feel greater ownership of the ideas discussed.

Assessing Student Understanding in Lecture-Discussion Lessons

The Lecture-Discussion Model, as described in this chapter, is designed to teach relationships in organized bodies of knowledge. This is similar to the goals for the Integrative Model but different from those for the Inductive, Concept-Attainment, and Direct-Instruction Models, which are designed to teach specific topics in the form of concepts or skills.

As described in the previous sections, the Lecture-Discussion Model is used to teach relationships among ideas, including concepts, generalizations, principles, and rules. Assessing understanding of these specific forms of content has been discussed in earlier chapters, so we will not examine it further here. Instead, we want to focus on the decisions teachers must make in assessing students' understanding of relationships among different ideas.

The ability to relate different topics depends on an understanding of the topics themselves, so assessment should involve both the specific topics and the relationships among them. As an example, consider the following item that could be used to assess Lorrie's students' understanding of reinforcement schedules.

Read the following anecdote and answer the questions that follow:

Mrs. Cortez collects homework on Mondays, Wednesdays, and Fridays, while Mrs. Amato collects it periodically but doesn't announce when she will collect it. (She averages three days a week on different days.) Both teachers score and return the homework each day after giving it.

1. Identify the type of reinforcement schedule each teacher is using.
2. Explain why it is that type in each case.
3. Based on our understanding of reinforcement schedules, which teacher is likely to be most effective in promoting students' efforts on homework?

This item accomplishes at least three goals:

■ It measures students' understanding of the concepts of fixed-interval and variable-interval schedules of reinforcement.
■ It measures their understanding of the differences between the two concepts.
■ It shows students how the topics they're studying can be applied to the real world.

In addition, being able to explain *why* the first was fixed interval and the second was variable interval requires higher-order thinking. Ideally, assessments should accomplish all of these goals.

As another example of asking students to apply information to a new situation, consider the following item:

Describe how the staging for the Greek play *Oedipus Rex* would be different if it were done in an Elizabethan theater.

In order to answer this question correctly, students must know the characteristics of Elizabethan theater and apply them to a Greek play. This information provides the teacher with a measure of the extent to which the schema for theater had been integrated in students' schemas.

Another way of measuring students' understanding of subordinate, coordinate, and superordinate relationships is to provide them with a list of concepts and ask them to arrange the concepts hierarchically. As an example, consider a lesson on vertebrates in a high school biology class. The teacher would provide the students with the following list of concepts related to vertebrates and ask the students to organize them hierarchically.

Reptiles	Birds	Vertebrates
Fish	Warm-blooded	Mammals
Snakes	Monotremes	Placentals
Frogs	Salamanders	Cold-blooded
Marsupials	Turtles	Lizards
Amphibians		

The hierarchy might then appear as shown in Figure 9.13.

Note that this item is similar to the diagnostic exercise described earlier in the planning section. The difference between the two is that this item would be used after the concepts had been covered and is explicitly designed to measure relationships between concepts.

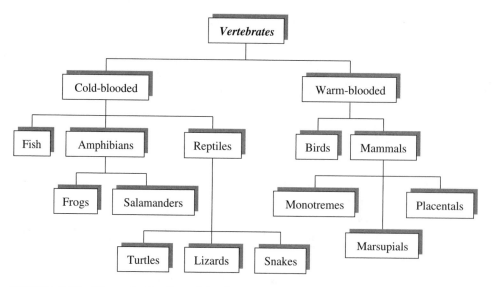

FIGURE 9.13   Hierarchy for Organizing Vertebrates

The examples we have given are only a few of the ways that learners' understanding of relationships among ideas can be assessed. Many more exist. Our reasons for offering them are to emphasize that instruction using the Lecture-Discussion Model focuses on relationships in organized bodies of knowledge and not on memorized information. With effort, and that focus in mind, you can continually improve your assessments, and with them the quality of your students' learning.

Summary

The Lecture-Discussion Model: An Overview

The Lecture-Discussion Model is a teacher-directed model designed to help learners understand relationships in organized bodies of knowledge. As opposed to content-specific models that focus on individual concepts, the Lecture-Discussion Model attempts to help students understand not only concepts but how they are related.

The Lecture-Discussion Model: Theoretical Perspectives

Grounded in schema theory and David Ausubel's concept of *meaningful verbal learning,* the model is designed to help learners link new with prior learning and relate the different parts of new learning to each other. The model is designed to overcome some of the most important weaknesses of the lecture method by strongly emphasizing learner involvement in the learning process.

Planning for Lecture-Discussions

Planning for lecture-discussion lessons involves identifying goals, diagnosing students' backgrounds, structuring content, and preparing advance organizers. The goal of teacher planning in this model is to ensure that new content is learned in a meaningful, related manner and integrated with previously learned ideas.

Implementing Lecture-Discussion Lessons

Lecture-discussion lessons begin with an introduction that draws students into the lesson and provides an overview of the lesson's focus. During the presentation stage, the teacher shares new information, linking it to students' schemas. Comprehension monitoring ensures that students understand new ideas; integration links these ideas to each other and to previously learned content. In the final phases, review and closure, students are further encouraged to integrate ideas.

Variations of the Model

Matrices provide alternate ways of representing content. One of their advantages is that they can store information that students can use in constructing new ideas.

Group processes can complement Lecture-Discussions by providing increased opportunities for student involvement and dialogue. Teacher planning is required to ensure that the groups function smoothly and that group tasks are integrated into the structure of the model.

Assessing Lecture-Discussion Lessons

Assessment with this model should focus on students' understanding of relationships among the topics they study and application of those topics to new situations. This requires alternate items that extend beyond the measurement of specific concepts.

IMPORTANT CONCEPTS

Advance organizers *(p. 306)*
Comprehension monitoring *(p. 317)*
Integration *(p. 319)*
Introductory focus *(p. 315)*
Lecture *(p. 307)*

Meaningful verbal learning *(p. 306)*
Review *(p. 319)*
Rote learning *(p. 306)*
Schema theory *(p. 303)*
Schemas *(p. 304)*

EXERCISES

1. Read the following case study and answer the questions that follow.

> Iris Brown is teaching her English class about parts of speech. She wants them to understand the function of different parts of speech in the total communication process. She also wants them to understand the relationship between the different parts of speech. She begins her class with a review of previously discussed material.
>
> "Who can remember how we started our unit on communication and parts of speech?" Iris asks.
>
> "... We said communication is ... the ... two-way sending back and forth of information that usually is done with language ... and we said that the parts of speech and the way we punctuate are ... parts of ... the whole process," Steve says haltingly.
>
> "Good Steve, and what did we say about parts of speech yesterday?" Iris continues.
>
> After thinking for a few seconds, Quiana replies, "We said that parts of speech are like building blocks in a house. The parts of speech are sort of like the ... like the building blocks for the way we communicate, and the way the blocks are put together determines the form of the message and what it means."
>
> "We also said words could be divided into naming words, action words, describing words and other words," Evelyn adds.
>
> "That's good," Iris smiles. "Now how did we describe these groups?"

The lesson continues with a discussion of each of these parts of speech.

   a. Describe the scope of the teacher's planning for the lesson.

   b. Identify and describe the two advance organizers in the case study.

   c. Diagram the organization of the material illustrated in the episode.

2. The following is a description of a college class involved in a discussion of teaching models. This is the last day of a three-day presentation.

   a. Identify the advance organizers in the lesson (some may be from previous lessons).

   b. Draw a hierarchy of the content contained in the lesson.

   c. Identify in the lesson where integration took place.

      1. Phyllis Peebles, the instructor, begins her Friday class with a review of her Monday and Wednesday class.

      2. "How did we begin the Monday session?" she asks.

      3. "Well," Ron says, "you said a teaching model is like a conceptual blueprint in that both are used to achieve some purpose. A blueprint is used as a guide for an engineering objective, while a teaching model is a guide to achieving content and process objectives."

      4. Arlene adds, "You noted that models can be grouped according to whether they emphasize cognitive, affective, psychomotor, or a special kind of cognitive goal called information processing."

5. "You said that our emphasis in here would be on information processing," Mary adds.

6. "Wednesday you began to deal with the information processing family,"Bob interjects.

7. "And you said you wanted to deal with each of the models separately so that they would remain clear and distinct in our minds," Martha adds.

8. Then George says, "You began the lesson on information processing models by stating that they are designed to help students handle stimuli and input from the environment and transform it into more meaningful output."

9. "You then went on to say that the models are grouped according to whether they are primarily deductive, inductive, or problem solving," Kay notes.

10. "You further broke the inductive models into the Integrative Model, the Inductive Model, and the Concept-Attainment Model, and the deductive models into Direct Instruction that teaches concepts and skills and the Lecture-Discussion Model," Russ adds.

11. "You also noted that while the Lecture-Discussion Model is primarily expository and deductive and the Integrative Model is inductive, they aren't as unrelated as you would expect because they can be used to process large amounts of information, but the way in which this is done differs."

12. "We also added that the Integrative Model is much more process oriented than is the Lecture-Discussion Model," Carol comments.

13. "You also suggested," Linda notes, "that Ausubel sees the nervous system as an information processing mechanism analogous to a discipline which organizes concepts hierarchically."

14. "Excellent," comments Phyllis. "You seem to have formed stable concepts of the ideas that we've discussed so far. Today I want to consider a new model. This information processing model is the Problem-Solving Model, designed to help students develop their ability to solve problems in the classroom and in the real world."

15. "This model combines both inductive and deductive modes of thinking. The first part of the model involves identification of some kind of a problem, and the rest of the model involves gathering information to explain or solve the problem."

16. Wayne interjects, "We learned that there are primarily three forms of knowledge we try to teach: concepts, generalizations, and facts. Which of these is the Problem-Solving Model designed to teach?"

17. "That's a good question," Phyllis notes. "But before I answer that I'd like to show you some examples of the Problem-Solving Model and see if you can answer that question yourself." The class then proceeds to analyze the examples presented and ultimately comes up with the answer to Wayne's question. (We examined the Problem-Solving Model in Chapter 7.)

DISCUSSION QUESTIONS

1. How are schemas acquired? Give at least three examples from common experience.

2. Though schema theory was described as the theoretical background for the Lecture-Discussion Model, it could be described as a framework for the other models presented to this point as well. Why, then, would it have been described specifically as the theoretical foundation for this chapter?

3. The Inductive Model was described as being based on constructivist views of learning. In what ways could lecture-discussion lessons be constructivist? Offer two specific ways.

4. What are the particular strengths of the Lecture-Discussion Model? What are its primary weaknesses?

5. What conditions might influence the effectiveness of advance organizers? Are they more effective with younger students or older? Are they more effective with new material or old? Are they more effective with abstract or concrete material?

6. Consider advance organizers in a broad sense. What kinds of aids and/or teacher behaviors can serve as organizers for students? What might be a metaphor for advance organizers in the affective domain? In the psychomotor domain?

7. The Integrative and Lecture-Discussion models appear to be quite different, but in reality they are similar in several ways. Identify at least three similarities.

8. Identify at least three similarities and at least two differences between the Lecture-Discussion Model and the Direct-Instruction Model.

9. How would David Ausubel react to the Inductive Model? The Integrative Model? The Direct-Instruction Model?

CHAPTER

10 Adapting Instruction to Improve Effectiveness

We have now discussed the major instructional models in this book. We emphasized the teacher-effectiveness research and research on cognitive views of learning, expanded the discussion to emphasize teaching for understanding, and stressed the importance of selecting different models for different instructional goals. These topics led to a discussion of a "models" approach to instruction.

The teaching models in this book focused on cognitive views of learning, which emphasize the importance of students' actively search for meaning. Cognitive views of learning developed in response to dissatisfaction with behaviorism as a basis for guiding instruction. Cognitive perspectives assume that students actively construct their own understanding rather than passively receiving that understanding from teachers or textbooks.

Chapter 2 introduced you to the essential teaching skills that form the foundation for teaching effectiveness. This discussion was followed by a description of higher-order and critical thinking that are integral to deep understanding of content.

Chapters 3 through 9 illustrated and discussed specific models, each designed to help students reach specific content goals while practicing social interaction and thinking skills. In the real world, however, teachers face many situations that require flexibility and adaptation in their instruction. This chapter is intended to illustrate that adaptability, which represents an even more advanced stage of teaching expertise.

When you've completed your study of this chapter, you should be able to meet the following objectives:

- Identify the model most effective for specific goals.
- Identify similarities and differences among the models.
- Identify elements of each of the models in a single teaching episode.
- Adapt elements of each model to reach particular goals.

To begin our discussion, let us look at a teacher adapting the models to best meet her students' needs.

Marita Eng is beginning a unit on sea animals with her fifth graders, and she plans to spend about a week and a half on it. She introduces the unit on a Monday by showing a large poster board with an outline on it that looks like this:

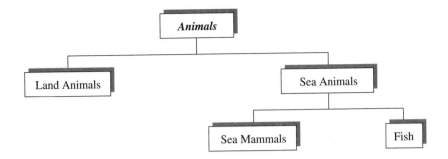

She begins her first lesson of the unit by saying, "Everyone, this is what we'll be learning about for the next few days. . . . Now let's look at the outline. What does it tell us? . . . Anyone?"

". . . It looks like . . . sea mammals and . . . fish are both . . . kinds of animals that live in the sea," Brad volunteers hesitantly.

"Good, Brad," Marita smiles. "Yes, when we see this kind of outline, it tells us, like we see up here," she nods, pointing to the outline, "that sea mammals and fish are both kinds of sea animals . . . and it also tells us that land animals and sea animals are both kinds of animals in general.

"Now," she continues, "today, we're going to look at this video, and we all want to be very good observers. Then we're going to be even better thinkers as we make conclusions based on what we see. So our goal for today is to learn to make good conclusions."

She then continues, "Now what makes a conclusion a good one? . . . Anyone?"

No one answers.

"What did we say we were going to do first when we look at the video?"

". . . Be good observers," Cal volunteers.

"Good, exactly," Marita smiles. "So how do our observations relate to our conclusions?"

". . . We use the observations to help us with our conclusions," Kim says after thinking about the question for a few seconds.

"Well done, Kim. That's right. We want to base our conclusions on our observations. . . . That's our goal for today."

Marita then starts the videotape, which shows a number of short scenes of whales and dolphins, such as a baby dolphin nursing from its mother, a baby whale being born, and a whale surfacing and "blowing" (exhaling). After a few minutes, she stops the tape and asks students to describe what they saw.

"A little dolphin was feeding from its mother," Brenda volunteers.

"The animals come up to the top of the water every now and then," Andre adds.

"Yes, and they blow water," Steve puts in.

"What do you think that blowing water is?" Marita queries.

No one answers.

Marita tilts her head back and blows a rush of air through her nose toward the ceiling.

"Breathing?" two of the children wonder simultaneously.

Marita smiles. "What do you think? . . . Does that make sense?"

". . . I don't think so," Andrew shakes his head. "That would mean their nose is on the top of their head."

". . . Why not?" Janine shrugs after thinking about it. "It could be there. We breath up when we lay on our backs."

Marita watches as students debate whether or not animals' noses could be on the tops of their heads for a few more minutes. They finally agree, in a few cases a bit reluctantly, that it is possible.

Wayne then interjects, "These animals look like fish but if they come up to breathe, and their babies are born like dogs and cats and stuff, they can't be fish."

"What must they be then?" Marita wonders.

". . . Mammals?" Letitia answers slowly with a question in her voice.

"How do you know?" Marita probes.

". . . If they breathe air, . . . and they nurse their babies, . . . and they're born like dogs and . . . you know, . . . they must be mammals."

"That's very good thinking," Marita waves and nods. "Remember that we said we were going to practice making conclusions. What Letitia just did is an example of that. Very well done, everyone."

Marita shows another part of the videotape, and more discussion follows. She continues this process until the end of the class.

She starts her Tuesday class by saying, "Yesterday we were talking about sea mammals, one kind of sea animal."

Pointing to 'sea mammals' on the hierarchy, she continues. "Let's look again at our outline. What did we find out about them?"

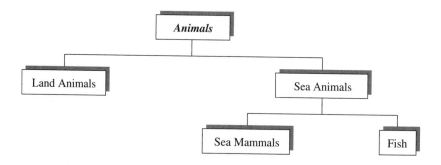

The class spends several minutes listing some of the observations and conclusions they made the day before, and Marita concludes the review by saying, "Now keep in mind what we know about sea mammals. Keep these ideas in mind while we talk about another kind of sea animal, fish. . . . We all know some things about fish."

She notes again, pointing to the hierarchy, "We know that fish are cold-blooded animals that breathe through gills and usually lay eggs to have babies."

Then she motions, "Let's look at the fish bowls. . . . Look over here," and she directs their attention to the two large fish tanks at the side of the room.

"Let's compare these fish to the mammals we learned about yesterday," she suggests. "How are they alike and how are they different?"

Students make several suggestions, such as identifying the gills on some of the fish and noting that they didn't go to the surface and "blow."

Marita continues the activity by showing some colored pictures of other fish. As students look at the pictures, they discuss how the pictures are similar to the fish in the bowl and the whales and dolphins they saw in the video. This discussion continues until the period is over.

Marita begins her Wednesday's class by reviewing Monday's and Tuesday's activities. She begins her review by asking about differences between fish and sea mammals.

Sharon comments, ". . . I think they're sort of hard to tell apart unless you're up close."

Maurice adds, "Fish can stay underwater the whole time, but mammals have to come up to the top to breathe."

Ray says, "They look quite a bit alike. They have fins on them . . . on their sides and tail."

Marita asks, "Why do you suppose the sea mammals and fish look so much alike when they are actually very different?"

No one answers.

"Well, what do we know about where they live?"

"They both live in the water," Tim shrugs.

"Good, Tim," Marita smiles. "What else?"

No answer.

"Okay, let me show you a few more pictures."

She shows the students a picture of an African grassland with gazelles and antelope on it, a jungle picture with chimpanzees, and another with orangutans.

After the students look back and forth from one picture to another, Juanita tentatively offers, "The animals in the same sort of place kind of look alike."

"What do you mean?" Kevin queries.

". . . Like the antelope and the . . ."

"Gazelle," Marita offers.

"Gazelle . . . whatever," Juanita goes on, "look alike. . . . See they both have long legs and stuff. . . . And the whale and the fish in the water. They look alike, too."

"What do the rest of you think?" Marita smiled.

"Yeah, the chimps and that other one look alike too, kind of," Emilio adds, pointing to the pictures with the chimpanzees and the orangutan, "and they both live in the jungle."

"Anyone else?" Marita encourages.

The class agrees that what Juanita and Emilio suggest seems to make sense, and then Marita asks, "What do we call 'where an animal lives'?"

". . . Their environment," Sandy offers after a couple of seconds.

"Good . . . yes, it's called their environment . . . and here we have three different environments, the ocean, grasslands, and the jungle.

"Now," Marita says with emphasis, leaning forward. "Let's see if we can describe a relationship between animals and their environment. . . . Think about it for a few seconds, and someone give it a try."

". . . Animals in the same environment look alike," Tina offered.

"What do you think everyone? Do animals in the same environment look alike?"

Some of the class members agree that they do and point to the examples that they already discussed. Others disagree and note that a wide variety of animals live on the plains other than antelope and gazelles. The class discuss the issue and finally conclude that animals in particular environments have characteristics that allow them to survive in those environments.

Marita then offers, "What we've been talking about is the ability of animals to *adapt* to their environments. Later we'll see that plants also adapt, but we'll wait to get into that."

Marita then asks students to summarize what went on during the period and closes the lesson for the day.

To begin Thursday's lesson, Marita has students offer some additional examples of adaptation, and then continues by saying, "There are actually two kinds of fish, those with backbones like ours and those with softer backbones."

She goes to her original outline and adds these categories below 'Fish' so it appears as follows:

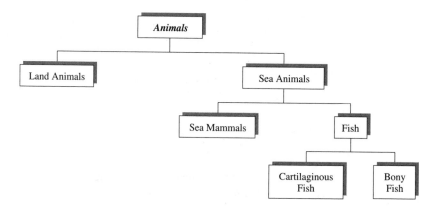

"We're going to change the routine a little today," Marita goes on. "I have a chart here, and some materials, and we're going to gather some information about the two different kinds of fish."

She displays the following matrix for the students.

	Examples	Gill Opening	Covering	Teeth	Reproduction	Circulatory System
Bony Fish						
Cartilaginous Fish						

Marita then continues, "We're going to work together today, and I've arranged for us to go to the media center where we'll have some books, video-discs, CD-ROMs, and information on the Internet that you can look at to gather your information. Now to get us going, I want two people working as a team to gather information about each part of the matrix. Work with your partner from your cooperative learning groups."

Marita asks one pair to volunteer to find examples of bony fishes, another pair to find information about the gill openings of bony fishes, a third pair to find information about the covering of bony fishes, and so on until all twelve cells of the matrix have been assigned to a pair. (Since she has twenty-six students in her class, two of the teams work as trios.)

The class goes to the media center and spends the rest of Thursday gathering information. They finish on Friday, come back to the classroom, and write their findings on a large piece of chart paper.

On Monday, Marita spends several minutes reviewing what they have done the previous week and then begins discussing the information in the chart by asking the students for similarities and differences in bony and cartilaginous fish, using questions periodically to clarify the information. The discussion continues for the remainder of class.

On Tuesday, Marita reviews the work of the previous six days again and has the students look at the two fish bowls again as they had the previous week.

"What do you notice?" she asks.

The students make several comments, and finally Joan asks, "Why are the fish in the bowl on the left moving around so slowly while the others are acting like they always do?

"That's a good question, Joan," Marita answers. "Let's see if we can figure out why."

"The fish aren't in the bowls they're usually in and they can't adapt," Gerald says with a big smile. "See what I learned last week, Mrs. Eng?"

"Good, Gerald," Marita smiles. "But how could we find out if that's true?"

After several seconds, Gabriella suggests, "Put them back the way they were."

"Yeah," "Hey," "Neat idea," "Okay," several of the students respond, so the class decides to follow Gabriella's suggestion.

While they wait to see what happens, the class discusses some possibilities. "What if the fish start behaving like they did before? . . . What will that tell us?" Marita queries.

The students offer some suggestions and discuss them, and Marita follows with other questions.

They turn back to the fish when Fran notes, "There's a film on one of the bowls."

"I know, I know," Javier jumps up excitedly. "We learned this week that fish are cold-blooded, and the water is cold so the fish don't move around as much."

This discovery leads to another investigation. The class measures the water temperature in the bowls and counts the number of times the gills move in the different water temperatures. As students gather the information, Marita records it on the board, and they continue with this process for the rest of the period.

On Wednesday, Marita guides the class through a summary of the entire unit, again looking at sea mammals and fish—both bony and cartilaginous, the process of adaptation, and how the environment affects the behavior of animals. She asks students to compare the behavior of the fish in the different water temperatures to their own behavior in the winter compared to the summer. This leads to a discussion of different ways of dressing and a comparison of warm-blooded and cold-blooded animals.

Marita then reminds the students that they will continue with their discussion of adaptation beginning the next day.

In the case study we've just read, we see how a teacher has used all or part of several different models to reach different goals in a unit. In some cases, such as Sue Grant's lesson on Charles's law in Chapter 4 or Tim Hardaway's lesson on the addition of two-digit numbers in Chapter 8, a single model was used exclusively: the Inductive Model for Sue and the Direct-Instruction Model for Tim. Often, however, teachers' goals are not as narrow or specific as Sue's and Tim's were, so effective teachers adapt the models, using portions of several of them to best help their students learn. This is what Marita did in her unit.

Let us look at how she combined and adapted the models in her unit.

Teaching Models: Adaptations

Examining Goals

To begin our discussion, let us think about Marita's goals. Among them were the following:

- To know that some mammals live in the sea
- To understand how animals adapt to their environments

- To understand differences between bony and cartilaginous fish
- To develop higher-order and critical thinking skills

In addition, student questions led to inquiry about the behavior of fish. Students formed hypotheses, gathered data, and made conclusions about the relationship between behavior and environment. Because of her expertise, Marita was able to capitalize on students' questions and turn them into an excellent learning experience. Let us turn now to some of the specific elements of Marita's teaching as she went through her unit.

She began by presenting a hierarchy as a way of organizing the information for her unit. Then she had students briefly discuss what the hierarchy represented and implied. The combination of the hierarchy and the discussion served as an advance organizer for her unit. While Marita's "organizer" didn't have all the characteristics of advance organizers that research identified (Corkill, 1992), her adaptation resulted in an effective organizer nevertheless. In this sense, her unit began as a form of the Lecture-Discussion Model, and the content of her unit was an organized body of knowledge—knowledge about sea mammals, bony and cartilaginous fish, the concept of adaptation, and the impact of environment on behavior.

In the first lesson of the unit, Marita showed the videotape of sea mammals. In this lesson she used the Inductive Model. The video provided the examples, she stopped the tape periodically to allow students to make observations and conclusions, and she guided their discussion according in terms of the structure of the Inductive Model. With her guidance, they arrived at the conclusion that mammals live in the sea as well as on land.

Let us look again at some of the dialogue.

BRENDA: A little dolphin was feeding from its mother.

ANDREW: The animals come up to the top of the water every now and then.

STEVE: Yes, and they blow water.

MARITA: What do you think that blowing water is?

CHILDREN: Breathing? [After Marita tilts her head back and blows a rush of air through her nose toward the ceiling.]

MARITA: What do you think? . . . Does that make sense?

ANDREW: I don't think so. That would mean their nose is on the top of their head.

JANINE: Why not? It could be there. We breath up when we lay on our backs.

WAYNE: These animals look like fish but if they come up to breathe, and their babies are born like dogs and cats and stuff, they can't be fish. [After the students discuss and finally agree that it is possible for animals to have their noses on the tops of their heads.]

MARITA: What must they be then?

LETITIA: Mammals?

MARITA: How do you know?

LETITIA: If they breathe air . . . and they nurse their babies . . . and they're born like dogs and . . . you know . . . they must be mammals.

Marita skillfully guided students as they discussed the information they gathered from the video. Her instruction was consistent with constructivist views of learning that stress active involvement, and she embedded her instruction in the general context of the Lecture-Discussion Model. Hers was a skillful adaptation of both models to help her reach her goals. The Lecture-Discussion Model was effective as an overall framework for her unit because the unit content was an organized body of knowledge involving interconnected ideas, and the Inductive Model effectively structured her first lesson because she was teaching a concept—the concept of *sea mammal.*

Marita began Tuesday, the second lesson of her unit, with another minilecture-discussion and another adaptation of an advance organizer, which included the outline and the statement:

> We know that fish are cold-blooded animals that breathe through gills and usually lay eggs to have babies.

Having provided the organizer, she turned again to an inductive procedure when she had the students compare fish to sea mammals, identifying their similarities and differences. This process continued into Wednesday, where she used the observations and conclusions that students had made to lead them to the concept of *adaptation.* Much of her instruction on Tuesday and Wednesday utilized the Inductive Model.

On Thursday, Marita turned to the Integrative Model and used an adaptation of cooperative learning. She provided the skeleton of a matrix and asked student pairs to gather information to be placed in it. While she could have—and perhaps should have—asked the students to suggest the categories, such as *skin covering,* that they would investigate in bony and cartilaginous fish, she chose to select the categories herself. This is a professional decision, one among the many that teachers make.

After students had gathered the information, Marita used the Integrative Model to guide the students' analysis. They looked for similarities and differences in bony and cartilaginous fish and formed explanations as they went along. Her analysis took her through Friday of the first week and Monday of the second week of her unit.

On Tuesday Marita planned to return to the discussion of different kinds of fish, but a question arose from the students' observations. Let's look again at some of the dialogue.

> **JOAN:** Why are the fish in the bowl on the left moving around so slowly while the others are acting like they always do?
>
> **MARITA:** That's a good question, Joan. Let's see if we can figure out why.
>
> **GERALD:** The fish aren't in the bowls they're usually in and they can't adapt. See what I learned last week, Mrs. Eng?
>
> **MARITA:** Good, Gerald. How could we find out if that's true?
>
> **GABRIELLA:** Put them back the way they were.

Joan's question provided the opportunity for an inquiry lesson. Marita capitalized on the opportunity by asking the students to try and figure out how they could answer the question. Gerald offered a hypothesis, and Gabriella suggested a way that data could be gathered to investigate the hypothesis.

As students waited to see if the behavior of the fish changed, Fran noted, "There's a film on one of the bowls," which was followed by Javier's comment, ". . . We learned this week that fish are cold-blooded, and the water is cold so the fish don't move around as much." Javier's point was essentially an alternative hypothesis, which led to a change in the direction of the investigation.

Students then investigated Javier's hypothesis by measuring the water temperature and studying the movements of the gills on each fish. While Marita might be criticized for not following up on the initial investigation with at least some discussion, she showed a great deal of expertise in adapting her instruction to the thinking of students consistent with the suggestions of constructivism. While we discussed constructivism as the foundation of the Inductive Model, we see that it can be used as a framework for the other models as well.

Synthesizing the Models

From the case study and our discussion, we see how effective teachers combine and adapt models to help them reach different goals, and we also see that many similarities exist in what appear to be very different models. We also see that models that seem to be grounded in different reference frames are highly compatible. For example, Marita had her students do a great deal of comparing, contrasting, and linking of new information to old. These processes, which appeared in the context of Inductive and Integrative lessons, are virtually the same as the process of *integration* when the Lecture-Discussion Model is used. Also, while the Lecture-Discussion Model and the Inductive Model appear to be grounded quite differently, Marita used them very compatibly. She established a conceptual framework with the Lecture-Discussion Model and then taught specific concepts, such as *sea mammals* and *adaptation,* using the Inductive Model within that framework. Combining and adapting the models in this way epitomizes effective teaching.

Models and Goals: A Review

From this discussion, we see that a key to teachers' decisions in using the models is a careful consideration of goals. Marita chose to begin her unit with the Lecture-Discussion Model because her unit goals focused on organized bodies of knowledge. She turned to the Inductive Model when her goals were for students to understand concepts, such as *sea mammals* and *adaptation,* and she moved to the Integrative Model when she wanted students to understand differences between bony and cartilaginous fish. Notice there that her goal was not to merely acquire a simple concept of bony and cartilaginous fish, but to understand similarities and differences between them. She could have chosen the Lecture-Discussion Model for this portion of her unit, but chose the Integrative Model instead because it gave her a greater opportunity to help her students practice higher-order and critical thinking—one of her goals for the unit.

When the inquiry question arose, Marita seized the opportunity to capitalize on an additional goal, one that hadn't been part of her original planning. Opportunities to capitalize on "incidental" goals often occur. The fact that Marita was able to turn it into a learning experience for her students is a tribute to her expertise as a teacher.

Marita didn't use the Direct-Instruction Model or the Concept-Attainment Model in her lesson. This is because her lesson goals didn't call for teaching a skill, which is effectively taught with the Direct-Instruction Model, and they didn't include reinforcing concepts for which the students already had partial understanding—a goal that could be reached with the Concept-Attainment Model. This is the way the models should be used in helping teachers reach their goals; they match the most effective model for the specific instructional situation.

Teaching Expertise: Beyond Instructional Models

In this final section of the book we attempt to place the models—as wholes or in parts—into proper perspective with teaching in general and, in doing so, discuss some basic principles upon which the models rest. To put the models in perspective, we would like to return to a point that was made in Chapter 1. There we said that

> a teaching model is not a substitute for basic teaching skills. A model cannot take the place of fundamental qualities in a teacher, such as knowledge of subject matter, creativity, and sensitivity to people. It is, instead, a tool to help good teachers teach more effectively by making their teaching more systematic and efficient. Models provide sufficient flexibility to allow teachers to use their own creativity. . . . Like a blueprint, a teaching model is a design for teaching within which the teacher uses all the skill and insights at his or her command.

The statement is a warning that the models described in this book are not panaceas for all the problems a teacher faces in trying to help students learn, and they will not automatically work magic in the classroom. They must be used by intelligent and sensitive teachers with clear ideas of what they're trying to teach; they cannot be followed mechanically according to a prescriptive format. They can help a teacher improve learning experiences for students but cannot by themselves make a bad learning environment a good one.

The models we have described are effective because they are based on fundamental principles of teaching and learning that go beyond the models themselves. These principles have been illustrated throughout the text. For example, the use of examples is critical in order for learners to effectively understand any concept, principle, generalization, or rule. We have tried to be consistent with this theme by illustrating each idea in the book with one or more examples. The case studies that we used to introduce each chapter are there for that purpose; they are examples that illustrate the concepts in the chapter. The concepts are sophisticated and abstract in many instances, but they are concepts nevertheless, so they require examples. In fact, their complexity and abstractness make the need for examples even greater then it is with more concrete and simpler concepts. The point here is that using examples, with or without the structured steps in a model, increases learning.

Another principle that underlies the models is the importance of clear goals and instructional alignment. Unless teachers are clear about what they are trying to accomplish, they have no way of determining whether or not they're getting there. Teaching models have alignment built into them, because each is designed to accomplish specific goals. However, Marita Eng's teaching reminds us that models don't substitute for basic professional judgment. Her goals for her unit were established in advance, but she capitalized on the opportunity to involve her students in inquiry when the opportunity arose. Her flexibility, both in using the models and in her overall approach to instruction, illustrates that models are tools to improve instruction, not rigid rules for teaching.

We have tried to demonstrate the relationship among planning, implementing, and assessing learning by presenting of each of the models in terms of these three phases. In addition, we have tried to be consistent with this approach by using objectives to communicate our planning, by teaching to the objectives, and by measuring your attainment of the objectives for each section. In this sense, we have made an effort to "practice what we preach."

We have made an effort to be consistent with what we are suggesting in one final way. We have encouraged teachers to adapt the models to their own particular needs, using parts of the models as they see fit. Our presentation of Marita Eng's unit illustrates this effort.

In addition to the specific strategies discussed in this book, there is an additional capability that we hope we've developed in the reader. This is the ability to recognize and seize opportunities to encourage students to practice their higher-order and critical thinking abilities. Doing this means taking advantage of the opportunity whenever it arises, as Marita did in her teaching. It is through active and critical thinking that students not only acquire deep understanding of the topics they study, but also the ability to add to and refine this understanding on their own. To illustrate this point, consider the following example.

A teacher is doing a lesson on ancient and extinct animals. In this lesson the teacher shows students pictures from a book and reads the captions under the pictures. Two of the pictures are shown below.

BRONTOTHERE

BRONTOSAURUS

The teacher, in reading the descriptions to the children, notes that the name *brontothere* meant thunderbeast and the name *brontosaurus* meant thunderlizard. The alert teacher then seizes on the opportunity to involve the students in a simple thinking activity. She asks them to note what the two names had in common and to recall the meaning of these names. With some prompting, the students generalize from the prefix *bronto* in each example to determine that it meant "thunder."

The important point here is that the teacher wasn't using one of the specific models per se, but she captured the essence of observing and generalizing in what amounted to a mini-inductive lesson. This entire process probably took less than 2 minutes, but students had an important learning experience. In this simple activity the students had a chance to practice higher-order thinking—specifically observing and generalizing, and they generalized about the prefix *bronto.* If teachers capitalize on these opportunities when they arise, they can do much to develop both their students' thinking and a depth of understanding of the topics they study, even if they don't use the models in structured lessons. Perhaps more important, in time students will develop the disposition to look for relationships on their own, which helps them develop as self-regulated learners, more responsible for their own growth and development.

Obviously, it isn't particularly important that students know what *bronto* means, but the skill they acquire in analyzing words and relationships in general, and the basic idea that the world makes sense and is understandable may be the best of what they take away from schools.

As another example, let's look in on a first-grade teacher, Bette Washington, as she reads a story to her students.

During the story, the word *dissolve* comes up.

"What's dissolve, Mrs. Washington?" Calvin asks.

After several futile attempts at explaining the concept, Mrs. Washington tries a different approach. (Think for a second how you would verbally explain this concept to a six-year-old.) She goes to the front of the room, gets a glass, pours water into it, and then pours a packet of sugar she has in her desk into the water.

"What do you see here?" she asks as she stirs the sugar.

"The sugar is gone," Andrew answers.

"Good, Andrew," Mrs. Washington smiled. "Where did it go?"

Andrew doesn't answer.

"What are some possibilities?"

". . . In the water," Karen answers with a shrug.

"Any other possibilities?" Bette asks.

". . . Maybe the air," Delmar suggests.

"Which do you think is more likely?" Bette probes.

After some discussion students conclude that the sugar must have gone into the water since that's where Bette poured it.

She finally says, "That's *dissolve,* everyone. We say that the sugar has *dissolved* in the water."

Bette Washington also displayed expertise and creativity in her teaching. She realized that for abstract concepts, such as *dissolve,* words are insufficient; students will understand only if they see a concrete example. Bette's creativity was in her ability to create an example on the spot. Her expertise was displayed in the fact that she did not merely show the students and tell them what they were supposed to see; she guided their understanding in a constructivist-oriented form of instruction.

As another example, consider a teacher of American literature who has students read biographical descriptions of authors followed by excerpts of their writing. Using selections from different time periods in our country's history, he then leads a detailed discussion in which the authors from similar time periods, such as post–Civil War, are compared. This group is then compared to authors who wrote in the 1920s. In all cases, students conclude, the authors' works are related to their life experience. The teacher has used no materials other than the textbook, but he has involved students in a creative activity requiring all the higher-order and critical thinking of a highly organized Integrative Model lesson.

Teachers with the insights demonstrated in these examples illustrate the best the models have to offer in terms of developing students' higher-order and critical thinking together with helping them acquire deep understanding of content. Whenever teachers ask students to identify trends, compare, and predict, they are capturing the essence of the models whether they use all the elements of a particular model or not. In doing so, they demonstrate expertise as teachers, and they contribute to increased student learning. We hope that your study of this text has contributed to that expertise.

Summary

Teaching Models: Adaptations

This chapter suggests that effective teachers consciously adapt and combine the models to best meet their instructional goals. While appearing different, the models are sometimes structurally quite similar and can often be effectively used in combination, such as introducing a lesson or unit with the Lecture-Discussion Model and then teaching specific topics within the lesson with the Inductive Model.

The choice of model depends on the teacher's goal. Social development goals are met by the Social Interaction Models. Goals involving concepts, principles, generalizations, and rules are effectively taught with the Inductive Model; goals involving organized bodies of knowledge can call for either the Integrative Model or the Lecture-Discussion Model; goals involving specific concepts and skills are efficiently taught with the Direct-Instruction Model, and more complex inquiry or problem-solving goals call for Problem-Based Learning Models.

Teaching Expertise: Beyond Instructional Models

Expert teachers capitalize on opportunities to promote both thinking and deep understanding of content when they arise. In doing so, they often teach hybrid minilessons involving one or more of the models. Understanding the models and the learning principles that are their foundation hopefully increases the likelihood that teachers will seize these opportunities.

D I S C U S S I O N   Q U E S T I O N S

1. Compare and contrast each of the models. Identify similarities in two or more of them and identify the ways in which they are different.

2. Compare the theoretical foundations for each of the models. In what ways are these foundations similar and different?

3. Constructivism is receiving a great deal of attention in education. Which of the models—other than the Inductive Model, which is based directly on constructivism—are constructivist in their orientation? How can each of the models be made more constructivist?

4. Which of the models are most effective for promoting higher-order and critical thinking? Which are least effective? Defend your answer with specific examples.

5. The Direct-Instruction Model has been criticized as being too behaviorist in its orientation. Is this criticism justified? Under what conditions might the criticism be justified? Under what conditions would the criticism lack justification?

6. Which models require the most sophisticated teaching skills? Which ones require the least sophisticated skills? Again, defend your response with specific examples.

EXERCISE FEEDBACK

Chapter 2

1d. Teaching efficacy is the belief that teachers can have an important positive effect on students. Shirley demonstrated this belief by saying, "I don't care. I'm pushing them harder. I think I could have done a better job last year. . . ." She accepted the responsibility for promoting learning and made every effort to ensure that it happened.

2a. Shirley began her math lesson within 1 minute of its scheduled starting time, she had her materials prepared and waiting, and she had well-established routines, as indicated by the fact that the students didn't have to be told how to pass in their papers.

3d. The class had studied adding fractions with like denominators, and she had them review the process before moving to a study of equivalent fractions.

4c. Shirley is emphasizing the fact that the problems they reviewed had like denominators. Emphasis is part of effective communication.

5a. Shirley's statement, "We're going to shift gears to where we want to add fractions when the denominators are not alike," is a transition signal. Transition signals are part of effective communication.

6c. Shirley's statements, "Now suppose I want to add half of this cake to a third of this one. . . . How much will I have?" and, "This is what we're going to begin today," were designed to provide an umbrella for the rest of her lesson. Earlier the class had been involved in review of adding fractions with like denominators.

7b. Monitoring is defined as the process of checking students' verbal and nonverbal behavior for evidence of learning progress. Shirley was alert and sensitive enough to recognize that Karen had given a correct but uncertain answer. She responded by recounting the shaded portions to confirm that Karen's thinking was valid. Her attention to Karen's uncertainty illustrates effective monitoring.

8d. In these paragraphs, Shirley guides the students in a summary of the lesson.

9a. The question, "How do we know?" asks students to provide evidence for a conclusion. Critical thinking is the process of making and assessing conclusions based on evidence.

10. Shirley's sensory focus was her drawings of the fractions. It was effective because the drawings were adequate attention getters, and all the information the students needed to understand the concept were observable in them.

11. Yes, Shirley's instruction was aligned. Her goal was for students to be able to add fractions with unlike denominators. In order to do so, they needed to understand equivalent fractions, so her lesson and seatwork assignment focused on finding equivalent fractions.

12. These paragraphs best illustrate equitable distribution. In each, Shirley calls on an individual student, asks the question first and then identifies the student by name, and calls on a different student in each question.

Chapter 3

1. Jim Felton used the Group Investigation-Model to help his students learn about nutrition. To do this, he divided students into teams and made each team responsible for investigating different topics, and asked each team to report on their findings.

   Jesse Kantor used Jigsaw II to help her students learn about amphibians. Different members of each team were responsible for different topics (e.g., circulatory system): these "experts" then taught other members of the team, and all members of the team were evaluated with a quiz covering all the topics.

2a. Knowledge of multiplication facts is convergent information best taught by the STAD model.

2b. Analyzing social issues suggests that the teacher is interested in process in addition to content. Designing a research project on voting would best be taught using the Group Investigation Model.

2c. This goal is content oriented and involves learning large bodies of interconnected information rather than discrete bits of information. Consequently, it would best be taught through Jigsaw II.

2d. Studying pollution through group projects would best be taught through Group Investigation.

2e. Helping students learn to research a topic would best be taught through Group Investigation.

2f. Knowing and understanding the four major food groups suggests that the teacher not only wants his students to understand basic facts about nutrition but also the interconnections between the facts. This goal suggests Jigsaw II.

2g. Knowing the names of capitals of states involves the learning facts. Facts are best taught through STAD.

3a. The targeting of group goals was suggested when Anya said, ". . . we're going to work on them together in groups." Group goals were also suggested when she said, ". . . when we take the quiz, each team will be scored on the basis of how much better team members improved."

3b. Individual accountability was suggested by Anya's statement that "your team's score will depend upon how well *all* the team members do—not just some."

3c. Equal opportunity for success was addressed when Anya discussed improvement points.

4a. One way to form teams is to divide students into quartiles, take the top and bottom students from the lowest and highest quartiles, then add them to the top and bottom students in the middle quartiles. Doing this, the first group would be composed of Juan, Ted, Kim, and Joan; the second group would have Bettina, Mary, Heather, and Lisa, and so on.

4b. Other factors to consider include gender, ethnicity, and ability to work together in groups. For example, note that the second group formed was composed of all females. If one of the teacher's goals was to teach boys and girls to work together cooperatively, then a better gender mix would be desired.

Chapter 4

1. *First,* each of the teachers used examples to illustrate the content they taught. For instance, Judy Nelson used her ball and globe, Suzanne Nelson used her demonstration and drawings, and Jim Rooney used his passage with the rules for forming possessives. *Second,* each of the teachers diagnosed the students' existing knowledge by asking open-ended questions. *Third,* each of the teachers put the students in an active role in the Teaming processing by encouraging them to discuss their developing understanding.

   Finally, each of the activities involved real-world tasks.

2. Judy Nelson's comment, "When we're done, we'll be so good at this that we'll be able to pinpoint any city in the world. Keep this in mind as we work today. . . ." was an attempt to establish positive expectations in her students.

3a. Generalization

3b. Rule

3c. Generalization

3d. Principle

4a. Immigration and economics

4b. Number and verb form

4c. Type of diet and cholesterol level

4d. Polarity and attraction

5a. Brief case studies could be used to illustrate this generalization. An example might be the following:

   > Enrique Rodriguez came home exhausted from a long day in the fields. The third year of drought had nearly destroyed his small farm in northern Mexico, and now he could barely grow enough corn and beans to feed his family of five.
   >
   > "We must do something," his wife said with concern as they sat quietly one evening. "The children are hungry."
   >
   > "I will go to the city," Enrique finally said with determination. "I will get the papers and see if we can go north of the border to find better work."

   Cases such as this illustrate the relationship between immigration and economics and could be effectively used with the Inductive Model. An alternative would be to use historical data displayed in charts that show how immigration is related to economics.

5b. Ideal examples would be sentences in the context of a reading passage. Some of the sentences would be written so that the subjects and verbs agree in number and others would have subjects and verbs that disagree. The teacher would then guide the students to identify the differences in the sentences.

5c. Like the generalization relating immigration and economicis, brief cases describing people and their diets together with their cholesterol counts would be good choices for examples. In addition, charts or graphs showing this relationship could also be used.

5d. To illustrate this principle, the teacher could have students experiment with actual magnets, calling their attention to the fact that some ends are labeled "S" and some "N."

6. A concept analysis might appear as follows:

Definition	A quadrilateral with opposite sides equal in length and all angles 90°
Characteristics	Opposite sides equal in length 90° angles
Examples	[Another example that appears at an angle]
Superordinate concept	Quadrilateral, parallelogram
Superordinate concept	Square
Coordinate concept	Rhombus

7a. Jim Rooney's sentences were concrete materials.

7b. Judy Nelson's beach ball was a model.

7c. Maps are also forms of models. We don't typically think of them that way, but they allow us to visualize what is too vast to be directly observed.

7d. Sue Grant's balloons were a form of concrete materials.

7e. Sue Grant's drawings were models.

8a. "What do you notice about the two pieces of paper?" is the more desirable question for the Inductive Model. It is open ended, which allows a variety of students to be called on quickly and ensures that the students will be able to respond successfully. It also allows the teacher to diagnose the students' background knowledge.

8b. "How do the two papers compare now?" is the more desirable question. Again, it is open ended and the same advantages we saw in 8a apply.

9a. The teacher used one example. The vials on the balance only established that the water was denser than the oil. The water poured on the oil established that the less dense material floated.

9b. They were concrete materials.

9c. The teacher would have to prompt the students to conclude that the water was denser than the oil. She would need to get them to say that the volumes were the same but that the mass of the water was greater, so the water was denser.

The students would readily see that the oil floated on the water. The teacher would then have to prompt the students to articulate the relationship between density and flotation; that is, "Less dense materials float on more dense materials."

9d. The teacher would present the students with additional examples and have the students explain what they saw. For instance, the teacher might drop an ice cube in water. Since it floats, we know that ice is less dense than water. She might also drop an ice cube in alcohol. Since the ice sinks in the alcohol, ice is denser than alcohol. (We can also conclude from these examples that alcohol is less dense than water.)

Chapter 5

1. Goals a, b, and d are all concepts and would be appropriate for the Concept-Attainment Model.

   Goals c and e would not be appropriately taught with the Concept-Attainment Model. Let's see why.

   (c) A teacher wanting students to know why two coffee cans roll down an incline at different rates has an objective that requires an explanation. Explanations include concepts but are broader than the concepts themselves. As such, they are not appropriately taught with the Concept-Attainment Model. A Problem-Based Learning Model, such as those presented in Chapter 7, would be appropriate.

   (e) A literature teacher who wants his students to know the time period during which Poe wrote has an objective that calls for factual information, that is: "Poe wrote in the first half of the nineteenth century" is a fact. Facts are not taught as the content goal in a Concept-Attainment activity.

2. Let's now consider sequences of examples for the concepts *gerund, soft,* and *miscible fluids.*

   (a) For the concept gerund, a sequence might be the following: (The positive examples are in italics. The sentences not italicized are the negative examples.)

   > *Hunting is a popular sport in many parts of the country. Walking is a major part of hunting,* and hunters get a lot of exercise.
   >   Susan and Jimmy were hunting together. *Suddenly glancing to the side of the road,* they saw another hunter chasing a deer out of the woods. Their hunting dog, Ginger, jumped out of their truck and also gave chase. *Running off the road isn't a good idea,* but this is what Jimmy did when he saw the bizarre events in front of him. Jimmy stared very disgustedly as he looked at his crumpled fender. He didn't know what to do.

   Obviously, there are many ways that a sequence of examples could be prepared to allow attainment of the concept *gerund.* The prepared sequence illustrates only one possibility. The sequence does, however, illustrate how the sequence can be embedded in the context of a short passage instead of being presented as a list of unrelated sentences. The important point is that each of the *yes* examples contains a gerund, while none of the *no* examples contains a gerund.

   (b) A sequence of examples for the concept *soft* might be the following:

1.	Piece of terrycloth	yes
2.	Piece of sandpaper	no
3.	Chamois skin	yes
4.	Diaper	yes
5.	Drinking glass	no
6.	Sponge ball	yes
7.	Toy car	no
8.	Wadded facial tissue	yes
9.	Piece of chalk	no

The positive examples could be indicated by smiling faces, plus signs, or the word *yes*. Note again that the *yes* and *no* examples do not always alternate. There is no rule that says every *yes* must be followed by a *no* or vice versa. Like the number of examples, the ordering of the examples depends on the judgment of the teacher.

(e) An appropriate sequence to teach *miscible fluids* might appear as illustrated here. Notice that the actual fluids should be used if the examples are to be most effective. Using the actual fluids (a form of concrete materials) allows students to directly observe the characteristics of the concept. If a compromise is required, a combination of actual fluids for some examples and models for the other examples would be the next most effective. The least effective form of example would be the use of words alone.

The following is a possible sequence.

1.	Water and alcohol	yes
2.	Alcohol and cooking oil	no
3.	Benzene and gasoline	yes
4.	Water and cooking oil	no
5.	Benzene and alcohol	no
6.	Water and hydrochloric acid	yes
7.	Oil and sulfuric acid	no
8.	Water and motor oil	no
9.	Benzene and toluene	yes
10.	Vinegar and water	yes
11.	Hydrogen and oxygen	yes

In some cases—water, cooking oil, alcohol, gasoline, motor oil, and vinegar—the actual liquids are easy to obtain, and in these cases they should be used. For the others, models are a reasonable compromise. The model could represent the different sizes of the respective elements and could show the mixing process. While words are most commonly used in an instance such as this, a model would be vastly superior.

3. The examples and sequences will be highly individual depending upon background knowledge and experience. Check with a fellow student or your instructor for feedback. Keep in mind as you design the sequence that *all* the positive examples must illustrate the concept and *none* of the negative examples can illustrate it. Also, use your imagination, and try to design the sequence cleverly to promote critical skills in the students.

4a. The examples of the concept in the anecdote are:

German Shepherd	fox
collie	wolf
beagle	

The other examples cited in the anecdote, such as Siamese cat, were the nonexamples (negative examples). The negative examples further clarify the concept by showing what it is not, while the positive examples show what the concept is.

4b. The characteristics cited in the anecdote are:

four legs prominent teeth
barks   hair

Note that none of these attributes alone is sufficient to describe the concept. Together, however, they provide an adequate description for the purposes of the teacher's lesson.

4c. The hypotheses that students offered were:

1. "It's an *animal.*"

2. "It could be *pet.*"

3. "I think it's *mammal.*"

7. "I think it's *dogs.*"

12. "Maybe it's *dog family.*"

4d. Michele's sequence was presented as follows:

Yes	1. German Shepherd	No	6. Siamese cat
No	2. Oak tree	Yes	7. Fox
Yes	3. Collie	No	8. Leopard
No	4. Magnolia tree	Yes	9. Wolf
Yes	5. Beagle		

Consider now a second partial sequence:

Yes 1. German Shepherd

No   2. Siamese cat

Yes 3. Wolf

No   4. Leopard

The sequence Michele used allowed students much more opportunity to practice their thinking skills than the second because the first few examples she used were more general and allowed for a variety of hypotheses. In the second sequence, *Siamese cat* as the first negative example would eliminate *animal* or *pet* as initial hypotheses, and *wolf* as the second positive example would probably cause the students to immediately identify the concept. The first sequence, in contrast, allowed many hypotheses that were successively narrowed until the concept was isolated.

4e. Michele could have further enriched the concept by including other positive examples, such as *jackal* and *coyote,* to broaden the concept for the students.

4f. Michele presented examples two at a time rather than singly. This is not critical and demonstrates the flexibility in the procedure. The only argument against this practice is that it might increase the cognitive load on young or inexperienced students to the point where they might have some difficulty processing the information.

4g. There were several points (e.g., lines 9 and 10) in the lesson where students voluntarily made the logic behind their answers explicit. Michele made a conscious effort to encourage this when she asked Phyllis to explain her hypothesis in line 4.

Chapter 6

1. **Phase 1**   Asking for similarities is part of phase 1.

2. **Phase 1**   The teacher continues to ask for similarities.

3. **JT**   Providing an example based on the information in the matrix supplies evidence for the earlier statement.

4. **Phase 3**   The teacher asks students to consider different conditions and suggest the outcomes of those conditions, which is a call for hypothetical reasoning.

5. **JT**   In asking, "What makes you say that?" the teacher asks the students to justify their thinking.

6. **Phase 1**   By again asking for similarities or differences, the teacher returns to Phase 1.

7. **JT**   Asking, "What makes you say that?" is another way of requiring students to justify their thinking.

8. **Phase 2**   "Why do you suppose idealism appears as a theme?"

9. **Phase 4**   Describing general patterns near the end of the lesson is a form of summarizing used to bring the lesson to closure.

10. **Phase 4**   The teacher continues to ask the students for summarizing statements.

11. **JT**   Again the teacher asks the student to justify her thinking by providing an example.

12. A variety of responses is possible. The following examples are offered as illustrations. They are not the only possible answers, and they are not necessarily the best possible answers.

Phase 1:

Look at the diameters of the planets. What do you notice here?

> The diameters of Jupiter, Saturn, Uranus, and Neptune are dramatically bigger than those of the other planets?

How do the planets' densities compare to their diameters?

> The planets with large diameters have low densities compared to the other planets.

Phase 2:

Why do you think the planets with large diameters have low densities?

> They are composed of materials that aren't very dense, such as gases.

Why do you suppose that Mercury's temperature varies so much—from 300° below 0 to 800° above 0?

> It rotates very slowly on its axis, so one side faces the sun for a long time and gets very hot, while the other side faces away from the sun for a long time and stays very cold.

It is generally believed that the earth is the only planet in the solar system that supports life as we know it? Why might that the case?

> It is the only planet with water?

> It is the only planet that has a livable average temperature—other than possibly Mars.

In spite of its large diameter, Saturn's gravity isn't much greater than the earth's. Why might that be the case?

> The density of Saturn is very low, so its gravity would be lower than would be expected for its size.

Phase 3:

Suppose Mercury rotated on its own axis much more rapidly than it presently does. How might that affect its ability to support life?

> It still wouldn't support life. It has no atmosphere. It is close to the sun, so it would still be very hot. It has no water.

Suppose that Saturn was a solid planet like the earth. How would that effect its gravity?

> Its gravity would be much greater than it now is.

Phase 4:

What kinds of general descriptions can we make about the planets in the solar system?

> The planets with large diameters have generally low masses and densities, so their gravities are lower than would be expected for their large size.
>
> The farther away the planets are from the sun, the colder they are.
>
> The farther away a planet is from the sun, the longer its year.
>
> All the planets rotate on their own axes.
>
> All the planets except Mercury and Venus have at least one moon.

Chapter 7

1a. The problem for the class was stray and unwanted pets.

1b. In representing the problem, the class decided on the following topics: pets in America, Humane Society, and the County Animal Control Division.

1c. The strategy that the class adopted was primarily fact finding or informational.

1d. They carried out the strategy by seeking information through interviews and printed materials.

1e. In evaluating their results, the class decided to launch a public information campaign about the problem of unwanted and stray pets.

1f. There was no evidence that the class analyzed the process.

2a. An event that the teacher could present might appear as follows: He could play excerpts of sounds considered to be musical and excerpts of sounds considered to be noise. After playing the excerpts, the teacher might say "Why was the first selection considered to be music and the second selection noise?"

2b. The teacher might begin the description of the event in either verbal or written form in this way:

> Mrs. Jones was a typical housewife in the town of Stevensville. She was married to a respected citizen, was the mother of three children, was active in civic groups, and she attended church regularly. However, on Saturday, June 17, the day of the annual community picnic, Mrs. Jones was taken aside and stoned to death by the rest of the

people in the town. Mrs. Jones had done nothing to deserve this execution, yet it was performed by most of the townspeople in front of the rest of the citizens who did nothing to prevent it. Why would this happen?

2c. The teacher's description of the event might appear as follows:

Hiroshima, a city of approximately 250,000 people, was located at the end of the main island of the Japanese chain. Hiroshima was not the largest city, nor was it the city with the bulk of the military supplies on the Japanese mainland. It was not the main cultural center of Japan. Yet this city was selected as the target for the dropping of the first atomic bomb in World War II. Why was Hiroshima selected as the first target when other places would seem to be more desirable?

2d. A description of the event could be:

Prior to the 1948 presidential election that pitted Truman against Dewey, public polls favored Dewey by a wide margin. In fact, on the night of the election, one prominent newspaper's headlines reported a victory for Dewey. According to the pre-election polls, Dewey was more popular, was felt to be better qualified for the presidency, and had powerful people on his side. Yet when the final tally was taken, Truman had won a tremendous upset victory. How could this have happened?

2e. One description of an event is the following:

The teacher places two beakers of colorless liquid (water and alcohol) on a demonstration table for the children to observe. The teacher then puts an ice cube into each of the containers of fluid. The ice cube floats on one of the fluids and sinks in the other. The two fluids appear to be the same, and the ice cubes are the same or nearly identical. The teacher would then ask why the object floats on one of the fluids and sinks in the other.

2f. In this case, the teacher might show the students pictures of apparently similar paintings. They could be similar in style, coloring, and framing. The teacher might say something on the order of the following: "The painting on the right sold for $5,000 while the painting on the left sold for $25. When the paintings appear to be similar, why should the one be so much more valuable than the other?"

3a. Ms. Stanley's actions in the lesson suggested that the lesson was preplanned rather than spontaneous. She had a content goal in mind (for students to understand factors that shaped the form that newspapers took) and came to class with the materials necessary for the activity.

3b. Students used primary data sources in pursuing their problem. An alternative secondary source would be to have students look up the information in a textbook.

3c. **(1)** Problem identification began when students compared the various newspapers. This phase of the model concluded when the teacher wrote, "What factors influence the size and composition of the daily newspaper?" on the board.

(2) Hypothesis generation took place when students offered their ideas (sports, advertising) about factors affecting newspapers and when Ms. Stanley wrote these on the board.

(3) Data gathering occurred in small groups as each group analyzed their individual newspapers.

(4) The data analyses were just beginning as time ran out. This is not an atypical problem for inquiry lessons, and teachers need to simply adjust to it. After having examined the hypotheses, students would cautiously generalize to include other instances.

4. Question **(1)** would be inappropriate for measuring process skills because it primarily covers content which has already been discussed in class. Consequently, what is being measured here is recall of information rather than process skills.

An important factor in measuring for process is uniqueness—that is, students are asked to analyze a problem not previously discussed. If the problem is previously unfamiliar, students' ability to analyze is being measured. If the problem has been discussed, the problem measures recall or comprehension of content rather than process abilities.

Question **(2)** is appropriate and directly measures students' ability to relate explanations and data. The question could probably have been described more specifically to provide better directions to students. For example, the illustrated item with the two cities is clearer and more specifiic. Again, however, remember that the explanation and the data on the cities must be unfamiliar to students or the teacher will be measuring recall of previously covered content.

Question **(3)** is also appropriate and measures students' ability to apply the information they've analyzed to develop a revised explanation. A combination of questions (2) and (3) would be excellent for measuring students' process abilities.

5. The anecdote illustrated an Inquiry problem as well as the H-DG-H cycle. The problem needing explanation was why Joan flared up at another teacher. The first hypothesis suggested to explain this phenomenon was that Joan was having marital problems. However, this hypothesis was not supported by the data, which indicated that Joan was happy both at home and at school. Having rejected this hypothesis, our inquirers then formed a hypothesis suggesting fatigue as a cause for Joan's behavior. Subsequent data seem to support this hypothesis, but the reader should note that no formal closure was reached

Chapter 8

Exercises 1 and 2 do not have clear-cut answers, and responses will be a matter of professional judgment. Our feedback is presented not as the "correct" answer, but rather as information designed to further stimulate your consideration and analysis of the material in this section. Please read the feedback to Exercises 1 and 2 with this idea in mind.

1. (a) Prime number, (c) square, (d) major scale, and (f) gerund are all concepts and can be taught with the Direct-Instruction Model. (b) To simplify arithmetic expressions following the rule: multiply and divide left to right and then add and subtract left to right is a skill and is also appropriate for the Direct-Instruction Model. (e) To understand that for nonmixing substances, less dense materials float on denser materials is a principle, and the model can be modified to effectively teach it. (g) To identify the relationships between the economy and geography of the North and South prior to the Civil War and how these factors impacted the outcome of the War is an organized body of knowledge. A model such as the Lecture-Discussion Model discussed in Chapter 9 would be more appropriate for teaching it. The reason the Direct-Instruction Model would be less appropriate is that the content described in the goal cannot be illustrated with a variety of examples as skills or concepts can, and as a result teaching the topic requires a different form of organization and presentation.

2. Responses to this item will vary widely. Select the topic and discuss the examples with your instructor or a colleague. The criteria for good examples are the same for the Direct-Instruction Model as they would be for the Inductive or Concept-Attainment Models.

3a. The four phases of the Direct-Instruction Model appeared in the lesson in the following ways:

Introduction: The introduction to the lesson occurred when Kathy linked the concept *antonym* to the superordinate concept *word pairs* and to the coordinate concept *synonyms,* which they had previously learned. Note that the introduction didn't contain any motivational component.

Presentation: This phase of the lesson occurred when Kathy defined the concept and illustrated it with examples.

Guided Practice: Guided practice occurred when Kathy presented examples and nonexamples of the concept and asked students for their own examples.

Independent Practice: The final phase of the model consisted of the students working on exercises that contained additional examples of antonyms.

3b. The most effective form of assessment would be to have the students write a paragraph in which a specified number of antonyms would be embedded.

3c. The lesson might be criticized in two ways. First, the concept *antonyms* was presented out of context. A better way of presenting the examples would be to have them embedded in the context of a passage. A second criticism is that Kathy might have more actively involved more students through groupwork and interaction.

Chapter 9

1a. Lecture-Discussion Model was used to plan in two ways: The first was to organize a unit of study on communication, and the second was to organize the lesson on parts of speech.

1b. There were two advance organizers illustrated in the anecdote. The first was used to organize the unit on communication and was a definition ("Communication is the two-way transmission of information that typically takes place through language"). The second was an analogy comparing parts of speech to building blocks and was used to organize the lesson on parts of speech.

1c. The organization for the unit as well as the lesson can be diagrammed as follows:

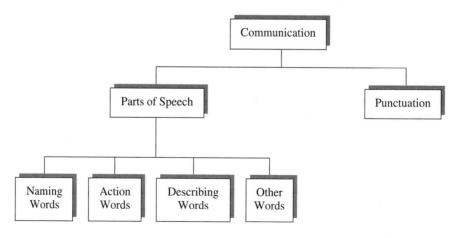

2a. There were three advance organizers mentioned in the lesson. Line 3 contained an analogy, and lines 8 and 14 contained descriptions.

2b. A hierarchical outline for the content presented would look like this:

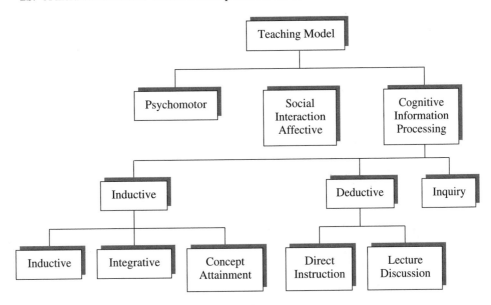

2c. Integration took place in lines 11 and 12, where the Integrative and Lecture-Discussion Models were compared and contrasted.

REFERENCES

Airasian, P. (1997). *Classroom assessment* (3rd ed.). New York: McGraw-Hill.

Alberto, P., & Troutman, A. (1999). *Applied behavior analysis for teachers* (5th ed.). Upper Saddle River, NJ: Merrill/Prentice Hall.

Alessi, S., & Trollip, S. (1991). Computer-based instruction: Methods and development. Upper Saddle River, NJ: Prentice Hall.

Alexander, P., & Murphy, P. (1998). The research base for APA's learner-centered psychological principles. In N. Lambert & B. McCombs (Eds.), *How students learn: Reforming schools through learner-centered education* (pp. 25–60). Washington, DC: American Psychological Association.

Anderson, J. (1990). *Cognitive psychology and its implications* (3rd ed.). New York: Freeman.

Anderson, L., Brubaker, N., Alleman-Brooks, J., & Duffy, G. (1985). A qualitative study of seatwork in first-grade classrooms. *The Elementary School Journal, 86,* 123–140.

Anderson, R. (1959). Learning in discussions: A resume/the authoritarian-democratic studies. *Harvard Educational Review, 29,* 201–216.

Aronson, E., Blaney, N., Stephan, C., Sikes, J., & Snapp, M. (1978). *The Jigsaw classroom.* Beverly Hills, CA: Sage.

Ausubel, D. (1963). *The psychology of meaningful verbal learning.* New York: Grune and Stratton.

Ausubel, D. (1968). *Educational psychology: A cognitive view.* New York: Holt, Rinehart & Winston.

Ausubel, D. (1978). In defense of advance organizers: A reply to the critics. *Review of Educational Research, 48,* 251–257.

Babad, E., Bernieri, F., & Rosenthal, R. (1991). Students as judges of teachers' verbal and nonverbal behavior. *American Educational Research Journal, 28*(1), 211–234.

Bandura, A. (1986). *Social foundations of thought and action: A social cognitive theory.* Englewood Cliffs, NJ: Prentice Hall.

Bandura, A. (1989). Social cognitive theory. In R. Vasta (Ed.), *Annals of child development* (Vol. 6, pp. 1–60). Greenwich, CT: JAI Press.

Bartlett, F. (1932). *Remembering.* London: Cambridge University Press.

Beck, I., & McKeown, M. (1993). Why textbooks can baffle students. *Learning, 1*(1). University of Pittsburgh: Learning Research Development Center, 2–4.

Bennett, S. (1978). Recent research on teaching: A dream, a belief, and a model. *British Journal of Educational Psychology, 48,* 27–147.

Berk, L. (1997). *Child development* (4th ed.). Needham Heights, MA: Allyn & Bacon.

Berliner, D. (1985, April). *Effective teaching.* Paper presented at the meeting of the Florida Educational Research and Development Council, Pensacola, Florida.

Beyer, B. (1983). Common sense about teaching thinking skills. *Educational Leadership, 41,* pp. 44–49.

Beyer, B. (1984). Improving thinking skills—Practical approaches. *Phi Delta Kappan, 65,* 556–560.

Blanton, W., Moorman, G., & Trathen, W. (1998). Telecommunications and teacher education: A social constructivist review. In P. Pearson & A. Iran-Nejad (Eds.), *Review of research in education* (pp. 235–275). Washington, DC: American Educational Research Association.

Bloom, B. (1986). Automaticity. *Educational Leadership, 43*(5), 70–77.

Blumenfeld, P. (1992). Classroom learning and motivation: Clarifying and expanding goal theory. *Journal of Educational Psychology, 84*(3), 272–281.

Blumenfeld, P., Pintrich, P., & Hamilton, V. L. (1987). Teacher talk and students' reasoning about morals, conventions, and achievement. *Child Development, 58,* 1389–1401.

Boyer, E. (1983). *High school: A report on secondary education in America.* New York: Harper & Row.

Bransford, J., Goldman, S., & Vye, N. (1991). Making a difference in people's abilities to think: Reflections on a decade of work and some hopes for the future. In L. Okagaki & R. Sternberg (Eds.), *Directors of development.* Hillsdale, NJ: Erlbaum.

Brooks, J., & Brooks, M. (1993). *In search of understanding: The case for constructivist classrooms.* Alexandria, VA: Association for Supervision and Curriculum Development.

Brophy, J. (1986). Research linking teacher behavior to student achievement: Potential implications for instruction of Chapter 1 students. In B. Williams, P. Richmond, & B. Mason (Eds.), *Designs for Compensatory Education Conference proceedings and papers* (pp. IV-121-IV-179). Washington, DC: Research and Evaluation Associates.

Brophy, J. (1987). On motivating students. In D. Berliner and B. B. Rosenshine (Eds.), *Talks to teachers* (pp. 201–245). New York: Random House.

Brophy, J. (1992). Probing the subtleties of subject-matter teaching. *Educational Leadership, 49* (7), 4–8.

Brophy, J., & Good, T. (1986). Teacher behavior and student achievement. In M. Wittrock (Ed.), *Handbook of research on teaching* (3rd ed., pp. 328–375). New York: Macmillan.

Brophy, J., & Evertson, C. (1974). *Texas teacher effectiveness project: Final report (Research Rep. No. 74-4)*. Austin: University of Texas, Research and Development Center for Teacher Education.

Brown, A. (1988). Motivation to learn and understand: On taking charge of one's own learning. *Cognition and Instruction, 5,* 311–321.

Brown, A. (1994). The advancement of learning. *Educational Researcher, 23,* 4–12.

Brown, A., & Campione, J. (1990). Interactive learning environments and the teaching of science and mathematics. In M. Gardner, J. Greeno, F. Reif, A. Schoenfeld, A. diSessa, & E. Stage (Eds.), *Toward a scientific practice of science education* (pp. 111–139). Hillsdale, NJ: Erlbaum.

Bruning, R., Schraw, G., & Ronning, R. (1999). *Cognitive psychology and instruction* (3rd ed.). Upper Saddle River, NJ: Prentice Hall.

Carlsen, W. (1987, April). Why do you ask? The effects of science teacher subject-matter knowledge on teacher questioning and classroom discourse. Paper presented at the annual meeting of the American Educational Research Association, Washington, DC.

Case, R. (1978). Intellectual development from birth to adulthood: A neo-Piagetian interpretation. In R. Siegler (Ed.), *Children's thinking: What develops?* (pp. 37–71). Hillsdale, NJ: Erlbaum.

Champagne, A., Klopfer, L., Solomon, C., & Cahn, A. (1980). *Interactions of students' knowledge with their comprehension and design of science experiments.* (pp. 188–950). Pittsburgh: University of Pittsburgh Learning Research and Development Center.

Chaskin, R., & Rauner, D. (1995). Youth and caring: An introduction. *Phi Delta Kappan, 76,* 667–674.

Clark, C. M., & Peterson, P. L. (1986). Teachers' thought processes. In M. C. Wittrock (Ed.), *Handbook of research on teaching* (3rd ed.). New York: Macmillan.

Clements, D., & Battista, M. (1990). Constructivist learning and teaching. *Arithmetic Teacher, 38,* 34–35.

Clifford, M. (1990). Students need challenge, not easy success. *Educational Leadership, 48* (1), 22–26.

Cognition and Technology Group at Vanderbilt. (1992). The Jasper Series as an example of anchored instruction: Theory, program description, and assessment data. *Educational Psychologist, 27,* 291–315.

Cohen, E. (1994). Restructuring the classroom: Conditions for productive small groups. *Review of Educational Research, 64,* 1–35.

Cohen E., & Lotan, R. (Eds.). (1997). *Working for equity in heterogeneous classrooms: Sociological theory in practice.* New York: Teachers College Press.

Cohen, S. (1987). Instructional alignment: Searching for a magic bullet. *Educational Researcher, 16*(8), 16–20.

Coleman, J., Campbell, E., Hobson, D., McPartland, J., Mood, A., Weinfield, F., & York, R. (1966). *Equality of educational opportunity.* Washington, DC: U.S. Department of Health, Education and Welfare.

Copeland, W., & Decker, D. (1995). *Video cases and the development of meaning making in preservice teachers.* Paper presented at the Annual Meeting of the American Educational Research Association, San Francisco.

Corkill, A. (1992). Advance organizers: Facilitators of recall. *Educational Psychology Review, 4,* 33–67.

Corno, L., & Snow, R. (1986). Adapting teaching to individual differences among learners. In M. Wittrock (Ed.), *Third handbook of research on teaching* (pp. 570–604). New York: Macmillan.

Cronbach, L., & Snow, R. (Eds.). (1977). *Aptitudes and instructional methods.* New York: Irvington/Naiburg.

Crooks, T. (1988). The impact of classroom evaluation practices on students. *Review of Educational Research, 58,* 438–481.

Cruickshank, D. (1985). Applying research on teacher clarity. *Journal of Teacher Education, 35*(2), 44–48.

Cuban, L. (1984). *How teachers taught: Constancy and change in American classrooms: 1890–1980.* White Plains, NY: Longman.

Cushner, K., McClelland, A., & Safford, P. (1992). *Human diversity in education.* New York: McGraw Hill.

Deci, E., Pelletier, L., & Ryan, R. (1991). Motivation and education: The self-determination perspective. *Educational Psychologist, 26,* 325–346.

Deci, E., & Ryan, R. (1987). The support of autonomy and the control of behavior. *Journal of Personality and Social Psychology, 53,* 1024–1037.

Dempster, F. (1991). Synthesis of research on reviews and tests. *Educational Leadership, 48*(7), 71–76.

Dewey, J. (1902). *The child and the curriculum.* Chicago: University of Chicago Press.

Dewey, J. (1916). *Democracy in education.* New York: Macmillan.

Dillon, J. (1987). *Classroom questions and discussions.* Norwood, NJ: Ablex.

Dinnel, D. & Glover, J. (1985). Advance organizers: Encoding manipulations. *Journal of Educational Psychology, 77,* 514–521.

Doyle, W. (1983). Academic work. *Review of Educational Research, 53,* 159–199.

Duffy, G., Roehler, L., Meloth, M., & Vavrus, L. (1985, April). *Conceptualizing instructional explanation.* Paper presented at the annual meeting of the American Educational Research Association, Chicago.

Duffy, T., & Cunningham, D. (1996). Constructivism: Implications for the design and delivery of instruction. In D. Jonassen (Ed.), *Handbook of Research for Educational Communications and Technology* (pp. 170–195). New York: Macmillan.

Dunkin, M., & Biddle, B. (1974). *The study of teaching.* New York: Holt, Rinehart and Winston.

Durso, F., & Coggins, K. (1991). Organized instruction for the improvement of word knowledge skills. *Journal of Educational Psychology, 83,* 108–112.

Eggen, P., & Kauchak, D. (1999). *Educational psychology: Windows on classrooms* (5th ed.). Columbus, OH: Merrill.

Eggen, P., & McDonald, S. (1987, April). *Student misconceptions of physical science concepts: Implications for science instruction.* Paper presented at the annual meeting of the National Association for Research in Science Teaching, Washington DC.

Elam, S., & Rose, L. (1995). The 27th annual Phi Delta Kappa/Gallup poll. *Phi Delta Kappan, 77* (1), 41–49.

Emmer, E., Evertson, C., Clements, B., & Worsham, M. (1997). *Classroom management for secondary teachers* (4th ed.). Needham Heights, MA: Allyn & Bacon.

Emmer, E., & Gerwels, G. (1998). *Classroom management tasks in cooperative groups.* Paper presented at the Annual meeting of the American Educational Research Association, San Diego.

Emmer, E., & Gerwels, M. (April, 1998). *Teachers' views and uses of cooperative learning.* Paper presented at the annual meeting of the American Educational Research Association, San Diego.

Evertson, C. (1987). Managing classrooms: A framework for teachers. In D. Berliner & B. Rosenshine (Eds.), *Talks to teachers* (pp. 54–74). New York: Random House.

Evertson, C., Anderson, C., Anderson, L., & Brophy, J. (1980). Relationship between classroom behaviors and student outcomes in junior high mathematics and English classes. *American Educational Research Journal, 17,* 43–60.

Feather, N. (Ed.). (1982). *Expectations and actions.* Hillsdale, NJ: Erlbaum.

Feuer, M., & Fulton, K. (1993). The many faces of performance assessment. *Phi Delta Kappan, 74* (6), 478.

Foos, P. (1992). Test performance as a function of expected form and difficulty. *Journal of Experimental Education, 60* (3), 205–211.

Gage, N. (1985). Hard gains in the soft sciences. Bloomington, IN: Phi Delta Kappa.

Gage, N., & Berliner, D. (1992). *Educational psychology* (5th ed.). Boston: Houghton Mifflin.

Gage, N., & Giaconia, R. (1981). Teaching practices and student achievement: Causal connections. *New York University Education Quarterly, 12,* 2–9.

Gersten, R., Taylor, R., & Graves, A. (1999). Direct instruction and diversity. In R. Stevens (Ed.), *Teaching in American schools* (pp. 81–102). Columbus, OH: Merrill.

Gillies, R., & Ashman, A. (1998). Behavior and interactions of children in cooperative groups in lower and middle elementary grades. *Journal of Educational Psychology, 90*(4), 746–757.

Good, T. (1979). Teacher effectiveness in the elementary school. *Journal of Teacher Education, 30*(2), 52–64.

Good, T. (1983). Research on classroom teaching. In L. Shulman & G. Sykes (Eds.), *Handbook of teaching and policy* (pp. 42–80). New York: Longman.

Good, T. (1987a). Teacher expectations. In D. Berliner & B. Rosenshine (Eds.), *Talks to teachers* (pp. 159–200). New York: Random House.

Good, T. (1987b). Two decades of research on teacher expectations: Findings and future directions. *Journal of Teacher Education, 37*(4), 32–47.

Good, T., & Brophy, J. (1986). School effects. In M. Wittrock (Ed), *Third handbook of research on teaching* (pp. 570–604). New York: Macmillan.

Good, T., & Brophy, J. (1997). *Looking in classrooms* (7th ed.). New York: HarperCollins.

Goodlad, J. (1984). *A place called school.* New York: McGraw Hill.

Grabinger, R. (1996). Rich environments for active learning. In D. Jonassen (Ed.), *Handbook of research for educational communications and technology* (pp. 665–692). New York: Macmillan.

Gronlund, N. (1993). *How to make achievement tests and assessments.* Needham Heights, MA: Allyn & Bacon.

Harmin, M. (1994). *Inspiring active learning: A handbook for teachers.* Alexandria, VA: Association for Supervision and Curriculum Development.

Harrington, H. (1996, April). *Learning from cases.* Paper presented at the annual meeting of the American Educational Research Association, New York.

Harris, D. & Eggen, P. (1993, April). The impact of experience on conceptions of expertise: A comparison of the thinking of veteran, first-year, and preservice reachers. Paper presented at the annual meeting of the American Educational Research Association, Atlanta.

Hayes, J. (1996). A new framework for understanding cognition and affect in writing. In C. Levy & S. Ransdell, (Eds.), *The science of writing* (pp. 1–28). Mahwah, NJ: Erlbaum.

Hiebert, E., & Raphael, T. (1996). Psychological perspectives on literacy and extensions to educational practice. In D. Berliner & R. Calfee (Eds.), *Handbook of educational psychology* (pp. 550–602). New York: Macmillan.

Hiebert, J., Wearne, D., & Taber, S. (1991). Fourth graders' gradual construction of decimal fractions during instruction using different physical representations. *Elementary School Journal, 91,* 321–341.

Hmelo, C. (1995, April). *The effect of problem-based learning on the early development of medical expertise.* Paper presented at the Annual Meeting of the American Educational Research Association, San Francisco.

Hmelo, C., & Lin, X. (1998). Becoming self-directed learners: Strategy development in problem-based learning. In D. Evensen, & C. Hmelo (Eds.), *Problem-based learning: A research perspective on learning interaction.* Mahwah, NJ: Erlbaum.

Holt, J. (1964). *How children fail.* New York: Putnam.

Hunter, M. (1984). Knowing, teaching and supervising. In P. Hosford (Ed.), *Using what we know about teaching.* Alexandria, VA: Association for Supervision and Curriculum Development.

Jencks, C., Smith, M., Acland, H., Bane, M., Cohen, D., Gintis, H., Heyns, B., & Michelson, S. (1972). *Inequality: A reassessment of the effect of family and schooling in America.* New York: Basic Books.

Johnson, D., & Johnson, F. (1994). *Learning together and alone: Cooperation, competition, and individualization* (4th ed.). Englewood Cliffs, NJ: Prentice Hall.

Kagan, D. (1992). Professional growth among preservice and beginning teachers. *Review of Educational Research, 62,* 129–169.

Kagan, S. (1986). Cooperative learning and sociocultural factors in schooling. In *Beyond language: Social and cultural factors in schooling language minority students* (231–298). Los Angeles: California State University; Evaluation, Dissemination and Achievement Center.

Kagan, S. (1994). *Cooperative learning.* San Juan Capistrano, CA: Resources for Teachers.

Katz, L., & Chard, S. (1989). *Engaging children's minds: The project approach.* Norwood, NJ: Ablex.

Kauchak, D., & Eggen, P. (1993). *Learning and teaching: Research-based methods* (2nd ed.). Needham Heights, MA: Allyn & Bacon.

Kauchak, D., & Eggen, P. (1998). *Learning and teaching: Research based methods* (3rd ed.). Needham Heights, MA: Allyn & Bacon.

Keislar, E., & Shulman, L. (Eds.). (1966). *Learning by discovery: A critical appraisal.* Chicago: Rand McNally.

Kellogg, R. (1994). *The psychology of writing.* New York: Oxford Press.

Kerman, S. (1979). Teacher expectations and student achievement. *Phi Delta Kappan, 60,* 70–72.

Kher-Durlabhji, N., Lacina-Gifford, L., Jackson, L., Guillory, R., & Yandell, S. (1997, March). *Preservice teachers' knowledge of effective classroom management strategies.* Paper presented at the annual meeting of the American Educational Research Association, Chicago.

Kilbane, C., & Herbert, J. (1998). *Judging the merits of case-based instruction on the Internet.* Paper presented at the Annual Meeting of the American Educational Research Association, San Diego.

King, A. (1999). Teaching effective discourse patterns for small-group learning. In R. Stevens (Ed.), *Teaching in American schools* (pp. 121–139). Columbus, OH: Merrill.

Klauer, K. (1984). Intentional and incidental learning with instructional texts: A meta-analysis for 1970–1980. *American Educational Research Journal, 21,* 323–339.

Klausmeier, H. (1992). Concept learning and concept thinking. *Educational Psychologist, 27,* 267–286.

Kloostermann, P., & Cougan, M. (1994). Students' beliefs about learning school mathematics. *The Elementary School Journal, 94,* 375–388.

Knowles, J. (1959). *A separate peace.* New York: Bantam.

Krajcik, J., Blumenfeld, P., Marx, R., & Soloway, F. (1994). A collaborative model for helping middle grade science teachers learn project-based instruction. *Elementary School Journal, 94,* 483–497.

Krapp, A., Hidi, S., & Renninger, K. (1992). Interest, learning, and development. In K. Renninger, S. Hidi, & A. Krapp (Eds.), *The role of interest in learning and development* (pp. 3–26). Hillsdale, NJ: Erlbaum.

Kuhn, D. (1999). A developmental model of critical thinking. *Educational Researcher, 28,* 16–25.

Lambert, N., & McCombs, B. (1998). Introduction. In N. Lambert & B. McCombs (Eds.), *How students learn: Reforming schools through learner-centered education* (pp. 1–22).Washington, DC: American Psychological Association.

Langer, J., Bartolome, L., Vasquez, O., & Lucas, T. (1990). Meaning construction in school literacy tasks: A study of bilingual students. *American Educational Research Journal, 27,* 427–471.

Lave, J. (1988). *Cognition in practice: Mind, mathematics, and culture in everyday life.* New York: Cambridge University Press.

Lave, J. (1990). The culture of acquisition and the practice of understanding. In J. Stigler, R. Schweder, & G. Herdt (Eds.), *Cultural psychology* (pp. 309–327). Cambridge, England: Cambridge University Press.

Lepper, M., & Hodell, M. (1989). Intrinsic motivation in the classroom. In C. Ames & R. Ames (Eds.), *Research on motivation in education* (Vol. 3, pp. 73–105). San Diego: Academic Press.

Maehr, M. (1992, April). *Transforming the school culture to enhance motivation.* Paper presented at the annual meeting of the American Educational Research Association, San Francisco.

Marshall, H. (1992). Seeing, redefining, and supporting student learning. In H. Marshall (Ed.), *Redefining student learning: Roots of educational change* (pp. 1–32). Norwood, NJ: Ablex.

Maslow, A. (1968). *Toward a psychology of being* (2nd ed.). New York: Van Nostrand.

Mayer, R. (1983). Can you repeat this? Qualitative effects of repetition and advance organizers from science prose. *Journal of Educational Psychology, 75,* 40–49.

Mayer, R. (1984). Aids to text comprehension. *Educational Psychologist, 19,* 30–42.

Mayer, R. (1997). Multimedia learning: Are we asking the right questions? *Educational Psychologist, 32*(1), 1–19.

Mayer, R. (1998). Cognitive theory for education: What teachers need to know. In N. Lambert & B. McCombs (Eds.), *How students learn: Reforming schools through learner-centered education* (pp. 353–378). Washington, DC: American Psychological Association.

Mayer, R. (1999). *The promise of educational psychology: Learning in the content areas.* Upper Saddle River, NJ: Prentice Hall.

Mayer, R., & Gallini, J. (1990). When is an illustration worth a thousand words? *Journal of Educational Psychology, 82,* 715–726.

Mayer, R., & Wittrock, M. (1996). Problem-solving transfer. In D. Berliner & R. Calfee (Eds.), *Handbook of educational psychology* (pp. 47–62). New York: Macmillan.

McCarthy, S. (1994). Authors, text, and talk: The internalization of dialogue from social interaction during writing. *Reading Research Quarterly, 29,* 201–231.

McCombs, B. (1998). Integrating metacognition, affect, and motivation in improving teacher education. In N. Lambert & B. McCombs (Eds.), *How students learn: Reforming schools through learner-centered education* (pp. 379–408). Washington, DC: American Psychological Association.

McDougall, D., & Granby, C. (1996). How expectation of questioning method affects undergraduates' preparation for class. *Journal of Experimental Education, 65,* 43–54.

McGreal, T. (1985, November). Characteristics of effective teaching. Paper presented at the first annual Intensive Training Symposium, Clearwater, FL.

McKeachie, W., & Kulik, J. (1975). Effective college teaching. In F. Kerlinger (Ed.), *Review of research in education* (Vol. 3). Washington, DC: American Educational Research Association.

McLeod, D. (1989). The role of affect in mathematical problem solving. In D. McLeod & V. Adams, (Eds.), *Affect and mathematical problem solving* (pp. 20–36). New York: Springer-Verlag.

Merseth, K., & Lacey, C. (1993). Weaving stronger fabric: The pedagogical promise of hypermedia & case methods in teacher education. *Teaching & Teacher Education, 9*(3), 283–299.

Morine-Dershimer, G. (1987). Can we talk? In D. Berliner & B. Rosenshine (Eds.), *Talks to teachers* (pp. 37–53). New York: Random House.

Morine-Dershimer, G. (1993, April). *What's in a case—and what comes out?* Paper presented at the Annual Meeting of the American Educational Research Association, Atlanta.

Morine-Dershimer, G., & Vallance, C. (1976). *Teacher planning* (Beginning Teacher Evaluation Study, Special Report C). San Francisco: Far West Laboratory.

Mostert, M. (1996, April). *Cognitive aspects of case-based teaching.* Paper presented at the annual meeting of the American Educational Research Association, New York.

Murphy, J., Weil, M., & McGreal, T. (1986). The basic practice model of instruction. *The Elementary School Journal, 87,* 83–95.

National Council of Teachers of Mathematics. (1989). *Curriculum and evaluation standards for school mathematics.* Reston, VA: Author.

National Council of Teachers of Mathematics. (1991). *Professional standards for teaching mathematics.* Reston, VA: Author.

National Research Council. (1996). *National science education standards.* Washington, DC: National Academy Press.

Nickerson, R. (1988). On improving thinking through instruction. In E. Rothkopf (Ed.) Review of

Research in Education (pp. 3–57). Washington, DC: American Educational Research Association.

Noblit, G., Rogers, D., & McCadden, B. (1995). In the meantime: The possibilities of caring. *Phi Delta Kappan, 76,* 680–685.

Noddings, N. (1995). Teaching the themes of care. *Phi Delta Kappan, 76,* 675–679.

O'Keefe, P., & Johnston, M. (1987, April). Teachers' abilities to understand the perspectives of students: A case study of two teachers. Paper presented at the annual meeting of the American Educational Research Association, Washington, DC.

Parke, C., & Lane, S. (1996/97). Learning from performance assessments in math. *Educational Leadership, 54*(4), 26–29.

Pearson, D., & Dole, J. (1987). Explicit comprehension instruction: A review of research and a new conceptualization of instruction. *Elementary School Journal, 88*(2), 153–165.

Perkins, D. (1992). *Smart schools.* New York: The Free Press.

Perkins, D., & Blythe, T. (1994). Putting understanding up front. *Educational Leadership, 51,* 4–7.

Perkins, D., & Unger, C. (In press). Teaching and learning for understanding. In C. Reigeluth (Ed.), *Instructional design theories and models* (Vol. 2, pp. 91–114). Mahway, NJ: Erlbaum.

Peterson, P., Marx, R., & Clark, C. (1978). Teacher planning, teacher behavior, and student achievement. *American Educational Research Journal, 15,* 417–432.

Peterson, P., & Walberg, H. (1979). *Research on teaching.* Berkeley, CA: McCutchan.

Pintrich, P., & Schunk, D. (1996). *Motivation in education: Theory, research, and applications.* Upper Saddle River, NJ: Prentice Hall.

Poole, M., Okeafor, K., & Sloan, E. (1989, April). *Teachers' interactions, personal efficacy, and change implementation.* Paper presented at the Annual Meeting of the American Educational Research Association, San Francisco.

Pratton, J., & Hales, L. (1986). The effects of active participation on student learning. *Journal of Educational Research, 79,* 210–215.

Prawat, R. (1992). From individual differences to learning communities—our changing focus. *Educational Leadership, 49,* 9–13.

Reckase, M. (1997, March). *Constructs assessed by portfolios: How do they differ from those assessed by other educational tests?* Paper presented at the annual meeting of the National Educational Research Association, Chicago.

Resnick, L. (1989). Introduction. In L. Resnick (Ed.), *Knowing, learning, and instruction: Essays in honor of Robert Glaser* (pp. 1–24). Hillsdale, NJ: Erlbaum.

Resnick, L., & Klopfer, L. (1989). Toward the thinking curriculum: An overview. In L. Resnick & L. Klopfer (Eds.), *Toward the thinking curriculum: Current cognitive research* (pp. 1–18). Alexandria, VA: The Association for Supervision and Curriculum Development.

Roblyer, M., Edwards, J., & Havriluk, M. (1997). *Integrating technology into teaching.* Upper Saddle River, NJ: Prentice Hall.

Rosenholtz, S.J., & Simpson, C. (1984). The formation of ability conceptions: Developmental trend or social construction? *Review of Educational Research, 54,* 31–63.

Rosenshine, B. (1979). Content, time and direct instruction. In P. Peterson & H. Walberg (Eds.), *Research on teaching.* Berkeley, CA: McCutchan.

Rosenshine, B., & Stevens, R. (1986). Teaching functions. In M. Wittrock (Ed.), *Handbook of research on teaching* (3rd ed., pp. 376–391). New York: Macmillan.

Roth, K., & Anderson, C. (1991). Promoting conceptual change learning from science textbooks. In P. Ramsden (Ed.), *Improving learning: New perspectives.* London: Kogen Page.

Rowe, M. (1974). Relation of wait-time and rewards to the development of language, logic, and fate control: Part one—wait time. *Journal of Research in Science Teaching, 11,* 81–94.

Rowe, M. (1986). Wait time: Slowing down may be a way of speeding up. *Journal of Teacher Education, 37*(1), 43–50.

Rumelhart, D. & Ortony, A. (1977). The representation of knowledge in memory. In R. Anderson, R. Spurs, & W. Montague (Eds.), *Schooling and the acquisition of knowledge.* Hillsdale, NJ: Erlbaum.

Rutter, M., Maughan, B., Mortimore, P., Ouston, J., & Smith, A. (1979). *Fifteen thousand hours.* Cambridge, MA: Harvard University Press.

Schmuck, R., & Schmuck, P. (1997). *Group processes in the classroom* (7th ed.). Madison, WI: Brown & Benchmark.

Schoenfeld, A. (1991). On mathematics as sense-making: An informal attack on the unfortunate divorce of formal and informal mathematics. In J. Voss, D. Perkins, & J. Segal (Eds.), *Informal reasoning and education* (pp. 311–343). Hillsdale, NJ: Erlbaum.

Schunk, D. (1994, April). *Goal and self-evaluative influences during children's mathematical skill acquisition.* Paper presented at the annual meeting of the American Educational Research Association, New Orleans.

Schwartz, B., & Reisberg, D. (1991). *Learning and memory*. New York: Norton.

Scruggs, T., & Richter, L. (1988). Tutoring learning disabled students: A critical review. *Learning Disability Quarterly, 11*(3), 274–287.

Sharon, S., & Sharon, H. (1988). *Language and learning in the cooperative classroom*. New York: Springer-Verlag.

Shulman, L. (1986). Those who understand: Knowledge growth in teaching. *Educational Researcher, 15*(2), 4–14.

Shulman, L. (1993, April). *Roles for cases in courses and programs*. Paper presented at the Far West Laboratory Conference on Case-Based Teaching, Tahoe, CA.

Singley, M., & Anderson, J. (1989). *The transfer of cognitive skill*. Cambridge, England: Cambridge University Press.

Slavin, R. (1986). *Using student team learning* (3rd ed.). Baltimore, MD: The Johns Hopkins University, Center for Research on Elementary and Middle School.

Slavin, R. (1995). *Cooperative learning: Theory, research, and practice* (2nd ed.). Needham Heights, MA: Allyn & Bacon.

Slavin, R., Karweit, N., & Madden, N. (Eds.). (1989). *Effective programs for students at risk*. Boston: Allyn & Bacon.

Slavin, R., Madden, N., Dolan, L., & Wasik, B. (1994). Roots and wings: Inspiring academic excellence. *Educational Leadership, 52*, 10–14.

Smith, L., & Cotten, M. (1980). Effect of lesson vagueness and discontinuity on student achievement and attitude. *Journal of Educational Psychology, 72*, 670–675.

Snyder, S., Bushur, L., Hoeksema, P., Olson, M., Clark, S., & Snyder, J. (1991, April). The effect on instructional clarity and concept structure on students' achievement and perception. Paper presented at the annual meeting of the American Educational Research Association, Chicago.

Spiro, R., Feltovich, P., Jacobson, M., & Coulson, R. (1992). Knowledge representation, content specification, and the development of skill in situation-specific knowledge assembly: Some constructivist issues as they relate to cognitive flexibility theory and hypertext. In T. Duffy & D. Jonassen (Eds.), *Constructivism and the technology of instruction: A conversation* (pp. 121–127). Hillsdale, NJ: Erlbaum.

Stepien, W., & Gallagher, S. (1993). Problem-based learning: As authentic as it gets. *Educational Leadership, 50*(7), 25–28.

Sternberg, R. (1998) Principles of teaching for successful intelligence. *Educational Psychologist, 33*(2/3), 65–72.

Stiggins, R. (1997). *Student-centered classroom assessment* (2nd ed.). Upper Saddle River, NJ: Prentice Hall.

Stipek, D. (1996). Motivation and instruction. In D. Berliner & R. Calfee (Eds.), *Handbook of educational psychology* (pp. 85–113). New York: Macmillan.

Stipek, D. (1998). *Motivation to learn* (3rd ed.). Needham Heights, MA: Allyn & Bacon.

Strong, R., Silver, H., & Robinson, A. (1995). What do students want (and what really motivates them)? *Educational Leadership, 53*(1), 8–12.

Suthers, D. (1998). *Representations for scaffolding collaborative inquiry on ill-structured problems*. Paper presented at the annual meeting of the American Educational Research Association, San Diego.

Sweller, J., Van Merrienboer, J., & Paas, F. (1998). Cognitive architecture and instructional design. *Educational Psychology Review, 10*(1), 251–296.

Taba, H. (1965). Techniques of inservice training. *Social Education, 29*, 44–60.

Taba, H. (1966). *Teaching strategies and cognitive functioning in elementary school children* (Project No. 2404). Washington, DC: USOE.

Taba, H. (1967). *Teachers handbook to elementary social studies*. Reading, MA: Addison Wesley.

Tennyson, R., & Cocchiarella, M. (1986). An empirically based instructional design theory for teaching concepts. *Review of Educational Research, 56*, 40–71.

Thelen, H. (1960). *Education and the human quest*. New York: Harper & Row.

Thompson, M., McLaughlin, C., & Smith, R. (1995). *Physical science*. Westerville, OH: Glencoe.

U.S. Bureau of the Census. (1994). *Statistics*. Washington, DC: Author.

Valencia, S., Hiebert, E., & Afflerback, P. (Eds.). (1994). *Authentic reading assessment: Practices and possibilities*. Newark, DE: International Reading Association.

Van Patten, J., Chao, C., & Reigeluth, C. (1986). A review of strategies for sequencing and synthesizing instruction. *Review of Educational Research, 656*, 431–471.

Villegas, A. (1991). Culturally responsive pedagogy for the 1990s and beyond. Princeton, NJ: Educational Testing Service.

Vito, R., & Connell, J. (1988, April). *A longitudinal study of at-risk high school students: A theory-based description and intervention*. Paper presented at the annual meeting of the American Educational Research Association, New Orleans.

Vygotsky, L. (1978). *Mind in society: The development of higher psychological processes* (M. Cole, V. John-Steiner, S. Scribner, & E. Souberman, Eds. and Trans.). Cambridge, MA: Harvard University Press.

Vygotsky, L. (1986). *Thought and language.* Cambridge, MA: MIT Press.

Wade, S. (1992). How interest affects learning from text. In K. Renniger, S. Hidi, & A. Krapp (Eds.), *The role of interest in learning and development* (pp. 531–553). Hillsdale, NJ: Erlbaum.

Wang, M., Haertel, G., & Walberg, H. (1993). Toward a knowledge base for school learning. *Review of Educational Research, 63*(3), 249–294.

Webb, N., Baxter, G., & Thompson, L. (1997). Teachers' grouping practices in fifth-grade science classrooms. *Elementary School Journal, 98*(2), 107–111.

Webb, N., Nemer, K., Chizhik, A., & Sugrue, B. (1998). Equity issues in collaborative group assessment: Group composition and performance. *American Educational Research Journal, 35*(4), 607–652.

Weiner, B. (1994a). Ability versus effort revisited: The moral determinants of achievement evaluation and achievement as a moral system. *Educational Psychologist, 29,* 163–172.

Weiner, B. (1994b). Integrating social and personal theories of achievement striving. *Review of Educational Research, 64,* 557–573.

Weinstein, R. (1998). Promoting positive expectations in schooling. In N. Lambert & B. McCombs (Eds.), *How students learn: Reforming schools through learner-centered education* (pp. 81–111). Washington, DC: American Psychological Association.

Wertsch, J. (1991). *Voices of the mind: A socio-cultural approach to mediated action.* Cambridge, MA: Harvard University Press.

White, R. (1959). Motivation reconsidered: The concept of competence. *Psychological Review, 66,* 297–333.

Wiggins, G. (1996/97). Practicing what we preach in designing authentic assessment. *Educational Leadership, 54*(4), 18–25.

Williams, S., Bareiss, R., & Reiser, B. (1996, April). *ASK Jasper: A multimedia publishing and performance support environment for design.* Paper presented at the annual meeting of the American Educational Research Association, New York.

Wittrock, M. (1986). Students' thought processes. In M. Wittrock, (Ed.), *Handbook of research on teaching* (3rd ed., pp. 297–314). New York: Macmillan.

Worthen, B. (1993). Critical issues that will determine the future of alternative assessment. *Phi Delta Kappan, 74,* 444–454.

Zahorik, J. (1996). Elementary and secondary teachers' reports of how they make learning interesting. *The Elementary School Journal, 96*(5), 551–564.

GLOSSARY

Academic rule: A relationship between concepts arbitrarily derived by people.

Advance organizers: Verbal statements at the beginning of a lesson that preview and structure new material and link it to students' existing schemas.

Affective domain: Dimension of the curriculum that focuses on attitudes and values and the development of students' personal and emotional growth.

At-risk students: Students in danger of failing to complete their education with the skills necessary to survive in modern society.

Authentic assessment: Assessments that directly measure student performance through real-life tasks.

Automaticity: The process of overlearning information and skills to the point where they can be accessed or used with little mental effort.

Callout: An answer given by a student before the student has been recognized by the teacher.

Caring: Teachers' abilities to empathize with and invest in the protection and development of young people.

Case: A specific kind of problem-based learning that presents students with a segment or sample of a professional problem or dilemma.

Characteristics: The defining features of a concept.

Checklists: Written descriptions of dimensions that must be present in an acceptable performance.

Closure: A form of review that occurs at the end of a lesson.

Cognitive apprenticeship: Learners learn by doing alongside an expert but also learn why they are performing a skill or procedure in a certain way.

Cognitive domain: Dimension of the curriculum that focuses on knowledge and understanding of facts, concepts, principles, rules, skills, and problem solving.

Combining pairs: A groupwork strategy that uses learning pairs as the basic unit of instruction but provides opportunities for the pairs to share their answers with another pair.

Comprehension monitoring: The process of informally assessing student understanding through questioning in lecture-discussion lessons.

Concept analysis: The process of describing a concept in terms of its characteristics, related concepts, examples, and definition.

Concepts: Categories, sets, or classes of objects, events, or ideas with common characteristics.

Connected discourse: Instruction that is thematic and leads to a point.

Constructivism: A view of learning that says that learners develop their own understanding of the way the world works rather than having it delivered to them by others (most commonly teachers) in an already organized form.

Cooperative Learning: A cluster of instructional strategies that actively involve students in group-work toward a common goal.

Coordinate concepts: Concepts with distinct characteristics, all of which are members of a larger class or category.

Critical thinking: The process of assessing conclusions based on evidence.

Definition: A statement that includes the name of the concept being defined, a superordinate concept, and the concept's characteristics.

Direct-Instruction Model: A teacher-centered strategy that uses teacher explanation and modeling combined with student practice and feedback to teach concepts and skills.

Discussions: An instructional strategy in which students share ideas with each other and engage in higher level thinking.

Emphasis: Signals that alert students to important information in a lesson that are communicated through vocal or verbal cues and repetition.

Equal opportunity for success: A concept within cooperative learning suggesting that all students, regardless of ability or background, can expect to be rewarded for their efforts if they make an honest effort.

Equitable distribution: A questioning pattern in which all students in the class are called on as equally as possible.

Essay items: Test questions that require students to organize information in making extended written responses to questions or problems.

Essential teaching skills: The critical teacher attitudes, skills, and strategies necessary to promote student learning.

Examples: Cases that illustrate a concept.

Feedback: Information about current behavior that can be used to improve future performance.

Focus: Instructional materials and techniques that attract and hold students' attention throughout the learning activity.

Generalizations: Relationships between concepts that describe patterns that often have exceptions.

Generative knowledge: Knowledge that can be used to interpret new situations, solve problems, think and reason, and learn.

Group goals: Incentives within cooperative learning that help create team spirit and encourage students to help each other.

Group Investigation: A cooperative-learning strategy that places students in groups to investigate a given topic.

Groupwork: A family of instructional models that use group interaction to supplement other strategies.

Heuristics: General, widely applicable problem-solving strategies.

Hypothesis: A tentative answer to a question or solution to a problem that can serve as the focal point of inquiry and can be verified with data.

Ill-defined problems: Problems with ambiguous goals and no agreed-upon strategy for solving them.

Individual accountability: A cooperative-learning principle requiring that each individual member of a cooperative-learning group demonstrate mastery of the concepts and skills being taught.

Inquiry: A scientific process for answering questions and solving problems based on facts and observations.

Inquiry Model: A teaching strategy designed to teach students how to investigate questions through the systematic gathering of facts.

Instructional alignment: The congruence, or match, among objectives, learning activities, and assessments.

Integration: In lecture-discussion lessons, the process of linking new information to prior learning and linking different parts of new learning to each other.

Intrinsic motivation: Motivation to engage in an activity for its own sake.

Introductory focus: The set of teacher actions at the beginning of a lesson designed to attract students' attention and pull them into the lesson.

Jigsaw II: A form of cooperative learning in which individual students become experts on subsections of a topic and teach that subsection to others.

Learning (behaviorism): A view of learning that focuses on changes in observable behavior that occur as the result of experience.

Learning (cognitive): A view of learning that emphasizes active processes in which learners attempt to make sense of what they study.

Lecture: A form of instruction in which students passively receive information delivered in an organized way by teachers.

Long-term memory: The permanent memory store in our personal information-processing systems.

Meaningful verbal learning: The acquisition of ideas that are linked to other ideas.

Meaningfulness: The extent to which a learner creates links or associations between an idea and other ideas.

Metacognition: The awareness of and control over our cognitive processes.

Modeling: The display of behaviors that are imitated by others.

Models: Representations of academic topics that allow us to visualize what we cannot observe directly (as in a model of the atom).

Monitoring: The process of constantly checking students' verbal and nonverbal behavior for evidence of learning progress.

Observational learning: The changes in behavior, thinking, or emotions that result from observing the behavior of another person (a model).

Open-ended questions: Divergent questions (or directives) that ask students to describe or compare and contrast information.

Organized bodies of knowledge: Topics that combine facts, concepts, generalizations, and the relationships among them.

Pairs check: A groupwork strategy that involves student dyads in checking answers that is primarily used with seatwork activities where students are working on problems with convergent answers.

Pedagogical content knowledge: The ability to represent topics in ways that are meaningful to learners, plus an understanding of what makes topics difficult or easy to learn.

Performance assessments: Evaluative tasks on which students are required to demonstrate their level of competence or knowledge by creating a product or a response.

Personal teaching efficacy: The belief that an individual teacher can have an important positive effect on his or her students.

Precise terminology: Teachers defining ideas clearly and eliminating vague terms from presentations and answers to students' questions.

Primary data sources: Individuals' direct observations of the events being studied.

Principles: A special kind of generalization in which relationships among concepts are accepted as true or valid for all known cases.

Problem-based learning: A teaching strategy designed to teach problem-solving skills and content and to develop self-directed learning.

Productive learning environments: Classrooms that are orderly and focused on learning.

Prompt: Any teacher question or directive designed to elicit a student response after the student has failed to answer or has given an incorrect or incomplete answer.

Psychomotor domain: Development of students' physical abilities and skills.

Questioning frequency: The number of questions teachers ask during learning activities.

Rating scales: An assessment instrument that contains written descriptions of evaluative dimensions and scales of values on which each dimension is rated.

Review: The process of summarizing previous work that creates a link between what has been learned and what is coming.

Rote learning: A form of learning that emphasizes the memorization of specific items of information rather than exploring relationships among topics.

Scaffolding: Instructional support that helps learners to perform skills and acquire new information.

Schema: Knowledge stored in people's memories as sets of interconnected ideas, relationships, and procedures.

Schema theory: A cognitive view of knowledge construction that says that the information people store in memory consists of networks of organized and interconnected ideas.

Scientific method: A view of knowledge construction and verification that emphasizes forming conclusions based on observation, developing hypotheses, and testing them with facts.

Secondary data sources: Other individuals' interpretations of primary data sources, such as information found in textbooks, encyclopedias, and other reference books.

Self-directed learning: A goal of problem-based learning that develops when students are aware of and take control of their learning progress.

Self-regulation: An individual's conscious use of mental strategies for the purpose of improving thinking and learning through the deliberate use of learning goals.

Sensory focus: The use of stimuli—concrete objects, pictures, models, materials displayed on the overhead, and even information written on the chalkboard—to attract and maintain attention.

Sensory memory: The part of our information-processing system that briefly holds information until we attend to it.

Skills: Cognitive operations with three essential characteristics: they have a specific set of identifiable procedures, they can be illustrated with a large and varied number of examples, and they are developed through practice.

Social Interaction Models: A cluster of instructional strategies that involve students working collaboratively to reach common goals.

Social structure: The characteristics of the classroom environment necessary for learning to take place and the roles of the teacher and students in that environment.

Sociocultural theory: A cognitive view of learning that emphasizes student participation in communities of learning.

Student Teams Achievement Division (STAD): A cooperative-learning strategy designed to teach basic facts, concepts, and skills through the use of multiability learning teams.

Subordinate concepts: Subsets or examples of concepts.

Superordinate concept: A larger category or class into which a concept fits.

Systematic observation: An assessment strategy that utilizes observations requiring teachers to specify criteria in terms of the processes they are assessing and take notes based on the criteria.

Task analysis: The process of breaking a skill into its component subparts.

Task specialization: A component within Jigsaw II requiring that different students have specialized roles in reaching the goals of a learning activity.

Teacher-effectiveness research: A body of classroom reseach that attempts to describe patterns of teacher behavior that influence student learning.

Teacher expectations: The inferences teachers make about students' future academic achievement, behavior, and attitudes.

Teaching models: Prescriptive teaching strategies designed to accomplish particular instructional goals.

Think-alouds: Conscious attempts to verbalize internal cognitive strategies.

Think-pair-share: A groupwork strategy that asks individual students in learning dyads first to think about a question or problem, to come up with an answer, and then to share it with a partner.

Transfer: The ability to apply a skill or knowledge learned in one setting to a different setting.

Transfer of responsibility: The gradual shift of control of learning from teacher to students.

Transition signal: A verbal statement that communicates that one idea is ending and another is beginning.

Wait-time: The period of silence both before and after a student responds.

Warmth: Teachers' abilities to demonstrate that they care for students as people.

Working memory: The portion of memory in which conscious processing of information occurs.

Zone of proximal development: A stage of learning in which a student cannot solve a problem or perform a skill alone but can be successful with the help of a teacher.

INDEX